AF265772

ANGLO-CATHOLIC CLASSICS

Writings produced, re-published or edited by the Oxford fathers (or their disciples) that underwrite the Anglo-Catholic tradition.

NASHOTAH HOUSE PRESS

Nashotah House Theological Seminary
2777 Mission Road
Nashotah, WI 53058

www.nashotah.edu

Cover design by Ben Jefferies

Printed 2022

NOTES AND QUESTIONS

ON THE

CATHOLIC FAITH AND RELIGION.

NOTES AND QUESTIONS

ON

THE CATHOLIC FAITH AND RELIGION.

THE NOTES AND ANSWERS COMPILED CHIEFLY
FROM THE WORKS AND IN THE WORDS OF

DR. PUSEY.

WITH A PREFACE BY THE REV. THOMAS THELLUSSON CARTER,

HON. CANON OF CHRIST CHURCH, OXFORD.

"It is a mistake not to say plainly, in matters of faith, what we mean."
Preface to Sermon, 'Prophecy of Jesus.'

"What I have believed, that I have ever taught, in the most explicit way that I could."
Letter to 'Record,' March 11, 1863.

LONDON:
WALTER SMITH AND INNES,
31 & 32, BEDFORD STREET, STRAND, W.C.
1891.

PREFACE.

It is, I suppose, generally agreed among those who desire to see the Catholic Faith, as inherited and received by the Church of England, more firmly and intelligently settled among us, that one chief need at this present time is the definite exposition of its principles in a methodical and collected form, with some real measure of recognized authority. Until quite lately it has been a state of continual progress—a constant succession of materials having been provided. Truths which had been obscured, or altogether ignored, have been restored to us. They have been tested by appeal to our acknowledged formularies, our standards of doctrine and traditional belief. They have been defended against various opposing forces, and have thus been subjected to severe criticism ; and now some of our chief witnesses, to whom we owe this restoration, have either passed away, or may not long be spared to us. After the heated controversy there is generally felt to be comparative rest, and among opponents a disposition to be more forbearing and tolerant. It seems, therefore, that the time has come for attempting what is needed—the gathering up of the gains of the conflict, and what we trust will live on, as the testimony of the past generation to Anglo-Catholic truth.

The present work is the first contribution to this much-desired object. It has been undertaken with an earnest zeal, evidently carried out with great pains, and, as far as I can judge, marked throughout by the utmost carefulness. The friend alluded to by the compiler in his introduction, to whose advice and assistance he has been much indebted, is well known to me as one in whom I have ever reposed entire confidence for theological accuracy, and a true balance of mind in dealing with questions of doctrine.

It will no doubt strike every one who enjoyed the blessing of personal acquaintance with Dr. Pusey, that to make him a standard of teaching and guide to truth, would have been repudiated by him with the utmost force of his intense nature. It seems, however, impossible for many reasons to regard him otherwise than in such a position. To me, to have been asked to bear my share in commending a work founded on this idea, has a very touching interest, lying deep among the most treasured remembrances of my whole life, and life-work. As a younger, with him as an elder, boy at Eton ; as a commoner at Christ Church, Oxford, with him as Professor living in the well-known house in the corner of " Tom Quad " ; as a guide and counsellor during the rest of his life, till the sad and ever-memorable day on which I knelt at the foot of the bed on which he lay taking his last sleep, in his simple cottage home at Ascot, with the few who there watched till his spirit had passed away, and his eyes were closed for ever on this world—he has ever been to me as a Pole Star in the regions of divine truth. And if in any man the love of Christ underlay and animated his exhaustive studies, his ever-ready and rich utterances, and his ceaseless efforts to bear witness to the truth, it was Dr. Pusey.

But far beyond any personal considerations, the selecting Dr. Pusey, as the compiler of this important work has done, as a standard of Anglo-Catholic teaching, rests on grounds which, Dr. Pusey alone being the dissentient, must I think, to all who have been conversant with the history of the Oxford movement, appear amply justified.

It has often been expressed as matter of surprise, that Pusey's and not Newman's name became the watchword of the Oxford movement. It is clear enough now, how exceedingly fortunate this was, considering the respective destinies of the two men. But as so often is the case in fixing names to represent things, an instinct founded on real reasons, though by apparent accident, prevailed, and amply supports the use. It is true that not he, but Newman, was the animating and commanding spirit of the Tractarian movement, and only accidentally, so to speak, was Dr. Pusey's name first publicly associated with it, because his initials happened to be attached to his Tract on Fasting. But his eminence and weight among the Tract writers, and his subsequent defence of their principles at all risk of consequences to himself, tended to make him their prominent and leading advocate.

Newman's record of the welcome with which he was received among the Tract writers, is well known. "I used," he says, "to call him ὁ μέγας." His great learning, his immense diligence, his scholar-like mind, and his simple devotion to the cause of religion, overcame one ; and great of course was the joy when, in the last days of 1833, he showed a disposition to make common cause with us—it at once gave us a position and a name. . . He was a man of large designs; he had a hopeful, sanguine mind ; he had no fear of others, he was haunted by no intellectual perplexities." This remarkable testimony does not give the whole account of the reasons why we are justified in looking on Dr. Pusey as a guide and standard, and a sufficient witness to what we very fairly claim to be the fruits of the late revival, and so our true inheritance, as acknowledged Anglo-Catholic doctrine.

Dr. Pusey, unlike Newman, was bred and nurtured in the highest Church of England piety and teaching of the time. The basis of his intellectual development was laid in the traditions which had descended, as was also the case with Mr.

Keble, from the days of the Non-jurors. To Pusey, as to
Keble, the increased study of Patristic Theology, and of Church
traditions, was the legitimate and proper development of his
antecedents. It was the natural or supernatural growth from
truth to truth, as "from grace to grace," without any conscious
break, or radical change. This gave Dr. Pusey such calmness of
conviction, such confidence in his position, such stability under
all opposition, such quietness in controversy, such firmness of
adherence to the Church of England's position, whatever might
be its difficulties or its drawbacks, such unshaken patience
and loving-kindness under censure and reproach in high places,
under ceaseless suspicion and evil-speaking at one time almost
everywhere. Yet I believe Dr. Pusey to have been always
absolutely true to the Church of England, and never to have
had any thought or looking beyond its limits, as his proper
home. Newman gives, in the passage already quoted, an
indication of his advances to the true groundwork of English
Catholicity, in his starting " The Library of the Fathers." He,
as Newman says, "advocated in 1836 his great project for a
translation of the Fathers, as those witnesses to whom we
have ever looked as our authorities in teaching." There
might have been added his share in establishing " The Library
of Anglo-Catholic Theology." Dr. Pusey speaks, as Newman
says, of what struck him (Pusey) "among the most hopeful
peculiarities of the movement "—" its stationariness." " He
made it (the remark) in good faith; it was his subjective view
of it" (*Apologia*, pp. 136, first ed. 1864).

Moreover, in his quiet study, and with his quiet heart, Dr.
Pusey was a true combatant. His whole disposition indeed was
to confine himself to Scriptural studies; and his desire, as is
well known, was to devote his life to complete a Commentary on
the Holy Scriptures, of which he gave such valuable samples,
the fulness and diffusiveness of which caused the difficulty
of carrying on the design with the assistance of others. But

his cherished design was hopelessly hindered by the repeated calls to come to the defence of imperilled truth, and apply the immense stores of his learning to some point of immediate attack.   His readiness in meeting every assault, and sustaining every position that had been assailed, thus tended to place him in the position of witness to a vast circle of truth, and caused his various writings to cover the whole ground of the theological controversies of his time.   Happily too he lived through the whole period of the fruitful discussions which have arisen out of the Catholic movement.   Nor did he ever fail, while all turned to him in every emergency, to enter the lists against all comers.   At the same time his sympathies were keenly alive ; and by his devotional instincts he was far more inclined to use his great powers in the promotion of piety than in the turmoil of controversy.   Even in controversy it was for truth and peace he strove.   His efforts for opening the way to re-union with the Church of Rome, his personal labour, as well as his writings with a view to such reconciliation, are well known.   Nor did they cease till, as he deeply felt, the decree of Papal Infallibility, 1870, closed the door against any such hope, till God in His providence in His own time, should re-open the way to friendly intercourse, with a view to the considera-tion of the questions now dividing us—an object which he had so much at heart.

Nor was this the whole extent of his sympathies.   He was always drawn to the devout side of the Evangelicals—their reverence of the Holy Scriptures, their love of Christ.   Nor only with them did his kindly feelings stay his desire for reunion.   He recognized in personal intercourse what was true in the piety and devotion of the more orthodox among Protestant Dissenters.   It was this combination of devoutness, and recognition of devoutness in others, together with his vast store of learning, and extensive experience, that renders Dr. Pusey's testimony so unique, so comprehensive, so wide in the

truest sense of the word, and at the same time so lovingly kind
and considerate.

In thus speaking of Dr. Pusey's singular position and high
authority, as a witness and guide beyond that of any teacher of
the Church of England in these latter days, as to the vast body
of Catholic Apostolic truth, our real inheritance, I would be
understood, as trusting that feelings of personal attachment and
grateful recollections have not led me to exaggerate the value
of his testimony.   In this trust I heartily commend this work,
on which my friend the compiler has bestowed so much labour
and loving care.

T. T. C.

CLEWER, *Septuagesima*, 1891.

INTRODUCTION BY THE COMPILER.

THIS volume is not put forth as a complete or systematic manual of theological instruction. It makes no such claim ; but the compiler humbly trusts that these pages will be found useful to many who are seeking for sound, sober, Catholic teaching on some matters of faith and religion.

As regards the imperfections of his book, he would plead that he did his best to get the work done by others, that he offered a large sum of money to a well-known Church Society to undertake it, but that while the proposal was heartily commended, no one could be found who was able to devote himself to the compilation. He then resolved to attempt the task himself, feeling that although many other men could have done it better, yet that he had two qualifications for the work—a grateful, loyal devotion to Dr. Pusey, and a very intimate acquaintance with his writings. After receiving the permission of Dr. Pusey's trustees he wrote to Canon Liddon, saying that before the book would be submitted to him for his final approval, a mutual friend would look through the proofs, to save him as much trouble as possible, as to any needful revision or alteration. Canon Liddon wrote in reply :

April 28, 1890.

"I have lately had much trouble with my head, and may have to go away for some time ; I mention this in case you should be able to send the book at an earlier date. I have entire confidence in ——'s judgment in all theological matters; he is learned, and quite free from crotchets; indeed, if he revises the proofs there would be no sort of necessity for my doing so."

The compiler has therefore good ground for thinking that had Dr. Liddon been alive, this book would have been published with some few words of commendation from his pen, and he acknowledges his great indebtedness to the friend of whom Dr. Liddon had such a high opinion, an opinion with which he presumes most heartily to agree.

The book is published at a very low price for two reasons: in the hope of a wide circulation, and to enable Churchmen to give a copy as a present to Working-men's Church Institutes. Many of the working-classes have only known Dr. Pusey as a High Church clergyman, who wittingly or unwittingly led people to Rome. This absurd prejudice exists still in the minds of some who would learn to know better if they carefully studied Dr. Pusey's writings. The working-classes and the poor would indeed be very ready to learn of Dr. Pusey, did they but know how exceeding great his interest in, and his love for them was. This challenge might be safely made to any controversialist: " Produce the volumes of any other noted English divine who speaks so often and so lovingly of the poor." Sometimes he speaks of them when it never would have been expected. Who, for instance, would have thought it likely in the opening pages of a learned treatise on the *Councils of the Church*, to find (pp. 3, 4) some earnest words on behalf of the poor? Let any reader of Dr. Pusey's sermons do as the compiler of this book has done, mark with his pencil all the passages he meets with, wherein Dr. Pusey pleads for the poor, and he will be astonished to find how numerous are the instances.

The working-classes and the poor are not the only Christians who need more instruction as to their faith and religion. So far as the compiler of this volume may venture to allude to his own experience, he would affirm that it is in the ranks of the upper classes where most theological, or rather untheological, ignorance is to be found. So strongly has he felt this to be the case, that, some fourteen years ago, he tried to get a small Church college established in London, where at certain periods all who desired it could come and be examined, and certificates of merit be awarded. The idea was that there should be three grades: the first for those who had not much time for study, and who were not otherwise well educated; the second for those with leisure and well educated; the third for those who wished to study continuously, deeply, and who could afford the time and bear the expense.

The new scheme of the London Diocesan Reading Union will, it is to be hoped, do a most useful work, as books are recommended for study and examinations to be held. It does not, however, augur well to see none of Dr. Pusey's books on the first list, while one work at least is recommended which is by no means "thoroughly sound," if one may judge by the notices of it in the best Church journals.

The perusal of some of Dr. Pusey's writings, followed by an examination, would be an invaluable benefit to many.

In the course of his numerous publications there is hardly any subject of importance or interest to the Christian student which he has not touched upon. On one of his pages will be found reverent and profound remarks on the doctrine of the Blessed Trinity, on another a word or two on such questions as "whether or no will animals live again?"

It may be well said here that Dr. Pusey would have been the very last man to set himself up as such an authority, that all or any should blindly pin their faith to his and say, "I believe this or that because Dr. Pusey teaches it." Like the Church of England, whose most devoted, loyal son he was, his authority for all that he taught was the teaching of the early

Church, as seen in the decrees of General Councils, accepted by the whole Church, and testified to in the writings of the Fathers. The reader, then, of this book, is not so much asked to accept the teaching of these pages as simply that of Dr. Pusey, but as the true Catholic teaching of the Church put forth by one of her most illustrious divines, who was also a most reverent and laborious student, and therefore not one likely to mislead or deceive.

His book on *Daniel the Prophet*, his preface to his *Councils of the Church*, a passage in his speech before the English Church Union, June 1867, may be referred to in proof of his being a careful and most painstaking student. The preface to his last edition of the sermon, the *Rule of Faith*, and his corrections of some criticisms on the *Manual for Confessors*, p. 27, show how scrupulously careful he was in the verification of statements and quotations. No one is perfect, and no one is master of everything, but it may well be asserted that there have been very few voluminous writers of the eminence of Dr. Pusey, whose inaccuracies have been so few and far between.

In his case this is the more remarkable, because he was continually forced into controversy, and we all know how that position is a sore trial to the honesty and accuracy of those who are in it. Whenever he made a mistake, no one, except an unscrupulous or bitter antagonist, could say that Dr. Pusey had been intentionally inaccurate. His well-known slip, as to the consecration of Archbishop Chichele (*Eirenicon*, Pt. I. p. 233), is so palpably a case of confusion of memory, that one wonders how any one with a spark of right feeling could have uncharitably put it down to anything else!

Controversialists of this class (if they know their Bibles well enough), might as well have seized on a passage in Dr. Pusey's *Eleven Addresses*, p. 126, wherein he treats of prayers for the dead, and alludes in proof to "the Apostle's prayer, as seems probable, for the departed Epaphroditus." Dr. Pusey probably knew his Bible as well, if not better, than any man in this century, and had the misprint "Epaphroditus" for "Onesiphorus" occurred in one of his controversial works instead of in one of his addresses at a Retreat, we should no doubt have had all sorts of sinister motives and designs attributed to him for making the slip!

As regards the fault in memory relating to Archbishop Chichele, the less said about it by Dr. Pusey's opponents the better, as the Archbishop is a witness in proof of the Papal usurpation being continuously resisted in England.

The compiler regrets that there is so much of the "Roman controversy" in these pages; but is there not a cause? Many seem to be under the delusion that as Roman Catholics dwell among us amicably as citizens, that they are amicable and tolerant as regards religion in general, and the Church of England in particular. The contrary is the fact, and of late years the energy and bitterness of their controversialists has been much and sadly on the increase. They do not gain much in the numbers they persuade into secession, but they do gain in political influence and on the press; and worst of all their opposition to the Church of England injures and unsettles the faith of numbers who cannot believe the "Gospel according to Rome." The Roman Catholic journals prove amply how fiercely the Roman communion in England opposes the Church, and if further proof be needed it is patent in the fact that Cardinal Manning's *Letter to Dr. Pusey*, 1864, which drew forth the *Eirenicon*, and which letter Dr. Pusey called a "death thrust," has just been republished.

The compiler hopes, however, that while the reader will find some pages given to the controversy forced upon us by those who seek the destruction of the Church of England, yet that the book on the whole will be a help as to those things which concern the peace of the soul, the deepening of the faith, and the increase of the desire more and more to love God and man.

b

It is much to be regretted that on the death of Dr. Newman, attempts were made to extol him and his former work for the Church of England, by depreciating Dr. Pusey and the labours of his life. Neither of these two good and eminent men would have liked any comparison to be instituted between them. The compiler is no doubt but one of many who feels that under God he owes a debt he can never adequately repay to Dr. Pusey; he had, so to speak, devoured his writings long before reading any of Dr. Newman's. Without making any comparison as to their gifts and their characters, it is simply a fact, which Cardinal Newman would have always admitted, that whatever before his secession he had done for the Church of England, Dr. Pusey, as the life-long champion of her claims, as teacher and spiritual adviser of her children, had done far more.

One book of Dr. Pusey's has not been quoted from, *An Historical Enquiry into the Causes of the Rationalist Character lately predominant in the Theology of Germany*, Pt. I., 1828; Pt. II., 1830. Dr. Pusey withdrew this book from publication; but it cannot be thought that he would object to the concluding sentence of this, his earliest work, being quoted as an encouragement to all the dutiful children of the Church of England—that is, the Catholic Church in England: "Be our faith rekindled, more energetic, more warm, more purifying, and the gates of hell will not prevail even for a time against this our portion of the Church of God."

CONTENTS.

PART I.

PART II.

MISCELLANEA.

CONTENTS. xxiii

CHURCH SEASONS.

NOTES AND QUESTIONS

ON THE

CATHOLIC FAITH AND RELIGION.

PART I.

FAITH.

> "For all thy rankling doubts so sore,
> Love thou thy Saviour still;
> Him for thy Lord and God adore,
> And ever do His Will."—JOHN KEBLE.

"BELIEF in general is an assent to that which is credible, as credible."

"The strength and validity of every testimony must bear proportion with the authority of the testifier. The authority of the testifier is founded upon his ability, and integrity" (and knowledge).

"If either ignorant or dishonest, his testimony may deceive."

"Human faith is an assent unto anything as credible, merely on the testimony of man."

"As that, there is such a city as Constantinople (to one who has not seen it); or that there was such a person as Cæsar."

"If we receive the witness of men, the witness of God is greater" (1 John v. 9).

"Divine faith is an assent unto something as credible upon the testimony of God."

"God has infinite knowledge and wisdom. God is Love. God is The Truth. From which internal essential and infinite Rectitude, Goodness, and Holiness, followeth an impossibility to declare or deliver that for truth which He knoweth not to be true."

"God then has spoken to us by His Son. The words His Father gave Him, He delivered to the Apostles. He prayed not only for them, but for them also who should believe on Him through their word."

"This was the true foundation of faith in all them which believed, that they took not the words which they heard from the Apostles, to be the words of the men which spake them, no more than they did the power of healing the sick, or raising the dead, and the rest of the miracles, to be the power of them who wrought them ; but as they attributed those miraculous works to God working by them, so did they also that saving word, to the same God speaking by them."—BISHOP PEARSON, *Exposition of the Creed.*

Is it always easy for the Christian to explain fully and clearly the grounds of his faith ?

"Few can adequately explain the grounds of their belief."[1]

"In the Gospel all is supernatural. It is above nature, in that it alone provides adequate remedies to the infirmities of human nature. Above nature are the life which it can produce, and the means by which it sustains that supernatural life, whether the Divine Word or the Sacraments of Christ, or the Sacrament of Prayer. Above nature is the whole office of the Holy Ghost, in the Church, and to individuals."[2]

"The difficulty of adequately explaining the grounds of your faith is occasioned by its Divinity. The Divinity of the object of your faith, and the Divine light of faith whereby you see it."[3]

You cannot satisfactorily explain or analyze love, trust, or

[1] Vol. 1872, p. 1. [2] *Id.* p. 3. [3] *Id.* p. 3.

the relation of soul to soul, the mystery of human filiation, eloquence, or the soul itself.

"But since then the soul has ways of knowing as to itself or others, more than it could explain or prove, since the soul of man has a nameless power over the souls of men to transfuse itself into them; to imprint on them for evil or for good its own thoughts, mind, will; shall not the Almighty God our Maker have means direct, convincing, demonstrating, *without circuit of proof* to impress on the soul, His creature, truth as to Himself? Has the Living God no means directly to infuse Himself into the soul which He has made, *impressing* upon it supernaturally His own Thoughts, Mind, Knowledge, Will?"[1] (Granting what cannot be denied, that God can do all this gracious work for and in the soul, we need not be dismayed because we cannot satisfactorily explain exactly *how* He effects this work of Love.)

"The denial of this power of God is the chief falsehood of rationalism."[2]

If a man cannot clearly demonstrate the proofs, and the truth of what he believes, must he not be always liable to doubt?

"Human reasoning ends in probability only. High probability it may be; moral, not absolute certainty. If the result of evidence be only that Christianity is highly probable . . . then our creeds should have run—'I believe that it is highly probable that there is one God the Father Almighty' . . ."[3]

"Faith is a God-given certainty."

"To the Christian every article of the Christian faith is as certain as his own existence. He is as certain that God *Is*, as that he himself is. Not 'opinions' or 'views,' but *knowledge*, a certain personal knowledge of God and of Christ . . . a knowledge which God infuses with His gift of faith into the soul."[4]

Again and again are we taught by our Lord and His Apostles, that faith has the certainty of knowledge.

"Jesus even likens the certainty of our knowledge that He came from God, to His Own Knowledge of the Father! 'I have

<hr>

[1] Vol. 1872, p. 8.   [2] *Id.* p. 9.   [3] *Id.* p. 11, 12.   [4] *Id.* p. 13.

known Thee, and these have known that Thou hast sent
Me.'"[1]

"Absolute certainty of knowledge is essential to revelation.
What is to 'reveal' but to unveil truth to us? To what end
should God reveal truth, except that we should know it?"[2]

"Christianity, then, claims a God-given certainty of God-
given truth.

Whence comes this Faith?

Remember always that faith is not of ourselves; it is the gift
of God (Eph. xi. 8); and that "no man can say that Jesus is
the Lord but by the Holy Ghost" (1 Cor. xi. 3).

"Faith from first to last is the gift of God. 'What hast
thou which thou hast not received?'" (1 Cor. iv. 7.)

As Christians may we see the more, that not of *ourselves*,
but of His rich mercy we bear that Glorious Name whereby
we are called, and have all the countless gifts which it
involves, the very least of which is greater than all creation
besides.[3]

*What would follow if the beginning of our faith were from
ourselves?*

"Then the beginning of our salvation would be from
ourselves, not from God, who in His love by His grace
'forecometh us in all things.'"[4]

*Can a man by his own unaided intellect discover and then
accept and believe the revelation of God—the Gospel?*

"Faith is the gift of God. In vain then will any who
have unhappily lost or impaired it, attempt to recover it by
a mere intellectual study of evidence. The object of faith is
one God. Unless we believe Him wholly, we do not believe
Him at all. If, on any ground, of their own repugnance men
disbelieve anything which God has revealed, then, whatever
else they hold is the conclusion of their own understanding,
not from God. They have, in fact, no faith. They believe
certain things of God, as a heathen may; they do not believe

---

[1] Vol. 1872, p. 15.   [2] *Id.* p. 18.   [3] *Sermons*, vol. ii. p. 300.
[4] *All Faith the Gift of God*, p. 5, vol. 1855.

in God. If, on the contrary, men seek faith from God, and by His grace submit themselves with their whole hearts to all which He has revealed, He will not let such err, in any matter which shall affect their salvation."[1]

"The natural man receiveth not the things of the spirit of God . . . neither *can* he *know* them because they are spiritually discerned" (1 Cor. i. 14).

"Even the angels behold God, not by their own created vision, but through the light of glory which God imparts to them. So with us, 'Through Thy light we shall see light'"[2] (Ps. xxxvi. 9).

Is the Christian to think little of intellect ?

So to do would be very wrong, for intellect, too, is a gift of God. It has its own reward if sanctified.

"'He who made all things for Himself,' must have prepared for those wonderful transcending intellects whose piercing thoughts are more like intuition than reflection, some separate lustre in that bright galaxy around His Throne. But only if tried, perfected, sanctified—intellect penetrated by the Spirit of God, irradiated by His Light, kindled by the glow of His Love, reflects to far ages the light which it has caught, illumines mysteries, guards truth. Great intellect may greatly serve God, if it first humbles itself to obey Him."[3]

"Unbelief, scepticism, rationalism, doubt, float harmless around the heart which believes in Jesus and meditates on Him. Disputing might as soon rend the sun from the heaven as Jesus from the heart which loves Him. The doubts of others cannot trouble our knowledge, nor the blindness of others our sight. You have not to win that faith for yourselves. The power of that faith was given you when you were 'born of water and the Spirit,' and Christ, antedating reason and your own choice, made you members of Himself and children of God. You have by His mercy to retain, not to gain, faith. You will not lose it while you lose not Him."[4]

[1] *All Faith the Gift of God*, vol. 1855, Pref. p. x. [2] *Id.* p. 25.
[3] *Id.* p. 23. [4] *Sermons*, vol. 1872, p. 29.

If faith were simply intellectual assent that the Gospel is true, would such faith be enough ?

Certainly not. It would not be a saving faith, it would be rather what is called *historic*, dead faith. That is the simple acknowledgment that such things were revealed, and such and such things really did happen.

What then is essential without which faith must be cold, weak, dry, and dead ?

"Love—faith without love has no root. For we are rooted and grounded in love."[1]

"Faith without love is the devil's faith. They believe and tremble. God is love. God is the object of faith. Faith then cannot for an instant be separated from love. Love, and you will not cease to believe."[2]

"Love is in all true faith as light and warmth are in the sun's ray."[3] Faith brings love, not love faith. Faith brought the Magdalene to her Saviour. "Yet she had not been forgiven had not her faith, love. First, our Lord says her sins are forgiven because she loved much."[4] Then He adds, "Thy faith hath saved thee."

"Faith which loves not, is not faith, it is dead. It is like a body without a soul."[5] "Love is the life of faith, both should grow together. The more we love the more we trust. Want of love is the cause of all want of faith. To preserve faith look above all things, in all things, unto Jesus the Author and Finisher of thy faith."[6]

"Do deeds of love for Him, to Him, following His steps, and so let love give life to thy faith."[7]

What is then the Christian's duty in regard to his faith?

"To guard it diligently with a sense of his responsibility to Almighty God, from whom it was received, to whom it is to be handed back unimpaired, through which the Christian has to stand accepted at the Judgment Seat of Christ."[8]

---

[1] *Sermons*, vol. 1872, p. 33.   [2] Vol. i. p. 5.   [3] *Id.* p. 6.
[4] *Id.* p. 9.   [5] *Id.* p. 12.   [6] *Id.* p. 14.
[7] *Id.* p. 19.   [8] Vol. 1872, p. 489.

"Man is responsible for his faith, because he is responsible for his acts whereby he loses it, and without which acts one by one, he would not have lost it." [1]

Must we be very careful not to disbelieve anything which God has revealed?

"He who wilfully rejects any truth proposed to him by God, does in fact reject God as the Supreme Truth, the Fountain of all truth, as he who disobeys any one command does, in fact, reject God as the Supreme God, the Rule and the Measure and Source of all good." [2]

"No one who departs from God, by departing in any one point from the revealed Will and Mind of God, has any standing-ground where to rest his foot." [3]

"But this is a characteristic of all who have parted with faith, that they began with some one point. They parted as they thought with one point of faith; the event showed that they parted with the faith itself." [4]

Name two causes of the prevalence of doubt.

"Sloth and pride."

"It is not inquiry, but a non-inquiring acquiescence in doubt which is the peril of this day. It costs much to disbelieve, it requires submission to our God and His grace to believe." [5]

THE ARTICLES OF THE CHRISTIAN FAITH.

To what is a Christian, as regards his faith, pledged?

"He is pledged at his Baptism to believe *all* the Articles of the Christian Faith, not this Article or that, for there never has been any heresy in the world but which has believed some one or more Articles of the Faith, . . . but not one form of religion in the world believes all the Articles of the Christian Faith, but the Church of Christ only. He cannot be a faithful Christian who does not keep, or endeavour to keep, the whole Faith. And as we know that in keeping God's commandments he who

[1] Vol. i. p. 296.   [2] *Real Faith*, p. 52.   [3] *Id.* p. 54.
[4] *Id.* p. 57.   [5] *Daniel*, p. 565.

'offends in one point is guilty of all,' so he who disbelieves
one Article of the Creed cannot rightly hold and believe the
others."—ISAAC WILLIAMS on the *Catechism*, vol. i. p. 68.

*Some seem to think that they may reject some one Article of the
Christian Faith without risk and injury : is this possible?*

"No.   As we have seen above, God the object of faith, is
One, and the substance of faith, is one.   Any deliberate
rejection of the faith in any one point is in fact a rejection of
the whole habit of faith." [1]

*Is it the declaration of the Apostle, that as there is one Lord
so there is one Faith?*

"Yes.   Holy Scripture does not know anything of Revelation
except as One Whole.   It speaks not of faith, but of *the*
faith ; not of another Gospel except to anathematize it, but of
The Gospel, *The* Word of God.   Everywhere it implies or
asserts that that which is revealed to our belief, is *One
Indivisible Whole.*[2]

*At Holy Baptism, the beginning of the Christian's life, what
summary of the Articles of the Christian Faith is proposed to
him?*

"The Apostles' Creed."

*At the time of sickness what is the minister directed to rehearse
to him?*

" The Articles of the Faith, reciting the Apostles' Creed."

*Ought the Christian to be content with a simple knowledge of
the Apostles' Creed alone?*

" Besides keeping God's holy will and commandments, and
learning the creed, the newly baptized are to learn all other
things which a Christian ought to know and believe for their
soul's health.   And they are to be called to use all diligence
to be rightly instructed in God's Holy Word."   The Christian
is not required to believe as an Article of the Faith, or requisite
or necessary to salvation, any thing that is not read in Holy
Scripture, nor may be proved thereby.

[1] *Real Faith*, p. 50.   [2] *Id.* p. 69.

" He will also see that the Nicene Creed and the Creed of St. Athanasius are to be thoroughly received and believed as well as the Apostles' Creed, because they may be proved by most certain warrants of Holy Scripture." [1] The Christian must also accept the authority of the Church as a faithful Witness and Keeper of Holy Writ.

If a man truly, simply, and reverently with all his mind and heart holds the Creeds, may he be said to believe all the Articles of the Christian Faith?

Yes, because therein he declares his belief in the Blessed Trinity.   He therefore believes and wishes to believe all that God the Father has revealed by His Son, all that God the Son had revealed by His Spirit.   In these Creeds he also declares his belief in the Holy Catholic Church, the Catholic Faith, the Catholic Religion.

He believes all that is taught of God and His Church, therefore he holds all the Articles of the Christian Faith, if he honestly holds the three Creeds.

What if some earnest, simple, but not very well instructed Christian, who prays to know and believe all that God has revealed, is ignorant of some one truth which he ought to believe?

" He might declare in some such words as these his confession of faith.   " I believe explicitly, all which I know God to have revealed to His Church, and implicitly, anything if He has revealed it, which I know not.   In simple words—' I believe all which the Church believes.' " [2]

What if a person has intellectual difficulties as to some one Article of the Creed, may he then reject it?

No.   " It is often the very condition of retaining faith altogether, to continue even for a long time to believe, without seeing, even if with all the diligence which a person can use, he cannot see the proof of an Article of Faith." [3]

" Lord, I believe ; help Thou my unbelief."

[1] Article VIII.   [2] *Eirenicon*, p. 7.   [3] *Rule of Faith*, p. 4.

THE THREE CREEDS.

What books may be used as helps to the study and understanding of the history and teaching of the Creeds?

Bishop Pearson's *Exposition of the Creed.*

Bishop Forbes on the *Nicene Creed.*

Norris' *Rudiments of Theology.*

Maclear's *Introduction to the Creeds.*

Harvey on the *Creeds.*

Jackson on the *Creeds.*

Dr. Pusey's Sermon—*The Responsibility of Intellect in matters of Faith.*

Brewer on *Athanasian Creed.*

MacColl on *Athanasian Creed.*

Waterland on *Athanasian Creed.*

Where will the reader find a defence against modern objections to creeds, and a vindication of their lasting necessity?

In Liddon's *Bampton Lectures.* A most helpful, as well as a most noble, Apologia in defence of the Faith.

Why do the Anglican and the Eastern Churches refuse to add to the number of the Creeds?

"It is very plain in Holy Scripture that there was from the first a *certain deposit of faith* committed to the Church everywhere. This deposit of faith is witnessed to by the Scriptures. ' For when it was first committed to St. Timothy, it is probable that St. Matthew's Gospel alone was written.' St. Jude speaks 'of the faith once for all delivered to the saints'; many passages imply that the revelation preached by the Apostles was one complete unchangeable whole. This being so, we can understand the Church having a great reluctance in any way to seem to add to the Creeds, and of course she has never added to the Faith." [1] " At Nicea, Constantinople, Ephesus, Chalcedon, when she decreed anything she established nothing *new ;* she did not enlarge *the* faith, but fixed it. The Fathers

[1] *Rule of Faith,* p. 9.

held, as St. Leo, that 'It is not lawful to depart by a single word from the doctrine of the Evangelists and Apostles, or to think otherwise of the Divine Scriptures than the Blessed Apostles and our fathers have learnt and taught.' Therefore the Church was always jealous of anything seeming to be new, as perforce not true." [1]

When grave necessity arose, she stated as in the Creeds the same old truths more fully. "With her antiquity and universality were ever the tests of truth : novelty, of error. On reflection we may well understand the reluctance of the Church to formulate and publish a creed or an article of faith, lest her declarations and explanations of old truths should be imagined to be the declaration of *new* doctrines unknown before, as not taught by our Lord or the Apostles."

Let us remember that "we who are the heirs of the ages of Christendom should cling with a peculiar loyalty and love to the great Nicene confession of our Lord's Divinity." But remember also that "The Nicene definition was wrung from the heart of the agonized Church, by a denial of the truth on which was fed, then, as now, her inmost life."—LIDDON'S *Bampton Lectures*, p. 437. Ed. 3.

Let us remember, too, that the "Faith is kept alive by prayer more than by definitions." [2]

THE BLESSED TRINITY.

The Athanasian Creed contains the most full and accurate statement of the doctrine, in possession of the Church. It is her Faith. "This is the Catholic Faith—that we worship one God in Trinity, and Trinity in Unity."

What about the difficulty of apprehending the doctrine ?

We must remember the finite imperfect mind of created man must not expect to comprehend the mystery of the Being of God. He must simply, with all humility, receive what God has chosen to reveal, and then believe and adore.

[1] *Rule of Faith*, p. 25.   [2] *Eirenicon*, part i. p. 45.

"The doctrine relating to the Infinite Nature of God. If we *could* grasp it, we should ourselves be God. Still the truths which God reveals, though they are above reason, are not contrary to enlightened reason." [1]

Are there any illustrations that may help us?

"Various ones have been suggested, but we must not press these likenesses unduly, else we shall fall into error. The best illustrations must of necessity be imperfect. They may have enough of likeness to shadow out some portion of the truth. They are unlike, because nothing can be *wholly* like the Divine Nature except Itself." [2]

Is not the creed of the Unitarian or Mahometan very simple, much easier for all mankind to receive, and therefore more likely to be true—that there is but one Divine Being?

It is not for us to settle what idea of God is the simplest, but to accept what God has revealed, whether it seem a simple statement or a profound mystery. Besides, the doctrine of the Blessed Trinity no more contradicts our reason than that God is eternal.[2] "We cannot conceive eternity looking backwards. We can conceive time lengthened out longer and longer and longer. We can think of continuance. We cannot think of Eternity without beginning. Let any one tell us how *God is;* how He Is, without beginning to be, and then He may ask us to explain how the Father can be God, and the Son God, and the Holy Ghost God, and yet one God." [3]

What consideration is a great help in contemplating the doctrine of the Blessed Trinity—that there are three Divine Persons in the One Godhead?

"This, God is Love, Infinite Love, and Infinite Love can alone content Infinite Love. We know in ourselves how unsatisfactory is unequal love. Until creation, according to Unitarianism and Mahometanism, God's was a lonely, unsatisfied Love. The creation of angels and mankind, could only yield to him a finite, unequal, imperfect love, so from all eternity God, who is Love, has had something wanting to the

[1] Vol. ii. p. 275.   [2] *Id.* p. 277.   [3] *Id.* p. 278.

perfection of His Love. This of course is untrue, for in the Divine Society of the Blessed Trinity is the perfect, eternal bliss of God. The Father loves the Son, and the Son the Father, and Both the Holy Ghost, the Bond of Both. Infinite Love is ever given and received. Perfect Love is ever satisfied, for Infinite Love is ever infinitely loved." [1]

As usual, has not God given to men more than they desired or deserved, in such revelations of His Being as He has vouchsafed?

Yes indeed. "He has revealed Himself not only as our Creator to claim our obedience, not only as our Lord to exact our service, not only as our Judge to whom we must give account, not only as a Father to demand our honour. He reveals all this and more, He reveals Himself not as a First Cause, a Creator who made us, because He was tired of being alone; but He reveals Himself as One Eternal, One Incomprehensible, One Almighty, One God, One Lord, yet not in the cold isolation of an unimpersonal God, but as existing in Three (Persons) of equal Glory—(in a Fellowship) of Infinite, Perfect Love." [2]

"God Himself is the Holy Blessed Three, and yet is One; His Eternal Being is one simple indivisible Essence, without parts, without passion. The Three Persons in the Co-equal Trinity, Father, Son and Holy Ghost are eternally; the Son everlastingly begotten of the Father, and the Holy Ghost proceeding from both; yet Father, Son, and Holy Ghost are perfectly One. 'They are not three Gods, but one God.' And this is the eternal bliss of God, that although three in person, they are in perfectness One God, and 'God is Love.'" [3]

> Eternal One, Almighty Trine,
> Since Thou art ours and we are Thine;
> By all Thy love did once resign,
> By all the grace Thy heavens still hide,
> We pray Thee keep us at Thy side—
> Creator, Saviour, Strengthening Guide.—JOHN KEBLE.

---

[1] *See* vol. ii. p. 278. [2] *Parochial and Cathedral Sermons*, p. 484. [3] Vol. ii. p. 387.

GOD THE FATHER.

Every Christian soul ought ever to be longing to love God more than it does.

To think of the great things He in His love has done for the soul, kindles and rekindles love with a new heat and glow.

To forget or never to think of some great work of love which God has done for the soul, must lessen and weaken our whole capacity of loving Him at all as He should be loved.

As far as we can, we should think of *all* the great things God has done for us, and not as so many do, think of *some* of them, and never dwelling much in thought upon the rest.

So, too, it is injurious to our faith and love, only to think of what our Lord has done for us, and seldom to think upon the love shown to us by God the Father and God the Holy Ghost.

The faith and the love of many Christians seem to be sadly imperfect in three most important ways.

They do not seem to think as they ought, of the love of God the Father, for the souls of men.

They seem, as regards God the Son, to remember only the work He did for them when here on earth, in the days of His suffering life, forgetting the work He is ever doing for them in Heaven.

As they think only of our Lord's work on earth, so too they think little of, or seem to be ignorant of, the unceasing long-suffering work of God the Holy Ghost on earth, in the Church Militant—in the souls of men.

To God the Father is due all the love, which by His grace our whole being can give.

Our Lord, our Saviour, is His gift to us. He gave Him to be our Saviour because "He so loved the world." In all eternity it was the resolve of the Blessed Trinity to make man.

The Father to create, the Son to redeem, the Holy Ghost to recreate.

"It would be heresy to represent God the Son as more loving to us than God the Father."[1]

"Our redemption is equally the fruit of the love of the Father and of the Son. It is set forth, as you know, in Holy Scripture, as the act of love of Both. 'God so loved the world that He gave His only begotten Son, that whosoever believeth in Him should not perish, but have everlasting life.' 'God commendeth His love towards us in that while we were yet sinners Christ died for us.' 'In this was manifest the love of God towards us, because that God sent His only begotten Son into the world, that we might live through Him.' 'Herein is love, not that we loved God, but that He loved us, and sent His Son to be the propitiation for our sins'"[2] (St. John iii. 16; Rom. v. 8; 1 John iv. 9).

The Father so loved us that "He spared not His own Son, but delivered Him for us all" (Rom. viii. 32).

Again and again does our Lord tell us that His Father sent Him.

So, too, our Lord tells us, that His Father at His prayer, shall give, shall send the Comforter, the Holy Ghost.

"That the Father loveth you, because ye have loved Me" (John xvi. 27).

It is of the love of the Father that we should be called the sons of God (1 John iii. 1).

After the General Judgment, the welcome into Heaven is to be in the name of the Father; "Come, ye blessed of My Father, inherit the kingdom prepared for you from the foundation of the world."

All that our Lord said and did for us, was in His Father's name, of His Father's commandment—to His Father's glory.

It was then our Lord's mission, our Lord's work, to bring souls to the knowledge of His Father, that they might love Him with all their heart, and mind, and soul, and strength.

---

[1] Vol. 1872, p. 238.　　　　　[2] *Id.* p. 239.

Remember that as the Three Persons of the Blessed Trinity are co-eternal, co-equal in glory, so too they are co-equal in love. That God is Love; and we must be most careful that nothing in thought, word, or deed, shall be contrary to this view of God.

Remember that in all your love to Jesus, in all you ask in His Name, in all that His love wins for you, bestows upon you, "it is that the Father may be glorified in the Son."

GOD THE SON.

It has just been said that many Christians do not seem mindful of the great work our Blessed Lord is still carrying on for them, and that they seem only to think of the work He did for souls when on earth. Do they think of all that He did for them as their Example, and does for them now as their Intercessor, or do they only think of what He suffered and did for them on the Cross?

"Jesus died for me" seems to be all that many Christians believe as to His work as their Saviour, whereas "we are also saved by His life" (Rom. v. 10).

To give us life in Himself is one great part of His Mission. He declares Himself to be the Bread of Life. That whoso eateth His Flesh and drinketh His Blood hath eternal life. And as St. John says, "He that hath the Son hath life."

"Not alone to die for us did the Son of God leave the glory of the Father, but to live for us, and in us, and through us, to conquer our great enemy, Satan.[1]

"When we were Baptized, little as we knew of the gift, we were translated from our birth in the old Adam to our birth in the New, from death to life. Then we were made partakers of Christ's Death, and also of His Resurrection, as St. Paul teaches (Rom. vi. 4), 'That we also should walk in newness of Life.' 'Our life is hidden with Christ in God, and when Christ, who is our life, shall appear, then shall ye also appear with Him in glory.'[2]

[1] Vol. iii. p. 441.   [2] *Id.* p. 151.

"Not only did Christ die for our sins, but also He gave us power to become the sons of God, and if sons, heirs, heirs of God."

Christ also came to save us by His preaching to us the Gospel, that is the Good News of God, as St. Paul said, "Thou hast the words of eternal life." As our Lord Himself taught, "He that heareth My word, and believeth on Him that sent Me, hath everlasting life."

He also gave us Himself as our Example. "Follow Me." "He left us an example to follow His steps."

He also became our Saviour not only by His Sacrifice on the Cross, but also by giving us power over temptation, power over Satan, power over sin.

He died to save us from eternal death. He rose to impart to us eternal life. He ascended into Heaven, to send to us the Holy Ghost, to give us faith in Him our Saviour, and to make us His members, to unite us to Himself.

One work of our Lord on earth is perhaps more lost sight of than any other. Sad indeed it is to think that anything we know our Lord did, or said, or suffered for us, should be forgotten. Think then of the Intercessions of Jesus. How He prayed for us all, in the days of His humiliation! "Neither pray I for these alone, but for all who shall believe in Me through their word" (John xvii. 20). Those prayers, the prayers of Him Who spake as never man spake, Who prayed when He was tired and worn with the toils and cares of His most suffering life; prayed too, often in the lonely hours of the night. Those prayers, also, helped in the work of your salvation.

These were His chief prayers on earth, for our salvation, "for to this end He came on earth." "He never prayed for Himself alone, whose whole Being was for His Father's glory in the salvation of mankind. His whole Being was Prayer, as in the Psalmist's prophecy—'I am Prayer' (xix. 4). Thirty years of intercession were the preparation of His Ministry in winning souls to His Father. Inwardly He was the perpetual

Intercessor for all around Him, for the whole human race. When praying, the heavens opened to Him ; when praying, He was transfigured; when praying in Gethsemane, He shed as it were great drops of blood."[1] Remember ever that Jesus as He suffered, also He prayed for thee.

Remember daily that "Jesus ever liveth to make intercession for us" (Heb. vii. 25). Intercession is spoken of as though it were *the* object of Jesus' life in heaven ; "Jesus is our High Priest; for us He intercedes by presenting Himself. He is the propitiation for our sins." Our Lord's life in heaven since His Ascension has been one unbroken intercession for us.[2]

Remember that while our Lord intercedes and prays for us in Heaven as our High Priest and as our Advocate, that He still works for us and in us on earth, and "all that is done in His Name by the Church on earth He is the doer of it. All that is done for souls on earth Jesus doeth it through the Holy Spirit ; through whom He indwells us; through whom He feeds us, through whom He guides us, through whom He gives us all that makes us fit for our union with Him ; and forgiveness of sins, our final salvation."[3]

In thinking of the Incarnation, especially at Christmastide, what is sadly lacking on the part of many ?

While rejoicing at the birth of Jesus their Saviour, they forget, and do not try to appreciate, as they ought, the fact that our Lord not only took that nature to humble Himself in it to the death of the Cross, but also marvellously humbled Himself in taking our nature at all.[4]

" To me more overwhelming, though not so touching, not so wounding, is the thought of the condescension, that God should will to have our human nature, however deified, for ever united with His Godhead, than even those dread sufferings of the Cross. They were indeed an unutterable extension of His Condescension, that God not only took our nature, but

[1] *Lenten Sermons*, p. 325.   [2] *Eleven Addresses*, p. 57.
[3] *Id.* p. 61.   [4] *See* vol. i. p. 65.

that God was—not blasphemed only face to face (that alas !
He is everywhere as God)—but that God was spat upon, God
was mocked, God was buffeted, God was crucified, God died !
But these sufferings, although infinite in degree and value, were
bounded in time.   His existence upon earth as man, His work
in meriting our salvation, was to be compressed within those
thirty-four years.   The condescension of that Union, whereby
His Divine and Human Natures are never to be divided, is
for Eternity.   In all Eternity we shall, in the Light of the Godhead, see the especial lustre of those glorious Suns, the sacred
Five, the blessed wounds which for us He received." [1]

Remember, then, that as we bless Christ for His sacrifice
and death upon the Cross, that we ever bless Him for becoming in His love for us, Incarnate.

"The humiliation of the Cross presupposes the humiliation
of the Incarnation.   Each has its own unfathomable depths of
Divine condescension and mercy." [2]

The Incarnation and the Passion is, and for ever will be,
the wonder and the glory and the moving cause of the adoration of heaven.   Beholding the depth to which the condescending love of God stooped in becoming man, beholding
the height to which that same love has raised man to sit in
heavenly places with Christ Jesus, for ever and for ever will
the song of men and angels be, " O come, let us adore."—
See Dr. PUSEY's *Sermons :—Jesus the Redeemer, God with us,
The Incarnation, A Lesson of Humility ;* LIDDON's *Bampton
Lectures ;* SADLER's *Emmanuel ;* RICKETT's *Saved by His Life ;*
WILBERFORCE *on the Incarnation ;* BRIGHT's *St. Leo on the
Incarnation.*

---

[1] *Eleven Addresses*, p. 25.   [2] Vol. i. p. 65.

GOD THE HOLY GHOST.

"It fills the Church of God, it fills
The sinful world around ;
¦ Only in stubborn hearts and wills
No place for it is found."—JOHN KEBLE.

¦ *What is commemorated at the great festival of Whit Sunday ?*

"That which has been called God's wondrous exchange. Half made on the Ascension, when Man in God was taken up into Heaven, and sat on His Father's Throne. The day of Pentecost *fulfilled* the promise of the Father, and as man now dwelt in God, so God in a new ineffable way, dwelt henceforth in man."[1]

Mention something of what God the Holy Ghost in His office and work does for man ?

As truly as the soul dwells in the body, even so God the Holy Ghost dwells truly and really in the hearts of the faithful, is the life of the soul itself, unites it to Christ ; is the fountain of all graces. "We receive not only gifts and graces from God, but His gift is Himself. He is to us Wisdom, Righteousness, Sanctification, Redemption, and that by the indwelling of the Holy Spirit.[2] As our Lord says : 'If a man love Me, he will keep My words, and My Father will love him, and We will come unto him, and make Our abode with him.' As in Ezekiel xxxvi.—'I will put My Spirit within you, and cause you to walk in My statutes.'"[3]

Not only does God the Holy Ghost indwell us working in our souls, but as St. Paul says, "Our bodies are His temples." It is not as if the Holy Spirit spoke to us only from without, or came upon us as a temporary influence, but He indwells us, abides *in* us.

It is a solemn thought of comfort that the 'Holy Spirit as God can indwell the human spirit ; but created spirits can only indwell the body or act upon it from without.—HUTCHINGS *on the Person and Work of the Holy Ghost*, p. 138.

[1] Vol. i. p. 440.   [2] *Id.* p. 441.   [3] *Id.* p. 442.

Does not the fact of the indwelling Presence of the Holy Spirit increase the heinousness of all sin ?

"This is the intense, sickening misery of sin, that it is brought close into the presence of God within us. To will a sin of thought, is to will it in the very Presence of God, not afar off, not in heaven, not under His Holy Eye alone, but *there*, where He came to hallow us, where by the voice of our conscience He pleaded with us, where if we held on in sin, we must first stifle our conscience, that is deaden His Voice, nay, cast Him forth." [1]

" Remember the Holy Spirit is given to us as the fountain of all grace, a Heavenly Inhabitant of soul and body, making us to partake of His own holiness and love. Therefore He is the life of our soul ; the author, inworker, perfecter, of all holy thoughts, words, and deeds ; the glow of our love, the strength of our hope, the upholder of our faith. He knits our souls in one, and knits them in Himself to God. He comes closest to us of the ever Blessed Trinity. Yet where one Person of the ever Blessed Trinity dwells, there dwelleth the undivided Trinity." [2]

"He that defileth the temple of God, him shall God destroy" (1 Cor. iii. 17).

Give, as may be with reverence, a summary of the various great works carried on by God the Holy Ghost.

He rules, guides, enlightens the Church, and only in, by, and through His operation is all her work done. He brings souls to Christ by conversion, He unites them to Christ in Baptism, making them children of God; He strengthens in Confirmation, He moves to repentance, He restores peace, He preserves in holiness, He warns, He comforts, He sanctifies, He guides, He leads into all truth, He helps to find it and to preserve it.

Nothing is done that is good in the Church or in the soul but He is the doer of it. No Sacrament administered is

---

[1] Vol. ii. p. 449.   [2] *Id.* p. 381.

worthily received but by His operation and His grace; no temptation resisted or good thought inspired, good word said, or good deed done, but by His Inspiration. Such is but a faint, poor sketch of His long-suffering and gracious work.

What is one great want in Christian devotions ?

"A more definite worship of God the Holy Ghost."— HUTCHINGS, p. 37.

Many do not seem to think that they may, and should, pray to the Holy Spirit, yet in our formularies He is separately supplicated, praised, or adored.   In the Litany, in the Glorias, in the Creed, in the Veni Creator, in the close of the Collects and Prayers.

What is the Sin *against the Holy Ghost ?* (St. Matt. xii. 31).

"First, what it is not.   It cannot be any sin from which men have ever repented, for wherever God has given repentance He has given pardon."[1]

"To fear lest we have committed the sin, or have been near committing it, is a proof we have not yet committed it."

"The sin of 'the blasphemy against the Holy Ghost' was not one sort of guilt, but many in one; it was the guilt of those who had the very Presence of their Lord, who witnessed His Love and Holiness, who saw the power of God; but out of envy and malice, obstinately resisted the light, and ascribed that which was the very working of the Spirit of Holiness to the unclean spirit."[2]

This sin was in its very nature unpardonable, not because God would not pardon it upon repentance, but because it cut off repentance from itself, turning into sin the very miracles of mercy which should have drawn it to repentance.

So in these days, though we do not see Jesus with our eyes, we do see the work that He does in souls through the Holy Spirit.   If a soul will deny Jesus to be its Saviour, will persevere in resisting the voice of Conscience, the plead-

---

[1] *Sermon on Blasphemy against the Holy Ghost*, p. 7.
[2] *Id.* p. 15.

ings and workings of the Holy Ghost within Him; if it continues in impenitence, if it continues to live in malice and hatred against all good, against God, and this sad condition hardens and hardens, till matured into its full ripeness of final obduracy, this may be the blasphemy against the Holy Ghost, and unpardonable.—See *Sermon* by Rev. T. CARTER *on the Sin against the Holy Spirit.*

St. Augustine says—"There is not in all Holy Scriptures a more important or more difficult question."

"When a man after the patience of God leadeth him to repentance, after his hardness and impenitent heart treasureth up unto himself wrath against the day of wrath and revelation of the righteous judgment of God, who will render to every man according to his deeds. This impenitence, in one word, hath no forgiveness, neither in this world, nor in the world to come, for that repentance only obtaineth forgiveness in this world, that it may have its effect in the world to come."

But this impenitence or impenitent heart may not be pronounced upon so long as a man lives in the flesh.

"One refuge there is against unpardonable blasphemy, that we take heed of an impenitent heart, and then it be not thought that repentance can avail aught unless the Church be kept to, in which remission of sins is given, and the fellowship of the spirit is preserved in the bond of peace."[1]—AUGUSTINE'S *Sermons on Lessons of New Testament,* xxi.

What other warning is given to us?

"To grieve not the Holy Spirit of God" (Eph. iv. 30).

"God the Holy Ghost cannot suffer as Jesus did, because He is only God, and God is impassable. Yet there must be something analogous to our created affections in that God is Love, and when His Love is repelled He seemeth to be pained."[2]

Think of the work of the Holy Ghost in individual souls.

"He ever offers His grace to the ever renewed millions of human souls."[3]

[1] See *Pusey's Sermon,* as above.
[2] *Eleven Addresses,* p. 73.
[3] *Id.* p. 74.

How is He treated in each ?

" Often rejected ; not listened to ; His temple defiled ; reason, on which He acts, stupefied by drink ; or intent on other matters, heedless of and despising His teaching ; indifference often, harder to love, than passionate rejection. No one can sum up all that the Holy Ghost has endured in His long-suffering love, within His own soul, and then think of the millions of souls He has indwelt ! "

" And, sad and awful thought, there is not a soul among the damned to whom He has not said, ' Listen to Me and it shall be well with thee.' There is not a soul among them who has not turned away and said, ' I will not obey Thee.' " [1]—*See* also DR. PUSEY'S *Sermon on Grieve not the Spirit of God.*

In what special way (too often forgotten by all) does the Holy Ghost help souls ?

" He maketh intercession for us."—*See* Rom. iii. 26, 27.

" Our prayers are helped by Him ; they are by Him intensified. He teaches us what to pray for, and to persevere in prayer. He is the life of our prayers, and may be said (in a way) to pray in our prayers. He expresses within the Holy Trinity the longings which He has suggested. " [2]

We are heard not only through the all-availing intercession of our Divine Lord ; but the Holy Ghost, who dwelleth in us, obtains through our supplications what He asks and knows to be best for us.

What sublime operation of the Holy Ghost is specially connected with the work of our Redemption ?

Our Lord was Incarnate by the Holy Ghost, of the Virgin Mary.

We must not expect to be able, neither should we seek, to understand or explain this mystery.

Only we must take care we believe the truth aright. " In the Birth of Jesus Christ, we acknowledge that He was made Man of the substance of His Mother. That as He was so made of the substance of His Mother, so was He *not* made of

---

[1] *Eleven Addresses*, p. 76. [2] *Id.* p. 82.

the substance of the Holy Ghost, whose essence cannot at all be made ; and because the Holy Ghost did not beget Him by any communication of His Essence, therefore He is not the Father of Him, though He were conceived by Him ; so too must we *not* believe that the Holy Ghost formed any part of Christ's flesh, of any other substance than of the Virgin, for certainly, according to the flesh, He was of the fathers, and was as to that, truly and totally, the Son of David and of Abraham."—PEARSON *on the Creed*.

Who then was conceived and born of the Virgin Mary?

"The only-begotten Son of God, Begotten by the Father before all worlds, for us men and for our salvation. Was Incarnate of the Holy Ghost of the Virgin Mary. Was conceived and born, taking to Himself the human nature, consisting of a Soul and Body, conjoining it with the Divine Nature in the unity of His Person."

"The Word was in this manner made Flesh, really and truly conceived in the womb of the Virgin ; not after the manner of men, but by a singular, powerful, invisible, immediate operation of the Holy Ghost."—*See* BISHOP PEARSON *on the Article "Was Incarnate."*

All Christians should daily say the hymn 'Veni Creator'; or at least frequently, as an ejaculatory prayer, the first line of it—

"Come, Holy Ghost, our souls inspire."

OUR SALVATION BY CHRIST.

"O call thy wanderer home
To that dear home, safe in Thy Wounded Side,
Where only broken hearts their sin and shame may hide."

JOHN KEBLE.

Why need Christ have suffered so much in the work of our redemption?

Could not the Creator repair His injured work without that hardness?

He could, but He preferred to " do it with injury to Himself, that that most odious and worst sin of ingratitude might no more find occasion among men. He took on Him exceeding toil, that He might hold man a debtor of exceeding love, and that the difficulty of redemption might admonish, of thanksgiving, him, whom the facility of creation had made less devoted."—St. Bernard. *See* Pusey's *Sermon on the Atonement.*

Was it in consequence of the prayers of men, or of their love in any way, that God resolved to save the world ?

No. " Herein is love, not that we loved God, but that He loved us, and sent His Son to be the propitiation for our sins " (1 John iv. 10).

Why could not man redeem man ?

Because " Man, even if one were created anew, free from that original stain, and in a state of grace, he could not redeem man, because he *owed* himself and all that he was already to God. This then is what is meant by the doctrine of satisfaction, not that God was under any necessity to redeem man ; but that if He did, for the redemption of the whole race of man there was needed a Divine Redeemer "[1] (Psalm xlix. 7).

The heinousness of sin is shown in that for it Jesus died. " The infinite love of the satisfaction of Jesus remedies that quasi-infinity of evil. Through the death of Christ the justice of God was set forth as well as His Divine Love."[2]

Did our Lord suffer for all mankind, or only for a certain number ?

He died for all.

Did the Sacrifice of the Cross plead for all who should ever live after our Lord's Crucifixion, and for those alive on earth when He was Crucified, and for all that ever lived before the Crucifixion ?

Yes, for all souls ; and all former sins that are forgiven "are forgiven for the sake of that One Propitiatory Offering,

[1] Vol. 1872, p. 241. [2] *Id.* p. 242.

and on that same principle that Precious Blood has ever since invested the whole earth." [1]

How then will any of the Heathen, Idolaters, or Heretics be saved ?

" If in good faith any such was what he was, living up to the light which he had whencesoever it came, and repenting where he did amiss. All Christendom would say as to such an one being lost, 'God forbid.' He would not be saved as Article XXIII. puts it, 'by that law which he professeth,' but he would be saved *in* it, by the one love of God the Father, who made him, and of God the Son who redeemed Him, and God the Holy Ghost who drew and in his measure sanctified him." [2]

What is meant by Satisfaction due to the Divine Justice ?

"That what was justly due to our sins, Christ paid ; the punishment which we justly deserved, Christ bore." [3]

The truth that Christ gave Himself for us is expressed in various ways. What form, since it is most loving, is most put into mouths by our All-Loving God ?

He gave His Life—He gave Himself in our *behalf*. It expresses more love to say " that He gave His life in our behalf," because it says that He was thinking of us, sacrificing Himself out of love for us. [4]

Mention some of the numerous passages of Holy Scripture in which we are told that Christ gave Himself for us—in our behalf.

" The bread which I will give is My flesh, which I will give for (*i. e.* in behalf of) the life of the world " (John vi. 51.)

"This is My Body which is given for you." " This cup is the New Testament in My Blood, which is shed for you " (Luke xxii. 19).

" As My Father knoweth Me, and I too know the Father, and I lay down My life for the sheep " (John x. 15).

"Who loved me, and gave Himself for me " (Gal. ii. 20).

" He loved us, and gave Himself for us, an offering and a sacrifice to God " (Eph. v. 2).

---

[1] Vol. 1872, p. 245.   [2] *Responsibility and Intellect*, p. 45.
[3] Vol. 1872, p. 246.   [4] *Id.* p. 249.

" Offered Himself to God, an offering and sacrifice for us "
(Eph. v. 2).

*What did St. Paul first teach as the foundation of the whole
teaching of the faith?*

" I delivered unto you first of all that which I also received,
how that Christ died for our sins according to the Scriptures;
and that He was buried, and that He rose again " (1 Cor. xv.
3, 4).

What was the price paid, the ransom given for us?

" The precious blood of Christ " (1 Peter i. 18, 19).

" We were far off (from God) but were made nigh (to Him)
by the Blood of Christ " (Eph. ii. 13).

" We were justified by His Blood " (Rom. v. 9).

" He suffered that He might sanctify us by His Blood "
(Heb. xiii. 12).

" We have redemption through His Blood, the remission of
sins " (Eph. i. 7).

" The Blood of Christ cleanseth us from all sin " (1 John
i. 7).

" He has purchased the Church with His own Blood " (Acts
xx. 28).

" God made peace through the Blood of His Cross, through
Him, as to the things on earth and the things in heaven "
(Col. i. 20).

*What must we always remember when we think, or hear of, or
receive in Holy Communion the Blood of Jesus?*

The Blood of Jesus is the Blood of Him Who is Very
God; Who for us and for our salvation became Man, shed for
the forgiveness of our sins.

What is meant by saying Christ suffered instead of us?

" Any statement of vicariousness, or atonement, or redemption involves what is meant by satisfaction to the Divine
Justice that what was justly due to our sins, Christ paid; the
punishment which we justly deserved, Christ bore." [1]

[1] Vol. 1872, p. 246.

Our Lord ever liveth to make intercession for us ; is He then now engaged in reconciling us unto God ?

No.   We were reconciled to God by the death of His Son (Rom. x. 10). We have already received the atonement (Rom. v. 11). God has reconciled us to Himself by Jesus Christ (2 Cor. v. 18).

"First, God gave reconciliation through the death of His Son, through the Blood of the Cross, then He gave by His Apostles the ministry of reconciliation, to win mankind to accept that restored favour. It is not that God is now reconciling the world ; He is converting it ; He *has* reconciled it. God has done the work of reconciliation. God's entreaty to souls through the voice of the Church speaking by the Holy Ghost is, "Be ye reconciled to God." [1]

JUSTIFICATION.

What is to be understood by Justification ?

"A real and not an imaginary process which takes place in the soul by the operation of God.   That process is both external and internal. Man is declared and accounted righteous because he is *made* righteous. The justified state is as a change from the state of sinfulness into the state of habitual grace and of Sonship. It is the contraction of a real and living fellowship with Christ, the Righteous and Holy One, such fellowship implying the remission of sin and the infusion of sanctification. It is the making over and imparting of the righteousness of Christ, so as to become inherent in the believer, who thus (no doubt imperfectly) becomes really just and well pleasing to God.—Bishop Forbes *on Article XI.*

In saying we are justified by faith only, is it meant that our faith justifies us by any quality of its own ?

"Certainly not.   Historical faith, whereby man assents to the Word of God, and the doctrines therein taught by God,

[1] Vol. 1872, p. 254.

even while the life is at variance with the belief, is a gift of God enlightening the mind, and it is to the man's own exceeding fault that it avails him not to salvation. Justifying faith must include in itself the belief in all the Articles of the Christian faith as far as any may attain to know them. To believe in God, is by believing to love Him ; by believing, cleave to Him, go to Him, and be incorporated in Christ's members. But this justifying faith does not justify us by any quality of its own, but simply brings us to God, who of His own free bounty and love justifies those who believe in Him." [1]

Does God in justifying us simply declare us righteous, or account us righteous ?

"God in justifying us, not only declares, but makes us righteous." [2]

"What He imputes that He also imparts." [3]

He creates in us an inchoate and imperfect, yet still a real and true, righteousness ; inchoate and imperfect because we all, while in the flesh, "in many things offend" ; yet real and true, because it is the gift of God and the first-fruits of His Holy Spirit.

What is the source of man's acceptance with God ?

"It is out of himself. It is not faith, it is not works, it is the mercy of God in Christ Jesus. It is God who justifieth, and that freely, without any deserts of ours either preceding or following faith." [4]

Faith, then, being the gift of God to us, what must follow, or rather what must be its fruit, and the proof of its being a living faith ?

GOOD WORKS.

Is it essential to a living faith, and necessary to our salvation, that good works be done by the grace of Christ (when they can be performed) ?

---

[1] *Justification*, vol. 1855, p. 5.　　[2] *Id.* p. 7.
[3] *Id.* p. 8.　　[4] *Id.* p. 21.

"Faith without works is dead. By works faith is made perfect."—*See* 1 James ii. 20, 22.

A saving faith is in short a "faith that worketh by love," as St. Paul says (Gal. v. 6).

How may Faith and Works be described?

"As one compound whole, even as in man in whom they exist, body and soul are one living man."[1]

Give an instance from Holy Scripture showing that the purpose of the heart being an inward act, faith is not for a moment separate from action.

St. Paul's "Who art Thou, Lord?" was followed up at once with "Lord, what wilt Thou have me to do?"[2]

May we then solely put our trust in either our faith, or in our good works, or in both together?

"We are to trust in nothing; or rather we are to trust only for salvation in our Lord and Saviour Jesus Christ. (*See* the Collect for Sexagesima.) We are not to trust in any thing that we do, though we may hope and pray, as in the Collect for Trinity XXV., that God will stir up the wills of His faithful people, that they, bringing forth the fruit of good works, may of Him be plenteously rewarded, for the sake of Jesus Christ our Lord."

"By grace are ye saved through faith; and that not of yourselves: it is the gift of God: not of works, lest any man should boast" (Eph. ii. 8, 9).

If God has given thee vivid faith, and disposed thy heart to bring forth fruit in good works, ought thou to rest content?

"No. As thou by faith beholdest the greatness of God and of His eternal Grace, His ineffable Holiness, Majesty, Glory, Goodness, Love, thou wilt know and feel the nothingness of all in thyself, whether faith or works save, as they are the gift of God."[3]

As thou probest thyself, thou wilt see the more thine own evil. But as thou ownest thine own evil and God's good, He will take away from thee thine evil, and crown in thee His

---

[1] *Justification*, p. 28. [2] *Id.* p. 29. [3] *Id.* p. 47.

own Good : as thou ownest thyself in thyself an unprofitable servant, He, owning in thee His own work, will say unto thee, " Well done, thou good and faithful servant; enter thou into the joy of thy Lord."

EVERLASTING PUNISHMENT.

What does the Church teach on this awful subject ?

In the Athanasian Creed she teaches, " they that have done good shall go into life everlasting, and they that have done evil into everlasting fire."

What two objections are made against this statement ?

That all have done evil, therefore according to this statement none will be saved.

And that "everlasting fire" does not mean everlasting punishment, but only a punishment for a certain time, the duration of it being known to God only?

What is the answer to the first objection ?

Neither the Church, or the Bible, or the Creeds teach that all who have done evil, must without doubt perish everlastingly. On the contrary, the Bible, the Church, the Creeds teach distinctly "the forgiveness of sins." Whoever has done evil (and who has not ?), but repents of all the evil he has done, without doubt will not perish everlastingly. Such is the Catholic Faith.

The Creeds are set forth more for the edification of Christians than for objects of misunderstanding by sceptical critics.

But does the Church teach that impenitent sinners will be everlastingly punished and shut out from heaven ?

" The Church pronounces no sentence on any individual soul. The final condemnation or acquittal of each and every soul rests with God. Her duty is the simple declaration of God's truth, that those upon whom God's curse falls at the day of judgment are lost, and for ever.

But does not the word " everlasting" only mean a very long unknown time?

In Romans xvi. 26 the same word is used of the Everlasting God, and if everlasting punishment does not necessarily mean punishment which never comes to an end, then too everlasting bliss in Heaven may also mean that the joys of Christ's saints may have a complete termination.

Moreover, it must never be forgotten, that our Lord has plainly given us to understand that after the sentence of everlasting punishment is pronounced, there is no cessation of it for ever, that is, no forgiveness and admission into Heaven.

Take, for instance, His declaration, " Their worm dieth not, and their fire is not quenched." He does not say their worm will eventually die, and after due time their fire shall be quenched.

Let us never forget our Lord's declaration, " The word that I spake, the same shall judge him at the last day."

Those who deny that our Lord taught what the Church has always held that He taught, incur an awful responsibility, for which they will have to render strict account.

State some of the most plausible objections.

God is Love; it is then impossible to believe that He could punish any of His creatures for their sins, for ever and ever. How can it be true?

We are to walk by faith, not by sight; there are many mysteries in revelation which faith can only accept, but which reason cannot explain.

" The mystery of evil in the works of God Almighty, All-wise, and All-good, can neither be explained, nor softened, on any system of religion or irreligion. But since the existence of evil in the works of God is wholly beyond reason, and yet we must believe in the Infinite Love and Goodness of our God, although we cannot in the least understand, why He who is All-Good, should have created that which He knew would become evil, then it were against reason to require as a condition of our belief that we should understand anything

D

bound up with the existence of that evil. Since we are wholly ignorant about the whole, it were vain to insist that we should fully understand a part." [1]

" Explain to me the mode of God's Being as a Spirit, and I will explain to you how God is Three in One. Explain to me the essence of God, and I will explain to you how that essence is eternally communicated by the Father to the Son, and through the Son to the Holy Ghost, and how the three Divine Persons eternally in-exist in One Another. Explain to me how the existence of evil at all, is consistent with the Infinite Wisdom and Power and Love of God, and I will explain to you the justice of eternal punishment. Explain to me His justice and love in the sufferings of the new-born infant, and I will explain to you how and why the Justice of God required that the innocent should bear the guilt of us sinners, and it pleased the Lord to lay upon Him the iniquities of us all. Explain to me the mode of the knowledge of God, and I will explain to you our own free agency, and the mystery of pre-destination and of the efficacy of prayer. Explain to me the act whereby God created out of nothing, and I will unfold to you all the mysteries of creation. Explain to me the nature of the spiritual body after the Resurrection, and I will explain to you how the same flesh shall arise. Make known to me how ' the reasonable soul and flesh is one man,' and I will make clear to you how ' God and man are One Christ.' " [2]

But surely, it is said, that it cannot be justice to punish a man's sin, which after all is finite, with punishment which is infinite ?

It is forgotten that a man's sin is against the Infinite Love and Majesty of God ; that there can be no injustice in God's saying to mankind, " Love and serve Me, and I will give you everlasting joy and bliss. Rebel and disobey, and love Me not, and I will reject you everlastingly."

Is it true that the testimony of the Primitive Church is against the doctrine of eternal punishment ?

------

[1] *Real Faith Entire*, p. 77.   [2] *Id.* p. 80.

No; as a Committee of Convocation (Canterbury) say in their report on Burial Rites, July 1877, " The belief in a state of eternal punishment as well as of eternal happiness was all but *universal* among the ancient writers."—*See* Last Charge of ARCHDEACON HARRISON.

Surely after this life and after the Judgment, a man may become convinced of the error of his way, and desire to change his whole manner of life, thought, word, and deed, and amend and love God ?

" Unchangeableness may be, for what we know, one of the laws of eternity. We know that it shall be of the blessed. Heaven could not be Heaven unless they were fixed in good. What ? See God face to face, love Him with that transforming, ever-inflowing love ; be ever with Jesus ; thank Him ; feel through and through, ' What Jesus 'tis to love,' and think it possible that one could again be ungrateful to His love, again sin against Him, again crucify Him ? No ; the impossibility of sinning must underlie all the bliss of Heaven." [1]

" And it may be an equal law of our moral nature that they who reject God in time, even to the end will by a continuance of that same fixed will, reject Him everlastingly." [2]

It must also be remembered that at the Judgment, sinners that are rejected by the Judge, are rejected with the terrible words, " Depart, ye cursed, into everlasting fire."

Repentance, conversion, change of heart is the result of the operation of the Holy Spirit. Is the Holy Spirit to indwell those who are cast out in the company of the devil and his angels? Is He to be bestowed once more with greater power, and to regenerate and convert the impenitent, those who have already here received and quenched the gracious gift ?

Is there another Pentecost, another Whitsuntide, for those under our Lord's judgment curse ? If there is to be another giving of the Holy Spirit, then we may ask, When did God say so ? Where is it written ? If the love, the life, the death of Christ and the indwelling presence and work of the Holy

---

[1] *Everlasting Punishment*, p. 10.   [2] *Id.* p. 11.

Spirit here fail to soften and win, what can succeed when all this has failed?

Remember, too, that in this life the Holy Spirit works often, not only directly in man, but upon man through man. Here, there is the help of good example, to counteract the harm of bad example. In Hell there is no good companionship or good example.

Moreover, if punishment of the reprobate is not eternal, from what did Christ by His Passion and Cross save sinners? From nothing, because those who deny eternal punishment practically teach that those for whom Christ the Saviour died, and yet did not win, and who Christ the Judge condemned as cursed, are yet to be admitted into Heaven after a certain amount of punishment, such finite penance being more effective than the sufferings and sacrifice of the Son of God, and the work and pleadings of the Holy Spirit!

" Never will any one in truth believe the Redemption by Christ, who does not believe in Hell. God became man to redeem—from what? From what, according to them, is equally remedied without it."

What lie accompanied the first temptation of a soul?

"Satan's—'Thou shalt not surely die.' He says now, God hath not said any shall perish everlastingly. We dare not be wiser than God, Who said by His Apostle, 'Knowing the terror of the Lord, we persuade men.' We dare not be wiser than our Lord, Who said, 'I will forewarn you whom ye shall fear : Fear Him which, after He hath killed, hath power to cast into hell ; yea, I say unto you, Fear Him.' "[1]

" Listen not to them who repeat to you the tempter's words, 'Thou shalt not surely die.' Listen not to those who would make Jesus a deceiver; but listen to Him Who was crucified for you ; listen to Him Who loves you ; so shall you for ever thank Him and bless Him, that the fear of hell scared you back from sin, and made you take refuge in Him, Who loves you more tenderly than a mother doth, in the Bosom of your God and His everlasting love."[2]

[1] *Everlasting Punishment*, p. 29.   *Id.* p. 30.

But will it not be to the dishonour of God, if evil in hell is to go on for ever ?   Where then would be the triumph of Christ, Who was manifested to destroy the works of the devil ? Would not the triumph be Satan's, if evil ever exists ?

" If it was not inconsistent with God's honour and glory to permit the existence, it cannot be inconsistent with His honour and glory to permit its endless existence."—MALCOLM MACCOLL *on Eternal Punishment,* p. 18.

Besides, to be kept in eternal punishment is certainly not to be in a state of triumph. The Cross has its triumph, in the multitude no man can number. If the power and love of the Cross did not save all, it was not that God failed, but that men refused salvation, and chose evil instead of good.

What amongst other things helped the early Christian martyrs to the endurance of their terrible sufferings ?

The belief that it was better to suffer however terribly for a time for Christ, than suffer eternally for the denial of Him.

" I say unto you, my friends, ' Be not afraid of them that kill the body, and after that have no more that they can do.   But I will forewarn you whom ye shall fear : Fear Him which, after He hath killed, hath power to cast into hell ; yea, I say unto you, Fear Him.'   This fear of being for ever separated from Christ in hell, strengthened the weakness of the flesh in Christian martyrs, as we see from the sayings of some of them ; this roused some who for the extremity of suffering had once denied Him to endure fearlessly all torments for Him : the dread of the eternal fire made that which consumed the flesh to be like Elijah's chariot of fire, which bore him above all of earth : this fire expelled the evil passions of the flesh : this Article of their faith, the unlettered barbarians knew of as belonging to the Primitive Creed, as much as the words of our Lord in the Athanasian." [1]—*See* also CANON LIDDON'S *Sermon, Whole Counsel of God.*   Examples from RUINART.

[1] *What is of Faith ?* p. 24.

Mention two places where the Church of England teaches the doctrine of Eternal Punishment.

In the Litany she bids us pray—"From Thy wrath, and from everlasting damnation, Good Lord, deliver us." And at the side of the grave, at the burial of the dead—"O holy and most merciful Saviour, deliver us not into the bitter pains of eternal death."

In 1864 a Declaration by 11,000 clergymen was put forth, affirming that the Church of England, in common with the whole Catholic Church, teaches, in the words of our Lord, that the punishment of the "cursed" equally with the "life" of the "righteous" is "everlasting."

What is the will of God as regards the salvation of all souls ?

God willeth that all men should be saved (1 Tim. ii. 4) ; but all men *will* not, to be saved.

Consider this. To the souls on the left hand at the Judgment Day the Judge does not say, "Ye cursed, of My Father," for, not *He* laid the curse upon them, but their own works ; and He says, "into the everlasting fire"—not, prepared for them, but "prepared for the devil and his angels."

"I," He saith, "prepared the kingdom for you, but the fire no more for you, but for the devil and his angels ; but since ye cast yourselves therein impute it to yourselves." [1]—St. Chrysostom.

Does not the Greek word usually translated "everlasting" only mean for many ages, and not for ever ?

The opinion of the Rev. J. Riddell, one of the best Greek Oxford scholars of his day, says, " That word was used strictly of eternity, an eternal existence such as shall be, when time shall be no more. In the New Testament it occurs seventy-one times ; of eternal life, forty-four times ; of Almighty God, His Spirit and His Glory, three times ; the Kingdom of Christ, His Redemption, the Blood of His Covenant, His

---

[1] *What is of Faith ?* p. 29.

Gospel, salvation, our habitation in Heaven, of the glory laid up for us, thrice; our inheritance, consolation, of a sharer of eternal life; of eternal fire, thrice; of punishment, judgment, destruction, four times." [1]

"O Jesus, Who hast made known to Thy servants another death, besides that which separates the soul from the body; deliver us not, we beseech Thee, into the bitter pangs of eternal death, and that we with all those for whom we are bound to pray, may escape the sad sentence of final separation from Thee; grant us, we beseech Thee, courageous and duti-ful hearts, truly and lovingly to accept Thy most true and merciful warnings; keep this Church and nation from believing a lie, and from denying or doubting any part of Thy Gospel; and perfect in us, the love of the truth, that we may be saved through Thy merits and mediation, Who livest with the Father and the Holy Ghost, one God, world without end.   Amen."— *See* JOHN KEBLE'S *Litany of our Lord's Warnings*, and CANON LIDDON'S *Sermon, The Whole Counsel of God.*

SIN.

Why do so many persons think so little of the dreadful nature and character of sin ?

From the great imperfection of their faith.   The more thoroughly a man believes in God, the greater his horror will be of sin, the more living, convincing, and real, will be his conviction, that sin—all sin—is a terrible, soul-destroying thing.

Can any one, however strong his faith, realize now how awful sin is ?

"The depth of its blackness, none can thoroughly know, save God Himself.   For God alone knows the infinity of that Love and Holiness against which we sin." [2]

"It is offence against Him, our Lord and God to Whom we belong by virtue of our creation, as His subjects, whom He

[1] *What is of Faith ?* p. 38.   [2] *Eleven Addresses*, p. 85.

created for His good pleasure and glory. It is rebellion against His most righteous Will, withdrawing from Him His lawful possession, our souls, and transferring them to His and our enemy, the devil, who disputes His sovereignty over us. It is offence against Infinite Goodness, bringing a black spot into his creation; a putrid foulness, marring its beauty, as He made it to be a mirror of some of His own perfections. It is a defiance of His power, as though He could not requite. It is contempt of Himself, the Infinite God."

"God created us to be like unto the angels; our spiritual sins are an imitation of the sins of devils, without the temptation of the enormous intellect at least of some of them. · Our fleshly sins are disordered below the beasts that perish."[1]

What is the worst of all sin, its blackest feature, and its misery?

The ingratitude of it, rejecting God, rebelling against God, treating Him, as if He had never done anything to win our love.

"If the mighty works, which have been done in you, had been done in Tyre and Sidon, they would have repented long ago in sackcloth and ashes?" (Matt. xi. 21).

This then should be the especial grief as well for our own sins as for others, that they are so contrary to the Love of God·

Name one great fault in the view which most persons take of their sins.

They think almost entirely of sins they have done, they do not think enough of their sins of *omission.*

"Sins which we have done, we can, at least, imagine; the things which we ought to have done, and which not to do was sin in us, are beyond all imagining. We have no measure whereby to calculate them. We noticed them not. They mostly left no wound. And yet one class of such sins occupies a very prominent place in our Lord's picture of the Day of Judgment. 'Inasmuch as ye did it not to one of the least of these, ye did it not to Me.'"[2]

[1] *Eleven Addresses,* p. 86.   [2] Vol. 1872, p. 308.

Have we not to fight against all sins, both of commission and omission ?

Yes. We have to fight against all the whole body of sin, and also to take special care and pains to fight against the sin that doth so easily beset us.

Most souls have some besetting sin, some one particular fault in their character.

" The besetting sin is that by which a soul most frequently offends God, and offends Him most." [1] It has the most excuses made for it, it is fallen into the quickest, with the least resistance; it fills the imagination most often. So often sin is sinned in thought, that it is most necessary for the soul to conquer it thoroughly.

Why is it most important that this sin should be conquered ?

" Because if by God's grace the sin which has the greatest hold over a soul, is conquered, victory over all other temptations will become easier." " Slay Goliath, and the Philistines will flee." [2]

What are two great proofs of the awfulness of sin ?

(1) The awful consequences of the one sin in Paradise— sorrow, sickness, death, all the misery in the world's history, known and unknown, in all those countless souls who have been created.

(2) The price paid for the redemption of sinners, the Sacrifice of the Son of God, proves the heinousness of sin.

" The Cross of Jesus is the measure of sin as an offence against God; it brings within the reach of sense that which before was confined to the domain of thought; it exhibits sin in its true light in relation to the Divine Essence. Sin is an outrage upon the Divine Goodness, when we prefer something vile to God. Jesus and Barabbas are coupled together, and Barabbas is preferred."

Sin despises the Wisdom of God, when we break the law of God : Jesus, the Eternal Wisdom, is mocked as a fool in the

---

[1] Vol. ii. p. 134.   [2] *Id.* p. 135.

court of Herod. Sin says, "God hideth His face, He will never see it."

Disbelievers in the Divine Omniscience; of Jesus it is written, they "blindfolded Him . . . and asked Him, saying, Prophecy who is it that smote Thee?" Sin abuses the long-suffering of God: Jesus bore insults, mockery, and blows in silence. "He was led as a lamb to the slaughter, and as a sheep before her shearers is dumb, so He opened not His mouth." Sin prostitutes the power of God when we employ the strength which He has given us against Himself: Jesus was nailed, hand and foot, to the tree, as if weak and over-taken by His enemies. Sin outrages the sanctity of God; the sacred form of Jesus was exposed to ridicule, while He "endured the Cross, despising the shame." Sin would cause God to die if it were possible: it would remove Him from the world: sin caused Him to die, it did remove Him in a way by which He had made it possible, when Jesus upon the Cross gave up the Ghost. God took a nature in which He could reveal what an injury sin had all along been to His unseen perfections. The scene on Calvary was an illustration of the outrages which sin perpetrated upon all the perfections and Titles of God. The Cross was the measure of sin, making manifest the assaults which sinners at all times make upon the Invisible Goodness. The Cross was to be henceforth an abiding revelation of the guilt of sin, so that men, by using their senses, might learn its nature as they behold the God-Man nailed to the tree.—*See* HUTCHINGS' *Some Aspects of the Cross*, p. 67.

Suppose a person really does not know which is his besetting sin, what then?

Pray to know, but "if thou canst not find out thy chief fault, apply thyself to any bad one. It is better to gather thyself to an earnest conflict with almost any one, than to lose thy time in debating which to grapple with. Whilst thou art en-gaged in earnest about one, God will disclose to thee others."[1]

[1] Vol. ii. p. 155.

Mention some of the awful effects of sin.

It "deadens faith."

It takes away a humble, joyous sense of God's Presence.

It injures and hinders the work of God in His Church. It gives cause of triumph and delight to all the enemies of God.

It injures the soul for ever.

It injures other souls. Sin seldom stops at ourselves; if what we do, that is wrong, is unknown to others, yet it injures our character, lessens our fervour and zeal (under God) for doing good.

It risks our salvation.

It must end in hell, unless by God's grace repented of.

Is God angry with us on account of any predisposition to any sin born with us ?

" A man is not the object of God's displeasure on account of the remains of his inborn corruption if he in earnest strive with it. If he strive not in earnest with it, he is the object of God's displeasure, not on account of the sinfulness of his nature, but on account of his own negligence as to that sinfulness of nature, or his sinful concurrence with it." [1]

Is this a lawful complaint ?—" My nature is sinful, and therefore I am the object of God's displeasure, and all is ill with me ? "

" The truth is we have an infected nature, a nature prone to evil, ready to burst out into sin unless it be kept down by grace. But by grace it may be kept down; although not wholly, yet increasingly ; so that the will should be more and more confirmed to the Will of God, the imagination wander less from God, the heart thirst more for God, and for nothing out of God, or contrary to or beside His Holy Will. What is evil ought to be continually lessened; what is good, if not sensibly yet imperceptibly, ought to be strengthened, increase, and grow; as the corn groweth, thou knowest not how, but the growth is, after a time, seen. Yet this infection within us, although of " the nature of sin," still, unless our will consent to

___
[1] Vol. ii. p. 334.

its suggestions, is not sin. *So long as, by God's grace, we master it, it is not sin, but the occasion of the victories of His grace.*" [1]

"People distress themselves by not owning this: they deceive themselves, if they make it the occasion of careless-ness." [2]

What is the great secret of success in resisting temptation?

Feeling a sense of one's own weakness, and ever praying to God to help. "Try then to resist the very first motions of temptation; it is then that thou art most in thy own power." [3]

As in wrestling, let not the adversary close with and grip thee.

What should encourage prolonged resistance till victory is gained?

"Each such resistance is an act of obedience to God; each, done by His grace, draws down more of His grace to thee; in each, His good pleasure will the more rest upon thee; by each, thou wilt become more a vessel of His grace and love, more fitted and enlarged for His everlasting Love." [4]

What blessed result comes from long-continued, well-endured temptation?

"Through all this conflict the more thou art tossed here, the more thou wilt learn to long for thy heavenly home, the Home of His rest and love. Thou shalt learn to long lovingly for that day when the remaining corruption shall be put off, and this body of sin have died through the body's death; but the body itself shall be instinct with new life, and conformed to the glorious Body of thy Lord." [5]

What if sometimes one fails, but by God's grace repents?

"In all eternity redeemed man cannot forget what he has been. His own special blessedness would be less if he could. For our bliss will be by God's mercy in the Infinite Love of our God; and we should know less of that Infinite Love if we did not know how much He had forgiven us, how His victorious

---

[1] Vol. ii. p. 333.   [2] *Id.*
[3] *Id.* p. 340.   [4] *Id.* p. 341.   [5] *Id.*

Love had won us to Himself.   St. Peter's bliss would be less if
he could forget that look which won him back to himself and
to His Lord." [1]

"The robber would not, if he could, be deprived of the
memory of his Lord's love, which pardoned that, his last
blasphemy on the Cross, accepted the confession which that
love itself had given, and admitted him alone of His redeemed
to His side in Paradise." [2]

" But since the memory of forgiven sin will intensify the
joy of Heaven, so penetrated will it be and transfigured with
Divine Love, then neither, by the grace of God, will it cast
any shadow over life's pure joys here.   Nay, rather there is no
true joy without it." [3]

"Our only joy can be, not in ourselves, but in God; not in
ignorance that we are sinners, or how deep our sins, but in
pouring out all our sins at the feet of Jesus, and in His
forgiveness." [4]

" And then man's true joy is in thankfulness to God, and to
Jesus, God-Man, for atoning, pardoning love.   So God trans-
mutes our poverty into the riches of His grace; our short-
comings into the overflow of His love; our badness into the
occasions of His goodness; our hateful memories of what is
hateful sin, into channels of His purifying grace, the joy of
redeemed love." [5]

*It has been said that people do not think enough of sins of
omission.   Is there one great sin of this description very common
amongst professing Christians?*

Yes; the neglect of Holy Communion.

Why is this such a great sin?

Because it is such a sin of ingratitude and disobedience,
despising our Lord's dying command.

*What is one awful effect of sin which is so continually forgotten
and ignored?*

The dishonour done to God, Whose Temples we are.

[1] *Lenten Sermons*, p. 398.   [2] *Id.*   [3] *Id.*
      [4] *Id.* p. 399.   [5] *Id.*

Impurity, as we are told, "defiles the Temple of God," and if any man defile this Temple of God, him shall God destroy. "For the Temple of God is holy, which Temple ye are" (1 Cor. iii. 17).

As a rule do not people in general, rather look upon sin as only likely to affect them at some future time, if it affects them at all? And then, thinking they will live long, say to themselves that, " When I am nearer death than now, no doubt I shall have done with sin, be sorry for it, and be forgiven" ?

Some no doubt think and act thus, but it cannot be too earnestly impressed upon all that sin injures us *at once*, and it is impossible to repent of sins too soon; the sooner the better, lest we "die in our sins."

Remember there is a great peril in little sins.

"The naked foot can stamp out a spark and feel no pain, but unheeded the spark may cause the destruction of a city."[1]

"The thin edge of a wedge is slight and fine; it may be used to break an oak to pieces."[2]

"A drop of water is soft, but continued drippings wear away stones."[3]

"Stop beginnings if you would stop short of the end."[4]

"The first slight deceit is a greater wound to the soul at first, than deliberate lying afterwards. Had the first slight sins not been done, conscience, fine and delicate, would not have been impaired; yielding to little sins is like taking away the barrier of a fence stick by stick."[5]

"Little sins then are perilous to the soul, because they break down the safeguards against sin with which God fences it in by nature; they accustom the soul to the thought of further sin ; they take off the snow-white fineness of the purity of a soul in grace ; they relax the earnestness of the soul ; they indispose it to good ; they dispose it to further evil ; they come between the soul and God ; they weaken the mind ; they blind

[1] *Par. and Cathedral Sermons*, p. 118.
[2] *Id.* p. 119.   [3] *Id.*   [4] *Id.*   [5] *Id.* p. 122.

the understanding ; they chill the affections ; they dull the soul ; they divide the heart ; they hinder it from trustful repose in God ; at the last, step by step, they estrange the soul from God, cause God to withdraw His grace from the soul ; they invite his attacks, who is ever at hand in wait for the careless soul." [1]

What is one terrible effect of "little sins" ?

" To have indulged in them often puts souls under the evil influence of others, who want them to add sin to sin, and do the worst.

".A man's or woman's bad companions will jeer at them as squeamish, or nice, or over-particular, that, having done whatever other lesser wrong they have done, they stop short of any further wrong which they wish them to do. They taunt them with what they did before, as if they were all of a sudden changed, or were insincere before, or are so now, or are acted upon by mere fear of man, or some motives of interest, or were all at once becoming scrupulous and ' turning saint,' as they say. How many souls have been stung into greater evil by such reproaches ! How have some tender, loving souls been goaded into deadly evil, and their own utter ruin by the taunt, ' You do not care for me if you will not do this ! ' And yet those who taunted them would not have dared to breathe the polluting thought of evil, had not lesser evil of the same sort gone before. People do not expect a stranger whom they meet to turn back with them and go their road." [2]

" Think of your conscience being laid open before you ; think of every thought, word, deed in your whole lives, minute after minute, in every year, month, day of your lives, being unfolded to you ; sins which you never saw ; sins to which you blinded yourselves, so that you could not see them ; sins which you thought lightly of, because so many besides you did them ; or because you were accustomed to them, or because you liked them ; or perhaps they seemed to give you what you wished for. And then to see how, in wasting the grace of God, you

[1] *Par. and Cathedral Sermons*, p. 128.　　　[2] *Id.* p. 133.

had wasted Eternal Love, Eternal Beauty, Eternal Glory, Eternal Bliss, and that irreparably." [1]

" And then pray for grace often to say—

" By the grace of God, not for the whole world would I do the least thing which shall displease my Saviour and my God." [2]

REPENTANCE.

Must repentance always accompany faith ?

It is inseparable from it, for if a man has a real saving, living faith in Christ, he must, believing all that Christ has done for him, be truly sorry that he has ever sinned.

What is required of persons to be baptized ?

" Repentance, whereby they forsake sin ; and Faith, whereby they stedfastly believe the promises of God made to them in that Sacrament."—*The Catechism.*

What is required of those who come to the Lord's Supper ?

" To examine themselves, whether they repent them truly of their former sins, stedfastly purposing to lead a new life ; have a lively faith in God's mercy through Christ, with a thankful remembrance of His death ; and to be in charity with all men."—See *The Catechism.*

" Notice that in the order for Morning and Evening Prayer, and in the order for the administration of Holy Communion, the Service commences with exhortation to repentance, confession of our unworthiness, acknowledgment that we have sinned ; and before communicating another special form of confession is put into our mouths.

" Whenever we approach God in prayer to supplicate or praise Him, *first* we should acknowledge our *unworthiness.*

Does the Church of England lay great stress on the necessity of repentance being heartfelt, sincere, and thorough ?

" The very titles with which she accompanies the name of

---

[1] *Par. and Cathedral Sermons,* p. 116.   [2] *Id.* p. 117.

repenta:ce show how deep and earnest her views of repentance are; she *never names it without some word* to express its reali'y." [1]

Much instruction on the repentant character of our Liturgy will be found in No. 86, *Tracts for the Times.*

Any taking the trouble to look through the Prayer-book will be astonished to find how the Church does, as Dr. Pusey says, accompany the word repentance with some term to express its reality. "True," "unfeigned," "truly," "humble," "unfeignedly," "worthily," "earnestly," "hearty," "aright," "thorough," "earnestly sorry"—such are the terms in which she exhorts to, and characterizes, repentance.

Does the Church of England teach that repentance should be for all sins, or for some only ?

She teaches that we should repent for *all* sins, *always*, and that we should strive by God's grace to amend continually. "Always," "all the days of our life," "daily," "unto our life's end," "all our days," "from all evil," "from all deadly sin," "all our sins," "all vices," "all worldly and carnal lusts," "in all things obey," "follow all such things as are agreeable to our profession," "all covetous desires," "ever more ready to follow," "utterly abolish the whole body of sin," "all virtuous and godly living," "all worldly and carnal affections," "always in a readiness to die." From all these expressions it is mani. fest that the teaching of the Church is thorough, hearty, humble repentance, and earnest, continual amendment in *every* way.

How does a man become truly repentant ?

"Repentance (as faith) is God's gift to the soul. The Goodness of God leads to repentance" [2] (Rom. ii. 4).

Can a man in any way move himself to repentance, as by simple meditation on our Lord's Sacred Passion, and so become truly repentant ?

"No; a man might remain ice-cold under the very Cross, unless Christ Himself kindle the heart with His piercing look of love. There is in the Passion a power of love to draw men from sin to Jesus, but this power it has, only because He

______
[1] *Letter to Bishop of Oxford*, p. 92.   [2] *Id.* p. 95.

imparts it. "I, if I be lifted up from the earth, will draw all men unto Me" (John xii. 32).[1]

"Remembering that repentance is our Lord's gift, then we should place ourselves at the foot of the Cross, and there in its light unfold the book of conscience.[2] There in union with His grief and bitter Sufferings confess we our sins, as He knows them; offer if not a broken and a contrite heart, yet one that willeth, longeth that He would break it. So seek for and pray for repentance."[3]

If a man repents of and forsakes his sin, is he to expect perfect peace, and freedom from temptation at once?

"No; for often against their own will souls are scourged by the thoughts when they have parted with their sin and loathe it. This is indeed of the mercy of God, for thus He tries them, as it were over again, and by their not consenting to these thoughts He gives them the victory, wherein they had been defeated; brings them again into the battle, that they being faithful soldiers He may crown them; and so do they obtain an intense hatred of sin, which otherwise they had never known."[4]

What on the whole is the general course of the life of repentance?

"The first stage of penitence has mostly, with deep sorrow, at least some tinge of deep joy; sweetness at the beginning of conversion; labour, hardships, temptations to struggle with as it proceeds; peace and repose at its end."—St. Isidore, *Sent.* 1, 2, v. c. 8. See also *Leeds Sermons*, p. 208.

While then we may expect that life-long paths of penitence will have many a trial in it, are we to be dismayed, because the path is so narrow, so long, so hard, so difficult?

No; encouragement to persevere is given at the outset in the most sublime and glorious manner possible.

Our Lord says, there is joy in the presence of the angels of God over one sinner that repenteth (Luke xv. 10).

[1] *Leeds Sermons*, p. 191. [2] *Id.* p. 197.
[3] *Id.* p. 201. [4] *Id.* p. 210.

The angels thus rejoice because of the joy of God !

He who thus rejoices over the sinner on his repentance may indeed be trusted lovingly to watch over him, and to help him along the path of penitence.

Describe the preciousness of repentance.

" With faith it is the beginning of the Christian life ; it accompanies it to the end ; the groundwork of conversion, the companion of faith, the enlargement of love, the soothing fosterer of hope, the condition of holiness, it leads to the mercies of Christ, it opens all the treasures of the love of God." [1]

Name one reason against trusting to a death-bed repentance, supposing we could be sure (which we cannot be) of being then in full possession of our senses.

" We have no instance recorded in Holy Scripture of a man not listening to the calls of God, rejecting Him up to the last, and then being converted, and repentant."

" The hour of the dying thief's repentance by the Cross of Jesus was not his last hour, it was his first." [2]

What is the characteristic difference between true repentance, surface repentance, or mere emotional sorrow ?

True repentance is life-long.

But if the sinner has truly repented, and has been assured through the ministry of reconciliation (absolution) that he is forgiven, need his repentance continue ?

" So far from ending with forgiveness, one might rather say it then begins. While the soul fears that it is unforgiven, its penitence is a penitence of fear. It dreads hell and the wrath of God. Its object is chiefly itself. Penitence of forgiven sin is a penitence of love." [3]

What is meant by a penitence of love ?

" It is ever chiefly taken up with the thought of God and the love of God. 'Against *Thee* only have I sinned.'" [4]

" This loving sorrow ought to live on, for it deepens as God's goodness to the soul deepens." [5]

---

[1] *Absolution*, ii. p. 41.   [2] *Lenten Sermons*, p. 213.
[3] *Id*. p. 221.   [4] *Id*.   [5] *Id*. p. 229.

How should we endeavour to take all pain and trouble that may come upon us, from or after our sins?

Humbly, penitently, lovingly; "with a 'we indeed justly.'" [1]

What is the difference between repentance and remorse?

"Remorse centres in a man's self. It dreads the temporal penalty of sin, and more or less distinctly its deserved doom. But while it is mere remorse it does not turn to God. When it listens to God's call, 'Truly repent for love of Me, thy Saviour,' if the call is answered 'remorse is transformed, spiritualized into repentance.' If the call is not listened to and obeyed, remorse must end in callousness or despair—death of the soul." [2]

How does true repentance prove it is not like remorse, centred in self?

"Pardon, cleansing, justifying, renewing, does not content the penitent," he must at once long to do something for God, something for souls. "Then shall I teach Thy ways unto the wicked, and sinners shall be converted unto Thee." [3]

Does the fear of Hell drive men to repentance?

Yes; if the penitent does not merely think of Hell as his due, but also as the doom from which our Lord would save him.

Fear of Hell quickens repentance, for it intensifies the love of the Redeemer. "Not for any slight cause did God redeem man; not for any slight cause were those Awful Sufferings which exuded those drops of Blood, or called forth that loud cry upon the Cross. God became man to die for men, and that unutterable woe are awful counterparts." [4]

Why should love ever be in true penitence?

Because the true penitent feels that it is against Love he has sinned, that Love moved him to repentance, and that Love forgave. "Very beautiful is pure created love, because it is God's highest creation, the image of His Being, Who is Love. But all conceivable love, which God has created or shall

<hr>

[1] *Lenten Sermons*, p. 234.   [2] *Id.* p. 244.   [3] *Id.* p. 252.   [4] *Id.* p. 255.

create, or could if He so willed create, were but finite ; but His love to each is Infinite ! And against this Infinite Love we have sinned." [1]

To be ever repentant, will not this sadden our lives ?

"Our only joy can be not in ourselves, but in God." [2]

"True joy can never be in partial ignorance of ourselves. Joy consists not in ignorance that we are sinners, but in pouring out our sins at the feet of Jesus, and in His forgiveness."

"Humility, repentance, hatred of sin, meekness and tenderness to our fellow-sinners, safety against relapse, thankfulness to God, growth in grace, all are involved in the vivid memory that we are forgiven sinners. The memory of forgiven sin will intensify the joy of Heaven. There is no true joy without it here. Natural joy cannot content the heart, which was made for God. God only can impart true joy. We have all sinned ; but if we repent, then ' Blessed are the mourners, for they shall be comforted.' " [3]

"The sorrow of forgiven love is a festival joy, for we sorrow because we have been unworthy of that infinite love wherewith God has loved us, wherewith He loveth us." [4]

"Grant us by Thy Holy Spirit evermore to rejoice in His Holy Comfort."—*Collect for Whitsunday.*

What should satisfy the penitent, having still to continue in a state of trial ?

The thought that if man when innocent was to be perfected through trial, much more when fallen. [5]

"Also the fact that our Lord, the Holy One, was perfected through suffering."

Give one good reason why we should prayerfully cherish the habit of repentance.

"Sin does us *lasting* injury ; each separate act of sin changes so far our moral nature and our trial. Each leaves its effect upon our souls." [6]

<hr>

[1] *Lenten Sermons*, p. 397. [2] *Id.* pp. 398, 399.
[3] *Id.* p. 399. [4] *Id.* p. 402.
[5] Vol. ii. p. 182. [6] *Id.* p. 183.

"They form habits, and these are a second nature. True repentance calls out the love of God to forgive, cleanse, repair, strengthen, the soul wounded by its sin."

When may we especially hope and pray after true repentance for restoration of the soul's health by the love of the Good Physician?

"At Holy Communion, when we are cleansed by His Body and washed by His most precious Blood."[1]

What if after sorrow for sin the soul sometimes sadly feels as if God were not near it, as if He had forsaken it?

"Remember the very desire to feel His Presence is His Presence. Thou couldest not feel, nor desire Him, but for His presence in thy soul."[2]

He taught thee to mourn, that thou mightest be comforted.

Ought not a sinner directly he forsakes his sin, and feels that, as he says, he has now turned to Jesus, to be at peace, and just simply rest in Him, leaving the future to God, and not worry himself with constant vigilance, self-examination, and prayers for perseverance?

Certainly, God does give peace and comfort to the true penitent, but in His own time and way, and often only after a long time of trial and discipline, the peace and comfort increasing as the penitent continues to walk humbly with God.

"Heaven must be won step by step, by the vigilant, careful walking of persons, who stand in awe and (in that degree) sin not, as knowing that 'God will bring every work into judgment, with every secret thing, whether it be good or bad.'"[3]

We must not only start on the narrow way, but also pray often for grace "so to follow the blessed saints in all virtuous and godly living, till we come to the unspeakable joys God has prepared for those that love Him."—*Collect for All Saints' Day.*

But surely, is it not rather true, what many teach, that if a man believes that Jesus is his Saviour, and often declares this to be.

---

[1] Vol. ii. p. 195. [2] Vol. i. p. 340.

[3] *Day of Judgment*, Preface, p. vi.

his belief, and then simply trusts in Him, he will be saved, and that the man who thus believes, if he fall, God will raise him up, his sins cannot be very bad, neither can he continue in sin, and so he must continue safe?

True, indeed, we cannot be saved, unless we believe on our Lord Jesus Christ; yet not by our faith only shall we be judged, but by our works. Our faith will rather be to our condemnation than salvation, if we have only *called* Jesus Lord, and not *done* the things which He said.

He has assigned us no other witness of our love for Him than this, "Keep my commandments." "False is every system which under the show of not trusting in works, would make a work of faith and look to its faith, as something of its own, and thinks to be saved by what it thinks faith." [1]

Christ has told thee that thou shalt be judged, not according to what thou persuadest thyself thou feelest, but by what thou dost—by thy works. The Precious Blood of Christ is the sole hope of thy salvation, but not without thyself. "In short we must pray, ever watch, ever fight the good fight, though hoping only in God our Saviour." [2]

Does the Church then teach us all to be vigilant, careful, prayerful, as to how we live, and to trust in nothing of ourselves?

Yes; she teaches us to pray to God, "without Whom nothing is strong or holy, to increase and multiply upon us His mercy; that we so pass through things temporal, that we finally lose not the things eternal."—*Collect, Fourth Sunday after Trinity.*

The Collects are full of this teaching—on our helplessness and need of dependence on God.

THE BIBLE.

"Blessed Lord, who has caused *all* Holy Scriptures to be written for our learning; Grant that we may in such wise hear

[1] *Day of Judgment,* p. 36.   [2] *Id.*

them, read, mark, learn, and inwardly digest them, that by patience, and comfort of Thy Holy Word, we may embrace, and ever hold fast the blessed hope of everlasting life, which Thou hast given us in our Saviour Jesus Christ. Amen."— *Second Collect in Advent.*

Why is it of the utmost importance that we reverence the Holy Scriptures, and pray that we may always read, think, and speak of the Bible reverently?

Because we are to remember that we shall have to give an account of our faith, as well as of our works.

"The rejection of truth as well as unholiness of life, will have to do with the final doom of man. It is Jesus who said, 'He that believeth not shall be damned.' Who those shall be, He alone is the Judge. Of this we are sure, that they will be those only, who, through fault of their own, reject Divine truth." [1]

"Men will be damned (condemned) for *wrong faith*, as well as for unholy lives." [2]

"But then the words which appealed to us in vain will bear witness against us. 'The word that I have spoken, the same shall judge him in the last day.'" [3]

Remember in speaking of or reading the Bible you cannot be too reverent.

For the Bible is the Word of God, and should therefore always be thought, spoken of, always read with a deep sense of holy awe.

"The first irreverence to any revealed truth may and has ended in atheism." [4]

"But of all hopeless cases, the most hopeless would seem unbelief engendered by levity." [5]

"The idle word; the repetition of the profane jest; the listening to it; may be, some pointed scoff at some un-understood character or phrase of Scripture; the first ashamedness

---

[1] *Preface to Daniel*, p. xxix. [2] *Sermon*, November 5th, p. 26.
[3] *Sermon; Will ye also?* p. 16. [4] *Sinful Blindness*, p. 28.
[5] *Responsibility of Intellect*, p. 51.

of truth, because it is old, or, as some will tell you, antiquated ; the first wish not to seem less advanced or enlightened than others, or less free from theological prejudice, or not to be behind the age (as it calls itself), or to be accounted as talented as any talented equal who may, alas! have lost his faith— these are the distant, and not always distant, preparations for the loss of faith. For they treat God with levity, and prefer the creature to the Creator." [1]

If we distribute Bibles to unbelievers, is that not enough for conversion ?

God of course may touch a soul, as He did St. Augustine when reading the Holy Scriptures ; but it "were difficult to find even an individual who had been converted from heathenism *solely* by the written Word. The Bereans but examined the Scriptures in which they *already* believed, to see whether the new Revelation brought to them by St. Paul agreed with 'the promise made to their fathers,' and that, in conjunction with, and in consequence of, St. Paul's preaching. To the Ethiopian eunuch who was diligently studying the sacred volume Philip was sent. There is not a syllable of Scripture, whether of the Old or New Testament, which was not written for persons already orally instructed, and actually provided with living teachers. On what ground then should we be emboldened to assume that it is itself to be the teacher ? Or how dare we employ it to an end for which God has given us no proof that He designed it ? How dare we risk its profanation by exposing it to heathen, from whom Satan has not yet been cast out ? Now should we not rather expect that the Evil Spirit will delight to scoff at and blaspheme what we have watched over with so little jealousy ? and this has been so." [2]

What is God's ordinary method of converting souls ?

* "But no ! a different history for His Church was traced by the finger of God at Calvary. As is the Head, such must the members be. It is not by the easy, unsacrificing multiplication

---

[1] *Responsibility of Intellect*, p. 53.   [2] *Occasional Sermons*, xii. p. 11.

of copies of the written Word, but by *self-sacrificing* labour; it is not by the written Word only, but through the Word of God, living in and quickening His chosen temples, sanctifying them, and testifying His own presence by the holy awe of the habitation wherein He dwells, that so great a work must be accomplished. No promise has He ever made to His written Word alone, but the contrary. 'Faith,' saith St. Paul, 'cometh by *hearing*, and hearing by the Word of God.' But it is the Word of God preached by them whom He had sent. For he says a few verses before, 'How shall they believe in Him, of whom they have not heard? and how shall they hear without a preacher? and how shall they preach except they be sent?'"[1]

In preaching to the heathen, or in expounding the Bible to Christians, what Apostolic caution should be remembered?

"Hold fast the form of sound words, which thou hast heard of me" (2 Tim. i. 13).

"The word 'deposit' became, as we shall see, a word set apart to denote the body of the Christian Faith, committed to the Church; a sacred deposit; to be faithfully guarded, not to be tampered with, not to be lessened, not to be adulterated, but to be kept for Him Who left it to her trust, not to be mingled with anything foreign from itself. 'Keep,' Vincentius paraphrases,[2] 'that which is committed to thee, not that which is invented of thee: that which thou hast received, not that which thou hast devised; a thing not of wit, but of learning: not of private assumption, but of public tradition; a thing brought to thee, not brought forth of thee; wherein thou must not be an author, but a keeper; not a master, but a disciple; not a leader, but a follower. *Keep the deposit.* Preserve the talent of the Catholic Faith safe and undiminished; that which is committed to thee, let that remain with thee, and that deliver. Thou hast received gold, render then gold; I will not have one thing for another; do not for gold render either

---

[1] *Occasional Sermons*, xii. p. 9.
[2] *Oxf. Tr.*, p. 63.

shamelessly lead, or craftily brass ; I will not the show, but the very nature of gold itself.' " [1]

"St. Paul says first to St. Timothy, ' Hold fast the form of sound words, which thou hast heard of me,' [2] a form or mould, in which he was to be formed or moulded, and on which he was to frame all his speech upon the faith and love which is in Christ Jesus. St. Paul gave him a sketch, as it were (ὑποτύπωσιν), which he was to follow in all his teaching. ' Imitate,' Theodoret paraphrases, [3] ' painters ; and, as they, attending to the originals with accuracy, picture to the life their likenesses, so do thou also keep the teaching delivered by me as to faith and hope, as a sort of archetype :' and another, [4] ' Live and teach, according to that form which thou hast received of me.' "

"A form or sketch of sound words is plainly not only a popular statement of truth, as that ' Christ died for us sinners,' but the very words in which it was to be conveyed, according to the pattern of which all other doctrinal language was to be formed. Whence it hath been observed, [5] how very much of formed statement of doctrine, such as afterwards became the theological language of the Church, occurs in the few remains of St. Ignatius, the immediate successor of St. Peter at Antioch."

But to make out, that the Church is the converter of souls, disparages the written Word of God?

God forbid. " Yet the power to read is a blessing if they who are taught it are to use it aright, and above all books to love the Book of God, and above all knowledge, the knowledge of God. In sickness, the power of reading the Bible is a cheering power; in health, it may prevent our abusing and forgetting God; in loneliness, it makes God our companion, and families it binds together ; when tottering it may save us from falling ; the fallen, by God's imparted power, it may raise

---

[1] *Rule of Faith*, pp. 6, 7.　　[2] 2 Tim. i. 13.
[3] *Ad loc.*　　[4] Primasius *ad loc.*
[5] See a very thoughtful article in the *British Critic*, No. 49.

up; those who stand, it may keep upright. By it, God's
Holy Spirit converteth (if need be), maketh wise, joyeth, en-
lighteneth the soul. The broken-hearted it bindeth up; the
wounds of sin it gradually healeth; it leadeth men on from
strength to strength, and to the dying Christian it opens the
everlasting gates, and shows him the golden streets of the
heavenly city, and the angels who shall conduct him to
Abraham's bosom. One dare not say more, lest a creature
should be praising the Word of God. It supersedes not the
labour of the minister; but it supports the doctrine and
exhortation, which out of that word he imparts prepares men
to understand it, and fixes it deeper." [1]

*Would it be enough for a missionary to teach the heathen to
pray to God, to fast, to give alms, to rehearse his Belief, and to
study the Bible?*

"No; these acts are in their several ways means of grace.
But the Sacraments are more. They are part of the glories of
the Incarnation of the Son of God. The foundation of all our
blessings, the means whereby we were originally united with
Christ, or are kept cemented with Him." [2]

*When seemingly unanswerable difficulties as regards the Bible
are proposed to the Christian in the name of Science, what is he
to do?*

"'To admit' a difficulty by attempting to explain it, and,
failing to explain it, leaves matters worse than before. If we
have nothing but weak explanations to give, the only honest
way is to bide our time, and to own, 'I do not know.' The
believer is certain that God's Word and His works harmonize?
If he knows not how to harmonize them he can afford to wait
the development, or to remain ignorant." [3]

"Knowing as we do know, the divinity of the Old Testament
as a whole, it cannot be essential to our faith that the truth of
details too should be matter of demonstration. We believe as
to the parts because we believe the whole. It is a poor, unin-

[1] Vol. iii. p. 308.

[2] Vol. iii. p. 345.   [3] *Preface to Daniel*, p. lxxxi.

telligent human faith, ignorant of the real character or grounds of faith, which cannot say, unconcerned about details, 'I do not know.'"[1]

"Lesser questions easily receive their light, or, without injury to the faith, remain for the time obscure, when the eye has once seen the central truth."[2]

"It is mere dust in people's eyes that some speak of the present conflict as a question of reconciling physical science and theology. For the real objection is, that God should reveal Himself to His creature man, in any way than by the operation of man's natural reason, or that He should tell man anything, 'beyond the grasp of eye or hand.'"[3]

Does not geology prove the account of the creation in Genesis to be untrustworthy ?

"What intervened between that creation 'in the beginning' and that remodelling for our habitation does not concern us, and on this God is silent. He tells us the first and the last, that He created all things, and that He prepared this our beautiful earth for us, and created all things in it, and ourselves. In the interval there is room for all the workings of God, which geology speaks of, if it speaks truly. The history of the creation in Genesis falls in naturally with it, in that it does not say that this our mysterious habitation which God has made the scene of such wondrous love was created 'in the beginning,' *i. e.* before the time of which it proceeds to speak. Another period of undefined duration is implied by the words, 'And the Spirit of God was brooding upon the face of the deep.' For action of course implies time, in which the action takes place. And this action was previous to that of the first 'day' of the creation, which begins, like the rest, with the words, 'And God said.'"[4]

"It is a certain fact that Holy Scripture does leave two spaces, unmeasured by time, subsequent to the first creation of the earth, and that these spaces being absolutely

[1] *Daniel,* p. 278.   [2] *Id.* p. 101.
[3] *Preface to Daniel,* p. xiv.   [4] *Id.* p. xx.

undefined, admit of those all but boundless periods which geologists claim." [1]

But have not the recent study of, and the discoveries in, geology disproved the reliability of the Bible in its account of creation ?

" The belief that creation at least dated backward for count-less ages, was current in the Church some fourteen hundred years before geology. ' Six thousand years of the world,' says St. Jerome, ' are not yet fulfilled; and what eternities, what times, what originals of ages, must we not think there were before, in which angels, thrones, dominions, and the other powers served God, and, apart from the vicissitudes and measures of times, subsisted at the command [of God !" [2]

Remember that many of the common objections brought against the credibility of the Bible, though they seem very. telling to those who have never arduously studied the grounds of their faith, seem to be very shallow and weak to theologians who have.

" Forty years of study have only shown me the more, both from language and the subsequent books of the Old Testament, the evidence of its genuineness, which I already believed on the authority of our Lord. In examining for my class the first volume of Dr. Colenso, I could only be amazed that any mind could be shaken by such argument. Faith of course could not." [3]

" This has been for some thirty years a deep conviction of my soul, that no book can be written in behalf of the Bible like the Bible itself. Man's defences are man's word; they may help to beat off attacks, they may draw out some portion of its meaning. The Bible is God's Word, and through it God the Holy Ghost, who spake it, speaks to the soul which closes not itself against it." [4]

" But if defences are weak, except as far as God enables us to build them on Himself, ' builds the house' through man, defences not built as He would have them will not only fall,

---

[1] *Preface to Daniel,* p. xxi.
[3] *Id.* p. xiii. 1867.
[2] *Id.* p. xvii.
[4] *Id.* p. xxv.

but will crush those who trust them. The faith can receive no real injury except from its *defenders*. Against its assailants, those who wish to be safe, God protects." [1]

"Man cannot give faith; man cannot demonstrate faith into the soul; he can but meet argument by argument, and little comes of it. ' Rarely, very rarely,' said one of much experience, 'have reasonings or discussions subdued or brought back wandering hearts.' The prophetic word is powerful, more powerful than any exposition of it; for it is the Word of God; it breathes with the Spirit of God; it burns with the love of God. It will lead you, for God will lead you, through it. Only give up your whole heart to Him who made you in His love. Say to Him, ' My God, I believe with my will, whatsoever Thou hast revealed; for Thou art the Truth. Thou canst not deceive, nor be deceived; ' and pray to Him." [2]

"These things about which God's creatures dispute so freely are not matters of keen intellectual subtlety, or trial of skill, or practice of acuteness, or exercise of greater boldness than our fellow-men venture upon. They are matters of certain truth which God has infallibly revealed, and in rejecting which truth, men reject God. If men through their own fault reject Him (of which not they, but He, the Searcher of hearts, is the judge), they are matters of life and death—of life and death eternal—of that everliving life in God in Heaven, or that deathless death apart from Him, in an everlasting loss of God in hell. It is Jesus, Who died for us, Who so loved us to die for us, Who in His love said it, that we might not die eternally; ' He that believeth not, shall be damned.' " [3]

What is the great power and strength—the very Rock of Faith?

First, ever remembering it is the gift of God, the work in us of the indwelling Spirit. Secondly, "The love of Christ Crucified is the guardian alike of personal purity, and of purity of faith." [4]

[1] *Preface to Daniel*, p. xxv.

[2] Vol. 1872, p. 74.

[3] *Id.* p. 76.

[4] *Id.* p. 29.

" Heed not how men would explain away our Lord's words, but listen to Himself, speaking in them.   The words of man, save as they contain anything of eternal truth, pass away with man.   The words of Christ live because He lives ; words from the Eternal Word instinct with His Divinity, alive with His love.   To you too, as you meditate on them, they will speak with a Divine force ; and you too will, by His grace, be able to say with joy, ' We have heard Him ourselves, and know that this is indeed the Christ, the Saviour of the world." [1]

" Amid all the thickening assaults on faith which surround you, and which perhaps will thicken yet more, until the days of Anti-Christ, one sure Rock there is, whereon if our feet be planted they will never be shaken, never slide, never stumble, never falter—a *personal loyalty and love for Jesus.*   If, towards the close of a long life, my experience can, in any degree, benefit any of you, my sons, it is this.   For forty-five years, out of duty, not out of curiosity, I have read more of unbelief than most, in every form, in every province and district where it has made its assaults.   I have read it until the flesh crept and the soul sickened, but our dear Lord's promise was fulfilled to me—' If they drink any deadly thing, it shall not hurt them ; ' and my safeguard was this—loyalty to, and I hope I may say, though all too poor, a love to our Divine Master.   For everything in some way ran up against Him and against His Word.   Many a book of evidence such as men used to write left me thankful that they were not my stay: personal trust in Jesus could not fail, for He who gave it upholds it." [2]

Where can there be found copious extracts from the Fathers on the sufficiency and the use of the Holy Scriptures?

In Dr. Pusey's *Eirenicon,* vol. i. appendix A.

Is it true that the Church of England regards those Scriptures commonly known as the Apocrypha, as ordinary human writings or legends?

" This is a very common mistake.   She holds them in the very highest esteem, and says of them in Article VI., ' The

[1] Vol. 1872, p. 31.   [2] Id. p. 227.

Church doth read them for example of life and instruction of manners.'"

"Both books of Homilies, in some forty-three places in all, quote, either in the body of the Homily or in the margin, the Deutero-Canonical books. They quote them as 'Scripture written by the Holy Ghost.' 'The Scriptures,' 'the Old Testament,' with the formula, 'it is written,' as 'the Word of God,' 'the infallible and undeceivable Word of God.' They quote them—together with other Scripture, and under the same formula—even together with words of our Lord Himself. Tobit with the formula, 'The Angel Raphael told Tobias,' is often quoted in proof that 'fasting, used with prayer, is of great efficacy, and weigheth much with God.' They tell us that 'Jesus, son of Sirach,. doth certainly assure us.' They quote Wisdom as 'the godly writing of Solomon,' telling us that 'we may know that which Jesus, son of Sirach, teacheth'; and quote Baruch as 'the prophet Baruch.'"[1]

"The points, also, for which the Deutero-Canonical Books are quoted, although not the great doctrines of the Faith, are some of them such as could only be known by revelation, as that pride was the beginning of man's departure from God, or the value of almsdeeds in reference to the forgiveness of sin, of the efficacy of fasting with prayer, or the peace of those departed after a holy life, or the efficacy of holy fear of God."[2]

"The Church of Rome, as in the Old Testament, so in the New, distinguishes between the books which it styles 'Proto-Canonici' and 'Deutero-Canonici.' The Anglican Church, in the case of the Old Testament, receives as authoritative and Canonical only the former class, regarding the 'Deutero-Canonical' as apocryphal. In the case of the New Testament, the Anglican Church declares (Act VI.)—'All the books of the New Testament as they are commonly received, we do receive and account them Canonical.' The books styled 'Deutero-Canonical' by the Church of Rome are, as above— Hebrews, St. James, 2 and 3 St. John, 2 St. Peter, St. Jude,

[1] *Eirenicon*, iii. p. 150.   [2] *Id.* p. 156.

the Apocalypse, and certain verses in the Gospels."—BLUNT'S *Theological Dictionary on Canon of Scripture.*

It is remarkable that "whereas the Deutero-Canonical books are quoted so often in the Homilies, that, amid the copious quotations from Holy Scriptures in the Council of Trent, one place only is quoted from them, and that only upon a matter of practice." [1]

How do the Homilies speak of the reading and knowledge of Holy Scriptures?

"Unto a Christian man there can be nothing either more necessary or profitable than the knowledge of Holy Scripture ; forasmuch as in it is contained God's true Word, setting forth His glory and also man's duty."

"For in Holy Scripture is fully contained what we ought to do, and what to eschew, what to believe, what to love, and what to look for at God's hands at length. In those books we shall find the Father, from whom ; the Son, by whom ; and the Holy Ghost, in whom, all things have their being and keeping up ; and these Three Persons to be but one God and One Substance. In these books we may learn to know our- selves, how vile and miserable we be ; and also to know God, how good He is of Himself, and how He maketh us and all creatures partakers of His goodness. We may learn also in these books to know God's will and pleasure, as much as for this present time is convenient for us to know. By the Word of God we shall be judged ; for the Word that I speak, saith Christ, is it, that shall judge in the last day. He that keepeth the Word of Christ is promised the love and favour of God, and that He shall be the dwelling-place or temple of the Blessed Trinity. This Word whosoever is diligent to read, and in his heart to print that he readeth, the great affection to the transitory things of this world shall be minished in him, and the great desire of heavenly things that he is therein promised of God shall increase in him. And there is nothing that so much strengtheneth our faith and trust in God, that so much

---

[1] *Eirenicon,* iii. p. 156.

keepeth up innocency and pureness of the heart and also of outward godly life and conversation, as continual reading and recording of God's Word."

"And in reading of God's Word, he most profiteth not always that is most ready in turning of the book, or in saying of it without the book; but he that is most turned into it, that is most inspired with the Holy Ghost, most in his heart and life altered and changed into that thing which he readeth; he that is daily less and less proud, less wrathful, less covetous, and less desirous of worldly and vain pleasures: he that daily forsaking his old vicious life, increaseth in virtue more and more. And, to be short, there is nothing that more maintaineth godliness of the mind and driveth away ungodliness, than doth the continual reading or hearing of God's Word, if it be joined with a godly mind and a good affection to know and follow God's Will."

"And those things in the Scripture that be plain to understand and necessary for salvation, every man's duty is to learn them, to print them in memory, and effectually to exercise them; and as for the dark mysteries, to be contented to be ignorant in them until such time as it shall please God to open those things unto him."—*Homilies*, pp. 1—8.

Is there a very good prayer for the use of those who would study the Bible, and in all humility help other souls to the knowledge of the truth?

Yes. "O Eternal Truth, and True Love, and Loving Light, our God, and our All, enlighten our darkness by the brightness of Thy Light. Irradiate our minds by the splendour of holiness, that in Thy Light we may see light; that we, in turn, may enlighten others, and kindle them with the love of Thee. Open Thou our eyes that we may see wondrous things out of Thy law, who makest eloquent the minds and tongues of the slow of speech. To Thee, to Thy Glory, to the good of Thy Church and people may we labour, write, live. Thou hast said, Lord, to Thine Apostles and prophets, their followers and interpreters, 'Ye are the salt of the earth,' 'Ye are the light of the world.' Thou hast said it, and, by saying it, hast done it. Grant to us then, Lord, that we too, like them, may be preachers of Heaven, sowers for eternity; that they who read, may, by the knowledge of Thy Scriptures, through the graveness and the weight of Thy promises and threats, despise the ensnaring entanglements of earth, and be kindled with the love of heavenly goods, and the effectual earnest longing for a blessed eternity. This be our one desire, this our prayer, to this may all our reading and writing and all our toil tend, that Thy Holy Name may be hallowed, Thy Holy Will be done, as in Heaven so in earth, Thy Holy Kingdom of Grace, Glory and endless Bliss where Thou wilt be all things, in all, may come to us. Amen." [1]

HORNE'S *Introduction.*

LEE *on Inspiration.*

WESTCOTT'S *Works.*

Commentaries by WORDSWORTH, DUNWELL, SADLER, DENTON, ISAAC WILLIAMS.

LITTLEDALE and NEALE *on the Psalms.*

INSPIRATION OF HOLY SCRIPTURE.

"The doctrine of the Inspiration of the Holy Scripture has been already instanced. There are few subjects, not involving directly the Faith in the Holy Trinity, which English Church-men probably feel so keenly as the Inspiration of Holy Scripture. For it is the foundation of all besides. What would it be then to them to hear questions as to the extent of its Inspiration, wherein Inspiration consisted, how much or how little the teachers of the Church might receive or teach, whether a Canonical book was necessarily inspired?" [2]

The reader is referred to Canon Liddon's Sermon, *The Worth of the Old Testament,* December 8th, 1889, wherein he

---

[1] See end of *Preface to Minor Prophets*, p. iv.

[2] *Supremacy*, p. 11.

emphasizes the great answer and argument against all impugners of the trustworthiness of the Old Testament Scriptures—"Christ our Lord has set His seal upon them."

"The Church of England maintains without reserve or qualification, the Inspiration and Divine Authority of the whole Canonical Scriptures, as not only containing but being the Word of God."—*Declaration of* 11,000 *Clergymen*, 1864.

"During the whole of my matured theological life, I have held verbal inspiration, nor, since we have no clear thoughts except as embodied in words, can I imagine any other." [1]

(1) "It is plainly of faith that all mankind except those who with Noah entered into the ark perished by the flood." [2]

"The letter of that history is of course true.   We may have our opinions, but we have no right to make our opinions, *i. e.* our interpretations of God's Word, when these interpretations have no authority from Holy Scripture or the Church, the measure of the meaning of God's Word."

(2) "Few things have been more mischievous than the attempt to square God's Words with facts imperfectly understood."

(3) "We cannot divide Holy Scripture or Christianity polypus-like, so that one part might be cut off and the rest remain in the same life as before.   It is one whole, and as in that beautiful system of our nerves, one prick at any extremity runs through the whole, and may carry death, so it would be with the Gospel if it were possible."

"This has been for some thirty years a deep conviction of my soul, that no book can be written in behalf of the Bible like the Bible itself. . . The faith can receive no real injury except from its defenders." [3]

---

[1] January 27, 1863 : *Letter to Rev. J. Williams.*
[2] Speech, Norwich Church Congress.   [3] *Preface, Daniel,* p. xxv.

THE BIBLE THE WORD OF GOD.

" How, to speak of facts to which yet our Lord pledges His truth—how should the known world have been drowned by a flood, or Noah be saved in the ark, or Lot's wife have become 'a pillar of salt,' or Jonah have lived in the fish's belly, or the men of Nineveh have repented at the preaching of one stranger, or mankind have sprung from one pair, or devils have possessed the bodies of men, or Sodom and Gomorrah have perished by that shower of fire and brimstone, or Israel have been fed with manna in the wilderness? I speak not of any true or probable interpretations of the facts which our Lord so authenticates for us. . . ." [1]

" It touches not faith in what way Lot's wife perished. But the facts abide. Are we wiser than He, who chose a stable for His birthplace, obscurity for the first thirty years of His life, the Cross for His bed of death, thenceforward to reign supreme over the wills and hearts and intellects of mankind. . . ."

" Who has ever since been adored as One God with the Father, though 'for us men and for our salvation He became man.' If we could not have conceived such a plan, if we could not even conceive of such a soul as that of Jesus, ever in inmost communion with the Father, ever declaring His absolute union of will with the Father, that He spake the words of the Father and did His works, and yet declaring in simplest words, 'I am in the Father, and the Father in Me'; 'I and the Father are one' (substance); 'I am the Way, the Truth, and the Life,' then it would seem to be no large demand upon our diffidence to own that Jesus would know better than we as to the facts of the Old Testament which He authenticates, and by which He points some of His teaching."

[1] Vol. 1872, p. 223.

MIRACLES.

"It might be over-taxing our powers, anyhow it is superfluous to attempt to work conviction as to most of the miracles of the Old Testament by independent evidence. They were evidence to those who saw them : to us, our Lord is the Evidence for them, and (I may say) for all things." [1]

"Everything before He came, looked on to Him ; everything since is grounded on Him, the One Foundation of the Church, of faith, of hope, of present knowledge by His Word, of holiness by His Spirit, of Life Eternal, which He is, as His Gift. 'Other foundation can no man lay than that is laid, which is Jesus Christ,' 'the same yesterday, to-day, and for ever.'"

[1] Vol. 1872, p. 224.

THE CATHOLIC CHURCH.

ONE, HOLY, APOSTOLIC.

> " From every region, race, and speech,
>   Believing myriads throng,
>   Till far as sin and sorrow reach
>   Thy grace is spread along."—JOHN KEBLE.

How many Churches are there ?

One only. As there is but one God, as there is but one Saviour, as there is but One Faith, so too there is, and can be, but One Church.

Why can there not be more than One Church ?

Because God is not the author of confusion, and having appointed but one Saviour, one Mediator between God and man, mankind are only saved by and through that one Saviour Who has founded but One Church.

Quote some passages of Holy Scripture in proof of this ?

" On this Rock I will build My Church " (St. Matt. xvi. 18).

" The Church of God, which He has purchased with His own Blood " (Acts xx. 28).

" Christ loved the Church, and gave Himself for it " (Eph. v. 25).

" He is the Head of the body, the Church " (Col. i. 18).

There is then but One Church, though we may speak of

the members of the One Church in different countries as of "Churches," or may distinguish them by the name of their locality, as "the Church of the Laodiceans" (Col. iv. 6); "the Church which is at Cenchrea" (Rom. xvi. 1); "the Churches of Asia' (xvi. 19).

All these Churches are of course parts of the one whole, being members of the One Body, whose Head is Christ.

It is then quite wrong to suppose or speak of a New Church being founded ?,

The Church may plant herself in places where she has not been before, and her members there would be the newly-formed portion of the Church in that locality, and not in the literal sense of the words a new Church.

When you speak of the Catholic Church, do you mean that large body of Christians who recognize the Bishop of Rome as their Supreme Infallible Head ?

Most certainly not.

Do you mean, then, the three great Communions, the Eastern Church, the Roman Catholic Church, and all in union with the Anglican Communion ?

No; this would not be a full and accurate description.

Do you mean by the Catholic Church, the Church Militant here on earth ?

No; the Catholic Church means the Church Militant on earth, together with all her members who have departed this life, and are now with Christ.

But can the Church be said to be ONE, since there is a great division in it — the Roman Communion claiming to be the Catholic Church, and refusing to hold communion with the Eastern and Anglican portions of the One Church of Christ ?

Much depends upon the meaning persons have in their minds when they say, "How can the Church be One when her members differ so much from each other?" In the first place, the Church may be one as to number, that is to say, there is but one Church. Secondly, it is possible, and it is the fact, that the members of this one Church on earth may differ, just as two brothers might differ who were yet of course children of the same parents, and members of one family. All Churchmen take this for granted, that Christ founded one Church, absolutely one only.

All agreeing then that Christ's Church is one in number, can she be said to be one as to agreement in doctrine?

Here again much depends on the full scope of the question in the mind of the questioner.

Christ's Church cannot teach two contradictory doctrines as necessary for salvation to be believed; that is quite certain.

She cannot teach one thing as of faith and necessary to salvation to be believed, in one century, and its opposite in another; that is quite certain.

She cannot, without a fresh revelation from God, declare anything as necessary to salvation to be believed now, which she has not taught, as of faith, before.

She is *the* Church of God, Christ is her Head, and the Holy Spirit her guide; she cannot then be self-contradictory.

It was, and is, and ever must be, the will of Christ that His Church everywhere should, as regards her members, be thoroughly at one, united in one common faith.

She *is* thus united concerning all that is really necessary to salvation. She holds, for instance, and teaches the Apostles' Creed, and all the faith of which it is the sum and symbol everywhere.

But ought not the Church to be so thoroughly united, that such should be the perfection of her unity, that there should be perfect agreement among all her members always everywhere, both as to the faith and all matters of pious opinion, and everything connected with the religion of Christians?

Such unity, as a matter of fact, does not and has not existed since the days of the Apostles. No one, however heartily he might yearn for the perfect unity and peace of Christendom, can pretend that such agreement has always existed.

How, then, can the Church be said to be one?

"How the Church is one the Church nowhere defines." [1]

"It cannot be simply the perfect harmony of men's wills. Hers is a 'supernatural and Divine unity.'" [2]

"Unity, in part, is the direct gift of God; in part, it is the fruit of that gift in the mutual love of the members of the Church; in part, it is a spiritual oneness wrought by God the Holy Ghost; in part, it is a grace, to be exercised by man, a consequence and fruit of that gift. In one way it is organic unity derived from Christ, and binding all to Christ, descending from the Head to the Body, and uniting the Body to the Head. In another, it consists in acts of love from the members one to another. Christ our Lord, God and man, binds us to Him by the indwelling of His Spirit, by the gift of His Sacraments, administered by those to whom He gave the commission so to do, by the right faith in Himself. We are bound to one another, in that we are members of Him, and by the love which He sheds abroad in our hearts through the Spirit, which He giveth us, and by common acts of worship and intercommunion." [3]

"Of these, the highest and chief is that which binds us to Christ Himself; our highest union with one another is an organic union with one another through union with Him.[4]

"*It is not chiefly* an *union of will* or *of mind or of love*, although these *ought to be the fruits of it* in its most perfect state, *but an union through* His indwelling Spirit."

"This oneness, then, is an actual mystical oneness inwrought by Christ our Head uniting the whole Church together in one with Himself in His Body; and actual oneness produced by grace corresponding to the Oneness of Father and the Son by nature." [5]

All who have been baptized have put on Christ, Jew, Greek, bond or free, male or female: "Ye are all one in Christ Jesus" (Gal. iii. 27).

[1] *Eirenicon*, pt. i. p. 45.   [2] *Id.*   [3] *Id.*
[4] *Id.* p. 46.   [5] *Id.* p. 47.

So too in Holy Communion. "We being many are *one* bread, and one body: for we are partakers of that one bread" (1 Cor. x. 17).

The Scriptural test of unity is after Baptism to continue in the Apostles' doctrine and fellowship, "in breaking of bread, and in prayers" (Acts ii. 42).

First, then, unity is organic, objective, inwrought by our Head Jesus, Himself through union with Himself by His Holy Ghost.

"Subjective unity is 'unison of wills,' and intercommunion with one another. This unity may be suspended while objective unity is maintained. Our duty is by prayer, by example, by speaking in love, by living each of us more and more up to the standard of our high calling, to promote unity, peace, and concord, throughout the Church."[1]

But is not all unity forfeited where the unity of intercommunion is suspended?

"No one in the face of Church history can or does maintain that all interruptions of intercommunion destroy unity."[2]

"There is then no ground to assume that suspensions of intercommunion (sad and mournful as they are) in themselves, hinder either body from being a portion of the Body of Christ."[3]

"We believe the prophecy to have been fulfilled, 'neither shall men learn war any more,' although peace has been in these last days the exception among Christians; we believe our Lord's words, that love is the test of His disciples, and that thereby shall they be known among men, although love and jealousy and self-interest and anger are far more visible."[4]

"Well then may we believe that the several Churches owning the same Lord, united to Him by the same Sacraments, confessing the same faith, however their prayers may be hindered, are still one in His sight, Whom all desire to receive; Whom all confess; Whose Passion all plead before the Father; in Whom alone all alike hope."[5]

[1] See *Eirenicon*, pt. i. pp. 58, 59.
[2] *Id.*　　[3] *Id.* p. 65.　　[4] *Id.*　　[5] *Id.* p. 66.

What should be the prayerful aim of all who are distressed at the differences between the members of the Church?

"To come to a better understanding with one another, not to cast out those who differ from them."[1]

"It is then a sad fact that '*entire visible unity* is not vouch-safed to the Church of these last days'; but does this sad fact prove that the Church is a complete failure, as some would therefore argue?"[2]

No; for "in spite of the injury caused by human misunder-standing and divisions, the Holy Ghost, though His work is much hindered, still carries on and keeps on the fulfilment of the Divine mission of the Church in the conversion and regeneration of mankind." "The increasing life of the Church will be accompanied doubtless with increasing love, and we must remember that holiness is even more distinctly foretold as a characteristic of the Church."[3] "Yet if holiness (as it is) may be imperfect, much more unity. For holiness is the very end of the dispensation of the Gospel, and the word of the Scriptures cannot be broken."[4]

"Moreover, sufficient stress has not been laid upon the note of sanctity, and its operation on the organic Church; perhaps because, inasmuch as God only knows those who are His, men prefer to deal with that which is tangible and visible, and therefore appeal perhaps too exclusively to the note of unity; and yet surely the same laws affect both.—BISHOP FORBES, p. 275. Article XIX.

How is the Church holy?

The Church is holy, because Her Head, Her Founder, is Christ. He gave Himself for it, that He might sanctify it; "that it should be holy, and without blemish" (Eph. v. 27). She is holy because the Holy Spirit indwells her, and works in and through her. She is holy, for she teaches holiness. She teaches God to His people. She is holy in Her doctrines;

---

[1] *Letter to Bishop of London*, p. 188.
[2] *Letter to Archbishop of Canterbury*, p. 10.
[3] *Id.* p. 19. [4] *Id.* p. 20.

the Sacraments she dispenses are holy; all that she does is in the Name of God.

But can it be said that Her members are holy?—and if it cannot so be said, How can the Church, while the evil are mingled with the good, be holy?

"Our Lord gave Himself for us, that He might redeem us from all iniquity, and purify unto Himself a peculiar people, zealous of good works" (Titus ii. 14).

Members of Christ's Church are holy, for they are temples of God indwelt by His Holy Spirit, and through Him made members of Christ, and children of God. We are then holy as to our position in Christ; so too if we hinder not the work of the Holy Spirit, but humbly obey God, and follow the motions of His grace, the teaching of the Holy Spirit, and receive the Holy Communion; then our union with Christ is deepened, perfected, and we truly grow in holiness.

Why is the Church called Catholic?

"It is called Catholic, because it is throughout the world, from one end of the earth to the other; and because it teaches universally and completely one and all, the doctrines which ought to come to man's knowledge concerning things both visible and invisible, heavenly and earthly; and because it subjugates in order to godliness every class of men, governors and governed, learned and unlearned; and because it universally treats and heals every sort of sins which are committed by soul and body, and possesses in itself every form of virtue which is named, both in deeds and words, and in every kind of spiritual gifts." "In this Holy Catholic Church, receiving instruction, and behaving ourselves virtuously, we shall attain the Kingdom of Heaven, and inherit Eternal Life, for which also we endure all toils, that we may be partakers of it in the Lord."—ST. CYRIL. BISHOP FORBES *on the Nicene Creed*, p. 280.

Or, as may be gathered from Bishop Pearson, the Church is Catholic because, *Firstly*, The most obvious and most general notion of this Catholicism, consisteth in the diffusiveness of the Church, grounded upon the commission given to the builders of it—"Go teach all nations" (St. Matt. xxviii. 19), whereby they and their successors were authorized and empowered to gather congregations of believers, and so to extend the borders of the Church, to the utmost parts of the earth.

Secondly. They called the Church of Christ "The Catholic Church," because it teacheth all things which are necessary for a Christian to know, whether they be things in Heaven or things in earth, whether they concern the condition of man in this life, or in the life to come.

Thirdly. The Church has been thought fit to be called 'Catholic," in reference to the universal obedience which it prescribeth, both in respect of the persons, obliging men of all conditions; and in relation to the precepts, requiring the performance of all the evangelical commands.

Fourthly. The Church hath been yet further called or reputed "Catholic," by reason of all graces given in it, whereby all the diseases of the soul are healed; all spiritual virtues are disseminated; all the works, and words, and thoughts of men are regulated till we become perfect men in Jesus Christ.

In all these four acceptions did some of the ancient fathers understand the Church of Christ to be "Catholic," and every one of them doth certainly belong to it. Wherefore I conclude that this Catholicism or second affection of the Church consisteth generally in universality, as embracing all sorts of persons, as to be disseminated through all nations, as comprehending all ages, as containing all necessary and saving truths, as obliging all conditions of men to all kinds of obedience, as curing all diseases, and planting all graces in the souls of men.—BISHOP PEARSON *on the Creed.*

What is meant by saying the Church is Apostolical?

That she was under God founded, spread, and organized, upon and by the Apostles, at and after the Day of Pentecost; that first in and from the Apostles, the Church received the full authority and power to start upon Her Divine mission, "Go ye and disciple all nations." From this time the Church received all that was necessary for Her to carry on Her Master's work, or rather from henceforth Christ by His Holy Spirit filled, sanctified, enabled the Church to carry on His works in her; to guard and witness and interpret Holy Writ; to know and teach all things necessary to salvation; to dispense all means of grace necessary to salvation; in short, to teach and *do* all that was necessary for the glory of God and the good of souls till Christ Her King should come again. And the Church so founded by the God of Order, was no undisciplined community, but a kingdom (not of the world), to have organization, constituted authority, settled government, and duly appointed officers.

"The Church has a principle of perpetuity imparted to it by God through His promise, who is her Head and Lord. Her succession of Bishops mounts up by a golden chain, link by link, to the Apostles, with whom and with their successors Christ promised to be always, even to the end of the world, and to the Second Coming; and through them as joints and bands, the whole body having nourishment ministered, and knit together, increaseth with the increase of God."[1]

Before the Incarnation was there one Church on earth?

"The Old Testament, in direct prophecy or type, is one large prophecy of the Redeemer and His Kingdom or Church. No sooner had disunion multiplied with the multiplying of man, but, in the second generation from Adam, He formed union through a Church, and 'men began to call upon the name of the Lord,' *i. e.* they began to unite in worshipping the Lord, and, amid the growing corruption, religion was no longer entrusted to the insulated care of single families."[2]

"God called Abraham *alone*, and blessed and increased him, and formed the Jewish Church out of him, that however largely it might spread, it might be bound in one by its origin

---

[1] *Occasional Sermons: Church the Converter of Heathen*, p. 13.
[2] *Id.* p. 14.

of one. He gave it also outward marks and signs between Him and it which, by severing it from others, might keep it one in itself." [1]

"Throughout prophecy there are two subjects spoken of—the Lord of the Church and the Church ; the Temple and He who filleth the Temple; the Bride and her King and Husband ; the City of God and its King ; the one fold and its Shepherd : and individuals have their interest in Him, as sheep in that fold, as citizens of that heavenly city, as children of that kingdom, as living stones built up in that 'spiritual temple' for an habitation of God through the Spirit." [2]

In what various ways is the Church spoken of, showing that there is but one Church, and her office, the conversion and "discipling" the world?

"The Church is the one mustard-seed which groweth up into a great tree, wherein the birds of the air lodge and are at rest. It is the one mass of leaven gradually spreading through the meal, and converting it into one substance conformable with itself. It is the one net cast into the sea, inclosing within itself those who will be gathered, and burst not through it, and landing the good on the blessed shore of everlasting life. The Apostles were fishers of men, in that they and all the successors in their office have this one commission, to gather people into this one net. The Church is the one vineyard, the one marriage feast unto which all are brought, the one candle giving light to all that enter in ; nay the title of *Kingdom* of God, *Kingdom* of Heaven, which our Lord everywhere gives to the Church, is in itself a parable expressing the same truth, that it shall be *one* well-ordered government, not broken down into many kingdoms, but absorbing all other kingdoms into herself, and enlarging herself so as to enfold them all, having God for its Ruler, its Redeemer, and for its Head, and Heaven for its end. And so, under its one Head, duly governed and ordered by His inferior ministers, and blessed with the union

[1] *Occasional Sermons: Church the Converter of Heathen*, p. 15.
[2] *Id.* p. 19.

and harmony of Heaven, and the peace and order of the blessed angels." [1]

"And when our Lord, in His Divine Prayer, which is the model of all our prayer, teaches us to pray for the spreading of His Gospel, He does so in no other way than in those large and full words, ' Thy Kingdom come.' " [2]

In the very earliest days of the Church, in the lifetime of the Apostles, was there any great observance of order in sending forth those who were to preach the Gospel ?

"The main principle which I pointed out was this : that it was not by the desultory efforts of individuals or self-constituted bodies, but by the Church as a whole, and by individuals, as subordinate to her and 'her instruments, that the world was to be converted." [3]

" From the first, the Apostles, even after they had received their commission from our Lord, were enjoined by Him to tarry at Jerusalem until they should 'receive power from on high,' and a visible mission in the sight of the whole Church. St. Paul, though expressly called by our Lord from Heaven as ' a chosen vessel to bear His Name before the Gentiles and kings,' still went not forth to his mission until they whom the Holy Ghost appointed had 'separated him and Barnabas for the work whereunto the Lord had called them, and laid their hands on them, and sent them away.' And this was their first commission, for he and Barnabas having been separated for the work, afterwards fulfilled their Apostolic office by their own Apostolic authority." [4]

St. Peter and St. John were sent to Samaria, Barnabas was sent to Antioch. All was done in order under the Apostolic authority of the Church.

How should Christians think of the Church ?

"Christ's Church is His body, the token and channel of His Presence, possessing as a whole (as we daily repeat of her) His attribute of ' Holiness,' because she is (Scripture saith) His

[1] *Occasional Sermons: Church the Converter of Heathen*, p. 22.
[2] *Id.* p. 23.　　　　[3] *Id.* p. 32.　　　　[4] *Id.* p. 34.

body, indwelt by His Divinity ; the body whereof He is the Head, and as such, living by His Life, moved by His Will, informed by His Spirit, imperishable, because as the head forsaketh not the members, so neither He the body He hath taken. She is one body, composed of the elder and more perfect Saints who are now perfected, and of us, as many of us as are yet in the Vine, and partake of His holiness, and are living branches. In her hath He ever dwelt by His Spirit, manifesting Himself by divers tokens, according to His Wisdom or her needs and faithfulness, by miracles, by the endurance of the martyrs, the courage of confessors, the perseverance of saints, the holy prayers of the devoted, the tears of penitents, the self-denial and toil of ascetics, the truth of evangelists, the charity of the bountiful, the humility of the poor, the hope and sure trust of the broken-hearted. She is one great mystery, consisting in Heaven of Angels and " just men, made perfect," and here below of such as being imperfect, are yet in the course of being perfected, and whom she is daily receiving into herself, under him her Head, that they may, in Him, be per-fected. And in her He is yet 'God with us,' in His Sacra-ments ; by the one whereof we are made members of Himself, we are taken out of our state of nature and the mere lineage of Adam, and made a part of that mystical body which does so truly belong to Him, as the Body which He took. And by the other, feeding on Him we live by Him and in Him and to Him, and He in us." [1]

What is the primary condition given in Ephesians iv. 11, 12 ?

" That we seek the truth in the Church which God founded, and as He founded it. 'He' (*i. e.* our ascended Lord, Whom from the right hand of God shed down His gifts upon men) 'gave some, apostles ; and some, prophets ; and some, evan-gelists ; and some, pastors and teachers ; for the perfecting of the saints, for the work of the ministry, for the edifying of the body of Christ ; *i. e.* He formed a Church with a regular ministry, some ordinary, some extraordinary, that in it, those

[1] Vol. i. p. 69.

whom in it He hath called to be saints, might be gradually trained up unto perfection, 'for the perfecting of the saints,' for the edifying or 'building up' of the body of Christ, until the whole were perfected." [1]

"Thus far we have ground only for praising God that He has, in His great mercy, assigned us our happy lot in an 'Apostolic Church,' whose Bishops have received their commission through a long unbroken line from the Apostles, whom 'He gave'; and that in this Church the pure faith is confessed, as He delivered it, neither adding to it nor taking from it." [2]

Was there, in the days of the Apostles, a full and settled regular ministry ?

"Yes; and the stress laid upon it would surprise many in these days if they attended to it at all." [3]

Mention one passage of Scripture proving this.

"And He gave some, apostles; and some, prophets; and some, evangelists; and some, pastors and teachers; for the perfecting of the saints, for the work of the ministry, for the edifying of the body of Christ; till we all come in the unity of the faith, and of the knowledge of the Son of God, unto a perfect man, unto the measure of the stature of the fulness of Christ. That we henceforth be no more children, tossed to and fro, and carried about with every wind of doctrine, by the sleight of men, and cunning craftiness, whereby they lie in wait to deceive ; but speaking the truth in love, may grow up into Him in all things, which is the Head, even Christ : from whom the whole body fitly joined together and compacted by that which every joint supplieth, according to the effectual working in the measure of every part, maketh increase of the body unto the edifying of itself in love" (Eph. iv. 11—17).

In what ways then is this well ordered Ministry essential to the growth of the body—the Church ?

"To its unity, to its connection with its Head, to its internal well-being, the avoiding of error, the growth of our faith and

---

[1] Vol. iii. p. 186.   [2] *Id.* p. 107.
[3] *Church and Heathen*, p. 37.

knowledge, and the supply of graces from Christ to the completion of His kingdom."[1]

How are we to regard the efforts at Evangelization made by those who do not belong to the Catholic Church?

"One would, of course, rejoice that Christ was made known to those who otherwise would not have heard of Him, even though 'the truth as it is in Him' should be at first imperfectly set forth. We may be glad, if in China, or some of the thousand isles of the Southern Ocean, the Roman Church or any of the maimed communities of Christians in our own land, may have borne His Name."[2]

Why is the belief in the Holy Catholic Church placed next to belief in the Holy Ghost in the Apostles' Creed?

"Holiness, Unity, Catholicity, are the attributes of His Church. Therefore is the belief in the Holy Catholic Church placed next to that of the Holy Ghost, since He, the Giver of life, present in the whole body, and proceeding from the Father and the Son, unites and sanctifies, and knits in one its several members throughout the world."[3]

While then it is by and through the Church that we are brought to and united to Our Saviour, what other unspeakable blessing do we owe her?

"The Church of God is the witness and keeper of Holy Writ. The Old Testament is received from the Ancient Church of God, the Jewish Church. The Catholic Church settled the rule and canon of the New Testament Scripture. By her authority it was finally determined what is Scripture and what is not Scripture."—GRUEBER'S *Catechism on the Church of England, the Ancient Church of the land,* p. 120.

Does the Church of England hold that there is and ever has been in the Church a duly authorized and constituted order of Ministry?

It is evident unto all men diligently reading the Holy Scriptures and ancient authors, that from the Apostles' time there have been these orders of ministers in Christ's Church;

---

[1] *Church and Heathen,* p. 39.   [2] *Id.* p. 55.   [3] *Id.* p. 59.

Bishops, Priests, and Deacons—which offices were evermore had in such reverend estimation, that no man might presume to execute any of them, except he were first called, tried, examined, and known to have such qualities as are requisite for the same; and also by public prayer, with imposition of hands, were approved and admitted thereunto by lawful authority. And therefore to the intent that these orders may be continued, and reverently used and esteemed, in the Church of England, no man shall be accounted or taken to be a lawful Bishop, Priest, or Deacon, in the Church of England, or suffered to execute any of the said functions, except he be called, tried, examined and admitted, according to the form hereafter following, or hath had formerly Episcopal Consecration or Ordination.

" When the day appointed by the Bishop is come, after Morning Prayer is ended, there shall be a sermon or exhortation declaring the duty and office of such as come to be admitted Priests; how necessary that order is in the Church of Christ; and also how the people ought to esteem them in their office."— *See* Ordinal in Prayer-book.

COLLECT.—"Almighty Giver of good things, who by Thy Holy Spirit hast appointed divers orders of Ministers in Thy Church."

The Exhortation calls attention to the dignity and great importance of the office of the Priesthood.

Can the Catholic Church teach anything contrary to the Faith once delivered to the Saints?

No. Individuals may fall into heresy, portions of the Church in various localities may impair, add to or subtract from the faith, but "the whole Church can never be led into any formal acceptance of error, by virtue of our Lord's promise. This is matter of Faith." [1]

Give an illustration in proof, ancient and modern.

In days of Athanasius large numbers of bishops were infected with the Arian heresy. The Church condemned it. In 1870 the Roman Communion created a new Article of Faith, that the Bishop of Rome is Infallible. The Anglican and Eastern

[1] *Eirenicon*, p. 93.

portions of the Catholic Church reject the dogma as a new and unwarrantable attempted addition to the Catholic Faith.

Is it true that the Church of England, at the time of the Reformation, separated herself from the Catholic Church, breaking away from and rejecting the Catholic traditions and teachings of the Church?

Most untrue. The statement is generally made by very ignorant persons, or by those whose interest it is to disparage and ignore the office and work of the Church of England.

What is her own testimony?

In the Preface to the Prayer-book, it is said : "We have rejected all such (alterations as were either of dangerous consequence) as secretly striking at some established doctrine or laudable practice of the Church of England, or indeed, of the whole Catholic Church of Christ."

"But so far was it from the purpose of the Church of England to forsake and reject the Churches of Italy, France, Spain, Germany, or any such like Churches, in all things which they held and practised; that, as the apology of the Church of England confesseth, 'It doth with reverence retain those ceremonies which do neither endamage the Church of God, nor offend the minds of sober men; and *only departed* from them in those particular points, wherein they were fallen both from themselves in their ancient integrity, and from the Apostolical Churches which were their first founders.'"— *Canon* XXX.

"The Primitive Church which was most holy and godly."— *Homilies*, 2 B, x. i. 2.

"The Primitive Church which was most pure and uncorrupt."—*Homilies*, 2 B, ii. 1.

"The Primitive Church in those times which was most pure and sincere."—*Homilies*, 2 B, ii. 1.

"The Primitive Church which was most uncorrupt and pure."—*Homilies*, 2 B, ii. 2.

"This truth and doctrine (concerning forbidding and

worshipping of images) was believed and taught of the old Holy Fathers and most ancient learned doctors, and received in the old Primitive Church which was most uncorrupt and pure."—*Homilies*, 2 B, ii. 2.

" About four hundred years after our Saviour Christ, there were no images used for worship, and received in the Church of Christ, which was then much less corrupt and more pure than it now is."—*Homilies*, 2 B, ii. 2.

" Those six councils which were allowed and received of all men."—*Homilies*, 2 B, ii. 2.

" And there is no doubt but that the Primitive Church next the Apostles' time was most pure."—*Homilies*, 2 B, ii. 2.

" The Primitive Church which is especially to be followed, as most uncorrupt and pure."—*Homilies*, 2 B, ii. 3.

" The judgment of the Primitive Church, which was most pure and sincere."—*Homilies*, 2 B, ii. 3.

" Whosoever through his private judgement, willingly and purposely, doth openly break the traditions and ceremonies of the Church, which be not repugnant to the Word of God, and be ordained and approved by common authority, ought to be rebuked openly."—*Article* XXXIV.

Although the Church of England is a portion of the One Catholic Church, is in short, The *Catholic Church in England; it is said she has ceased to be a true portion of the Catholic Church by her denying its visible Head, the Bishop of Rome.*

The Church of England does not any more than the Eastern Church own the monarchy of the Bishop of Rome. " In the time of Henry VIII. the English Church submitted to the abolition of appeals to Rome, and what it then submitted to, it has since concurred in. But if anything is clear in Christian antiquity, it is that such appeals are *not of Divine right.*" [1]

" What was not of Divine right cannot become such. That only is Divine law which was given by God." [2]

<hr>

[1] *Eirenicon*, p. 66.   [2] *Id.* p. 72.

" The African Church in the fifth century, not only forbade appeals to parts beyond the seas, but excommunicated throughout Africa any one who should so appeal." [1]

" The primacy of the Bishop of Rome is not denied by the Church of England, for she acknowledges general councils which owned it." [2]

Primate means " first among equals," not absolute supreme infallible monarch.

Why was the Bishop of Rome allowed the pre-eminence of honour amongst bishops ?

Because, as testified by the Council of Chalcedon, Rome was the seat of the Empire, and therefore to its throne the fathers reasonably gave privileges.

It has been said that the Church of England denies the perpetual Divine voice of the Church; if so, can she be as she claims to be, a true portion of the Catholic Church?

The Church denies no authority, power, right, prerogative, privilege, gift of any sort whatever, wherewith the Church has been endowed by Christ. Those who say she denies or rejects the Living Voice of the Church are Roman opponents who claim for their Communion, that it is the whole Church. The Church of England does deny the Bishop of Rome to be the living voice of the Church; she does deny a decree of any Roman Council to be the voice of the whole Church ; she accepts nothing, in short, but what the whole Church accepts as taught of God. In this she is thoroughly Catholic. She does not see the perpetual necessity of defining or declaring Articles of Faith. God the Holy Ghost in His own time may cause the whole Church to unite in a general council to do what seemeth Him good. But " meanwhile He exercises the office of teacher, by teaching the children of God, by giving them the supernatural gift of faith as of grace ; and He maintains everywhere in the Church the tradition of the great body of faith infallibly fixed." [3]

<hr>

[1] *Eirenicon,* p. 76. [2] *Letter* in reply to Rev. A. GURNEY, Dec. 7, 1865.
[3] *Eirenicon,* pt. i. p. 93.

Is not the Church of England rightly described as the Protestant Church of England?

No. She nowhere claims to be anything else but a pure portion of the One Catholic Church. The word Protestant does not occur in the Prayer-book; she speaks of the Catholic Church, the Catholic Religion, Catholic Faith in the Creeds. She prays for the good estate of the Catholic Church in her prayer for "all conditions of men." She speaks again and again of the "Holy Church universal," "the Universal Church," "the Church," "the Holy Church," "Christ's Church," "the whole Church," "the Church of Christ," "the Church of God."

Is it not the case that the word Protestant does occur in the Coronation Service?

Yes; the Sovereign promises to uphold the Church in England against her enemies, against those who, while professing themselves Catholics, behave in a very uncatholic and schismatic way, and are her bitter opponents—*i. e.* the Roman Catholics.

In this same Coronation Service the Sovereign swears to defend the Catholic Faith. And the Communion table is called the "Altar" forty times or so.

What do persons mean when they say they are Protestants?

Generally speaking, they mean they are not Roman Catholics; or, that they do not believe that the Catholic Church has three Holy orders of ministers, Bishops, Priests, and Deacons; and that they take a very low view of the Sacraments, looking upon them more as mere signs and ceremonies, than as sanctifying and life-giving means of grace.

The Church of England does *protest*, and protest most strongly, against the uncatholic claims of the Roman Communion; and in so doing she agrees with the Eastern Church.

But she recognizes no such thing as *the* Protestant Church, or *the* Protestant Faith. When the term is used by the

American Church it is simply meant to disavow sympathy with the attitude, position, and distinctive doctrines of the Roman Schism. It is much to be regretted that the American Church ever formally adopted such an unsatisfactory title.

Do not some professing Christians unjustly suspect Churchmen who dislike to be called Protestants ?

Yes. "It implies a papistical leaning to dislike the term 'Protestant,' the rejection of which is to argue a leaning to Romanism ; it does not belong historically to our Church, but to the Lutherans, and was still used exclusively of them, in the memory of some of the younger among us. It has nowhere been adopted by our Church in any formulary or document of hers ; nay, it was in 1689 altogether repudiated by the representatives of the inferior clergy at least, the Lower House of Convocation, who would not even allow of the phrase, 'The Protestant religion in general, and the Church of England in particular,' lest they should thereby seem in any way to identify themselves with the Foreign Churches." [1]

"It is always more real to describe ourselves by what we are, than to state merely what we are not, lest in time our faith should shrink into the mere denial of error instead of being a confession of the truth." [2]—BISHOP COTTERILL, *The Genesis of the Church ;* HOOKER'S *Ecclesiastical Polity ;* PALMER'S *Treatise ;* BISHOP MOBERLY'S *Great Forty Days.*

PRAYER.

If a man says a prayer or two on rising, and again before going to sleep, will not such devotion be enough ?

Would that all invariably said but one word of prayer morning and evening ! Let any one humbly search the Scriptures, and see whether he ought to be content, praying a little or praying much. Remember our Lord's Example.

"Continue instant in prayer." "Watchful therein, with all

---

[1] *Letter to Bishop of London*, p. 12.　　　　[2] *Id.* p. 13.

perseverance," "at all seasons." "Men ought always to pray, and not to faint"—"pray without ceasing."

No one can doubt but the command to pray often earnestly, continuously, for all things, always, is as plain as any of the plainest commands of God.

But if a man is very busy pressed for time?

We shall be judged according to what we have, not according to what we have not. If we have little time we must do our best "to give of that little."

But how can a very busy person be often praying?

"Most businesses," says a good doctor of our Church, "have wide gaps, all have some chinks, at which devotion may slip in. Be we never so urgent or closely intent upon any work (be we feeding, be we travelling, be we trading, be we studying), nothing can forbid but that we may together wedge in a thought concerning God's goodness, and bolt forth a word of praise for it; but that we may reflect on our sins, and spend a penitential sigh on them; but that we may descry our need of God's help, and despatch a brief petition, a 'God be praised,' a 'Lord have mercy,' a 'God bless,' or 'God help me,' will no wise interrupt or disturb our proceedings."—ISAAC BARROW.[1]

What comfort is there for the busy who have not much time for prayer?

"God does not look on the length of the prayers, but on the desire of the heart."

"Longing desire prayeth always though the tongue be silent. If thou art ever longing, thou art ever praying. When stayeth prayer? When desire groweth cold."—ST. AUG. on the N. I. *Sermons.*[2]

"He then cannot be said to have any care about continued prayer, who passes any day between morning and evening without it, who lets his thoughts run on through the day on his daily business, without checking them to offer at least some brief prayer to God; who begins a work without asking God to bless it; who receives a mercy, or his daily food, without

[1] Vol. iii. p. 230.   [2] *Id.* p. 415.

blessing Him ; who comes into his daily temptations without asking God to deliver him from them ; who is beset by any care, and casts it not on God ; who does not labour.to fix his heart, like David, upon God, that he may praise Him ; who does not consider prayer (whatever he may yet have come up to) as the main business of life, as it will be of life eternal, and so does not wish or strive at least to interpose it at all intervals he may have ; who does not at least divide each day into portions, and begin, at least, each such portion with some prayer." [1]

Name one most useful important prayer, seldom thought of, seldom used ?

"Prayer morning by morning, to be enabled to pray : 'Lord, teach, help me to pray.' " [2]

Mention the reason why all should say, at least a secret word or two of prayer, when the thought comes into the mind to pray.

"That thought to pray cannot come from thyself or from the Evil One, it must come from God." [3]

If we expect our prayers to be heard, what are the necessary conditions ?

"The conditions of prayer which shall be heard are— (1) A right faith : 'in My Name.' (2) A right life : 'if My words abide in you.' (3) That we be members of His body : 'If ye abide in Me.' (4) Confidence as to the very subject of our prayer : 'believing that ye shall have them '; and (5) perseverance." [4]

What must we be careful about, remembering that we are to pray in His Name ?

That we ask not in His Name, thinking of Him other than as He is, "Very God of very God." Not wishing anything to be granted unless He too wills it. Not dreaming of asking for anything, for any fancied deserts of our own, but for His sake only. Praying as Jesus prayed, in the spirit of His prayer, "Not as I will, but as Thou wilt."

---

[1] Vol. iii. p. 230.   [2] *Id.* p. 237.
[3] *Id.* p. 238.   [4] *Id.* p. 241.

Whence comes our right, that we may use, and dare to use, His Name?

"The best prayer is the humblest; remember our very *faith entitles us not* to it; it belongs to us not by any act of our own, but by His, adopting us, re-creating us, giving us a 'new name,' even His own, as having been re-created in Himself; and putting It into our mouths and emboldening us to utter it."[1]

Name one most important reason against the neglect of prayer.

To pray not, is to lose one's sense of dependence upon God; prayer proves that we feel our dependence upon Him.

"Prayer is dependence upon God. Not to pray must be spiritual pride, the most dangerous state."[2]

Name one reason why the prayers of many seem so unsatisfactory, so comfortless, so useless.

Because from want of honest self-examination and serious consideration in view of the Judgment, they forget or they ignore the fact, that they are not in perfect charity with all men, or are not wishing, praying, and trying to be so, more than they now are.

Of what sort should our first prayer always be?

One acknowledging our *unworthiness* to approach God even in prayer.

What have been called the two wings of prayer?

"Charity and fasting are the wings of prayer; fasting as a token and means of self-abasement; charity to man as a token of our love to God, Whom we see not, and drawing down His ineffable love to us through Whom we love; charity in forgiving wrong, charity in showing mercy in our prayers, as we hope to have other's prayers for us; charity especially in self-denying almsgiving to Christ's poor."[3]

Why do so many persons find it so difficult to pray without wandering thought and distractions?

From not always trying to live in the recollection of God's presence.

"Such as we are at other times, such will our prayers be.

---

[1] Vol. iii. p. 250.   [2] *Id.* p. 253.   [3] *Id.* p. 260.

God helps us in our prayers, as without Him we cannot pray ; but He doth so in proportion as we admit His aid in the rest of our life. We cannot pray as we ought unless we live as we ought. Our prayers will partake of our other infirmities. We cannot at once collect ourselves, and become other men in the presence of God, from what we were just before." [1]

"We cannot keep our thoughts disengaged at prayer if they are through the day engaged ; we cannot keep out vain thoughts then, if at other times we yield to them." [2]

"We must live more to God if we would pray more to God." [3]

"This, then, is the chief, the most comprehensive remedy against distraction in prayer, to see that we be not distracted amid the manifoldness of the things of sense at other times." [4]

What is the best model of prayer ?
Our Lord's prayer, of course.
May we in reverence ask why so ?
First, because our Lord gave it ; and secondly, He who knows our infirmities so well, teaches us *how* to pray—in short sentences.

"The best models of prayer consist of brief petitions as suited to men in need ; for when they really feel their need they use not many words : 'Lord, save us, we perish,' is the cry of need. And so the petitions of the pattern of all prayer, our Lord's, are very short, but each containing manifold prayers. So are the Psalms in prayer or praise : 'Blot out mine iniquities,' 'Create in me a new heart,' 'Cast me not away from Thy presence,' 'Save me by Thy name.' Such are our own primitive prayers, collects, litany, sentences, asking much in few words. Even our longest prayer 'for the Church Militant' is made up in fact of a number of separate prayers." [5]

Give a few simple rules and encouragements to pray.

[1] Vol. iii. p. 268.　　　　　[2] *Id.* p. 269.
[3] *Id.* p. 270.　　　[4] *Id.*　　　[5] *Id.* p. 281

"The name of Jesus itself often repeated is a volume of prayer."[1]

"Pray *modestly*, as to the things of this life : *earnestly*, for what may be helps to your salvation : *intensely*, for salvation itself, that you may for ever behold God, love God."[2]

"Practise in life whatever thou prayest for, and God will give it thee more abundantly."[3]

Pray to persevere, trying to pray better.

Remember Jesus in Heaven ever prayeth for us. "He presents before the Father the tokens of His passion in that human nature which for us He took to plead for us. How should he not obtain all things for whom, in whom, Christ prayeth? Prayer in faith, hope, charity, humility is the voice of God in our secret hearts. What should hinder it from ascending to the Presence of God, to be presented by Him, not for our unworthiness, but for His worthiness?—Who gave it to us, gives to it the value of His own Blood."[4]

Jesus ever prays for me; shall I not then ever pray for His sake, Who loved and gave Himself for me?

Why should we have humble confidence in prayer, and ever believe that no good prayer is unavailing?

We pray in Jesus' Name. "We hear no answer, we see no sign; perhaps until we are in eternity we shall never know what became of the prayer. But it had an inward power, a Divine might from God to God, a covenanted omnipotency with the Omnipotent. God has pledged His truth, that is Himself, that, if it has been asked according to His will, He will give it. God became man to give us this power over Himself."[5]

What is a great fault in the prayers of many?

They consist so much in supplication, they contain so little of praise and thanksgiving. "Our prayers would be quite changed, they will be transfigured as they shall have more of thanksgiving in them."[6]

---

[1] *Letter to Bishop of London*, p. 79.   [2] Vol. ii. p. 178.
[3] *Id.* p. 179.   [4] *Id.* p. 180.
[5] *Lenten Sermons*, p. 323.   [6] *Id.* p. 331.

What so spoils prayer, even in people whose hearts are right with God ?

"It is only while we think of our poor, wretched, thankless selves, that we can mistrust God or pray so coldly. Go out of yourselves, and go forth into that Ocean of love wherein thou art bathed. Thank God for what He has made thee, the object of His love, the son of His love in the well-beloved Son; nay, one with Him, 'in whom He is well pleased.'"[1]

"Thank God for all the blessings which you know, as they are showered daily upon you; thank Him for having saved you from any sin and misery; for enabling you to check any temptation; for keeping from you any which you would not have resisted; thank Him for all His unmerited love, and that He has concentrated on you all the wonders of His Redemption; that He died for you, as much as if in all this wide world of the redeemed there had been none to die for besides."[2]

And in daily life remember there is nothing too small to thank God for.

Mention another fault in the private prayers of many.

"They do not pray heartily and enough for *others ;* our dear Lord never prayed for Himself alone, neither do you. It were a poor thing, if it were possible, to get to Heaven by one's self. What? To think to reach the abode of eternal love, and God Who is Love, and bring none with us whom we have at least by our prayers won to God."[3]

"I said, 'If it were possible to be saved alone.' I should almost doubt whether it were possible, quite alone; it would be well-nigh impossible, for it would be to be saved without love."[4]

"Pray, as far as God gives you now, simply, humbly, earnestly, regularly, perseveringly, for others with yourself; unite your prayers to your Redeemer's prayers; your prayers for others will return into your own bosom; God will hear for yourself your prayers for others, and it will be part of that Ocean of

---

[1] *Lenten Sermons*, p. 332.   [2] *Id.* p 333.
[3] *Id.* p. 337.   [4] *Id.* p. 338.

H

joy into which you shall enter, that as the prayers of others have been heard for you, so shall there be some there, who, through your prayers shall have been won to your faith in God, to love of God, to everlasting life in God."—Rev. W. H. HUTCHINGS *on Prayer;* LIDDON'S *Some Elements of Religion.*

FASTING.

Does the Church of England in any way enjoin or encourage fasting?

Very plainly. She appoints certain days of fasting or abstinence. She bids her children pray for grace to use "such abstinence, that, our flesh being subdued to the Spirit, we may ever obey Thy godly motions in righteousness, and true holiness, to Thy honour and glory."—*First Lent Collect.*

She directs that adult candidates for Holy Baptism be exhorted to prepare themselves by fasting, as well as by Prayer. In the last prayer of the Commination Service she bids her people pray, "Be favourable to Thy people who turn to Thee in weeping, fasting, and praying."

"Now, beloved, ye have heard, first, what fasting is, as well that which is outward in the body as that which is inward in the heart. Ye have heard also that there are three ends or purposes whereunto, if our outward fast be directed, it is a good work that God is pleased with; thirdly, hath been declared, what time is most meet for to fast, either privately or publicly. Last of all, what things fasting hath obtained of God, by the examples of Ahab and the Ninevites. Let us therefore, dearly beloved, seeing there are many more causes of fasting and mourning in these our days, than hath been of many years heretofore in any one age, endeavour ourselves, both inwardly in our hearts, and also outwardly with our bodies, diligently to exercise this godly exercise of fasting in such sort and manner, as the Holy Prophets, the Apostles, and divers other devout persons for their time used the same."—*Homilies, S.P.C.K. Edition,* p. 309.

Name some of those who, after fasting, received special help or mercies from God.

"Ahab, David, Moses, Elijah, Samuel, Esther, Ezra, Nehemiah, Daniel, Anna." [1]

What is the Scriptural reason for fasting?

When our Lord came to this world as our Saviour, " He took not away suffering and self-discipline, but hallowed them, uniting them with His own sufferings, and giving them thereby efficacy which, in themselves, they had not. He sanctified fasting by His example. He gave it virtue by His Passion. He filled it with His Spirit, and so made it a token of His disciples, and a channel of grace. He placed it at the outset of His teaching; He prefixed it, in His Own Person, to His ministry; He left it as a solemn memorial of Himself, as part of the bridal dowry of the Church, a mark that we are the children of the Bride-Chamber, now widowed for the time, and in sorrow for His absence, until we be admitted to the marriage supper of the Lamb. ' The days will come when the Bridegroom shall be taken from them, and then shall they fast in those days.' How then are we His disciples if we fast not? Should we not rather wonder that we do anything but fast, since all our days are days of His absence?" [2]

THE INVOCATION OF SAINTS.

What does the Church of England teach?

She condemns the Romish doctrine in Article XXII.

In the majority of Romish catechisms and manuals of instruction you will only find it taught, that it is lawful to desire and to ask the Saints to obtain help for us by their intercessions, but the popular forms of prayer and litanies go far beyond this.

What is really the popular Roman teaching and practice?

The encouragement of, and the uttering of, direct addresses to The Virgin, or to some great Saint for favours and helps of all sorts; appealing to them as if they of their own power could

[1] Vol. i. p. 183.　　　　　[2] *Id.* p. 184.

bestow the favour asked ; appealing to them as if God would be more likely to listen to them than to our own prayers, which He has promised to hear for Christ's sake.

But surely, it is argued, He is more likely to listen to the intercession of the Saints praying for us, than to our prayers ?

All who pray are heard for Christ's sake only.

It is forgotten that God the Holy Ghost prays in us.

Is it wrong or vainly superstitious for any, in their private prayers to God, to express their desire to Him that the saints may pray for them ?

It would be very difficult to prove that such a desire, expressed to God in prayer, could be wrong in any way.

" The safer way is to pray for them to Him, of Whom and through Whom and to Whom are all things, our God and our All, Who according to the current Roman explanation also reveals to them the desire of those below to have their prayers." [1]

Give one or two specimens of the Invocation, rightly condemned by the English Church.

" Mary, give me patience and strength."

" O Mary, our great Mediatrix ! "

" Thou art the Dispenser of all graces."

> " O Jesus, Mary, Joseph, deign,
> Our souls in heavenly ways to train ! "

Are these Invocations only of recent origin ?

They are not to be found in antiquity. The New Testament, the writings of the Fathers, the inscriptions in the Catacombs, all bear witness that these invocations are new and uncatholic.

" No one can look uncontroversially at such occasional addresses as there are to martyrs in the fourth century (and those chiefly prayers at their tombs through their intercession for miraculous aid of God), and such books as *The Glories of Mary, The Month of Mary,* and say that the character of the modern reliance on, and invocation of, Saints was that of the

---

[1] *Preface to Paradise of the Soul,* p. xi.

Ancient Church. No one could (it should be thought) observe how through volumes of St. Augustine or St. Chrysostom there is no mention of any reliance except on Christ alone, and how in modern books St. Mary is held out as 'the refuge of sinners,' as having 'the goats committed to her, as Christ the sheep,' as 'the throne of grace,' to whom a sinner may have easier access than to Christ, and seriously say, that the ancient and modern teaching and practice are the same. We could preach whole volumes of the sermons of St. Augustine or St. Chrysostom to our people to their edification and without offence; were a Roman Catholic preacher to confine himself to their preaching it would (it has been said among themselves) be regarded as 'indevout towards St. Mary,' as 'one whose religion was more of the head than of the heart.' "[1]

Why is this direct invocation of saints for what God alone can give objectionable ?

"The exclusive address of unseen beings has an obvious tendency at once to fall into a sort of worship; it is too like the mode in which we address Almighty God to be any way safe; the exclusive request of their intercessions is likely at once to constitute them intercessors in a way different from God's servants on earth, and (which is the great practical evil of these prayers in the Roman Church) to interfere with the office of the Great Intercessor."[2]

What are the distinctions drawn by Archbishop Ussher between any practice which may be found in the early Church, and the Roman practice of the Invocation of Saints ?

(1) That in the Ancient Church mental addresses were confined to God, as knowing the thoughts; in the Romish they are made to the saints also.[3]

(2) In the Ancient Church they spoke doubtfully, whether the saints know the details of our wants; in the Romish it is held as a point of faith that they hear men's prayers.

(3) In the Ancient Church the saints were applied to only

---

[1] *Preface to Paradise,* p. viii.
[2] *Letter to Bishop of Oxford,* p. 198.   [3] *Letter to Jelf,* p. 105.

in the same way as the living; in the Romish, " formal and absolute prayers are tendered to them."

(4) In the Ancient Church they are addressed only as joint petitioners; in the Romish, as advocates and mediators by virtue of their own merits also.

(5) In the Ancient Church the seeking the prayers of the Saints interfered not with our " boldness to approach the Throne of Grace "; in the Romish, the Saints are held out as an easier and more acceptable way for a sinner to approach God; in the Ancient Church persons were taught chiefly to look to their own prayers; in the Romish to the intercession of saints.

(6) And principally, in the Ancient Church the prayers of the saints were requested as fellow-servants; in the Romish, invocation is attributed as a part of the worship due to them, in Bellarmine's words, " an eminent kind of adoration."

JESUS THE OBJECT OF DIVINE WORSHIP.

What is the ordinary method and form of prayer?
That which is addressed to God the Father through Jesus Christ our Lord.

May we address prayers directly to Jesus, and to the Holy Ghost?
Jesus being God, certainly we may pray to Him direct; the Holy Ghost being God, to Him also we may pray direct.

"Since then," says St. Augustine, "we serve both the Father and the Son and the Holy Spirit with that servitude which is called ' Latreia,' and we hear the law of God enjoining that we should show this to no other but the Lord our God only; doubtless our one and only God is the Trinity Itself, to which one and alone we by right of piety owe such a servitude." [1]

" *But does not the fact that God the Son has become Incarnate,*

---

[1] *Lenten Sermons*, p. 438.

become man, make some difference; in short, ought we to pray to and worship Jesus just as we do God the Father?"

"Nor plainly, does the humility of the Incarnation make any difference herein.   For He deified our nature in Himself by taking it; He could and did, empty Himself of the visible glory of His Godhead; He could not, by becoming man, cease to be God.   He became man, 'not by conversion of the Godhead into flesh, but by taking of the Manhood into God.' 'We worship not a creature,' says St. Athanasius; 'God forbid,' for such an error belongs to heathens and Arians.   But we worship the Lord of the creation, the Word of God Incarnate." [1]

Is it right or wrong to offer the worship due to God only, to the Humanity of Jesus, or to any portion of it, as to His Heart, His Hands, His Wounds?

We may in reverent contemplation think of any of His sufferings for our salvation, and say in the words of the hymn—

> "See from His Head, His Hands, His Feet,
> Sorrow and love flow mingled down."

We may think of and pray, "By Thine Agony and Bloody Sweat, Good Lord, deliver us;" we may supplicate our Lord by the memory of His Thirst, or any of His Sufferings to help us; *but in worshipping Jesus, we must be careful, both in our thoughts and words, not in any way to think or say anything that implies we offer Divine Worship but to Him only.*

"And neither severing the Body, being such, by Itself apart from the Word, do we worship it; nor, wishing to worship the Word, do we remove Him from the Flesh; but knowing, as I said before, the Scripture, 'The Word was made Flesh,' we own Him, although being in the flesh, to be God." [2]—ST. ATHANASIUS.

Is the Humanity of our Lord by Itself to be worshipped?

"His Personality is not human, but Divine; when, then, we adore Christ our God, we adore not His Deity and His Humanity separately, but His Deity clothed with His Humanity.

[2] *Lenten Sermons,* p. 439.   [3] *Id.* p. 440.

This the Church of God proclaimed that she had received from the first, that 'God the Word Incarnate, with His own Flesh, was worshipped,' rejecting with anathema the opposite heresies, that Christ is worshipped in two natures, thus introducing two acts of worship, one appropriated to God the Word, the other appropriated to the Man." [1]

Is it right to say that the Humanity of Christ, or any part of His Human Nature, e. g. His Sacred Heart, is an object of Divine Worship, because though distinct it is indivisible from the Divine Person ?

Jesus, the God-Man, the Lord God Incarnate, is *the* Object of Divine Worship.

" If any one dare to say that the assumed Humanity ought to be adored and glorified with God the Word, and co-addressed as one with another (for he who adds 'with' manifestly points to the adoration of one with or besides another), and does not rather with *one adoration* honour Emmanuel, and ascribe one glorification on account of the fact that the Word was made Flesh—let him be Anathema."—S. CYRIL. [2]

Suppose a Christian could now see our Lord on earth with His Glory veiled, and were to fall at His Feet and adore, he would not be adoring the Sacred Feet only, he would not be adoring the Human Nature of Christ by itself; he would be adoring Jesus, and Jesus only, Who is God, and Who has assumed that Human Nature.

In short, no other worship is to be given to Our Lord but the very highest of all possible worship—that which is due to God, and God only.

Let not any forget or transgress the Command given to the Hosts of Heaven.

" When He bringeth the First Begotten into the world, He saith, and 'let all the Angels of God worship Him.' "

Special devotions to our Lord, *e.g.* to His Five Wounds, are not wrong. Only those who use them rightly, find such

---

[1] *Lenten Sermons*, p. 441.

[2] *See* DR. PUSEY, *Letter to Bishop of London*, p. 113.

devotions the greatest help and consolation, and a vivid way of expressing their love to our Lord.

The cause of their neglect, and of their misuse, has been in the want of true devotion to the Person of our Lord.

Blame none who use them not; use them only in a true, Catholic, intelligent, humble way; and "we should bear in mind that these were part of our ancient inheritance, and they flow so naturally from the contemplation of our Blessed Lord's Humanity and Passion, that we must have misgivings whether we should ever have lost them, or be now to such an extent without them, had our devotion to the Person of our suffering Redeemer been what it ought."[1]

"Had it been deeply impressed upon us that He is 'Very God and Very Man,' and that everything that He wrought or suffered for us had therefore an infinite value; or had we contemplated His Sacred Humanity as they only may venture who think habitually of His Human Nature as wholly taken into God; we could hardly have ceased to have dwelt reverentially on each single act and moment of His Life and Passion."[2]

"With regard to devotions in reference to the Five Wounds which our Blessed Lord received for us, they are, I believe, on the very principle of the deepest petition of our Litany: 'By Thy holy Nativity and Circumcision; by Thine Agony and bloody Sweat; by Thy Cross and Passion.' Those Wounds are the Wounds of Him who being Man was also God; they are the Wounds which the prophet foretold that we too should gaze upon, and gazing on 'they shall look on Him Whom they had pierced, and shall mourn for the sins whereby we pierced Him.' They are Wounds which shall be beheld in the Day of Judgment, when they who persevered in piercing Him anew, shall wail not in penitent sorrow, but in despair. 'Behold He cometh with clouds; and every eye shall see Him, and also which pierced Him; and all kindreds of the earth shall wail because of Him.'"[3]

---

[1] *Preface to Surin*, p. xxviii.   [2] *Id.* p. xxix.

[3] *Letter to Bishop of London*, p. 180.

"Why should we not gaze on them in thankful love now, that we may not behold them then in terror?

Why, when dwelling upon His Passion, should we not dwell on every circumstance in it which the Holy Ghost has caused to be set down for us, and implore Him by *every* Deed of His Love to have mercy upon us?"

Remember then, "the Sacred Flesh of Jesus being the Body of God, is worshipped with Divine worship *in* God, since Christ is not divided; and we, worshipping Him, *separate not* the Body from the Word, nor the Word from the Body, but worship our One Uncreated Lord; the Word, Who for our sakes took the Manhood into Himself, the Only Begotten, with that Holy Temple which He came and took."[1]

THE SACRAMENTS.

What is the twofold mission of the Catholic Church?

By preaching and teaching, spreading everywhere the knowledge of the Lord, to bring souls to believe the Gospel, and to repent. Also to *make* them Christians, and to preserve their union with Christ in and by the Sacraments.

What is the charge given to Priests at their Ordination?

"Be thou a faithful dispenser of the Word of God, and of His Holy Sacraments, in the name of the Father, and of the Son, and of the Holy Ghost." And to each Priest is given the Bible, with the commission, "Take thou authority to preach the Word of God, and to minister the Holy Sacraments in the congregation."

How many Sacraments hath Christ ordained in His Church?

"Two only, as generally necessary to salvation, that is to say, Baptism, and the Supper of the Lord."—*Church Catechism.*

Does this mean that there are only two Sacraments?

No; but that there are two only generally necessary to salvation. The Church here implies that there are other rites which

______
[1] *See* DR. PUSEY'S *Sermons at Leeds*, p. 331.

might have the name, though not of this high dignity, nor "universally necessary," nor "ordained by Christ Himself."

"Precisely this distinction is made in the Homilies, which recognize several Sacraments in that larger sense; at the very time that in the same language in the Articles they distinguish between them and the two great Sacraments. 'As for the number of them (the Sacraments), if they should be considered according to the exact signification of a Sacrament, namely, for visible signs, expressly commanded in the New Testament, whereunto is annexed the promise of free forgiveness of sins, and of our holiness and *joining in* Christ, there be but two; namely, Baptism, and the Supper of the Lord. For although Absolution hath the promise of forgiveness of sins, yet by the express word of the New Testament, it hath not this promise *annexed and tied to the visible sign*, which is imposition of hands; for this visible sign (I mean laying on of hands) is not expressly commanded in the New Testament to be used in Absolution, as the visible signs in Baptism and the Lord's Supper are; and therefore Absolution is *no such Sacrament as Baptism and the Lord's Supper are*, and though the ordering of ministers hath this visible sign and promise, yet it lacks the promise of remission of sins, *as all other Sacraments besides the above-named do*. Therefore neither it *nor any other Sacrament else, be such Sacraments* as Baptism and the Communion are. But in a general acception, the name of a Sacrament may be attributed to anything, whereby an holy thing is signified.'"[1]—*Homily on Common Prayer and Sacraments.*

State shortly the eminence of the two great Sacraments.

"Baptism is the one we acknowledge to be the re-birth of God the Holy Ghost, the grafting into Christ, whereby we are taken out of our state of nature, and our supernatural life in Christ is begun in us; the Holy Eucharist is eminently our life, the Crown of the Christian being, our closest union with Christ, the great invention of our Blessed Lord's love, to make

[1] *Letter to Bishop of Oxford*, p. 98.

Himself present to us and in us, as He is nowhere besides in this earth." [1]

The two Sacraments which flowed from the Side of Christ are essential to the Christian life.

"Confirmation enlarges the gift of Baptism, and was counted of old a supplement to it, or almost a part of it. The Sacrament of Penitence were not needed if we ever kept faithfully the gift in Baptism : it is but the second plank given to us by the mercy of God after shipwreck. The Sacrament of Matrimony hallows an allowed yet not the highest state of the Christian. Orders are directly but for one class, although that class was instituted for the good of all, and its offices are necessary to all. The Unction of the Sick is not held to be necessary to salvation. But Baptism clothes us with Christ, and in the Holy Eucharist He is Himself our Food." [2]

Where is Ordination spoken of as a Sacrament?

In the Homily of Common Prayer and Sacraments.

Where is Holy Matrimony spoken of as a Sacrament?

In the Book of Homilies, Part I., in the Homily against Swearing.

Does the Church of England teach that Sacraments are, as it were, merely outward ceremonies, useful for Christians to observe, or does she teach that they are really and truly most valuable channels of grace?

She teaches, as we have seen, that Holy Baptism and Holy Communion are two great Sacraments generally necessary to salvation. She also teaches (*see* Article XXV.), that "Sacraments ordained of Christ be not only badges or tokens of Christian men's profession, *but rather they be certain sure* witnesses, and effectual signs of grace, and God's good will towards us, by the which He doth work invisibly in us, and doth not only quicken, but also strengthen and confirm our Faith in Him."

In Article XXVII. she teaches Baptism is not only a sign

<hr>

[1] *Eirenicon*, pt. iii. p. 91.　　　　　[2] *Id.* p. 92.

of profession and mark of difference, whereby Christian men are discerned from others that be not christened; but it is also a sign of Regeneration, or New Birth, whereby as by an instrument they that receive Baptism rightly *are grafted* into the Church.

As regards Holy Communion, in the Homily on the Sacrament, we "must be sure to hold that in the Supper of the Lord there is no vain ceremony, no bare sign, no untrue figure of a thing absent; but, as the Scripture saith, The table of the Lord, the Bread and Cup of the Lord, the Memory of Christ, the Annunciation of His Death; yea, the Communion of the Body and Blood of the Lord."

As regards the two great Sacraments, remember—

"Without the birth there can be no room for sustenance; and so, without Baptism, can there be no Communion; but neither will the birth support life without after-nourishment, so neither will it avail to have been born even of God, unless the life which is of God be supported by the means appointed by God. It will not profit us to have been Baptized unless we continually seek renewal and strengthening of that life by His Body and Blood."[1]

HOLY BAPTISM.

What sparkles in that lucid flood
Is water by gross mortals eyed ;
But seen by faith, 'tis Blood
Out of a dear Friend's side.

JOHN KEBLE.

What does the Church tell us are the benefits we receive in Holy Baptism ?

We are made members of Christ, children of God, and inheritors of the Kingdom of Heaven. We receive then the inward and spiritual grace of a death unto sin, a new birth unto righteousness, being by nature born in sin, and children of wrath we are hereby made children of grace.

[1] Vol. iii. p. 347.

Where in the Prayer-book are we most plainly told of the great work done for us in Holy Baptism?

In the Office for the reception of a child into the congregation of Christ's flock after the administration of Private Baptism. "Seeing now, dearly beloved brethren, that this child is by Baptism regenerated and grafted into the body of Christ's Church." In the same Office the child "is now, by the laver of regeneration in Baptism, received into the number of the children of God, and heirs of Everlasting Life." And in the order. for Confirmation, the candidates are declared regenerate by Water and the Holy Ghost.

If a man lives a good moral life, and says he believes that Christ is the Saviour of the world, but declines to be baptized, saying he thinks it not necessary, may he be regarded as a Christian?

Most certainly not. No man is a Christian till he is baptized. It is Baptism which makes him a Christian. To be a Christian, one must not only believe in Christ, but must put on, be joined on to Christ; as the Church teaches, by Baptism—"Man receives that which by nature he cannot have." —See *Office of Baptism for such as are of Riper Years.*

What great blessing in Baptism have we hitherto not directly mentioned?

The Remission of Sins.

Quote a few passages from Holy Scripture proving this and the necessity of Baptism, and what God does for us in that Sacrament.

John iii. 3—5: "Verily, verily, I say unto thee, Except a man be born again, he cannot see the Kingdom of God. Nicodemus saith unto him, How can a man be born when he is old? can he enter a second time into his mother's womb, and be born? Jesus answered, Verily, verily, I say unto thee, Except a man be born of water and the Spirit, he cannot enter into the Kingdom of God."

Mark xvi. 16: "He that believeth and is baptized shall be saved; but he that believeth not shall be damned."

Acts ii. 38, 39 : " Repent, and be baptized, every one of you in the name of Jesus Christ for the remission of sins, and ye shall receive the gift of the Holy Ghost. For the promise is unto you, and to your children."

Acts xxii. 16 : " Arise, and be baptized, and wash away thy sins, calling on the name of the Lord."

Gal. iii. 26 : " Ye are all the children of God by faith in Christ Jesus. For as many of you as have been baptized into Christ have put on Christ."

Titus iii. 5 : " Not by works of righteousness which we have done, but according to. His mercy He saved us, by the washing (or font) of regeneration, and renewing of the Holy Ghost."

1 Peter iii. 21 : " The like figure whereunto even baptism doth also now save (not of the putting away of the filth of the flesh, but the answer of a good conscience toward God), by the resurrection of Jesus Christ."—*See* SADLER'S *Church Doctrine Bible Truth*, pp. 49, 50.

These passages show plainly that in Holy Baptism we are new born, our sins washed away. We have become members of Christ, our salvation has been bestowed, and we are to beware that we live according to our high calling.

In the Epistles are the members of the Apostolic Churches all assumed to be Saints, i. e. Holy ?

Yes.—*See* SADLER'S *Church Doctrine Bible Truth ;* see also the *Sacrament of Responsibility and the Second Adam, and the New Birth*, by the same author.

These books of Mr. Sadler on Holy Baptism are simply invaluable to all who want to know and understand the Scriptural Doctrine of Holy Baptism.

Does the Church of England insist upon the necessity of Baptism, and the responsibility of the Baptized, as strongly as any other portion of the Catholic Church ?

Yes. Nowhere in the Church is the true Catholic Doctrine of Holy Baptism, and the vital importance of this great Sacrament, more strongly insisted upon.

"When any such persons, as are of riper years, are to be baptized, timely notice shall be given to the Bishop, or whom he shall appoint for that purpose, a week before at the least, by the parents, or some other discreet persons; that so due care may be taken for their examination, whether they be sufficiently instructed in the Principles of the Christian Religion; and that they may be exhorted to prepare themselves with Prayers and Fasting for the receiving of this holy Sacrament."—First Rubric: *Baptism of those of Riper Years.*

"The people are to be admonished, that it is most convenient that Baptism should not be administered but upon Sundays, and other Holy-days, when the most number of people come together; as well for that the Congregation there present may testify the receiving of them that be newly baptized into the number of Christ's Church; as also because in the Baptism of Infants every man present may be put in remembrance of his own profession made to God in his Baptism."—First Rubric: *Public Baptism of Infants.*

In both these rubrics we see how careful the Church of England is, that her children should be reminded of the importance and dignity of this great Sacrament, taking care, as she does, to order that it be administered in language the congregation can understand. Indeed, it has been remarked that in the Roman Communion, the Sacrament of Baptism has not been "unduly exalted, but on the contrary depreciated." Not that she has ever denied its necessity, but that she dwells so oft and continually upon the importance of other Sacraments, that the dignity of the Sacrament of Baptism has been rather cast in the background.[1]

Sadler, in *Church Doctrine Bible Truth*, p. 177, remarks— "Judged by their respective services, Baptism has a far higher position in the English than in the Romish Church, for the whole of the English Baptismal Office has to do with Baptism itself; its institution by Christ, the grace and promises connected with it, and its teaching; whereas in the Romish

<hr>

[1] *Letter to Bishop of Oxford*, p. 114.

Office, the administration of the Sacrament itself is thrust into a corner, and four-fifths of the Service have to do with other ceremonies, as outward signs of some inward spiritual graces conferred by them, such as the priest breathing on the infant; the priest placing his hands on its head; the exorcising and benediction of the salt; the making the infant taste the salt; three separate exorcisms of the infant itself before its Baptism; the application of saliva before Baptism, and anointing with oil before Baptism, and another anointing with oil after Baptism; so that in the copy of the Ritual Romanum which I have now before me, out of ten pages occupied by the Baptismal Service, not two have to do with the Sacrament itself."

All these adventitious ceremonies (especially as some of them, *e.g.* the exorcisms, are supposed to be means of grace in themselves) must detract from the witness of the Church to the grace of Baptism itself, as a Sacrament of Christ's institution.

"Remember whoever of us have been Baptized into Christ, were Baptized into His Death. 'By Baptism we have been made partakers of the Cross, the Death, the Passion, the Burial, the Resurrection of Christ: we have been joined to Christ; His Death and Life are ours'; that henceforth 'the whole body of sin,' sin in all its members, and all the parts of which the old man is composed, may be utterly 'destroyed,' that we may no longer 'serve sin,' may serve it no more than the 'dead' who is freed from sin. For the life that ye now live is not your own, but from God, and 'to God, in Jesus Christ our Lord,' in Whom we His members are"[1] (Rom. vi. 11).

CONFIRMATION.

Does the Church of England exhort her members to take great care as to the religious bringing up of young children?

Yes. Not only in the exhortation to Sponsors in the

[1] Vol. iii. p. 53.

Baptismal Office, but also in the rubrics at the end, she says—
"The Curate of every parish shall diligently upon Sundays and
Holy-days, after the second Lesson at Evening Prayer, openly in
the Church instruct and examine so many children of his Parish
sent unto him, as he shall think convenient, in some part of
this Catechism.

"And all Fathers, Mothers, Masters, and Dames, shall cause
their Children, Servants, and Apprentices, (which have not
learned their Catechism,) to come to the Church at the time
appointed, and obediently to hear, and be ordered by the
Curate, until such time as they have learned all that is here
appointed for them to learn.

"So soon as children are come to a competent age, and can
say, in their mother tongue, the Creed, the Lord's Prayer, and the
Ten Commandments; and also can answer to the other questions
of this short Catechism; they shall be brought to the Bishop.
And every one shall have a Godfather, or a Godmother, as a
Witness of their Confirmation."—*See* first three Rubrics at end
of Catechism.

"Indeed the care of children, one may well know to be the
sign of a standing or a falling Church, as we see it daily to be
of a standing or a falling family; and our Church in her
happier days amply provided for it."[1]

"She gave them to her ministers as the prime of their
charge; nay, she made it one main office of one order of her
Ministers, to 'catechize children,' and through the Bishop, she
requires all her Deacons to promise so to do."

"In her Litanies, or solemn supplications to Almighty God,
she thought especially of them, and inserted a petition not
for 'fatherless children' only, whom we all should pity, but
for all 'young children' as much needing her pity and her
prayers."

*Besides her exhortations to bring up children in the fear and
admonition of the Lord, what else does the Church most strictly
enjoin concerning their spiritual welfare?*

[1] Vol. iii. p. 302.

That they are to be brought to the Bishop to be Confirmed by him.

Does the Church then think it very necessary to give this order?

Very necessary indeed, for she also rules at the end of the Order of Confirmation, that none be admitted to Holy Communion till Confirmed, or ready and desirous to be Confirmed.

May Confirmation be called a Sacrament?

Certainly; because it has all that appertains to the nature of a Sacrament, namely, an outward and visible sign, the laying on of hands; and the inward and spiritual Grace, the Gift of the Holy Ghost.

But has not the Holy Ghost been already given in Holy Baptism?

Yes; then the person Baptized was made a child of God, a member of Christ, and a temple of the Holy Spirit. In Confirmation, the Holy Spirit perfects His work in *strengthening* the Baptized person to walk answerably to his Christian calling.

What if a Baptized person declines to be Confirmed?

In the first place, he is debarred from the reception of Holy Communion, and so his very salvation is endangered. Secondly, he is declaring his disbelief in Christ's Church by disobedience to her plain teaching; thirdly, he is giving scandal, *i. e.* offence; a cause of stumbling to weak and ignorant brethren, teaching them to despise a gift of God, and is acting very wrongly in thus breaking the traditions and ceremonies of the Church through his private judgment (Article XXXIV.). Moreover he is despising Christ's Apostles, after whose example Confirmation is enjoined and administered. Lastly, he despises the gift of the Holy Spirit.

ABSOLUTION.

What other expression does the Church use explanatory of Absolution?

Remission of sins.

When are sins first remitted or put away?

At Baptism.

Where is this stated?

In the Nicene Creed. "I acknowledge one Baptism for the remission of sins."

If a person (as all of us do) sins after Baptism, what is necessary to obtain Absolution, pardon, forgiveness, or remission of his sins?

He must repent, he must confess his sins to God, he must firmly purpose amendment; and if his sins have in any way injured his fellow-man he must endeavour to make restitution or reparation as far as he can.

If a man cannot quiet his own conscience, what does the Church advise him to do?

She says through her minister in the exhortation before Communion, that if persons after bewailing their own sinfulness, confessing themselves to Almighty God with full purpose of amendment of life, cannot quiet their own consciences; and if there be such an one "let him come to me, or to some other discreet and learned Minister of God's Word, and open his grief; that by the ministry of God's holy Word he may receive the benefit of Absolution, together with ghostly counsel and advice, to the quieting of his conscience, and avoiding of all scruple and doubtfulness."

Does the Church of England teach and allow private confession to a priest?

Most certainly; she advises it in certain cases, as we have just seen.

Does she insist upon it as necessary to salvation?

Certainly not. She teaches that repentance and confession of sin to God and firm purpose of amendment are necessary. She says to her children, You *may* confess to a priest—not you *must.* "In the English Church, confession is purely voluntary." If a Roman Catholic were to neglect confession it would be a perfect neglect of the law of his Church.[1]

Does she ever urge this private Confession to a priest upon her members ?

In the Order for the Visitation of the Sick, she directs that the sick person be moved to make a special confession of his sins, "if he feels his conscience troubled with any weighty matter."

Where does the Church of England teach that her priests have the authority and power to Absolve ?

She ordains them, saying, "Receive thou the Holy Ghost, for the office and work of a Priest in the Church of God, now committed unto thee by the imposition of our hands. Whose sins thou dost forgive, they are forgiven," &c. And in the Order for Morning and Evening Prayer, she declares that God "hath given power, and commandment, to His Ministers, to declare and pronounce to His people, being penitent, the Absolution and Remission of their sins." In the form of Absolution in the Order for the Visitation of the Sick, the Church declares that our Lord Christ "hath left power to His Church to absolve all sinners, who truly repent, and believe in Him."

And in the Homily on Common Prayer and Sacraments, "Absolution hath the promise of forgiveness of sins."

Suppose persons to be truly repentant, and to have confessed their sin to God in private, and then in the public confessions of the Church to have again thought of and confessed their sins to God—might they believe that the Absolution pronounced in Church by the Priest applies to them, and that they may believe they have the assurance of God's forgiveness ?

It would be very difficult to prove that they have no right to think so.

[1] *Preface to Holy Communion, a Comfort to the Penitent,* p. xi.

Why then is there any need for the practice of Private Confession?

Because of the simple fact that many "'consciences *are* burdened,' especially after bad relapses, and that many do need still further help and comfort than they receive in the public and more general Absolution in Church." Thus, some may individually feel a need of Sacramental Absolution.[1]

Granting what cannot be truthfully denied—that souls, if they feel the need, are invited by the Church to seek the benefit of Absolution in private, after secret confession of the sins that trouble them; still are there not many strong objections to the use of the privilege?

It would be difficult to name anything good that has not been objected to in one way or another. All the objections that are made against Confession only hold good as regards Confession *misused*, not rightly used.

Rightly used, that is, when the priest is a faithful minister, and the penitent simply in earnest, there is absolutely no objection that can truthfully be sustained.

There is, however, a widespread objection arising from the dread of priestly authority, and that private confession would make that authority to be more claimed and to become more powerful.

"Men ignore the fact that Confessions are made in private by priests as well as by the people. They, too, are as much under authority in this respect. And confession being voluntary, it is idle to speak of authority as liable to abuse."[2]

No doubt an *unfaithful* minister might try to use his influence wrongly on this or any other occasion, as *e.g.* for political purposes; but the faithful minister would never anywhere, at any time, attempt to "lord it over any part of God's heritage."

But might not the Priest be very unwise or inexperienced, and so give unwise counsel and do harm?

---

[1] *Preface to Entire Absolution*, p. i.
[2] Vol. 1885, *First Preface*, p. xi.

It is to be remembered that the Church of England leaves her children *free* to *whom* to open their griefs. So that they can, if they choose, as they ought, to go to some faithful and wise priest.

Still there is this objection. Going to Confession must tend to make at all events some souls very morbid, very scrupulous, and so they will lose their self-dependence, and lean too much on this help outside themselves.

A faithful and wise priest would, of course, do all he could to help the penitent against losing any sense of his own responsibility, and would do all he could to help and encourage him to live a healthy, vigorous, Christian life.

Still there is the danger of suggesting or teaching sin by indiscreetly questioning the penitent?

Certainly, some most unwise manuals have been published and occasion given for this objection to be made. But here again the objection does not hold, where Confession is made to a faithful and wise priest.

Evil influence, evil talk, dangers of this sort may exist anywhere on the face of the earth wherever two souls or more may meet, but still we trust each other in common and important affairs of life very much.

" We do not disuse medicines for the body because poisons have been administered through carelessness, or disorders wholly mistaken, and so treated as to bring death, not life ; or even the infection of mortal diseases been unsuspectingly conveyed ; nor do men cease to take advice as to their estates, because ignorant or dishonest lawyers have at times ruined their clients. People are content to run risks in one case, because they value their lives or estates. They magnify the risks in the other, because they either value not their souls, or dislike the cure, or think they cannot be lost." [1]

Where is there a learned and practical defence of Confession?
In Dr. Pusey's *Preface to Manual of Abbé Gaume.*
Allowing then that there have been some unfaithful, unwise

[1] *Preface to Entire Absolution,* p. xiii.

priests who have betrayed their trust, or in some ways injured souls, the *abuse* does not invalidate the *use*, and it may be safely said that God would never let any one of His children suffer in the least, who in simple faith sought help at the hands of one of His wise and faithful Ministers.

"There can be no doubt, as those experienced in this matter well know, that, humanly speaking, early confession, by the blessing of Almighty God, would have saved many a soul from their subsequent sin and misery."[1]

It must also be remembered that most of the objections against Confession to God privately, before a Priest, come from persons who have never used this help for the soul, or from those who have been prejudiced against it by the slanders of others. It should also be remembered that of those who rightly make use of this private Confession, few ever entirely give up its use, unless unavoidably prevented by circumstances from availing themselves of this Sacramental help, and moreover those who go to Confession themselves, do not dissuade others from going.

Would that the advice contained in the Prayer Book 1549 were more generally known and followed.

" Requiring such as shall be satisfied with a general Confession not to be offended with them that do use, to their further satisfying, the auricular and secret confession to the Priest ; nor those also which think needful or convenient for the quietness of their own consciences, particularly to open their sins to the Priest, to be offended with them that are satisfied with their humble confession to God, and the general Confession to the Church : but in all things to follow and keep the rule of charity ; and every man to be satisfied with his own conscience, not judging other men's minds or consciences ; whereas he hath no warrant of God's Word to the same."

This Prayer-book was declared by the compilers of the subsequent Book to have been "done by the aid of the Holy Ghost."

[1] *Preface to Entire Absolution*, p. xiii.

See also Act for the Uniformity of Common Prayer A. 5 et 6 Edward VI. as follows—

"The Archbishop of Canterbury and certain of the most learned and discreet Bishops, and other learned men of this realm, having as well eye and respect to the most sincere and pure Christian religion taught by the Scriptures as to the usages of the Primitive Church, should draw and make one convenient and meet order, rite, and fashion of common and open prayer and administration of the Sacraments, to be had and used in his Majesty's Kingdom of England and Wales, the which at this time, *by the aid of the Holy Ghost*, with one uniform agreement is of them concluded." [1]

"When there hath been a very godly order set forth by authority of Parliament, for Common Prayer and administration of the Sacraments to be used in the mother tongue within this Church of England, agreeable to the Word of God and the Primitive Church, very comfortable to all good people desiring to live in Christian conversation," &c. [2]

It has been suggested that Priests advise the comfort of absolution to be sought from them in private, in order to enhance their authority over souls, is this so?

If any Minister of God does anything of the sort he would of course be desecrating his holy office. On the other hand, by undue authority to put off people from the reception of any means of grace, would not be to act like the Ministers of Him who bids us "restore in the spirit of meekness those overtaken in a fault," and "to lift up hands which hang down, and the feeble knees." [3]

But may not persons, without deep true sorrow for sin, make the Priest believe that they are truly penitent, and then receive Absolution?

Such deceit there has always been. "We do not," says St. Cyprian, "anticipate the judgment of the Lord, who will come to judge, but that if He shall find a sinner's penitence

<hr>

[1] *Entire Absolution*, pt. ii. p. 61.   [2] *Id.*
[3] *First Preface*, vol. 1855, p. xv.

full and entire, He will then ratify what has here been determined by us; if, however, any have deluded us by a feigned penitence, God, who is not mocked, and who looketh on the heart of man, will judge of those whom we have not seen through, and the Lord will correct the sentence of His servants."[1]

It must be remembered, as pointed out before, what great stress is laid by the Church upon repentance being true and real, and against pronouncing Absolution without due caution. She only orders the Priest to absolve the sick person "if he humbly and heartily desire it."

No one, especially the young, should unduly be hurried or pressed into the use of Confession. As far as possible, every one seeking this help, should have been thoroughly instructed, and have an intelligent knowledge of what they are about to do; no one thus instructed, would, if they were not very wilfully inclined to trifle with the things of God, make a light or wrong use of them.

What is the great comfort of Absolution to the true penitent?

"The very craving of the heart is satisfied; our sins, when we are fit to receive the blessed words, are forgiven at once. The effects of sin upon the soul may often have to be worked out by sorrow and toil, but forgiveness is not put off to a distant day. As soon as God's Priest in His Name has promised His forgiveness on earth, the sins of the true penitent are forgiven in Heaven. 'Whosoever sins ye remit, they *are* remitted unto them.'"[2]

What does God do for the Penitent, through the ministry of His Priest in Absolution?

"He conveys His own sense of pardon to the soul of the Penitent, sets him free from the guilt of his past sins, opens to the blessed influx of His grace the channels which sin had stopped, and often pours at once large grace and love into the soul."[3]

---

[1] *Preface to Holy Eucharist, Comfort to Penitents,* p. xv.
[2] *Entire Absolution,* pt. i. p. 35.   [3] *Id.* pt. ii. p. 3.

But, after all, does not the Church of England, in the Book of Homilies (on Common Prayer and Sacraments) deny that Absolution is a Sacrament? [1]

The Homily really states nothing of the sort, but the exact contrary. It plainly declares Absolution to be what it is, a Sacrament, in that it says, " neither *it*, nor any other Sacrament else, be *such* sacrament as Baptism and the Communion are." The reason being that by the express word of the New Testament the promise of forgiveness of sin " is not tied to the visible sign, which is imposition of hands."

Why has it been always taught that Holy Baptism and the Holy Eucharist are the two great Sacraments?

" These are symbolized by the Water and the Blood which flowed from our Redeemer's side." [2]   " These two great Sacraments derive into us the very life of our Lord." [3]   " They are the appointed channels for applying the Atonement to the soul." [4]

Absolution, then, is a Sacrament, though, as the Homilies express it, " no such sacrament," as Baptism and the Communion are.

If a man was Baptized as an adult, and had truly repented of all his sins before his Baptism, would he be judged for those sins hereafter?

" Sins before Baptism come not into judgment at all, they belonged to one who *is not*. In Baptism he was buried and died, and a new man, with a new life and a new principle of life, was raised through the resurrection of Christ." [5]

How about grievous sins after Baptism?

" They are remitted by Absolution, and if the penitent be sincere is an earnest of the judgment of Christ, and is confirmed by Him." [6]

---

[1] " No; this is a very common mistake, and it is even made by the Editor of the Book of Homilies in the edition published by the Society for Promoting Christian Knowledge; " see Index, *Absolution not a Sacrament*, p. 377.

[2] *Eirenicon*, pt. i. p. 20.   [3] *Letter to Jelf*, p. 25.
[4] *Id.* p. 40.   [5] *Entire Absolution*, pt. i. p. 24.   [6] *Id.*

Will such sins be ever mentioned to the penitent again when he appears before the Judgment seat of Christ?

It is best not to dogmatize on such a solemn question. We know that for all we do wrong, in thought, word, or deed—sins of omission as well as commission—we shall have to give account.

"The whole detail of the judgment of each soul rests with the Judge, our Lord; enough for the penitent to know that he must appear before the Judgment seat of Christ; that according to his sincerity the Lord may ratify or annul the judgment of His servants (the Priests)." [1]

Give a short summary of what the Church of England teaches as to the use of Private Confession to a Priest.

The Church, our mother, would not bring all her children, with their varied tempers, needs, languishings, sicknesses, under one rigid, unbending rule. She shows, in the Exhortation to the Holy Communion, that she would deal, not with laden consciences only, but with timorous, scrupulous, doubting, tender souls, the lambs of the flock of Christ, otherwise than she would with those, who seem to themselves, or are, the strong or the whole. One thing only she excludes where she excludes anything, "*compulsory* confession"—"that any man should be bound to the numbering of his sins"; "as if," adds Hooker, "remission of sins otherwise were impossible." But short of this, in that Exhortation she strives with an austere, anxious love, to rouse the conscience, not only as to overt, but as to secret, mental sins. "If any of you be in malice, envy, or any other grievous crime"; and then after words which may well shake the soul through and through, "lest after taking of that Holy Sacrament the devil enter into you, as he entered into Judas, and fill you full of all iniquities and bring you to destruction, body and soul, 'she straightway insists on the necessity of a quiet conscience,' and invites such as otherwise cannot quiet theirs, to open their griefs, that by the ministry of God's Holy Word they may receive the benefit of Absolution." [2]

---

[1] *Entire Absolution*, pt. i. p. 24. [2] *Id.* pt. ii. p. 9.

Confession, then, in the English Church is not compulsory?

No ; nothing can be clearer than this. But, as we see, both in the Exhortation before Communion, and in the Order for Visitation of the Sick, she does, in certain cases, most strongly advise and urge it.

Seeing, then, that Confession to a Priest is allowed in the English Church, speaking by her Prayer-book, is it not the fact that the teaching of the Bishops, at and since the times of the Reformation, was not in favour of Confession being used in the Church of England?

First, we will take the testimony of Bishops Ridley, Latimer, and Jewel. Bishop Ridley (died 1555) : " Confession unto the Minister which is able to instruct, correct, and inform the weak, wounded, and ignorant conscience—indeed I ever thought might do much good to Christ's congregation, and so, I assure you, I think to this day."—*Letter to one Master West: Works, Parker Society*, p. 318.

Hugh Latimer, Bishop of Worcester (died 1555) says : " But to speak of right and true Confession, I would to God it were kept in England, for it is a good thing."—*Sermon on the Third Sunday after Epiphany.*

Bishop Jewel (died 1571) : " The difference between us and our adversaries in this whole matter is not great. . . . Touching private confession if it be discreetly used, to the greater comfort and better satisfaction of the penitent, without superstition or other ill, it is not in anywise by us reproved. . . . Thus much only we say, that private confession if it be made unto the minister is neither commanded by Christ, nor necessary to salvation."—*Defence of the Apology*, pt. ii. vi. div. i.—*See* CANON COOKE *on Absolution*, 1874, p. 122, 123, 124.

Bishop Lewis Baly, Bishop of Bangor, died 1632 (a strong opponent of the Church of Rome), in his *Practice of Piety*, fifty-first edition, published 1714, says : " Though others may comfort with good words, yet none can absolve from sin, but only those to whom Christ hath committed the Holy ministry and word of reconciliation: and of their absolution Christ speaketh—'He that heareth you, heareth me.' In a doubtful title you will ask the counsel of a skilful lawyer; in peril of sickness you will know the advice of the learned physician; and is there no danger in dread of damnation for a sinner to be his own judge?"

"And verily there is not any means more excellent to humble a proud heart, nor to raise up an humble spirit than this spiritual conference between the pastors and the people committed to their charge. If any sin therefore troubleth thy conscience, confess it to God's Minister; ask his counsel, and if thou dost truly repent, receive his absolution; and then doubt not, in *foro conscientiæ*, but thy sins be as verily forgiven on earth as if thou didst hear Christ Himself, in *foro judicii*, pronouncing them to be forgiven in Heaven. 'He that heareth you, heareth Me.' Say this, and tell me whether thou shalt not find more ease in thy conscience than can be expressed in words."—*See* Appendix to CANON COOKE'S Work on *The Power of the Priesthood in Absolution.*

Bishop Cosin (died 1672):

"For the better preparation thereunto (receiving the Holy Communion) as occasion is, to disburthen and quiet our consciences of those sins that may grieve us, or scruples that may trouble us, go to a learned and discreet priest, and from him receive advice, and the benefit of Absolution."— *Works*, vol. ii. p. 121, *Ang. Cath. Lib.*

Archbishop Wake (died 1737):

"The Church of England refuses no sort of confession, either public or private, which may be 'any way necessary to the quieting of men's consciences, or to the exercising of that power of binding and loosing which our Saviour Christ has left to His Church."[1]

"We have our penitential Canons for public offenders. We

---

[1] *Letter to Upton Richards*, p. 244.

exhort men if they have any, the least doubt or scruple, nay, sometimes though they have none, but especially before they receive the Holy Sacrament to confess their sins."

We propose to them the benefit, not only of ghostly advice, how to manage their repentance, but the great comfort of Absolution too, as soon as they shall have accomplished it.

Mention some eminent Bishops and Divines who witness to the use and help of Private Confession in the Church of England.

Dr. George Hakewill.

Francis Mason (died 1621).

Dr. Richard Crakanthorp (died 1624).

John White, D.D.

Bishop Lancelot Andrewes (died 1626).

Dr. John Donne, Dean of St. Paul's (died 1631).

George Herbert, D.D. (died 1632).

Joseph Meade (died 1638).

Francis White, D.D., Bishop of Ely (died 1638).

Bishop Montague (died 1641).

Archbishop Ussher (died 1655).

William Chillingworth (died 1644).

Bishop Hall (died 1656).

Dr. Hammond (died 1660).

Dr. Peter Heylin (died 1662).

Bishop Sanderson (died 1662).

Archbishop Bramhall (died 1663).

Adam Littleton, D.D.

Anthony Sparrow (died 1685).

John Pearson, D.D., Bishop of Chester (died 1686).

Matthew Scrivener (died 1688).

Dean Comber.

Timothy Puller, D.D. (died 1693).

John Isham, D.D.

Symon Patrick, D.D., Bishop of Ely (died 1707).

William Nicholls, D.D. (died 1712).

Robert South, D.D. (died 1716).

Dr. Fiddes (died 1725).
Charles Wheatly, M.A. (died 1742).
Bishop Wilson of Sodor and Man (died 1755).
Richard Cecil (died 1810).
Dr. John Hey (died 1815).
Bishop Tomline (died 1827).
Bishop Herbert Marsh (died 1839).
See CANON COOKE's excellent treatise.

In the primitive Church was Private Confession to a Priest compulsory before Communion, or urged upon all as necessary ?

"It is certain that the early Church had no obligatory Confession except that of overt acts of sin, with a view to public penitence." [1]

Can a Priest of bad character absolve a penitent ?

No one truly repentant would seek absolution at the hand of a priest of bad reputation; such a penitent would naturally seek the spiritual help of one of good character. The Church, however, in Article XXVI. says : "Neither is the effect of Christ's ordinance taken away by their wickedness, nor the grace of God's gifts diminished from such as by faith and rightly do receive the Sacraments ministered unto them ; which be effectual, because of Christ's institution and promise, although they be ministered by evil men."

If a man has true repentance of his sin from love of God and hatred of sin, does God forgive that man although he does not confess his sin to a Priest to receive the comfort and grace of Absolution ?

"We may believe that when God does give such grace, He does forgive the sins, but such persons would miss the comfort of the authoritative remission of their sins." [2]

Yet we may fully believe that any sin will be forgiven by God upon a deep and entire repentance, for the merits of our Lord and Saviour Jesus Christ alone. "And surely one cannot see the blessed lives and death-beds of persons who without confession to man, live in the true faith and fear and love

---

[1] *Note de Tertullian,* p. 408.   [2] *Letter to Times.*

of God, and our Lord Jesus Christ, without believing that they are in the full grace and favour of God."[1]

It is a question for each one's own conscience—shall I, need I, ought I, to make use of this great help provided for the soul?

HOLY COMMUNION.

*" It is my Maker, dare I stay :
My Saviour, dare I turn away ? "*
                    JOHN KEBLE.

Why was the Sacrament of the Lord's Supper ordained ?

"For the continual remembrance of the sacrifice of the death of Christ, and of the benefits we receive thereby."—*Church Catechism.*

Is it not enough to go and receive Communion for the strengthening and refreshing of our souls ?

No; as we are told in one of the exhortations in the Communion Office, "It is our duty to receive this Communion in remembrance of the sacrifice of Christ's death."

What is verily and indeed taken and received by the faithful in the Lord's Supper ?

"The Body and Blood of Christ."—See the *Church Catechism.*

Then in the Holy Communion there is a remembrance of the sacrifice of the death of Christ, and also a great blessing received by Communicants ?

Yes.

Name one important part of preparation for the Holy Communion much neglected by many.

"We should come to the Holy Communion, examining ourselves whether we repent us truly of our former sins, steadfastly purposing to lead a new life, having a lively faith in God's mercy through Christ, with a thankful remembrance of His death, and being in charity with all men. And so, too, if we would come rightly to that Holy Sacrament, we should remember that our Church has united mercy to His poor

---

[1] *Letter to Saunders News Letter,* 1871.

K

with the Sacrament of His Body and Blood, and bade us ere we approach to receive Him, to remember Him in His poor, that so 'loving much,' we, who are otherwise unworthy, may be 'much forgiven'; we 'considering' Him in His 'poor and needy,' may be permitted to behold Him; and for Him, parting with our earthly substance, may be partakers of His Heavenly."[1]

Name one glorious benefit much forgotten by Communicants.

"Christ indwells us. By His indwelling us, we become one with Him, He with us, and we become *like* Him."[2]

How does Bishop Andrewes speak of the Celebration of the Holy Eucharist, and the mistakes of some concerning it?

"For many among us fancy only a Sacrament in this action, and look strange at the mention of a Sacrifice, whereas we not only use it as a nourishment spiritual as that it is too, but as a means also to renew a 'covenant' with. God by virtue of that Sacrifice, as the Psalmist speaketh. So our Saviour Christ in the institution telleth us, in the twenty-second chapter of Luke and twentieth verse, and the Apostle in the thirteenth chapter of Hebrews and tenth verse. And the old writers use no less the word Sacrifice, than Sacrament; Altar, than Table; offer, than eat, but both indifferently to show there is both."[3]

Give one of Dr. Pusey's summaries of the doctrine of the Holy Eucharist.

"(1) That the Holy Eucharist is the great and central act of Christian worship, our closest nearness to God.

"(2) That, while repudiating any materialistic conceptions of the mode of the Presence of our Lord in the Holy Eucharist such as I believe is condemned in the term, 'Corporal Presence of our Lord's natural Flesh and Blood,' *i. e.* as though His Precious Body and Blood were present in any gross or carnal way, and not rather sacramentally, really, spiritually; I believe that in the Holy Eucharist the Body and Blood of

---

[1] Vol. i. p. 73.
[2] *See* PUSEY's *Parochial Sermons*, vol. ii. pp. 359, 360.
[3] Vol. 1855, *Extracts from Writers in the Later English Church*, p. 46.

Christ are sacramentally, supernaturally, ineffably, but verily and indeed, present 'under the form of bread and wine,' and that 'where His Body is, *there* is Christ.'

" (3) That, thankfully believing that 'the offering of Christ once made is that perfect Redemption, Propitiation, and Satisfaction for the sins of the whole world, both original and actual, and that our Blessed Lord Himself, having finished upon the Cross that One Oblation of Himself,' doth now, while ever living to make intercession for us, add nothing to the Infinite Merits of the superabundant Satisfaction of that, His One Sacrifice, which would suffice to redeem a thousand worlds ; I also believe that as in all our prayers, 'through Jesus Christ our Lord,' we plead in word that one meritorious Sacrifice, so in the Celebration of the Holy Eucharist, the Priest presents and pleads to the Father that same Body which was broken for us, and the Blood which was shed for us, therein sacramentally present, by virtue of the Consecration, which our Great High Priest in His perpetual Intercession for us, locally present in His natural Body at the Right Hand of the Father, evermore exhibits before the Father for us. . . . These truths I hold not as opinions, but as matters of Faith." [1]

" Dr. Pusey also sought to make good, in regard both to Holy Scripture and the Fathers, the teaching of the English Church, in contrast with that of school-men as to the continuance of the visible elements in their natural substances." [2]

If others object, and say the doctrine of the Real Presence is not true, how should you act ?

Argue not ; pray that the objector may be led to believe what he now denies.

" If any allege to thee any imagined laws of matter (whereof we know nothing) whereby it should be supposed that our Lord's Precious Body and Blood could not be spiritually, supra-locally present under those outward forms, and would reduce thee to the belief of a presence, varying and uncertain,

---

[1] *Sermon :* " *Will ye also go away ?* " p. 26.
[2] *Preface,* vol. 1855, p. vii.

elicited by, and dependent upon, the faith, whereby we do receive the grace thereof, say to thyself, ' Of the laws of the spiritual body I know nothing; one thing I know, that the Truth has said, " This is My Body." '

> ' I believe whate'er the Son of God hath told ;
> What the Truth hath spoken, that for truth I hold.'

And then remember how holy men cautioned of old, ' Touch not the Body of Christ with a fevered hand ; ' ' Abstain from all uncleanness, and then take the Body and Blood of Christ, and carefully guard thy mouth by which the King has entered.' " [1]

" We should regard the Holy Eucharist both as a Sacrament and as a commemorative Sacrifice. As a Sacrament, in that He, our Redeemer, God and Man, vouchsafes to be ' our spiritual food and sustenance in that Holy Sacrament.'

" As a commemorative Sacrifice, in that He enables us therein to plead to the Father, that one meritorious Sacrifice on the Cross, which He, our High Priest, unceasingly pleads in His own Divine Person in Heaven." [2]

Can we think too highly of the Sacrament of the Holy Eucharist ?

Impossible. " What is that Sacrament whereby, in the words we so often hear, ' We dwell in Christ, and Christ in us ; we are one with Christ, and Christ with us ' ? Were this vouchsafed to us once only in our lives, had we to look forward to It as one gift once given, what would men think of It, how prepare for It ? But now that we can scarce count our communions past, it is thought much if God have His half-hour of thanks, and men go and forget what manner of men they have been." [3]

" Oh, what inner joy do they lose, who know only of a ' virtue' coming forth from Him in Heaven, or perhaps only some engraced act of ours making remembrance of His love ! Oh, how sore a loss of that deep well of love, not to know that

---

[1] *Sinful Blindness*, p. 30.
[2] Vol. 1855, *Preface*, p. vi. [3] Vol. 1872, p. 465.

He Who took our flesh to die for us, to ransom us, to live to make intercession for us, took It also to give It to us, that He might so ineffably unite us with Himself! How sore a loss for love, not to know when He comes to us, when we are to prepare to meet Him, when our souls may go forth to await Him, and, hushed with a holy awe, may receive Him, under the ruined mansion of our souls! The faith was as entire in the century which still saw St. John, as when Christian thought and devotion had dwelt upon it, for it rested on our Lord's Divine Word, 'This is My Body'; 'He that eateth Me shall live by Me.' It was antecedent to philosophy, it was not affected by it, it will survive or (as seems likely) it will win philosophy. For one thousand years, until the unhappy Berenger, not a light cloud overshadowed it, and that, too, soon passed away. By It in those centuries of fiery trial, Martyrs were strengthened to confess Him Whom they had received, Who dwelt in them; by It passion was lulled; in It the wise found their wisdom; practical minds their strength; mystical minds found a higher mysticism in It; even heretics bowed down before the love of God in It."[1]

Can any who profess belief in Christ safely neglect the Sacraments?

"Although all shall not be saved who partake of the Holy Sacraments, there is no revealed method of salvation without them. There is no revealed salvation from original or actual sin (and this parents should in these days well remember) without Baptism; without the Holy Eucharist there is no life."[2]

But do not many persons deny that there is anything of a Sacrificial Character in the Holy Eucharist?

Yes; many deny this, under a great misapprehension of the doctrine.

What is the mistake they make?

They fancy that it is taught that our Lord is re-sacrificed in some mysterious way, that He is sacrificed over again, or that

[1] Vol. 1872, p. 285. [2] Vol. iii. p. 334.

in some way He is offered up to complete and fill up something that may be lacking in His Sacrifice on the Cross of Calvary.

What does the Church teach us ?

That our Lord upon the Cross "made thereby His One oblation of Himself once offered, a full, perfect, and sufficient Sacrifice, Oblation, and Satisfaction, for the sins of the whole world."—See *Prayer of Consecration.*

How then can it be said, that in any sense the Holy Eucharist is a Sacrifice ?

In the words of Bishop Jeremy Taylor, "It is the greatest solemnity of prayer, the most powerful liturgy and means of impetration in this world. For when Christ was consecrated on the Cross and became our High Priest, having reconciled us to God by the death of the Cross, He became infinitely gracious in the eyes of God, and was admitted to the celestial and eternal Priesthood in Heaven, where, in the Virtue of the Cross, He intercedes for us, and represents an eternal sacrifice in the Heavens on our behalf. That He is a Priest in Heaven appears in the large discourses and direct affirmatives of St. Paul. That there is no other Sacrifice to be offered but that on the Cross, it is evident because He hath once appeared in the end of the world to put away sin by the sacrifice of Himself; and therefore, since it is necessary that He hath something to offer, so long as He is a Priest, and there is no other sacrifice but that of Himself offered upon the Cross, it follows that Christ in Heaven perpetually offers and represents that Sacrifice to His Heavenly Father, and in virtue of that, obtains all good things for His Church."[1]

"Now what Christ does in Heaven, He hath commanded us to do on earth, that is, to represent His Death, to commemorate His Sacrifice by humble prayer and thankful record, and by faithful manifestation and joyful Eucharist, to lay It before the eye of our Heavenly Father, so ministering in His Priesthood and doing according to His commandment and

[1] *Letter to Bishop of London*, p. 27.

example, the Church being the image of Heaven, the Priest the minister of Christ, the Holy Table being a copy of the Celestial Altar, and the Eternal Sacrifice of the Lamb slain from the beginning of the world being always the same. It bleeds no more after the finishing of It on the Cross, but It is wonderfully represented in Heaven and graciously represented here by Christ's action there, by His commandment here. And the event of it is plainly this: that as Christ in virtue of His Sacrifice on the Cross intercedes for us with His Father, so does the Minister of Christ's Priesthood here; that the virtue of the eternal sacrifice may be salutary and effectual to all the needs of the Church both for things temporal and eternal.

" And therefore it was not without great mystery and clear signification, that our Blessed Lord was pleased to command that the representation of His Death and Sacrifice on the Cross should be made by breaking of bread and effusion of wine to signify to us the nature and sacredness of the Liturgy we are about, and that we minister in the Priesthood of Christ, Who is a Priest for ever, after the order of Melchisedec; that is, we are ministers in that unchangeable Priesthood, imitating in the external ministry the prototype Melchisedec, of whom it was said, ' He brought forth bread and wine, and was the Priest of the Most High God'; and, in the internal, imitating the antitype or the substance, Christ Himself, Who offered up His Body and Blood for atonement for us; and by the Sacraments of bread and wine and the prayers of Oblation and Intercession, commands us to officiate in His Priesthood in the external ministering like Melchisedec; in the internal, after the manner of Christ Himself."—*Worthy Communicant*, chap. i. sect. iv.[1]

Give the teaching of another great English Bishop who, like Bishop Jeremy Taylor, was a strong opponent of Rome.

" ' In the Eucharist, as a Sacrament, we eat our ransom.' As St. Augustine says, we receive spiritually ' the Body of our

[1] *Letter to Bishop of London*, p. 28.

Lord Jesus Christ which was given for us, His Blood which was shed for us.' In the same Eucharist as a Sacrifice, we, in representation, plead the One Great Sacrifice which our Great High Priest continually presenteth for us in Heaven. In Heaven He presenteth ever before the Father in person, Himself mediating with the Father as our Intercessor ; on earth He invisibly sanctifies what is offered, and makes the earthly elements which we offer to be sacramentally and ineffably—but not in a carnal way—His Body and Blood. For although once for all offered, that Sacrifice, be it remembered, is ever Living and Continuous—made to be continuous by the resurrection of our Lord."—BISHOP PHILPOTS, of Exeter, *Pastoral Charge*, 1851.

Quote one well-known English Bishop of the seventeenth century.

" Nay, show Him forth ye must. That we will by a sermon of Him ; nay, it must be *hoc facite*. It is not mental thinking, or verbal speaking, there must be actually somewhat done to celebrate this memory. That done to the holy symbols that was done to Him, to His Body and His Blood in the Passover, break the one, pour out the other, to represent now how His sacred Body was 'broken,' how His precious Blood was 'shed.' "—BISHOP ANDREWES.

Many other witnesses may be cited, proving that the Church of England has always held the Catholic Doctrine of the Eucharistic Sacrifice.[1]

What results from the forgetfulness of the Eucharistic Sacrifice ?

" From the obscuration of Eucharistic truth which has prevailed since the Reformation, our Lord's Intercession has been looked upon much more as an act of prayer than of Sacrifice. Hereby the whole typology of the Books of Moses—as representing the ceremonies of the great day of atonement, whereby the atonement by slaying, being made outside the veil, the blood was carried, still as atonement, by the high priest into the Holy of Holies once a year—is entirely lost ; a poverty of

---

[1] See *Dr. Pusey's Letter to Bishop of London*, pp. 20—38.

conception with regard to the present work of Christ, the continued presentation of those Sacred Wounds, of that Glorious Body which once hung upon the tree, and now, without words, pleads by its very presence within the Holy of Holies, at the Father's right hand, is engendered ; and the deep cry of the Church, involving its belief in the Everlasting Propitiation of the Son of God, loses its significance."—BISHOP FORBES *on the Articles*, p. 223.

Is not the doctrine of the Eucharistic Sacrifice denied in Article XXXI. ?

The Article says—"The Offering of Christ once made is that perfect Redemption, Propitiation, and Satisfaction for all the sins of the whole world, both original and actual ; and there is none other satisfaction for sin, but this alone. *Wherefore* the sacrifices of Masses, in the which it was commonly said, that the Priest did offer Christ for the quick and the dead, to have remission of pain or guilt, were blasphemous fables, and dangerous deceits."

" Plainly, then, by the force of the word 'wherefore' she rejects no sacrifice which does not interfere with this." [1]

" In celebrating the Holy Eucharist she pleads to 'God, Who of ' His 'tender mercy did give' His 'only Son Jesus Christ to suffer death upon the Cross for our redemption, Who made there by His one oblation of Himself, once offered, a full, perfect, and sufficient sacrifice, oblation, and satisfaction for the sins of the whole world.' But that sacrifice once made lives on in Heaven. There our Lord, Who shall come down to judge, as He went into Heaven, still bears the marks of the wounds which for us and our Salvation He received, effulgent with the Glory of His Godhead, irradiant with His Divine love. There He pleads that all-Atoning Sacrifice, there for these over eighteen hundred years has He lived to make intercession for us, generation after generation ; yea, for each one of our sinful race. But since His perpetual intercession for us (which is an article of Faith contained in plainest words

[1] *Eirenicon,* pt. i. p. 27.

of Holy Scripture) does not interfere with that One Atonement made upon the Cross, neither does any pleading of that One Meritorious Sacrifice which was finished there, in that: to the *Merits* of that one Oblation our dear Lord Himself adds nothing. It sufficed for the sins of the whole world. That one Sacrifice we plead in every 'through Jesus Christ our Lord,' with which we end each prayer. Our Lord, as we confess to God, 'did institute, and in His Holy Gospel command us to continue a perpetual memory of that His precious Death until His coming again,' that we might plead to the Father that same Sacrifice. In the Holy Eucharist we do in act what in our prayers we do in words."

What does Article XXXI. protest against?

The Article is directed against the heretical idea of any reiteration of Christ's Sacrifice on the Cross in the Holy Eucharist, and against another wrong idea, that the Sacrifice on the Cross was for Original Sin, the Eucharistic Sacrifice for sin committed after Baptism.

"Not *any* doctrine of the Eucharistic Sacrifice is condemned by the Article, but only such doctrine as should add to the virtue of that full, perfect, and sufficient Sacrifice, Oblation, and Satisfaction for the sins of the whole world, which our Lord Jesus Christ made, when He suffered upon the Cross for our Redemption." [1]

"The key to the meaning of the Article is in the words 'wherefore' and 'satisfaction.' Any construction which condemns a doctrine of Eucharistic Sacrifice consistent with the first sentence of the Article makes it self-contradictory, inasmuch as the Article expressly confines itself to excluding any notion which would militate against the perfection of the offering of Christ once made upon the Cross, as being the only 'Satisfaction for Sin.' For 'there is but one real true and proper Sacrifice, viz. the offering which the Incarnate Son of God made of Himself upon the Cross to the Eternal Father.'"
—BISHOP FORBES *on the Articles*, p. 608.

[1] *Unlaw*, p. 49.

"For myself I think this argument of Bishop Forbes unanswerable."—DR. PUSEY.[1]

From whence do the objections to the doctrine of the Eucharistic Sacrifice come?

First, from the ignorant idea that the Church teaches that our Lord is in any way Sacrificed *over again*, and from not remembering, that although the Sacrifice on the Cross was finished for ever, then and there, yet He Who then suffered has to present and for us plead that Sacrifice.

"In that many of the objections flow from an inadequate belief in the doctrines of the perpetual Priesthood of our Lord and His unceasing intercession for the whole Church, it is to be feared that some hold, rather, that having made His one Oblation upon the Cross, He has now ceased from any exclusively priestly function. Is their idea of His intercession more than that of an oral, all-prevailing prayer? But God hath said, 'Thou art a High Priest for ever.' And He is not in such wise a High Priest that He can be imagined separate from the Sacrifice which He once offered—for that Sacrifice was Himself; that Sacrifice was His Manhood, never to be divided from His Godhead. He has carried within the Veil that Holy Body, once wounded for our transgressions, and those very wounds which He showed to St. Thomas, now resplendent in glory still move the Father to look upon the face of His Anointed, and for His sake freely to give us all things, and as this is no derogation therefrom that we, in the Holy Eucharist, with all our prayers present unto the Father the same Holy Body, present in an ineffable way by the words of consecration."—BISHOP FORBES *on the Articles*, p. 623.

Does not the Book of Homilies reject all notion of Eucharistic Sacrifice?

The passages alleged are two; one in the Homily concerning the Sacrament, the other in that for Whitsun-Day. The first is this, "We must then take heed, lest of the memory It be made a Sacrifice."

[1] *Unlaw*, p. 49.

The other is, " Christ commanded to His Church a Sacrament of His Body and Blood, that they (the Romans) have changed it into a sacrifice for the quick and the dead."

The whole passage stands thus : " But before all other things, this we must be sure of specially, that this supper be in such wise done and ministered as our Lord and Saviour did and commanded to be done, as His Holy Apostles used it, and the good fathers in the primitive Church frequented it. For, as that worthy man, St. Ambrose, saith, 'He is unworthy the Lord that otherways doth celebrate that mystery than it was delivered by Him ; neither can he be devout that otherways doth presume than it was given by the Author.' 'We must then take heed, lest of the memory It be made a Sacrifice ; ' lest, of a Communion, it be made a private eating ; lest of two parts we have but one ; lest, applying it for the dead, we lose the fruit that be alive. Let us rather in these matters follow the advice of Cyprian in the like cases, that is, cleave fast to the first beginning, hold fast the Lord's tradition, do that in the Lord's Commemoration which He Himself did, He Himself commanded, and His Apostles confirmed."—*Homily on Sacrament*, p. 473.

The argument follows from what the Homily has said just before, in its protest against being gazers instead of eaters. But note how the Homily says we are to be careful lest of *two parts we have but one ;* and the great necessity of *doing that in the Lord's Commemoration which He Himself did.* All that He did was Sacrificial.

" The Occasion, the Paschal Supper, in which it was instituted, was sacrificial, the Acts accompanying the Institution, the 'taking' of the elements, the 'giving of thanks' over them, the 'breaking' of the Bread, were sacrificial ; the words ' Do this,' 'Offer ye this,' 'in remembrance of Me,' or 'for My memorial,' were sacrificial ; and the Object for which all was said and done was sacrificial."—GRUEBER'S *Catechism*, p. 72.

As regards the passage in the Homily for Whitsun-Day, the context before and after shows that the Homily is only speaking against the *distinctive* alterations and additions of the Roman Communion.

Is it prophesied in the Old Testament that Worship in the Kingdom of Christ should be Sacrificial?

Yes. "And this is the name wherewith He shall be called, The Lord our Righteousness. For thus saith the Lord; David shall never want a man to sit upon the throne of the House of Israel; neither shall the priests the Levites want a man before Me to offer burnt offerings, and to kindle meat offerings, and to do sacrifice continually" (Jer. xxxiii. 16, 18).

"From the rising up of the sun even unto the going down of the same My Name shall be great among the Gentiles ; and in every place Incense shall be offered unto My Name, and a Pure Offering (or mincha, *i. e.* offering of fine flour or bread), for My Name shall be great among the heathen, saith the Lord of hosts" (Mal. i. 11).

Again, in Isaiah lvi. 6, 7, we read, "The sons of the stranger, that join themselves to the Lord. . . . Even them will I bring to My holy Mountain, and make them joyful in My house of prayer : their burnt offerings and their sacrifices shall be accepted upon Mine Altar ; for Mine house shall be called a house of prayer for all nations." This place also must refer to the times of the Christian Church, and yet burnt-offerings and sacrifices are spoken of as offered conjointly with prayers.

"The tenor of these Prophecies demand that in the spiritual Kingdom of the Messiah, *i. e.* in the Church of Christ, there should be ministers under Him, who may in some true and proper sense be called priests, and offer up worship which may, in some equally true and proper sense, be called Sacrifice." —*See* Sadler's *One Offering*, pp. 14, 15.

"The very words, 'This is My Blood of the New Testament,' are framed upon those whereby the Old Covenant at Mount Sinai was sanctioned through the sprinkling of real blood of a Sacrifice, appointed by God to shadow out the Atoning Blood which was shed upon the Cross." [1]

On what does the whole doctrine of the Eucharistic Sacrifice depend?

"The doctrine of the Eucharistic Sacrifice depends upon the doctrine of the real Objective Presence." [2]

"Also the doctrines of the Eucharistic Sacrifice and of Eucharistic Adoration are involved in the doctrine of the Real Presence." [3]

Our Lord *is* the Sacrifice for our Sins.

He is ever presenting Himself as our Sacrifice before His Father in Heaven.   We are ever pleading Him as our Sacrifice on the Altar on earth.

Is it right to say He IS *the Sacrifice for our sins?*

"He is the propitiation for our sins."   "He ever liveth to make intercession for us" (1 John ii. 2 ; Heb. vii. 25).

In the *Encyclical Letter of the Lambeth Conference, July* 1888, the Bishops in their exhortation on "*Definite* Teaching of the Faith" say, "We most earnestly press upon the Clergy the importance of taking, as the central thought of their teaching, our Lord Jesus Christ as the Sacrifice for our sins, as the Healer of our sinfulness, the Source of all spiritual life."

In short we must ever think of our Lord as our Living Sacrifice, as the Ever-Living Sacrificed One, as the "Lamb that was slain," as the Ever-Living Victim still bearing the marks of the wounds of Calvary ; as the One Who for us was dead, but now liveth for us evermore.   His continual Offering is of Himself.   Before His Father He is ever presenting Himself for us.

"Our dear Lord in His Glorious Body does ever, in the Presence of the Father, make Intercession for us : His Meritorious Sacrifice and Passion live on there : those Scars, more glorious than all created light, shine with the effulgence of His Godhead, through all the compass of Heaven, and, pleading His Atoning Death, obtain Mercy and Pardon for us sinners." [4]

---

[1] *Presence of Christ in the Holy Eucharist*, p. 27.
[2] *Eirenicon*, pt. i. p. 25.   [3] *Sermon : This is My Body*, p. 40.   [4] *Id.* p. 25.

There is, then, no doubt that the Catholic Church teaches that our Lord Jesus Christ is really present in the Sacrament of Holy Communion ?

Absolutely no doubt whatever. Though, alas! many professing Christians who do not believe the doctrine deny that the Church teaches it.

Give some proof that she does teach it.

First, let us see what the doctrine is. It is this, that "our Blessed Lord does not say, 'This is a figure of My absent Body,' nor does He say, 'This has altogether ceased to be bread, and is the same Body in the same way as that which you see with your bodily eyes,' but simply, 'This is My Body.'"[1]

The presence of which our Lord speaks has been termed Sacramental, supernatural, mystical, ineffable, as opposed, not to what is real, but to what is natural. The word has been chosen to express, not our knowledge, but our ignorance, or that unknowing knowledge of Faith, which we have of things Divine surpassing knowledge. We know not the manner of His presence, save that it is not according to the natural Presence of our Lord's Human Flesh, which is at the Right Hand of God, and therefore it is called Sacramental. But it is a Presence without us, not within us only; a presence by virtue of our Lord's words, although to us it becomes a saving presence received to our Salvation through our faith. It is not a Presence simply in the soul of the receiver, as "Christ dwells in our hearts by Faith"; or as, in acts of Spiritual, apart from Sacramental, Communion, we, by our longings, invite Him into our souls. But while the consecrated elements, as we believe (because our Lord, and God the Holy Ghost, in Holy Scripture call them still after consecration by the names of their natural substances, and do not say that they cease to be such)—while the consecrated elements remain in their natural substances, still, since our Lord says, "This is My Body," "This is My Blood," the Church of England believes that "under

---

[1] *Presence of Christ in Holy Eucharist,* p. 21.

the Form of Bread and Wine" so consecrated, we "receive the Body and Blood of our Saviour Christ." And since we receive them, they must be there, in order that we may receive them. We need not then (as the school of Calvin bids men) ascend into Heaven to bring down Christ from above, "For He is truly present for us truly to receive Him to the Salvation of our souls, if they be prepared by repentance, faith, love, through the cleansing of His Spirit for His Coming."

Both interpretations of His sacred words, as well that which says, "This is not bread, and nothing else but His Body," and that other, "This is a figure of His absent Body," introduce that into them which does not lie in them. Christ hath said, "This is My Body"; He saith not by what mode. We believe what He, the Truth, said. Truth cannot lie.

Many deny, do they not, that the doctrine of the Real Presence is to be found in the writings of the Fathers?

Few who have really studied the Fathers have dared to make this denial. Dr. Pusey in his letter, *Unlaw*, to Canon Liddon, says : "I collected in the briefest compass in which I could condense them, sayings of the Fathers containing that doctrine. I would venture to recommend to any one, before he slights that belief, just to survey them. Anyhow it might make them hesitate whether it was quite safe to speak very vehemently against what they taught."

Do not those Churchmen who believe in the doctrine of the Real Presence also believe in the doctrine of " Transubstantiation" ?

No. This is simply an assertion made by unlearned controversialists. In June 1867 some of the leading English clergymen published a declaration on the doctrine of the Holy Eucharist. The first article of the declaration is a protest against the doctrine of Transubstantiation. It says : "We repudiate the opinion of a Corporal presence of Christ's natural Flesh and Blood, that is to say of the presence of His Body and Blood as they are in Heaven, and the conception of the mode of His Presence, which implies the physical change of the natural substance of the bread and wine commonly called Transubstantiation."

"Holy Scripture, taken in its plainest meaning, affirms both that the outward elements remain, and still that there is the Real Presence of the Body of Christ. And I may, in the outset, say, that when the Articles reject Transubstantiation they themselves explain what they mean to reject—a doctrine which 'is repugnant to the plain words of Holy Scripture,' *i. e.* those words in which our Lord and St. Paul speak of the natural substances as remaining. The Articles call it also 'a doctrine which overthroweth the nature of a Sacrament,' in that the outward and visible part is supposed to have no real subsistence. They except against no statement which does not imply the natural substances cease to be."[1]

"To receive literally, then, those words of our Lord, 'This is My Body,' does not necessarily imply any absence or cessation or annihilation of the substance of the outward elements."[2]

"It is an unauthorized inference from our Lord's words, that the bread and wine are no longer there; so also, and even more, is it, that the words mean only, 'This represents, is a figure of, My absent Body.' "[3]

"In the early Church, then, we find it assumed or urged without misgiving that the consecrated elements nourished; we find it even assumed that the whole material element was absorbed into the human body."[4]

"The presence of the Body and Blood of Christ 'under the form of bread and wine' is a miracle inscrutable to human reason. The 'substance' of the bread and wine is a term of human philosophy as to created things, and therefore, since its meaning appears to have undergone a change subsequently to the time when it was introduced into matters of belief in th. Western Church, it may the rather be asked that that meaning should be defined."[5]

"Our belief of a Sacramental change, by reason of the real

---

[1] *Presence of Christ in the Holy Eucharist,* p. 14.   [2] *Id.* p. 16.
[3] *Id.* p. 25.   [4] *Doctrine of the Real Presence,* p. 154.   [5] *Id.* p. 161.

Objective Presence, does satisfy the language of the Fathers and corresponds with the whole of their teaching, that the elements remain, but that under them are present the Body and Blood of Christ." [1]

Under these poor outward forms, His creatures of Bread and Wine, "the faithful verily and indeed take and receive the Body and Blood of Christ." [2]

It is then not true, that belief "in the real Objective Presence involves any physical change in the natural elements (of bread and wine), which are the veils and channels of our Lord's unseen Presence." [3]

Now give a Summary of proofs that the Church of England teaches that we DO *receive the Blessed Body and Blood of Christ our Lord and Saviour, under the form of bread and wine in the Sacrament of the Holy Eucharist.*

"She teaches then that" Sacraments ordained by Christ Himself "are means" whereby God doth work invisibly in us; "means whereby we receive the inward part or thing signified" by "the outward and visible sign"; and that they are "pledges to assure us thereof"; that "the inward part or thing signified in the Sacrament of the Lord's Supper is the Body and Blood of Christ, which are verily and indeed taken and received by the faithful in the Lord's Supper"; that "Almighty God, our Heavenly Father, hath given His Son our Saviour Jesus Christ to be our Spiritual Food and sustenance in that Holy Sacrament"; that this is "a Divine thing to those who receive It worthily"; that then "we spiritually eat the Flesh of Christ and drink His Blood; then we dwell in Christ, and Christ with us, we are one with Christ and Christ with us"; that we "come there to the Body and Blood of Christ"; "receive His Blessed Body and Blood under the Form of Bread and Wine, that at His Table we," if we be faithful, "receive not only the outward Sacrament, but the

---

[1] *Doctrine of the Real Presence,* p. 314.
[2] *The Presence of Christ,* &c., p. 14.
[3] Vol. 1855, *Sermon IV., Preface,* p. vii.

Spiritual thing also ; not the figure only, but the truth ; not the shadow only, but the Body " ; " spiritual food, nourishment of our soul, a heavenly refection, an invisible meat, a ghostly substance " ; that " Christ " is our " refection and meat " ; that that Body and Blood are present there ; for " in the Supper of the Lord there is no vain ceremony, no bare sign, no untrue figure of a thing absent " ; that " the bread " which " is blessed " or " consecrated " with our Lord's words, " This is My Body," is the Communion or partaking of the Body of Christ ; " that the Cup, or Wine, which is blessed or conse-crated with His word, ' This is My Blood of the New Testament,' is to such as rightly, worthily, and with Faith receive the same, the Communion or partaking of the Blood of Christ " ; that if we receive rightly " we so eat the Flesh of Jesus Christ the Son of God, and drink His Blood, that our sinful bodies are made clean by His Body, and our souls washed through His most Precious Blood " ; we are made " partakers of His most Precious Body and Blood " ; and so, " partakers of Christ " Himself, God and Man ; that God Himself vouch-safes to feed those who duly receive these Holy Mysteries, with spiritual Food of the most Precious Body and Blood of His Son our Saviour Jesus Christ ; " that " the Body and Blood of Christ which were given and shed for us, " thus " given to us, " taken, eaten," and drunken by us (plainly, if we persevere), " preserve our bodies and souls unto Everlasting Life " ; and (as is implied by the very prayer) are " a means towards that perse-verance ; a salve of immortality, and sovereign preservative against death " ; a deifical Communion ; " the pledge of eternal health, the defence of faith, the hope of the Resurrec-tion " ; " the Food of immortality, the healthful Grace, the conservatory to Life Everlasting." [1]

But is there not one place in the Prayer-book where the Church of England plainly denies the doctrine of the Real Presence, namely in what is called the Black Rubric, which is inserted

---

[1] *See* DR. PUSEY *on the Real Presence*, pp. 234—237.

after the close of the Order of the Administration of the Holy Communion ?

Those who know anything of the history of this rubric, and of its insertion in the Prayer-book, know just the contrary to what is alleged by those who make this objection. The Bishops were asked to deny that our Lord's Blessed Body and Blood were present in the Sacrament "really and essentially." *This they refused to do ;* but they agreed to deny " a Corporal Presence " of Christ's natural Body and Blood, meaning that they were not present, corporally, that is, after the manner of a body, which of course we all know they are not. As Cardwell says, *Hist. of Conf.* p. 35 : " Its (this rubric's) removal (in 1559) clearly shows that the Church could not then be brought to express an opinion adverse to the Real Presence." It was restored in 1661, and its reappearance may likewise be employed to show that the Church at that time also was unwilling to make any declaration on that important tenet. To prevent misapprehension on this point, the words, " or unto any real and essential presence, there being, of Christ's natural flesh and blood," were altered to the very different expression, " or unto any corporal Presence of Christ's natural Flesh and Blood."

Our Lord then being present in this Holy Sacrament, it cannot be wrong to adore Him as there present ?

No ; for He is to be adored, being God.

But to adore our Lord, as being especially present in the Holy Eucharist, can this be right ?

No one should dream of localizing.

" We do not think that we are localizing the Infinite God if we conceive of Him in space, and adore Him in the highest Heavens. Yet He comprehendeth the Heavens, not they Him, the Infinite. We do not think that we are tying down our Lord's Divine Nature if we believe that He, our Lord and God, is, as He promised, specially present where two or three are gathered together in His Name, in our churches, or in the mountains and caves and dens of the earth, in the prison-house or the Catacombs. We think it no derogation to Him, the Infinite God, that He did not abhor the Virgin's womb, or that He lay in the manger amid the brute cattle, or was bound in swaddling-clothes. Believing, as we believe, we should, with the Magi, have fallen down and worshipped the speech-less Infant, knowing Him to be God, the Word. We should have thought His raiment, as Man, no hindrance to our ador-ing Him. Why then should we think it too strange a thing for His marvellous condescension, that He should now give us 'His Blessed Body and Blood under the form of bread and wine'?"[1]

"Or how should His Body which He gives us, not be His living, life-giving Body? Or how should His life-giving Body be apart from His Godhead, which makes It life-giving? Or how, since His Godhead is present there, should we not adore? We do not adore the Sacrament, as when He was upon the earth we should not have adored His raiment, even although the touch of it conveyed the hidden virtue from Him, the source of life and healing. But Himself, wheresoever or howsoever He is present, we are bound to adore."[2]

Mention two Rubrics bearing on the subject, which are con-tained in the Order for Administration of the Holy Commu-nion.

"When all have communicated, the Minister shall return to the Lord's Table, and reverently place upon it what remaineth of the consecrated Elements, covering the same with a fair linen cloth." "And if any remain of that which was consecrated, it shall not be carried out of the Church, but the Priest and such other of the Communicants as he shall then call unto him, shall, immediately after the Blessing, reverently eat and drink the same."

Is the term " Celebration" in the Prayer-book?

Certainly. The Rubric just after the Prayer for the Church Militant says, "When the Minister giveth warning for the Celebration of the Holy Communion"; and again in the second

---

[1] DR. PUSEY *on the Real Presence*, p. 335.   [2] *Id.* p. 336.

Rubric at the end of the Service, the Celebration of the Lord's Supper is mentioned.

The Homily concerning the Sacraments speaks of the "public Celebration of the memory of His Precious Death at the Lord's Table."

But is not the word " Altar " rejected by the Church of England as distinctively Roman ?

As has been said before, it is used over forty times in the office for the Coronation of the Sovereign of England, moreover the " Altar of the Lord " and the Lord's Table are synonymous terms. (*See* Ezek. xli. 22 ; Mal. i. 7. *See also* Heb. xiii. 10, and 1 Cor. x. 16—22.)

Ought the Holy Communion to be received in both kinds ?

Yes. "The Cup of the Lord is not to be denied to the Lay-people : for both the parts of the Lord's Sacrament, by Christ's ordinance and commandment, ought to be ministered to all Christian men alike."—*Article XXX.*

Without entering into all the excuses that have been put forward in defence of the modern Roman custom of denying the Chalice to all Communicants, it is enough to say that it must be always best and safest to follow the example of our Lord in everything when we can. At the institution of this Holy Sacrament, He gave both kinds to the Apostles.

"It seems to be questioning His wisdom to deny that there must be some special gift in the cup also. In what glowing words the Church of old spoke of 'the living Blood,' 'the life-giving Blood,' 'the precious Blood,' 'the atoning Blood,' 'the saving Blood,' 'the Blood of our Redeemer,' 'the Cup of Salvation'; 'of our drinking our ransom'; of drinking 'not water from the rock, but Blood from His Side.' The words with which it is administered among us, 'The Blood of our Lord Jesus Christ, which was shed for thee, preserve thy body and soul unto everlasting life.'" [1]

"Vasquez and Lugo both admit that it is the more probable opinion that there is some special gift in the Cup. Lugo

[1] *Eirenicon,* pt. iii. p. 328.

says that Franc. Blanco, Archbishop of Compostella, who was present at the Council of Trent, said, that such was the unanimous opinion of the Fathers (there), but that they were unwilling to define it inopportunely lest an occasion of outcry should be given to the heretics, wherewith agree the words of the Council itself (Sess. XXI. c. 3), where it is cautiously said, 'As pertains to the fruit, they are deprived of no grace necessary to salvation, who receive one kind only.'"[1]

"It did not say absolutely 'no grace,' but 'no grace necessary to salvation,' where, not without reason, that expression appears to have been added, 'no grace necessary,' and this Vasquez adds, 'on the ground that the command to communicate was fulfilled by the reception of one kind only.' He notices also that this Council, although it says 'Christ, whole and entire, is received under one kind only,' does not say that the entire (*integrum*) Sacrament, but a true (*verum*) Sacrament is received; and he sums up this part by saying: 'We grant that according to this our opinion, the laity, to whom one kind is denied, are deprived of some grace, yet not necessary to salvation, and this the Council did not mean to deny.'"

"They cite, moreover, Clement VI. (A.D. 1341), who granted the Cup to a king of France, 'ad majorem gratiæ augmentum,' to the greater increase of grace. 'Therefore,' adds Lugo, 'because both kinds give more grace than one.'"[2]

It is also, to say the least of it, a very grave matter of doubt, whether Communicants not receiving the chalice of the precious Blood, fully do as the Scripture saith, "Shew forth the Lord's death till He come."

As the Prayer-book teaches: "We ought always to remember the exceeding great love of our Master and only Saviour Jesus Christ, thus dying for us, and the innumerable benefits which by His precious blood-shedding He hath obtained to us; He hath instituted and ordained holy mysteries as pledges of His love, and for a continual remembrance of His death, to our great and endless comfort."

---

[1] *Eirenicon*, pt. iii. p. 329.   [2] *Id.* p. 330.

It is important to remember how Holy Scripture lays especial weight, not upon the death of our Lord only, but upon the shedding of His Blood.[1]

"The ends of the Sacrifices were various,—the Passover, and the burnt-offering, and the peace-offering, the sin-offering of ignorance for the priest, the congregation, the ruler, or the private person; the trespass-offering or the sin-offering,—but in all the blood was sprinkled. And so we come to the New Testament, the substance of these shadows, to Him Whom through these shadows the devout under the law looked on to, and was justified by his faith in Him Who was to come. And there, these meet us, not only that actual sacrifice and the history of His precious blood-shedding in the Gospels, but all the statements of the efficacy not of the death only, but of the Blood of Christ."[2]

Rom. iii. 25 : "Whom God hath set forth to be a propitiation through faith in His Blood."

Rom. v. 9 : "Much more then, being now justified by His Blood, we shall be saved from wrath through Him."

Eph. i. 7 : "In Whom we have redemption through His Blood."

Eph. ii. 13 : "But now in Christ Jesus ye who sometimes were far off are made nigh by the Blood of Christ."

Col. i. 20 : "And having made peace through the Blood of His Cross, by Him to reconcile all things unto Himself."

Heb. x. 19 : "Having therefore, brethren, boldness to enter into the holiest by the Blood of Jesus."

1 John i. 7 : "And the Blood of Jesus Christ His Son cleanseth us from all sin."

Rev. i. 5 : "Unto Him that loved us, and washed us from our sins in His own Blood."

Rev. v. 9 : "Thou art worthy to take the book, and to open the seals thereof; for Thou wast slain, and hast redeemed us to God by Thy Blood."

"Since then there was a special value in that precious Blood-

---

[1] *Letter to Bishop of London*, p. 120.   [2] *Id.* p. 121.

shedding, 'there must be some special value in receiving that precious Blood.'"[1]

To the reception of the Chalice, also, there has always been attributed one special gift; that of spiritual gladdening.[2]

FASTING BEFORE COMMUNION.

Should communicants receive Holy Communion fasting, or not fasting?

By all means, if they possibly can, they ought to receive the Holy Communion prior to the reception of any food.

" Fasting Communion has a twofold aspect—(1) with regard to the well and strong, and as the general rule, and (2) with regard to the delicate and sickly."

There is no doubt that in itself the practice of Fasting Communion has been from the time of these irreverences among the Corinthians, an universal custom and rule in the universal Church. It was the practice in the second century, and St. Augustine thinks that it was one of those things which St. Paul says, "I will set in order when I come"; whence St. Augustine says, "It is given to be understood that what is varied by no diversity of custom was ordained by Him." (Eph. v. 4.) Cat. inguis Januarii c/n 8. It is not a written law of the Church.

Divine laws are such as the two primary Laws, and the precepts of Holy Writ about faith and morals. These are binding at all times and in all places. Human laws are positive arbitrary laws, because men may enact, change, and abolish them. It is then very wrong when some among us have spoken of non-fasting Communion as a deadly sin, or even as sacrilegious. If there had been anything irreverent in receiving the Body and Blood of our Lord after food, our Lord would not have instituted it (as He did). If people say that it was to connect the old dispensation with the new, our Lord was the founder of both; again, if there were any intrinsic

---

[1] *Letter to Bishop of London*, p. 123.   [2] *Id.* p. 164.

irreverence, the last Communion of the sick would not by express provision be allowed after food; again, it is allowed everywhere that the Christmas midnight Communion should be after the food taken a few hours before, without any intervening sleep, and (as lately) when Christmas Day was on the Monday, the day before was no fast. But the division of the day at midnight is only arbitrary. When the day begins at sunset it is the same day; there is no difference in principle or in the nature of the act itself. Again, in the Roman Church also, the non-fasting Communion cannot be accounted intrinsically wrong, since it was customary, it has been said, for the kings of France and Spain to be allowed to take some broth before Holy Communion, and King James II. was allowed to receive the Sacrament after slight refreshment on account of his health. When persons say, "It is a deadly sin," they must mean that it is against an express and known law of the Church. The sin is in the formal contempt of the law or the legislator.

But it appears that although there is a pious custom from the earliest times, there is no law the infringement of which would involve contempt. People would hardly say that the neglect of Ash Wednesday was anyhow a mortal sin. We should be very slow in multiplying mortal sins. There are many cases, when from delicate health a person might be unable to go out (certainly in winter) at an early hour, without having taken something, or where for months together there is only late Communion.[1]

"Isidore, embodying in his own statement the words of St. Augustine, states it as explicitly as words could express it, that in honour of so great a Sacrament, the Lord's Body should enter the mouth of a Christian before any other food."[2]

"The rule of the Ancient Church, of which we have evidence towards the close of the second century, was of the nature of a positive law. Had there been any intrinsic irreverence, in

---

[1] *Letter of* DR. PUSEY, *December* 1874.

[2] *Preface to Real Presence*, p. xxv.

taking food before receiving the Body and Blood of Christ in the Holy Eucharist, our Blessed Lord would not so have instituted it. Old Canons also dispense with its observance in the case of the sickly; and the Latin Church allows the Holy Eucharist to be received after food, by the dying. But to those who hold with Calvin the whole rule is unmeaning, they would, if they spoke their minds (as in ordinary life they do), account it superstitious. If we only ate 'mere bread and wine' in remembrance of our Lord's death, there would be no more reason for fasting before we received it than for fasting before we heard in Church the history of His Passion. The theory of the Calvinists being, that Sacramental and non-Sacramental Communion is one and the same, there could be no more reason for fasting before Sacramental than before non-Sacramental Communion. But then the practice of the Primitive Church, 'the custom kept throughout the whole world,' as St. Augustine says, implies a different belief from that of the School of Calvin." [1]

Give two reasons for thinking that the Church of Englana approves of Communicating fasting.

She directs that adults be exhorted to prepare themselves with prayer and *fasting* for the receiving of the Holy Sacrament of Baptism. She of course regards the Holy Communion as a Sacrament of equal dignity, and therefore would not be likely to discourage any from fasting before Reception who could do so. It has been thought by some that the Church in advising the sick to give timely notice to the Curate of their wish to communicate therein, implies fasting Communion.

This would be very difficult to prove, yet it does seem remarkable why, if for want of warning received in due time, the Curate cannot Celebrate, and yet be able, as the rubric directs, to instruct and exhort the sick person.

The practice of Fasting Communion is certainly nowhere forbidden by the Church of England; it seems to be one of those most excellent Catholic Customs which could not be

---

[1] *Preface to Real Presence,* p. xxvi.

observed by all, and so is left by her to the consciences of her children to observe it or not as they honestly think best.

"As regards Evening Communions, it is difficult to understand how any who believe that in Holy Communion we receive the Body and Blood of Christ, can have anything to do with them." [1]

There can be no doubt that the Church of England is in favour of Fasting Communion, and opposed to Evening Communion, from the simple fact that she continually appeals in all she teaches and commands to the example of the Primitive Church, where there is no doubt fasting before Communion was *the* Custom, and Evening Communions unknown.

FREQUENT COMMUNION.

Are we not likely to Communicate more worthily, if we only Communicate very rarely?

"We do nothing well which we do not do habitually. The worst prayers are those which are most seldom said: the most indevout worshippers in Church are those who, in proportion to their abilities, come here the least frequently: the coldest and most profitless Communions are those of the most occasional communicants." [2]

SPIRITUAL COMMUNION.

"Learn at least gradually 'Spiritual Communion' on other days, when thou mayest not receive Him in His Sacrament. All prayer calls Him into the soul. 'When I call upon my God,' exclaims a Father in reverent awe, 'I call Him into myself.' 'Thou callest upon God, when thou callest God into thee. Thou invitest Him, in a manner, into the mansion of thy heart.' But it is a more solemn act, consciously to call our Lord into ourselves." [3]

<hr>

[1] *Letter, December* 1874.　　　[2] *Lenten Sermons*, p. 361.
[3] Vol. i. p. 413.

"Communions in spirit detain Jesus in the soul which He hath visited, and prepare the soul to long for His fuller Presence." [1]

Bishop of Brechin's *Defence ;* Sadler's *One Offering.*

HOLY MATRIMONY.

> " Only kneel on—nor turn away
> From the pure shrine where Christ to-day
> Will store each flower ye duteous lay
> For an eternal wreath."
>
> Keble.

What is Holy Matrimony ?

"An honourable estate instituted of God in the time of man's innocency, signifying unto us the Mystical Union that is betwixt Christ and His Church."

State the Scriptural doctrine as to Holy Matrimony.

"Three in person they are in perfectness One God, and 'God is Love.' In some shadow of this oneness God willed eternally to make us His creatures. Even in Paradise God instituted that two should be one. He made the oneness the closer, in that He took from Adam part of his very self : that as, in the All Holy Trinity, the Son is from the Father, co-eternally, the oneness should be shadowed out, as far as it could be, in His creature : and the woman was formed not apart, as other creatures were, not as a daughter only, but of the very substance and strength and firmness of the man. And man and woman were again to become one. But for the Fall there would have been no passion in love, and loving intercourse ; no shame, no distress, no pain in child-bearing ; but there would have been perfect union of love. For in Paradise, too, God said, ' They twain shall be one flesh.' One they were, by origin one of the other ; one they should be in their offspring : one they should be, in that they were to live through life for one another alone : one they should be in the

---

[1] Vol. i. p. 414.

oneness of their mutual love and their one will, whereby their souls should be knit together in one : one through the blessing of Almighty God, Who made them, what He declared them, no more twain but one." [1]

"The oneness of marriage shadows forth that spiritual oneness whereby Christ and the whole company of the redeemed are so one, that He vouchsafes to speak of Himself as not complete without them : Himself, 'the Head of the Church,' 'His Body, the fulness of Him who filleth all in all.' But since marriage is this high and wondrous image of the union of the soul with Christ, how holily ought it to be compassed, entered upon, lived in !" [2]

What then is the Christian idea of marriage ?

"As gathered from the Holy Scriptures and the teaching of the Church, it is a sacred and a serious ordinance of God, whereby two persons are indissolubly bound together until death, for the discharge of mutual duties and functions closely connected with this world and the world to come. It is the figure and representation of the Incarnation of our Lord God, bearing an exceedingly close analogy to that Divine mystery in both its nature and its laws ; so much so, that in any difficult moral questions relating to marriage, the true key will be most readily and securely found in the laws of the Incarnation. It is ordained to be the foundation of the human and of the extension of the supernatural society; because, through it, God wills to be perpetually creating those predestined to be the members of His Son's mystical Body; and thus it is a designed means of fulfilling the great purpose for which God was made Man. The true marriage covenant is the earthly analogue of the covenant between God and humanity, and enshrines in a wonderful but most practical manner the image of the mutual obligations of that marvellous grace."—JOHN WALTER LEA, *Sanctity of Marriage*, p. 4.

"It is an ordinance founded on the principle of duality in unity, as 'God and Man are one Christ.' It is a union of

---

[1] Vol. ii. p. 388. [2] *Id.* p. 390.

the whole being, not of the body only; 'as he that is joined
to the Lord in one spirit,' as well as a 'member of His body';
and as the Incarnation is the union of whole Godhead with
whole Manhood.　It is indissoluble, as the hypostatic union
is never to be divided.　It is a union of two only (as against
polygamy or polyandry), as there are but two natures in the
hypostatic union, and as God says of the Bride (whether
humanity in the abstract or the regenerate humanity which
individually and still more collectively is the 'extension of the
Incarnation'), 'My love, My undefiled, is but one,' thus
'every man' is to have 'his own wife,' and 'every woman'
'her own husband.'　It is a sacred covenant on the one side
of perfect love and a gift of equal participation in all honour
and goods, as the Lord's humanity is glorified 'with the glory
which' He 'had with' 'the Father' before the world was;
and as the members of His Body shall 'sit' with 'Him'
in 'His' throne even as 'He' is 'set down with His'
Father in His Throne: and as Christ loved the Church and
gave Himself for it.　On the other side is a loving subjection,
for 'the head of the woman is the man,' as 'the head of
every man is Christ,' the Man, the God-Man; and 'The
Head of Christ is God,' the Essential Godhead, the head of
the Humanity even of God.　These are enough for the present."
—LEA, *Sanctity of Marriage*, p. 5.

How should husband and wife love each other?

As Christ loveth the Church.

" Christ loved in the Church an undying beauty, which He
would give her.　He loved all souls, not for what they were,
but for what He should make them.　We love after the pattern of Christ.　When we love in one another that deathless
beauty of the soul which Christ gives; when we love in despite
of defects, which Christ will, by His grace, remove; when
we are patient and forbearing with what Christ has not as yet
removed, looking and longing for His transforming grace now,
yet onwards still to that 'mighty working whereby He shall
subdue all things unto Himself.'　To love the beauty of the

body, save as the soul shines through it, is not love like Christ. Poor, fading, a shadow only of that which shall never fade, is any beauty of the body. Beautiful above the stars of Heaven, more piercing than their lustre, and undying, is the beauty of the soul in grace. Look then to that in one another which shall live on and shine on in the heavenly courts when all riches of this earth shall be dissolved; yea, when what is now of this earth, but from our Maker's hands, not from our marring of His work, shall be transformed into the glory of Christ." [1]

"This love shall grow with years, as the love of Christ and the grace of Christ, which is the beauty of the soul, grows and is enlarged in each. This love shall be refined and purified by sickness and the wasting of the body, as the soul shall, through God's chastening, purifying hand, lay aside its dross, and glow the more with the beauty of the grace of Christ. This love shall not decay, much less die, even after the body's death. For souls which are united in Christ shall not be separated from Christ; they shall live on still, one in the one love of Christ. In Heaven there shall be 'neither marrying nor giving in marriage,' but there shall be love; love, pure, holy, happy, like that of the Angels of God in Heaven, who are ever filled with the love of God, ever behold the face of God, are ever over-streamed with the radiancy of that love which issues forth from the eternal fountain of love." [2]

Is marriage indissoluble ?

A true, lawful, valid, Christian marriage, that is, a marriage which had no impediment to prevent its being a proper marriage, can never be dissolved by any earthly power.

The Christian man and woman are joined together in Holy Matrimony "till death us do part." And "those whom God hath joined together, let no man put asunder."

"God made one, Adam first, to mark the oneness of marriage and make it a law of nature, appointing 'that out of man (created in His own image and similitude) woman should take

<hr>

[1] Vol. ii. p. 392.   [2] *Id.* p. 393.

her beginning, and knitting them together, did teach that it should never be lawful to put asunder those whom He, by matrimony, had made one.' Between those two, and consequently between all other married, to be born from them, He willed that there should be one indivisible union; for Adam could be married to no other save Eve, since no other had been created by God. Nor could Eve turn to any other man than Adam, since there was no other in the world. Infringe not then this sanction of God, and unity of marriage, and degenerate not from your first parents Adam and Eve. 'If divorce had been good, Jesus says, God would not have made one man and one woman; but having made one Adam, would have made two women, had He meant that he should cast out the one, and bring in the other; but now, by the mode of creation, He brought in this law, that each should have throughout the wife which he had from the beginning. This law is older than that about divorce, as much as Adam is older than Moses.'"[1]

"All the souls which God would ever create are His, and He could have called them into being at once. Yet, in order to designate the unity of marriage, He willed to create but one. So our Lord argues against divorce. 'Have ye not read that He which made them at the beginning made them male and female?' They both together are called *one man*, and therefore should be of one mind and spirit also, the unity of which they ought faithfully to preserve."[2]

"And wherefore one? Seeking a seal of God, *i. e.* worthy of God; for from religious marriage, religious offspring may be most hoped from God; and by violating that law, those before the flood brought in a spurious, unsanctified generation, so that God, in His displeasure, destroyed them all. And take heed to your spirit, which ye too had from God, which was His, and which He willed in time to create. He closes as He began, with an appeal to man's natural feeling, 'Let none deal

[1] *Minor Prophets*, p. 609. LAPIDE and ST. CHRYSOSTOM.
[2] *Id.* p. 609.

treacherously against the wife of his youth.' He hateth putting away. He had allowed it for the hardness of their hearts, yet only in the one case of some extreme bodily foulness, discovered upon marriage, and which the woman, knowing the law, concealed at her own peril. Not subsequent illness, or any subsequent consequence of it, however loathsome (as leprosy), were a ground for divorce, but only this concealed foulness, which the husband found upon marriage. The capricious, tyrannical divorce, God saith, He hateth; a word naturally used only as to sin, and so stamping such divorce as sin."[1]

" To treat marriage as dissoluble is not only to undermine its sanctity, but to subvert its essential law. It goes far towards virtually abolishing it altogether, and substituting a mode of union other than that ordained by God."[2]

" Its immediate evil is vast; its potential evil almost incalculable, yet this desperate and well-nigh fatal error has been already effected among us by the action of the Divorce Law (of the State, not the Church), which permits those legally divorced to enter into other legal unions as though the former husband or wife were dead."[3]

"Since the laws of the State sanction divorce, also the so-called marriage of divorced persons during the lifetime of their partners. And, since continual efforts are being made to legalize marriage contracted within the degrees (of affinity) forbidden by God, what should be the duty of all professing Christians?"[4]

" As one man we ought to resolve that nothing should ever induce us to condone in public or in private life violations of God's law of marriage. No 'position,' secular or ecclesiastical, no previously high character or 'respectability,' no legality, no worldly indifference, no fear of being called bigots, no consideration whatever should induce us to treat, or to

---

[1] *Minor Prophets*, p. 609.
[2] LEA, *Sanctity of Marriage*, p. 6.
[3] *Id.*   [4] *Id.*

designate adultery as anything but adultery, or incest as anything but incest. Of course I do not mean that we should go
about the world reviling others, or blazoning their evil report
everywhere. No pure-hearted, loving Christian could for a
moment think of this. But I mean that, as a truly noble
Christian man will, when necessity arises, treat a swindler as a
swindler, a liar as a liar, a thief as a thief, yet without any
violation of the Christian law of charity ; so we should also,
regarding the same royal law, resolve to treat the legalized
adulterer as an adulterer still, though legalized, and the incestuous person, whether legalized or not, as an incestuous person
still. In other words, let us show by our actions that we do
regard the law of God, and the Catholic interpretation of that
law by the Universal Church of God, as the one and only law
for us, and that, in comparison, human laws are as though they
were not. Let us be charitable, but on our part also consistent ;
and let it be seen and known what Word we believe, and what
Laws we obey, all the more plainly should the law of the land
happen to be against them." [1]

CELIBACY OF THE CLERGY, IS IT DESIRABLE ?

"I am not advocating celibacy, my lord, as the *general*
rule of the Church, nor imposing upon others 'a yoke which
I touch not with one of my fingers' : nor have any of us so
done. But surely there is room for all ; and, while the peaceful duties of the country pastor can often be even better
discharged, perhaps, by a married priest, 'ruling well his own
house, and having his children in subjection in all gravity,'
a pattern of domestic charities, there are surely duties enough
in the Church where celibacy may have its proper place, and
where there is much room for the exhibition of the sterner
grace of self-denial, foregoing all the highest earthly joys which
cheer us on our pilgrimage, passing alone and isolated through

[1] LEA, p. 47.

the world, and *visibly* living only for his Master's work, and to gather in his Master's scattered sheep. If the degraded population of many of our great towns are to be recovered from the state of heathenism in which they are sunk, it must be by such preaching of the Cross, wherein it shall be forced upon man's dull senses that they who preach it have forsaken all to take it up and bear it after their Lord."[1]

What is the real Catholic teaching concerning the marriage of the clergy?

"The proposition that the celibacy of the Priesthood is not *jure divino* is absolutely Catholic. It has ever been regarded as a matter of pure discipline, varying with the different ages and the necessities of the Church."—FORBES *on the Articles*, p. 627.

And, as regards marriage, that they should be married once only.

"The Scriptural argument from 1 Tim. iii. 2, 'Let a bishop be the husband of one wife,' is irrefragable on both sides. To look with contempt upon married bishops and priests, is to be wiser than Holy Scripture, which allows them to be married. On the other hand, the words seem to mean, that the Bishop should have had altogether one wife only, not merely had one wife at once. For a rule which forbade to bishops only to have one wife at once, would, in itself, allow other Christians to have more, contrary to the original institution of marriage and our Lord's expressed words. For St. Paul's direction is of the nature of a positive, although divine law; it does not in itself express a breach of the seventh commandment. This would be expressed by some words denoting the offence, as those other words ('Not given to much wine, not a striker,') express in themselves direct breaches of moral duty. To inculcate a moral duty upon a particular class, would not, of course, set others free to break it; but to enact a positive law for a particular class, does imply

---

[1] *Letter to Bishop of London*, p. 172.

that the rest are free from that law. The law in–the New Testament, that the Bishop should be ‘the husband of one wife,’ is analogous to the law in the Old Testament, that the High Priest should marry none but a virgin.”[1]

“But it is not the question what any one had done before he was converted; St. Paul is speaking not of this, but of the selection of Bishops and Deacons, out of those already converted and Christians. To a Christian, polygamy is adultery. One who would prove that the rule to be ‘the husband of one wife’ meant, that a Bishop should not have two wives at once, ought first to show that any Christian could. For, if there were no polygamists among Christians, no one, of course, could be found to be a Bishop who was such.”[2]

The rule of St. Paul appears to have been embodied at once, in this sense, in the law of the Church. For the earliest Fathers who speak on the subject, speak of it, not as a matter of a private opinion, but as forbidden by the law of the Church that such as had been married twice should be ordained. The Apostolic Canons guard both sides. They provide that the Clergy should “not put away their wives, under pretence of piety,” and that one who after Baptism had been involved in two marriages, was not to be admitted to Holy Orders. The third Apostolic Canon says, “Let not a Bishop, or Priest, or Deacon cast out his wife on pretence of piety; if he do cast her out, let him be excommunicated; if he persevere, let him be deposed.” The thirteenth provides, “He who has been engaged in two marriages after baptism, or has a concubine, cannot be a Bishop or Priest, or Deacon, or altogether of the ecclesiastical order.” The very words of this Canon are remarkably retained in Origen, “The twice married can neither be Bishop, nor Priest, nor Deacon, nor widow”: and in Tertullian, “No one can be a Priest, than who, as a layman, has been only once (*semel*) a husband” (*De Exp. Cast.* c. 7); and in St. Jerome, “The twice married cannot

---

[1] *Tertullian*, p. 420.   [2] *Id*. p. 422.

be chosen into the ecclesiastical order." It is directly quoted by St. Basil in his second Canonical Epistle (*Ep.* 188, can. xii. t. iii. p. 275). "The Canon altogether excludes the twice married from the Ministry."[1]

St. Chrysostom (on Tit. i. 6, *Hom.* ii. p. 283, *Oxf. Tr.*) is very distinct.

"Why does he bring forward such an one? To stop the mouths of those heretics who condemned marriage, showing that it is not an unholy thing in itself, but so far honourable, that a married man might ascend the Holy Throne; and, at the same time, reproving the wanton, and not permitting their admission into this high office who contracted a second marriage. For he who retains no kind regard for her who is departed, how shall he be a good president? And what accusation would he not incur? For you all know, that, though it is not forbidden by the laws to enter into a second marriage, yet it is a thing liable to many ill constructions."[2]

May the Christian widower or widow think that hereafter there will still be some special bond, tie, or sacramental character, or mark, when reunion takes place with the one who has gone before?

"There are surely many Christians whose hopes being beyond the grave, their love too is beyond the grave; who can love no second with a husband's love, because they still love the first; who, looking to be reunited, though as the angels of God in heaven, after this earth, cannot on this earth displace that union by another; their *union continues still*, though invisible."[3]

"There, in that abode of love, shall no special holy love be lost. God has not formed us, yea, bidden us, in this our nursery for the Heavenly life, to love one another in all our several relations, that all this after life should cease. He has not bound us in those varied sweet bands of love—fathers,

---

[1] *Tertullian*, p. 422. [2] *Id.* p. 424.
[3] *Proposed change in Marriage Law*, p. 13.

mothers, children, brothers, sisters, husbands, wives, friends, or those wider circles through which love radiates here—that the love which is from Himself and which He has made part of the undying soul shall die."[1]

"But take then that other, in one way, yet deeper mystery, to which God has appointed that love of father and mother should, in a degree, yield, that feeling, over which man at first has power, which, when allowed, becomes part of himself, so that thenceforth it lives on bound up with his life; which, when hallowed by God, ends in a oneness which time, severance, age, death, breaks not; nay which, through death, becomes like the love of God, the love of the Unseen, to be renewed where there is neither marrying nor giving in marriage, in adoring love before the throne of God. Man could assign this or that ground of his married love. He could not explain to himself the whole."[2]

What must Churchmen think of marriages with the sister of a deceased wife, and all such unhallowed unions ?

"The celebration of such marriages is but the first act, which rivets all the difficulties which follow. It cements an union, indissoluble by human law, allowing of no subsequent marriage, forbidden by the law of God. Marriage by human law, fornication according to the Divine, a life-long fornication, tinselled over by the sanctions of man, and perhaps, by the ceremonial of a profane ritual, blessed in the name of God Who curses it. What if the conscience of either party wake, or be better informed when too late? What if it should begin to doubt, when bound by the law of marriage to that which, if the marriage itself is against God's law, is sin ? "[3]

But can such marriages be wrong since they are sanctioned by the Church of Rome ?

The Church of Rome is supposed to forbid and condemn the marriage with a deceased wife's sister. But the Bishop

---

[1] Vol. ii. p. 263.
[2] Vol. 1872, p. 5.   [3] *God's Prohibition*, p. 43.

of Rome *does* dispense in such cases, that is, give leave for these incestuous unions to be formed.

Why are such dispensations given, if these marriages are contrary to the laws of God?

This is a question Roman Catholics must answer satisfactorily if they can. Cardinal Manning in a published letter, May 10th, 1882, says the dispensations are given for "grave reasons, and to avoid greater evils."

What the greater evils may be, are not clear. If a widower takes into his house his dead wife's sister to act as his house-keeper, and as mother to his children, there is no evil in it. If he live sinfully with her, that is very terrible, a sin of incestuous fornication. If he is married to her after a dispensation from the Pope, incest is incest still, for God has not sanctioned what He has cursed, and the evil has become worse than before, because the state of sin is declared to have God's approval, otherwise the dispensation would not have been granted.

Have Roman Catholic Theologians and Divines held that the Pope cannot give a dispensation for marrying a wife's sister, because to do so would be to contradict the law of God?

"Yes; that was held by a great many authorities; for instance, St. Thomas Aquinas, St. Buonventura, and a great body of school-men afterwards. Both the school-men and the canonists say that the Pope could not dispense in those cases, because it was against the law of God. I think that one of the strongest passages is by John Turrecremata, an eminent theologian and canonist in the confidence of Pope Eugenius, by whom he was sent to the Council of Basle, and was made a Cardinal. In answer to some who alleged that such dispensations had been given, he says, 'We have not seen this'; 'nay, on the contrary, when the King of France, now reigning as Dauphin, he applied that, his wife being dead, he might contract marriage with her sister: the matter was examined before me (*coram nobis*) by the command of the Lord Eugenius, to whom the cause was committed, and it was judged that the Pope could not dispense *quod non poterat Papa dispensare.'* "[1]

Is there now any doubt about the lawfulness of these dispensations to marry a wife's sister in the Roman Communion ?

Now that the infallibility of the Pope is with Roman Catholics an article of faith, they cannot now question his right to grant these dispensations. As Dr. Pusey said before the Parliamentary Commission, 1847, "I should have thought that the whole question turned upon the Infallibility of the Pope."[2]

Does the Greek Church allow marriage with a wife's sister ?

No ; they are held to be incestuous, unlawful, and void from the beginning.

As regards the proposed relaxation of the laws of marriage, proposed by the advocates of marriage with the wife's sister, what should Christians think ?

"As regards any permission to marry a wife's sister, such a relaxation as this contemplated can bring no blessing, as contrary to the law of God. I would say that such relaxation is opening a question which, when opened, cannot be closed. The marriages now in question are but the first outworks ; if they were conceded, further questions would be raised, which it would be impossible to meet on any principle. The next step is that of the uncle and niece, which is allowed and practised commonly in the countries held up for our pattern in this. But such marriages as introduce a confusion of relations seem contrary to nature itself, as St. Ambrose observed of old. It is unnatural that a woman should be first cousin of her own children, in one relationship on an equality, in the other requiring reverence, and so on. Or, again (in the case of the wife's sister), that the children of the two marriages should be both brothers and sisters and first cousins. And yet this is but the very beginning of such changes ; nor if this principle be sacrificed, can any consistent limit be placed short of the very deepest incest."[3]

[1] *Evidence before Commission*, p. 43.   [2] *Id.* p. 43.   [3] *Id.* p. 53.

"These relaxations would sacrifice those who wished to cherish the natural affections towards the wife's family, to those who wished to make the sister-in-law the second wife. An instinctive feeling of propriety has made it a rule of society that persons whom the law allows to marry cannot remain under the same roof unmarried. In whatever degree the marriage law is relaxed, in that degree are domestic affections narrowed." [1]

" It may be worthy the attention of the commissioners that a change of the civil provisions as to marriage does not alter the duties of the clergy, who remain under the Canons. They could neither celebrate such marriages *nor consider persons so united as married in the sight of God*. There are, however, ulterior, though in fact great, evils, threatening the breaking up of those domestic habits which are so great a blessing to the English nation. The great evil is the contradiction to the law of God." [2]

Upon what principle is the Scriptural, and therefore the Church, law based ?

On the truth that man and wife are not " twain," but " one flesh " (St. Matt. xix. 6).

HOLY ORDERS IN THE CHURCH OF ENGLAND.

What is meant by the doctrine of Apostolical Succession ?

"It means that all men who have a right to be considered duly appointed Ministers of Christ, have received from Himself a commission to minister in His name, conveyed in an outward and visible manner, by what in fact is termed Ordination, in a direct line from the holy Apostles to whom our Lord first imparted it."—*Apostolical Succession*, OLDKNOW, p. 3.

" The doctrine of the Apostolical Succession implies the necessity of a commission, outwardly and visibly conferred, to authorize a man to act as a Minister of God, and the fact that

---

[1] *Evidence before Commission*, p. 53.   [2] *Id.*

such a commission was intended by our Lord to be conveyed, in a regular course from the Apostles, to all those who are entitled to minister in His name at the present day."—OLD-KNOW, p. 10.

What does the Church of England teach as to the importance of the doctrine of Apostolical Succession?

The Church of England rejects the ministry of all who have not been thus ordained, even though they come from foreign countries, thus seeming to imply the absolute necessity of episcopal ordination to confer the ministerial character, for, by the most universally admitted rule of Christian Communion, all who are constituted Christ's Ministers in any one portion of His Church, carry with them their character and commission in every other into which they may migrate. So much for our Church's judgment of the necessity of episcopal ordination. That such ordination is considered by it as conferring a share in the commission of the Apostles, may be not less conclusively established. True it is, our Church nowhere categorically affirms this; but it does more, it acts on it as indisputable. It deals with the Apostolic Succession, not as a theological dogma, but as an *awful reality*, as a main part of the economy of grace, as an act of Christ's Kingly government, as His promised presence with His Church to the consummation of ages. "All power is given unto Me in Heaven and in earth. Go ye, therefore, and teach all nations. And, lo! I am with you alway, even unto the end of the world."

"The full and undoubting persuasion of this mighty fact is the only warrant which can authorize me to confer, or you to receive, Holy Orders, according to the Form which our Church appoints. For how could any Bishop dare to say, 'Receive the Holy Ghost, for the office and work of a Priest in the Church of God, now committed unto you by the imposition of our hands,' with the awful words which follow? How, I ask, could any mortal man dare to give such a commission in such terms, unless he were confident that he has received authority so to give it, either immediately from Christ Himself (which is not pretended), or from, and through, those to whom our Lord Himself said, ' As My Father has sent Me, even so send I you ' ? In like manner, how could you, without the most impious rashness, seek such a commission at the hands of any man, of whom you were not assured that he has received from God authority to confer it?

" I repeat, therefore, that while our Church abstains from pronouncing on what is necessary to the Christian ministry elsewhere, it both requires Episcopal ordination for its own ministers, and affirms that those who have been so ordained to preach the Word and to minister the Sacraments have the assurance of the Holy Spirit accompanying their ministrations, derived to them in succession from the Apostles of our Lord."—*Ordination Sermon of Bishop of Exeter*, pp. 27, 28 ; 1843.

In Article XXIII. it is declared—" It is not lawful for any man to take upon him the office of publick preaching, or ministering the Sacraments in the Congregation, before he be lawfully called, and sent to execute the same. And those we ought to judge lawfully called and sent, which be chosen and called to this work by men who have publick authority given unto them in the Congregation, to call and send Ministers into the Lord's vineyard."

See also Preface to the Ordinal as follows :—

" The form and manner of making, ordaining, and consecrating of Bishops, Priests, and Deacons, according to the order of the Church of England.—The Preface.—It is evident unto all men diligently reading the Holy Scripture and ancient Authors, that from the Apostles' time there have been these Orders of Ministers in Christ's Church : Bishops, Priests, and Deacons. Which Offices were evermore had in such reverend Estimation, that no man might presume to execute any of them, except he were first called, tried, examined, and known to have such qualities as are requisite for the same; and also by publick Prayer, with Imposition of Hands, were approved and admitted thereunto by lawful Authority.   And therefore, to the intent that these Orders may be continued, and reverently used and esteemed, in the Church of *England ;* no man shall be accounted or taken to be a lawful Bishop, Priest, or Deacon in the Church of *England*, or suffered to execute any of the said Functions, except he be called, tried, examined, and admitted thereunto, according to the Form hereafter following, or hath had formerly Episcopal Consecration, or Ordination."

Give another summary and explanation of the doctrine of the Apostolical Succession.

"It is recorded by St. Matthew that our Blessed Lord concluded the Apostolic Commission with these words : 'I am with you alway, even unto the end of the world.'   But the Apostles are dead, and the end of the world has not yet come ; therefore if these words apply to the men, as such, and not the *office*, it is evident that either (1) the Lord Jesus believed that the end of the world would come during the lifetime of the eleven Apostles—in which case He was mistaken, or (2) He made a false promise, which He did not intend to fulfil.   Can such frightful blasphemy be uttered ?   'God forbid ; yea, let God be true, but every man a liar.'   If, on the contrary, as all Christian antiquity testifies, the words apply to the office, and not the men, it follows that here we have the proclamation, at the mouth of the Head of the Church, of the principle of the Apostolical Succession."—G. R. ROBERTS' *Reply to Capel*, p. 5.

Give a definition of Apostolical Succession.

"By Apostolical Succession I mean the transmission in an unbroken succession, generation after generation, of the Apostolic office.   In its plenitude this office is found in the Episcopate, and therefore upon the unbroken succession of the Episcopate depends the validity of the Orders, and by consequence of the Sacraments of a Church.   The Apostolic office, to which bishops succeed, embraces the following essential functions—Consecration of Bishops, Ordination of Priests and Deacons ; Preaching, Baptism, Confirmation, or 'Laying on of hands upon those that are baptized '; the celebration of the Holy Eucharist, Absolution and Benediction whether in Holy Matrimony or other offices. Of these functions some are delegated to the priesthood ; namely, Preaching, Baptism, the Celebration of the Holy Eucharist, Absolution, Benediction. Hence the priesthood exercises a portion, and but a portion only, of the Apostolic Office ; and that, too, by delegated authority. Deacons, who constitute the third and lowest order, whilst they share in the exceptions which distinguish the priesthood from the Episcopate, cannot preach without the Bishop's express licence, neither can they Celebrate the Holy Eucharist, nor absolve, nor give benediction, nor marry—Holy Matrimony being a Sacrament according to the Homily. Preaching, then, and Baptism are the only two Apostolic functions which are delegated to the Diaconate. The Deacon's Office, to quote from the Prayer-book, is to assist the Priest in Divine service, and specially when he ministereth the Holy Communion, and to help him in the distribution thereof, and to read Holy Scriptures and Homilies in the Church, and to instruct the youth in the Catechism, in the absence of the priest to baptize infants and to preach, if he be admitted thereto by the Bishop. And furthermore, it is his office where provision is so made to search for the sick, poor, and impotent people of the parish, to intimate their estates, names, and places where they dwell unto the Curate, meaning the parish priest, who has 'Cure of souls,' that by his exhortation they may be relieved with the alms of the parishioners, or others."—*See* GRUEBER'S *Catechism on Holy Orders.*

The Church of England as a true portion of the One Catholic Church of Christ has a valid ministry: she has then Bishops duly consecrated, Priests rightly ordained, Deacons properly set apart for their Office ?

Yes ; of this there is no doubt. Anglican Orders are valid. This, in answer to her enemies, has been proved over and over again. There is absolutely no doubt upon the point.

Name some of the numerous Authors who have defended the validity of Anglican Orders.

> Courayer.
> Percival.
> Mason.
> Haddan.
> Bailey.
> Lee.
> Littledale.
> Churton.
> Morse.

"The Council of Trent was asked by Pius IV. to declare the Elizabethan Bishops unlawful, and it expressly refused to do so. Pope Julius III. addressed a Brief to Cardinal Pole in 1554, desiring him to absolve and reconcile the Bishops and Priests made in Edward VI.'s time, but not directing him to re-ordain them."—LITTLEDALE *on Anglican Orders*, p. 9.

Does the Anglican Church deny the validity of the Orders of the Roman Communion ?

No ; she believes in their validity. In her charity and in her reverence for true Catholic principle, she holds that Roman Orders are to be accounted true and valid.

Aquinas says, in the name of the Western Church, " A Priest consecrates validly in heresy or schism although he sins in so doing."

Are we to believe that Presbyterians and Wesleyans receive nothing in their Sacraments ?

"Without · imitating their harshness, we, in our turn, would say, since the Church of England is the Catholic Church in England, and Episcopacy is an Ordinance of God, to abandon it is sin ; the degree of that sin, or its effects, we are not called upon to pronounce on ; nor would we ; only, as watchmen, we are bound to warn against this, as against every other sin, and the more against this, because men are now so careless about it."[1]

[1] *Letter to Bishop of Oxford*, p. 150.

" But while maintaining that they only are commissioned to administer the Sacraments, who have received that commission from those appointed in succession to bestow it, we have never denied that God may make His own Sacraments efficacious even when irregularly administered ; we should trust it might be so." [1]

" We would point out to those who are of our Communion, this security in remaining in her, to those who, or their forefathers, have deserted her, the superior safety in returning to her." [2]

" As to the Presbyterians, they deny, in regard to the Holy Communion, what we believe, and their account of their Communion is somewhat less than what we mean by a spiritual Communion. For they speak rather of ' ascending in mind into Heaven, and feeding upon Jesus there by faith,' than of praying Him to come by His Spirit into the soul. I mean that the Calvinist Confessions seem to me to speak rather of man's part than of His, of what faith enabled by Him does, than of what it receives. Still, be this as it may, they speak of a religious act, and although (as some of them say) there is no need, to this end, of anything outward, and what they describe might be done in every prayer, still, doubtless, He whom they seek is found by them for that which they seek. They seek a spiritual Communion, and doubtless God admits them to that spiritual Communion with Him which they desire. Nay, in Baptism He gives them more than they know of or believe." [3]

What did Bishop Hall write of Episcopacy?

The loss of Episcopacy, when it seemed for the time that it could not be had, Bishop Hall looks upon with "pity"; and its voluntary rejection he entitles, " to cast mire in the faces of the blessed Apostles, who received it from their God and Saviour, and by the guidance of His Spirit ordained it ; those who had abandoned it he ' beseeches and adjures by that love

---

[1] *Letter to Bishop of Oxford*, p. 152.
[2] *Id.* p. 158.   [3] *Eirenicon*, i. p. 272.

they profess to bear to the truth of God, by that tender respect they bear to the peace of His Zion, by their seal to the Gospel of Christ, by their main care of their happy account one day before the tribunal of the most righteous Judge of the quick and dead, to lay all this that he had said seriously together,' 'and' for God's sake and his own, not upon groundless suggestion to abandon God's truth and ordinance and adore an idol made of the ear-rings of the people, and fashioned out with the graving-tool of a supposed skilful Aaron, 'and for you,' he adds, ' my dearly beloved brethren at home, for Christ's sake be exhorted to hold fast to this Holy Institution of your Blessed Saviour, and His unerring Apostles, and bless God for Episcopacy.' "[1]

Is Episcopacy of Divine Institution ?

Yes.

But how can this be proved ?

Episcopacy is from the Apostles' time.   The Preface to the Ordinal declares this.   In the prayer, " Almighty God, giver of all good things, who by Thy Holy Spirit has appointed divers orders in Thy Church."   See the Form for the ordering of Deacons and Priests and the Consecration of Bishops.   This prayer is worded a little differently in the Form for the ordering of Deacons, but the truth is taught that the Apostles were inspired to choose Deacons—that God appointed divers Orders of Ministers, or by the Holy Spirit appointed divers Orders. Episcopacy and the Priesthood, to which the Diaconate is the probationary step, are Divine, for they are Apostolic, *i. e.* from the Apostles who were so taught, and received the appointment of God.

Where there is no proper belief in Apostolical Succession, in the necessity of a validly-ordained Ministry, is there any proper faith in " the Sacraments" ?

Is not the rejection of Apostolical Succession accompanied with a low and inaccurate view of the Sacraments ?

Yes. " The doctrine of Apostolical Succession, and that of the

<hr>

[1] *Letter to Bishop of Oxford*, p. 172.

N

Sacraments viewed in the abstract, would to most, probably, not seem at first sight to be so connected together, that a false view of the one would involve error upon the other, much less that the denial of the one should entail a fundamental change in the other. Yet so it has been. It seems as though people had been deterred by an instinctive dread from taking upon themselves the office of administering the Holy Eucharist with the full consciousness of its mysteriousness. It is too awful for man to undertake unbidden; he cannot invest himself with the belief that, in Hooker's words, 'in blessing visible elements' he has the power to 'make them invisible grace,' any more than he can give himself the Commission so to do: man's belief in this awful privilege, so surpassing human thought, must come from above; he can only believe it, when he has solemnly been invested with it. Accordingly where people have acted without this commission there they have unconsciously lowered the doctrine. In the thoughts of many Wesleyans at least, 'means of grace' will signify—not the Holy Eucharist, but their own peculiar discipline, their 'class-meetings' or the 'love-feasts.' They have often lost even the abstract belief, that the Holy Communion is any way more solemn, or attended with more mysterious blessing." [1]

"And so likewise as to other bodies, the further any have departed from the doctrine of the Apostolic Succession, so much the lower has their doctrine of the Sacraments become." [2]

"I do not mean any disparagement to any pious Presbyterians; but believing the Holy Eucharist to be what we in common with the whole ancient Church know It to be, we cannot but know that they who receive It worthily have a much greater closeness of union with our Lord than they who do not. Presbyterians have what they believe—we, what we believe." [3]

The doctrine of the Apostolic Succession is rejected by Presbyterians and others, how is it treated by Roman Catholics?

[1] *Letter to Bishop of Oxford*, p. 160.

[2] *Id.* p. 161.   [3] *Eirenicon*, i. p. 274.

They teach that Mission, Jurisdiction, valid Ordination, all depend on the Bishops of Rome on their succession, and on submission to them. They also deny that the English Church has the Apostolic Succession, and deny that she is a portion of the true Church—that is *the* Catholic Church in England.

Why do they deny this?

"Since there cannot be in the same place two successors of the Apostles, the admission that we have the Apostolical Succession must on principles which they cannot but acknowledge altogether exclude them. Hence it has been observed, 'The objections against the validity of the English ordinations have been almost exclusively devised and employed by the Romanists of England and Ireland; who, having revolted from their own Churches, resorted to every imaginable expedient to establish their new community, *per fas et nefas*, on the ruins of the Church of Christ. The Churches of the Roman Communion were in part deceived by the artifices and falsehoods of these men; but notwithstanding the errors and prejudice which they created, many theologians of that Communion were fully persuaded that our ordinations were valid. Hence also the great displeasure which was excited by Courayer's writing his able defence of our orders. It was objected to him at the time, "It" interposed an obstacle to the conversion of many "English."'"[2]—PALMER *on the Church*, vol. ii. p. 152.

What was Dr. Pusey's opinion of the attacks made by Roman Controversialists on the validity of Anglican Orders?

"On our English ordinations it is enough to refer to the words of Mason, Courayer, Bramhall (with the important additions of the very careful editor, the Rev. A. W. Haddan, *Ang. Cath. Lib.*). I have examined in turn every objection made to them, and it has seemed to me that Roman Catholic controversialists took up easily any objection which might for the moment serve their turn."[2]

"There is absolutely no doubt that our succession is valid, that our Bishops are the successors of those through whom

<hr>

[1] *Letter to Bishop of Oxford*, p. 174.   [2] *Eirenicon*, i. p. 270.

God planted the Gospel here: and so our Church is the appointed channel of God's gifts and the instrument of salvation for us. This is the first question to us, antecedent to anything else without us; no gifts, no helps to devotion, no. holiness, no sympathies, no beauty of system, no truths abroad, no contradictions at home, are any grounds whatever for abandoning the Church in which God has placed us. Nothing can be an adequate ground for any one except a conviction on adequate grounds, patiently tested and over-powering, apart from any cause of excitement that she is not the Church, and that to stay in her, being rent from the Body of Christ, is peril to his soul. I own I do not myself see how any one is to come to this conviction. For myself I am accustomed to dwell upon two tests which are given in the ancient Church. It is to be assumed as an undoubted fact that we have the succession—that if there is any descendant of the ancient British Church (that I mean which God planted here by successors of the Apostles as the instrument of salvation, and the channel of His gifts and Sacraments, and which He continued unto the Reformation): it is our own. (Unless the Church in England expired at once and is no more), ours is that Church—for no other has the line of descent." [1]

"The agents of the Roman Church have 'sought' many 'false witnesses' in order to invalidate our succession and our orders; and when she has 'found none' has resorted to so many frivolous pretences." [2]

"The Apostolical Succession then is not an abstract argument, but a tangible fact, the value of which any plain man can feel. Any one can understand that our Lord promised to be with the Apostles and with their successors to the end of the world, nor do any other even claim to be the successors of the original Bishops of our Church who were ordained by Apostles or Apostolic men, except those who now fill those Sees, the Bishops of the Anglo-Catholic Church. The Romanist Bishops

---

[1] *Letter*, Nov. 3rd, 1845.
[2] *Letter to Bishop of Oxford*, p. 174.

were but of yesterday, nor do they even pretend to be Bishops of our Sees; they assume only to be Bishops *in partibus infidelium* (till 1851); among us they are only the delegates of the Bishop of Rome; and thus they acknowledge themselves schismatics. The Roman Communion in this country has, as well as the Dissenters, separated itself from those who have received their commission from the head of the Church. To quote again the tranquil and learned writer just cited,[1] 'The Romish party in these countries committed schism in separating from the Communion of the Church and the obedience of their legitimate pastors in the reign of Elizabeth. It is certain that during the reign of Henry VIII. and his successors until the eleventh year of Queen Elizabeth's reign there were not two separate Communions and worships in England. All the people were subject to the same pastors, attended the same churches, and received the same Sacraments. It was only about 1570 that the Romish party at the instigation of foreign emissaries separated itself and fell from the Catholic Church of England.' A society formed in this manner by voluntary separation from a Church of Christ was totally cut off from the unity of the Catholic Church, nor is it to be alleged in reply that the new community was recognized by the Roman Bishops and some of the Western Churches; for this only proves that the Roman Bishops encouraged schism, and other Churches were misled by their excessive veneration for the Roman See, and by the misrepresentations of the enemies of the Church of England; therefore their sanction to the new community being given on erroneous information could not afford any justification of it. 'It is evident then that the whole separation or schism was originated and effected by the Roman Pontiffs and their adherents, not by the churches among us. I repeat it as a fact which ought never to be forgotten "that we did not go out from them, but, as the Apostle says, they went out from us." '"[2]

"The Pope indeed sent a titular Bishop to them in 1625,

---

[1] PALMER.   [2] *Letter to Bishop of Oxford*, p. 176.

whose successor went to France in 1629, and returned no more; and up to the present time the Romish community has not had any Bishops; for although the vicars-apostolic (as they call themselves) pretend to the Episcopal character, this character is by no means essential to their office; their successors may be priests or monks, and they have no ordinary power over the English Romanists, being merely deputies of the Roman Pontiff, who may revoke their commissions without any trial at his own will and pleasure. Consequently as vicars-apostolic they have no Episcopal jurisdiction in England, and as titular .Bishops *in partibus infidelium* they have no jurisdiction anywhere. Therefore they are not, properly speaking, Bishops; and the Romanists of England are devoid of any apostolical succession of Bishops, not to speak of some serious difficulties which affect the validity of their orders in these countries, and which will be considered elsewhere."—PALMER, pt. ii. c. 6.

" It was a principle acknowledged by the universal Church, and formally ratified by the Council at Nice, that in one place there could be but one Bishop." "One God, one Christ, one Bishop," was the exclamation of the Roman people when the Emperor proposed to them to have two Bishops to govern the Church in common. "We are not ignorant," says Cornelius to St. Cyprian, "that as there is one God, one Christ the Lord whom we have confessed one Holy Spirit; so there ought to be one Bishop in a Catholic Church." "There can be but one representative of the chief Shepherd in one place." "There can be but one Bishop in a Church at a time, and one judge as viceregent of Christ." "Since there can be no second after the first, whoever is made after him who ought to be alone is not a second Bishop, but is none." Whence the martyr St. Cyprian designates such an appointment as "setting up a profane altar, erecting an adulterous chair, offering sacrilegious sacrifices against the true Priest."[1] "Again then, my lord, the doctrine of the Apostolic Succession, so far from having any connection with Romanism, is a bulwark against it."[2] "The Romanists

---

[1] *Letter to Bishop of Oxford*, p. 178.   [2] *Id.*

account the promises to St. Peter to be confined to their single See; the Anglo-Catholics, with the Primitive Church, that they are inherited by the Bishops universally; Rome has in her corrupt days ever essayed to entrench on the independent authority of Bishops as of Churches; she would have them derive their authority immediately through her existing Bishop, not together with her Bishop from the one Bishop. The doctrine of the Apostolic Succession involves our independence from the undue authority of Rome. Whatever priority of dignity there may be, the Bishop of the smallest city is as much the representative of the chief Bishop as the patriarch of the greatest." [1]

May the charge of irregularity well be retorted on the Roman impugners of Anglican orders ?

Yes indeed. "While four Bishops were carefully warned each to use the consecrating words in the case of Parker, it had been in the occasional practice both of East and West to admit as valid, Consecration by one Bishop. There is a case of a single Consecration in the history of St. Athanasius, another in that of St. Heliodorus, and in the ancient Scot-Irish Church, in spite of the great multitudes of Bishops that were in Ireland, the practice was constant. Nay, even in the case of the Papal See there were tremendous irregularities. If we may believe Luitprandus, John XII. ordained a deacon in a stable; and another of the Popes, Pelagius I., was himself consecrated by two Bishops and a Presbyter, as Anastasius bears witness."

"To charges, moreover of laxity, as to enforcement of Episcopal ordination after the Reformation, as in the well-known case of Whittington, Dean of Durham, and the others who in Elizabeth's time were instituted into benefices; all one can say is, that it was wrong, exceptional, and speedily remedied. But more than that, it was distinctly an inheritance of pre-Reformation times. Benefices and Bishoprics had been held by non-ordained persons: even by children."—BISHOP FORBES *on Articles*, p. 721.

[1] *Letter to Bishop of Oxford*, p. 179.

SACERDOTALISM.

What is popularly understood by the term Sacerdotalism ?

It is a word now chiefly used by Controversialists ; the users imply certain charges, and then protest against those ministers of God whom they have accused.

What are these accusations ?

They say that English clergymen arrogate to themselves Divine Powers.   That they stand as obstacles instead of helps between the soul and God; that they wish to Lord it over God's heritage, to tyrannize over souls, to domineer over conscience.

What is the answer to these charges ?

First, it may be readily granted that, in the Roman Communion for instance, there have been real grounds for these charges being brought, and it may be the case that a few English clergymen have in these days given some occasion for these charges being made.   Granting so much, the accusations are, as they are constantly fashioned, either ignorant or deliberate slanders.

If those who bring these slanders were to push their principles to a logical conclusion, they would be in a most awkward position.   The principles are simply these.   " No man shall stand between me and my Maker," or " I do not require the help of man in anything that concerns my soul and God." This really means " I will settle for myself the Canon of Scripture ; I do not believe in the Holy Catholic Church ; I shall advise persons to Baptize themselves, to Confirm, and Communicate themselves ; even to preach to themselves." In short, the cry of Sacerdotalism, if it means simply a protest against priests arrogating to themselves rights, privileges, authority, prerogatives beyond their due, is quite right.   But, meaning, as it nearly always does, a denial of any authority in the Church, of any ministry of man, duly appointed by Christ Himself, then it is quite wrong.

"What angel in Heaven, said one, not yet emancipated from his Puritan education, yet one who confessed his own sins to the Priest, could have said to man as our Lord did to Peter, 'Feed My sheep, Preach, Baptize, Do this in remembrance of Me? Whose sins ye retain they are retained; and their offences in Heaven pardoned, whose faults you shall on earth forgive.' What think we? Are these terrestrial sounds, or else are they voices uttered out of the clouds above? The power of the ministry of God translateth out of darkness to glory; it raiseth men from the earth and bringeth God Himself down from Heaven; by blessing visible elements it maketh them invisible grace; it giveth daily the Holy Ghost; it hath to dispose of that Flesh which was given for the life of the world, and that Blood which was poured out to redeem souls; when it poureth malediction upon the head of the wicked, they perish; when it revoketh the same, they revive. O wretched blindness, if we admire not so great power; more wretched if we consider it aright, and, notwithstanding, imagine that any but God can bestow it!"[1]—HOOKER, vol. v. 771.

Is this question of Sacerdotalism a very important one?

Very much so. "My own strong conviction is that the issue of the battle in the English Church will depend very mainly on the issue of that which is now waged against that which is called 'Sacerdotalism.' People attach, doubtless, different meanings to the word; but what is really included in its rejection, is the belief of any medium between the soul and God. It involves primarily the rejection of Sacraments, and therein of any absolving power committed to the priesthood; and secondarily, any authority in matters of faith, other than the conscience of each individual, recognizing as true in Holy Scripture what commends itself to its individual judgment."[2]

"The attack has been dexterously begun. 'Sacerdotalism' suggests the idea of human weakness and arbitrariness. People are taught to think that men put the Sacraments in the place

---

[1] *God and Independence*, p. 22.
[2] *Will ye also go, &c.?* Preface, p. iv.

of Christ.   They appeal to men's love for our Divine Redeemer, and forget that the self-same argument may be turned against the mediation of our Lord Himself, as coming between the soul and God.   This has been before now in our own times." [1]

"But men say, there can be no special priests under the Gospel, because St. Peter says of all Christians that they are 'an holy priesthood to offer up Spiritual Sacrifices, acceptable to God by Jesus Christ.'   Would God all Christians knew their calling and obeyed it !   It would be a very different world.   But not a few, I fear, who, to get rid of the belief of any special priesthood under the Gospel, appeal to the universal priesthood of Christians, would be startled at being reminded, that, as Christians, they, one by one, had a portion in our Redeemer's Priesthood ; that they were Priests, and had, as Priests, 'sacrifices' to offer 'acceptable to God by Jesus Christ,' to be offered to Him, in union with the One Adorable Sacrifice.   Imagine one saying to you, one by one, my sons, abruptly but earnestly, 'Thou art a priest, holy through Him Who hallowed thee ; take heed to the Sacrifices which thou hast to offer, that thou neglect them not, that thou offer them not blind, or lame, or maimed, but holy and without blemish as a reasonable service.' " [2]

"Let those who rightly say that all Christians are members of an Holy Priesthood, be careful before they declaim against a special and God-appointed ministry (taken from amongst themselves), that they as Priests offer sacrifices continually—sacrifices of themselves as St. Paul says (Rom. xii. 1), of their alms, of their passions ; above all, the sacrifice of self-denial, and of a broken and contrite heart." [3]

If the Ministers of God are fiercely opposed when sincerely trying to do their duty as stewards of the mysteries of God, what is proved by this opposition ?

That their mission is with power.

"Men set themselves against religion and the religious, the

<hr>

[1] *Will ye also go, &c. ?*   Preface, p. vi.
[2] *God and Independence,* p. 30.   [3] See *Id.* p. 31.

Church or the Priesthood, only when and because they feel their power on God's side against them. What men despise they do not oppose. 'They kill us, they do not despise us,' were true words of a French priest as to 'the reign of reason' in the first French revolution." [1]

What is the Latin heading to Article XXXII. " Of the Marriage of Priests " ?

" De Conjugio Sacerdotum." [2]

Priests then have received a Divine Commission, and the help of the Holy Spirit accompanying their ministrations. What, then, should their conduct be ?

" As regards your commission (the Priesthood) the less you ever speak of it to others, except with all meekness, to warn them of their duty as members of the Church, the more useful will your ministry commonly be. But the more you reflect on it yourselves in a devout, lowly, heart-searching spirit, the better fitted will you be for your holy office—for the more deeply will you be impressed with the vast extent of your obligations, and the woeful deficiency of your performances. Oh, my friends! how precious is the 'treasure we have in these poor miserable earthen vessels!' Can any one of us be proud of its being intrusted to him? Do we not all feel with shame and fear, and deep humiliation our utter unworthiness to bear it?—our utter inability, by our own strength, to use it effectually, to any of the gracious purposes for which it was conferred? Be it our comfort, that one main reason why we have it, is that, 'the excellency of the power may be of God, and not of us.' While therefore you are conscious of your own infirmity, aye, and it may be of negligence, beyond the excuse of mere infirmity, in 'stirring up the gift that is in you by the putting on of hands commissioned by God to bestow it,' still be ye, as the Apostle was, 'troubled' indeed on every side, but not distressed; perplexed but not in despair. Rely on him, His grace is sufficient for ye : for His strength is made perfect in weakness.

[1] *Minor Prophets*, p. 177.   [2] See *Letter, Unlaw*, p. 47.

"I know how reluctant man is to admit or to bear this truth. It is opposed to our natural notions, and, therefore, is assailed on every side. Some think they have effectually disposed of it, by calculating the chances, which, in every particular case, may have broken a link in the chain of succession during the long line of eighteen hundred years, as if God would not sustain His own ordinance, if it be indeed His. Others, and the more numerous class of objectors, taunt us with our want of the sanctifying grace of the Spirit, in proof that we have not 'received the Holy Ghost for the office and work of a Bishop or Priest, in the Church of God'; as if we claimed for the commission that it gives the assurance of internal sanctification. Alas! we know and feel that it does not. We know, that, whatever ought to be its effect on our own hearts, it too often leaves them, through their own hardness, earthly, worldly-minded, unsanctified, as before. But shall God's promise therefore fail? Was that promise made to the minister, or to the office? Was it made for the sake of Him who is ordained, or for their sake towards whom he is to exercise his ministry? To all who call themselves Church-men the Twenty-sixth Article of the Church will give the answer; and will silence, if anything can, the ignorant clamour which calls it forth. They will there read, that 'Forasmuch as in the ministration of the Word and Sacraments, evil ministers do not the same in their own name, but in Christ's, and do minister by His commission and authority, their wicked-ness diminisheth not the grace of God's gifts, the Sacraments, which be effectual, because of Christ's institution and promise, although they be ministered by evil men.'"—*Ordination Sermon*, BISHOP OF EXETER, 1843, p. 28.

Do those priests who are invidiously called Sacerdotalists believe that they are as said, "coming, as they ought not, between souls and God?"

"Priests who believe that God has given authority to the Priest to pronounce forgiveness in His Name, and that He Himself confirms to the penitent what is so pronounced in His

Name, do not think that the Priest comes between them and God and they know that they themselves are wrongly accused of 'substituting the Sacraments for Christ,' *i. e.* the modes of His operation, or in the Holy Eucharist, His Presence for Himself." [1]

Why is it so many persons echo the cry of " Sacerdotalism," and think and assert, that the Priest places himself or the Sacraments as hindrances and obstructions between the soul and God?

Because they do not sufficiently remember that Christ works for souls in His love, in His Church; that " to the true Christian all is Christ, all is full of Christ." " Do not speak then, my brethren, any more (if any of you have) of persons placing this or that instead of Christ, the Church, or the Sacraments, or the Ministers of Christ. 'Who is Paul, and who is Apollos,' says St. Paul, 'but ministers by whom ye believed.' What, again, is the Church but 'the Body of Christ'? What are Sacraments, as our Church teacheth us, but 'means ordained by Christ Himself, whereby we receive the inward grace' and presence of Christ? How can any place the means of receiving Christ 'instead of Christ' when his very hope is to receive thereby the grace of Christ and Christ Himself, the author of grace? What is Baptism but that whereby 'we put on Christ'? What says St. Paul of the Holy Eucharist? 'The cup which we bless, is it not the Communion of, or communication of, the Blood of Christ? The Bread which we break is it not the Communion of the Body of Christ?'" [2]

Is it not true that the more God in His love does for us, the less some people believe and appreciate what He does for them in His love?

Yes. "They stumble at His Wisdom in ordering His own Creation; at His Holiness in punishing sin; but most of all they stumble at His Goodness and condescension. They have a greater quarrel with His condescension than with all His other attributes. They have stumbled and still stumble at God the Son becoming Man, and taking our

---

[1] See *Eirenicon,* i. p. 410.　　　[2] Vol. ii. p. 383.

flesh in the Virgin's womb ; they stumble at the humility of the Crucifixion ; they stumble at His placing His Manhood at the Right Hand of God ; they stumble at the simplicity, power and condescension, which He uses in the Sacraments ; they stumble at His giving us His Flesh to eat ; they stumble at His forgiving sins freely ; and again and again, they stumble at His making us members of Himself, without waiting for our own wills ; they stumble at His condescension in using our own acts, to the attainment of our degree of everlasting glory." [1]

" It is the overwhelmingness of God's condescension at which His creatures rebel. They would allow God, had He so willed, to help them after their own fashion, to give them faculties whereby they might know of Him what they wished. But that God should be so very nigh to man, that He should become one with man, that He should not abhor the Virgin's womb, that He Who is and was God should die for man, the pride of man staggers at the humility of God." [2]

" He chooses to carry on to us, through men like ourselves, the blessings which He gave to us in 'His Son, made after the likeness of our sinful flesh '; and as in the regeneration, or renewal of all things at the end of all, 'when the Son of Man shall sit in the Throne of His Glory,' they also (He tells them) 'shall sit on twelve thrones, judging the twelve tribes of Israel.' 'So did He join them to Him in the present work of the regeneration of the world.' Jesus, God-Man Himself, is the chief corner-stone, and in Him the whole building is fitly joined together. Yet St. Paul saith, He built us 'on the foundation of the Apostles and Prophets,' so 'to grow unto an holy temple in the Lord.' Them He made as 'pillars' of His Church their names—'the names of the twelve Apostles of the Lamb' He placed 'in the twelve foundations of the wall' of the Holy City, 'the holy Jerusalem,' that great city which descended out of Heaven from God, having the glory of God, 'even the Church of God.'" [3]

<hr>

[1] *Minor Prophets*, p. 93. [2] Vol. 1872, p. 138.

[3] Vol. iii. p. 394.

Whatever grace my soul receives through the ministrations of God's Priests for its spiritual good, Who is the Giver and Doer of such good ?

"Jesus. What is done in His name, He is the Doer of it. Man, as we know, visibly poureth water on the child or adult in the name of the Holy Trinity; man placeth his hand on the person to be confirmed, or on the penitent, or on the oblations with the words of Consecration, 'This is My Body,' 'This is My Blood,' and Jesus Baptizes with the Holy Ghost; Jesus forgiveth the sins of the penitent, and washes them away in His Own Blood. Jesus makes the elements of this world His Body and Blood." [1]

LIDDON'S *Sermon : ' Sacerdotalism.'*

LAITY IN SYNODS.

In these days when so many are wishing to do away with all idea of Church authority, or of a Church ministry, what assertion is frequently attempted ?

The attempt is constantly being made, to make out that all Christians, or indeed all persons, have an equal right and voice in the government and work of the Church.

In what particular way is this shown ?

In the endeavour to prove that there should be no such thing as a purely clerical synod, but that all laymen have an equal right with the clergy to be present, discuss, and vote.

What is the answer to the claim ?

There is no objection to the legitimate and formal expression of the mind of the faithful laity on questions affecting the spiritual or temporal interests of the Church. By books, letters, conferences, congresses, petitions; in all sorts of ways the laity can make themselves heard, and their influence felt.

But it is contrary to Church principles and practice that laymen be admitted on equal terms with equal rights along with the clerical members of a Church synod.

"I can but say, as the result of a long and careful study,

[1] *Eleven Addresses*, p. 61.

that the records of the primitive ages completely refute the notion that either the laity were constituent members of synods, or that the consent of the laity was necessary to the obligation of the spiritual laws by which they were bound. I have searched through the records of five centuries, and have not found a single instance in proof of either assertion."

Laymen were present in (or rather at) synods for many purposes; as learners or spectators, as witnesses to give evidence, as prosecutors to make complaints; occasionally perhaps as advocates; as officials to keep order at the command of the Emperors. But in these cases they were present as State officers, not as laymen, and (as at the Council of Chalcedon) were carefully distinguished from the synod itself. Sometimes, also, they were present, of course in their civil capacity, to add the sanction of temporal law to the spiritual law of the Church; but as constituent members of the councils, or as representatives of a lay order adding anything to their spiritual authority—*never*.

"I speak of danger because there is danger. It is true that we can place laymen in synods, but we cannot give them any authority in the Church; they can hamper the action if the synod pleases to allow it; but they can add nothing to its power. As a layman myself, I am not afraid to speak out; for though I am jealous enough for the real rights of my order, I think I know what their limits are. The laity have enormous influence—that is their right; authority in the Church in spiritual things they have none. The ancient Church knew nothing of it; Christ did not give it them, and nothing short of a revelation can give it them now. Setting aside, then, as we must do, the consideration of the imperial action in respect to synods as useless and unprofitable both in principle and in fact (for if admitted it would prove nothing to the present purpose); we find as the result of the inquiry now completed not one instance of constituent lay member-ship in synods, nor *à fortiori* of the laity having any co-ordinate authority there. If then the admission of the laity to ecclesiastical synods with rights of membership and co-ordinate votes is to be introduced among us, which God forbid; it must be done on grounds alien from the principles of antiquity, and diametrically contradictory to its invariable practice."—J. W. LEE *on Laity in Synods,* p. 49.

Is it from any jealous, narrow, hostile spirit that the Laity are not admitted into synods of the Church with co-ordinate authority with other members?

"God forbid! They are in some sense the very life of the Church. We cannot do without their hearty co-operation in all matters of spiritual interest; we want their confidence, their prayers, their wisdom, their counsel, their practical sagacity, their prudence, energy, and active sympathy; but we want above all the good Spirit of God to bind all orders and degrees together in truer love and holier unity, that whatever the future may have in store for us we may be ready, and that the one body being fulfilled with the One Holy Spirit may more and more increase, edifying itself in love until we all attain to the measure of the stature of the fulness of Christ."— J. W. LEA, p. 58.

How were matters of doctrine decided or attested in the early Church?

"Matters of doctrine were always exclusively decided or attested by those whom the Apostles left to succeed to such portion of their office, as uninspired men could discharge—the Bishops of the Universal Church." [1]

"The laity were present as witnesses, not even as Jury, much less as Judge." [2]

"To sum up: St. Cyprian states without hesitation and in the most varied ways, that the entire spiritual authority in the Church of Christ had been given by Christ Himself to the Bishops. Every principle, whether of doctrine or discipline, was laid down by the Bishops exclusively." [3]

Are there any plain proofs that the Laity did sit in synods with co-ordinate authority with the Bishops?

---

[1] *Councils,* Preface, p. xiii.   [2] *Id.* p. 83.   [3] *Id.* p. 89.

"The amount of evidence that Bishops alone had a definite voice in synods, is, throughout the history of the Church, in proportion to the detail in which the account of those synods is given. The evidence must in its own nature be incidental. No one questioned them; the Bishops alone had that definite voice. No one, then, went about to prove it. The word Synod by the very force of the term meant the Council of Bishops.[1]

"Testimonies have already been given during the period of the six first general councils, and far down into the ninth century (A.D. 889). That on the one hand those laymen who had most influence in the Church, the Christian Emperors, wholly disclaimed having any voice in matters of faith, and that the Bishops on the other hand, during that earlier period, spoke of decisions in matters of faith as intrusted to themselves by God."[2]

THE ANOINTING OF THE SICK.

Does the Church of England forbid the Anointing of the Sick?

"There is nothing to hinder the revival of the Apostolic and Scriptural Custom of Anointing the sick whensoever any devout person may desire it. It is indeed difficult to say on what principle it could be refused."—BISHOP FORBES *on the Articles*, p. 474.

In the Preface to the Prayer-book we are told, "For we are fully persuaded in our judgments (and we here profess it to the world) that the Book, as it stood before established by Law, doth not contain in it anything contrary to the Word of God, or to sound Doctrine, or which a godly man may not with a good Conscience use and submit unto, or which is not fairly defensible against any that shall oppose the same."

This Book was declared, as we have noticed above, to be

---

[1] *Councils*, p. 34.   [2] *Id.* p. 35.

agreeable to the Word of God and the Primitive Church.—
II. Act of Uniformity, Ed. VI.

The Ornaments' Rubric says that such Ornaments of the Church and of the Ministers thereof, at all times of their Ministration, shall be retained and be in use as were in this Church of England by the Authority of Parliament, in the second year of the reign of King Edward the Sixth.

A Vessel to hold holy oil to be used for the anointing of the sick was one of the Ornaments here referred to.

Moreover, in Canon XXX. the Church of England declares she retains with reverence those ceremonies which do neither endamage the Church of God, nor offend the minds of sober men.

What is the form for the Anointing of the Sick in the first Prayer-book of Edward VI.?

The English Church even in the unhappy time towards the close of the reign of Edward VI., virtually sanctioned it. The first Prayer-book in his reign had a special Prayer for "the Anointing of the Sick" with this direction—

"If the sick person desire to be anointed, then shall the Priest anoint him on the forehead or breast only, making the sign of the cross, saying thus—

"As with this visible oil thy body outwardly is anointed, so our Heavenly Father, Almighty God, grant of His Infinite Goodness that thy soul inwardly may be anointed with the Holy Ghost, Who is the Spirit of all strength, comfort, relief, and gladness. And vouchsafe for His great mercy (if it be His blessed will) to restore unto thee thy bodily health and strength to serve Him, and send thee release of all thy pains, troubles, and diseases both in body and mind. And howsoever His goodness (by His Divine and unsearchable Providence) shall dispose of thee; we, His unworthy ministers and servants, humbly beseech the eternal Majesty, to do with thee according to the multitude of His innumerable mercies, and to pardon thee all thy sins and offences committed by all thy bodily senses, passions, and carnal affections; Who also vouchsafe mercifully to grant unto thee ghostly strength by His Holy Spirit, to withstand and overcome all temptations and assaults of thine adversary, that in no wise he prevail against thee, but that thou mayest have perfect victory and triumph against the devil, sin, and death; through Christ our Lord, Who by His death hath overcome the Prince of Death, and with the Father and the Holy Ghost evermore liveth and reigneth God, world without end. Amen."

"This Prayer-book was declared by the Parliament to have been written 'by the aid of the Holy Ghost.' The statement so often quoted from the Act for substituting 'the second book,' that the first was a 'very godly order, agreeable to the Word of God and the primitive Church,' and that the doubts raised about 'it were rather by the curiosity of the minister and mistakers, than of any other worthy cause, shows that, even in those evil times, no slur was ever cast upon the Scriptural practice of anointing the sick."[1]

Is this the " Unction of the Sick" which seems to be rejected in Article XXV.?

No; it is "Extreme Unction" which is mentioned there. The prayer beseeches God to restore the sick person to his bodily health.

As may be seen in their Manuals of Instruction, Roman Catholics though praying for the recovery of the sick, yet practically reserve the administration of the Sacrament of Unction to cases where recovery seems unlikely, which practice certainly does not seem according to the Scriptures (James v. 14, 15). Their Manuals teach that the Sacrament of Extreme Unction is to be given where there is *"danger of death in sickness."*

"Had the Roman Church adhered to the Catholic practice following strictly the directions of St. James, we could never have had the mention of 'the corrupt following of the Apostles,' for that language relates to the then custom not to anoint the sick until they were 'in extremis,' so that the Council of

____
[1] *Eirenicon,* i. p. 222.

Trent had to provide, that, 'if the sick should recover after receiving this Unction, they may again be aided by the succour of this Sacrament when they should come into a like peril of life.' " [1]

The Article XXV. plainly means by the "corrupt following of the Apostles," "that what St. James directed with a view (at least in part) to the restoration of health, was administered only when in man's sight such restoration was impossible." Had they in the Roman Church retained the practice, as the Greek Church retains it, we should doubtless have retained it also.

Give a simple statement of what Anointing the Sick is.

"Unction with oil is a mystery, in which while the body is anointed with oil, God's Grace is invoked on the Sick to heal him of spiritual and bodily infirmities." [1]—*Statement in Russian Catechism.*

(KEMP on the *Unction of the Sick ; Pamphlet* by W. CROUCH.)

THE BLESSED VIRGIN MARY.

"Ave Maria ! Thou whose name
All but adoring love may claim."

JOHN KEBLE.

Why do we speak of St. Mary as " The Blessed Virgin " ?

There are certainly two and all-sufficient reasons. First, because the Angel Gabriel addressed her as " highly favoured ; the Lord is with thee, and blessed art thou among women." Again he tells her, " Thou hast found favour with God, and the Holy Ghost shall come upon thee, and the power of the Highest overshadow thee. Therefore, also, that Holy thing which shall be born of thee shall be called the Son of God." She is then declared to be blessed among women by the angel; and must be blessed, indeed, among and above all women, above all souls, and all creation under God, as the Mother of our Lord and Saviour Christ.

[1] *Eirenicon,* i. p. 219. [2] *Id.* p. 227.

Being then the Mother of our Lord Jesus Christ, what sublime title has been truthfully and reverently given to her?

"'The Mother of God.' The doctrine expressed by that great title 'Theotokos' is a matter of faith, an essential part of the doctrine of the Incarnation."[1]

Do not some persons object and protest against this title?

Yes; and their objection springs from their misbelief, or disbelief, in the doctrine of the Incarnation of the Son of God.

How so?

As the "Te Deum" expresses it: Christ, the King of glory; the everlasting Son of the Father; when He took upon Him to deliver man, He did not abhor the Virgin's womb. As Article II. expresses it—"The Son, which is The Word of the Father, begotten from everlasting of The Father, the Very and Eternal God, and of one substance with the Father, took man's nature in the womb of the Blessed Virgin of her substance, so that two whole and perfect natures, that is to say the Godhead and manhood, were joined together in One Person never to be divided."

Our Blessed Lord is a Divine Person from all eternity, and when He became Incarnate He did not cease to be the person He was before; for then He could not have said, "Before Abraham was, I am." The nature He took of the substance of His Mother was human; He who took it—the Person who was born—was Divine.

"It would of course be absurdity, heresy, and blasphemy, to say that the Virgin was the Mother of our Lord's Godhead, implying that The Eternal had no existence till born of her; but the Human Nature which God the Son, by the operation of the Holy Ghost, assumed of her substance, was so united to the Divinity that the Person born of the Virgin was God as well as man."—*See* BLUNT'S *Dictionary; Article,* "*Theotokos.*"

The Catholic doctrine is this—Jesus, who is God the Son, decreed from all eternity to take our Nature upon Him, and to be born of a pure Virgin.

---

[1] *Eirenicon,* pt. ii. p. 21.

This, the Incarnation of the Son of God, took place by the operation of the Holy Spirit, and He was made very Man of the substance of the Virgin Mary. He was born of her, and so He became her Son, and so she became His mother. To say that the title "Mother of God" may not be given to the Virgin, is to say that He who took human nature of her substance and was born of her was not God.

If by the operation of the Holy Ghost, the Blessed Virgin only became the mother of a good and holy man, then God is not our Saviour; the Jews did not crucify the Son of God; we are yet in our sins, and the whole world unredeemed.

But thanks be to God for ever and for ever, "the Son of Mary is not a distinct human person mysteriously linked with the Divine Nature of the Eternal Word."—LIDDON's *Bampton Lectures*, chap. v.

Isaiah xlix. 26: "All flesh shall know that I the Lord am thy Saviour and thy Redeemer, the mighty One of Jacob."

Isaiah vii. 14: "Behold, a Virgin shall conceive, and bear a Son, and shall call His name Emmanuel: God with us."

What of the objection that Jael, the wife of Heber, who killed Sisera, was declared to be blessed among women?

Except that such an objection has been made, and is often repeated by serious persons, the absurdity and irreverence of it would deprive it of all claims to notice; the Virgin's transcendent honour was prophesied long before her birth.

Jael killed a man in his sleep, and thereby rid a country of its oppressor, after his army had been routed and himself worn out in flying for his life.

The Virgin bare Him who is the Saviour of the whole world, the Healer of the nations, the Prince of Peace.

Did not our Lord Himself say: "That they who hear the Word of God and keep it, are blessed, rather than his own Mother"? (Luke xi. 27).

Yes; and no doubt the greatest privileges bear with them the greatest responsibilities. The twelve Apostles were specially blessed by our Lord; they were to sit on twelve

thrones with Him. Yet one, Judas, fell and lost his blessing.
The Virgin did not only have the glorious ineffable honour of
being our Lord's Mother, but she also did most humbly and
faithfully ever hear the Word of God and keep it (Luke i. 45;
ii. 19—51).

And to the end of Her Son's suffering life on earth she was
faithful, and was found at the foot of the Cross. So she had
the blessing that all faithful disciples have, and being also the
Mother of our Lord, and never speaking or acting so as to
forfeit the blessing of that sublime honour and privilege, truly
she was, is, and ever will be "Blessed indeed among women."

"For God in all eternity pre-ordained her who was to be
Theotokos, or the Mother of God; He endowed her with all
those qualities with which it was fitting she should be endowed.
God raised her to a nearness to Himself above all choirs
of Angels or Archangels, dominions or powers; above the
Cherubim who seems so near to God; above the Seraphims
with their burning love, close to His Throne."[1]

"It is self-evident that she stood single and alone in all
creation, in all possible Creations, in that in Her womb, He
who in His Godhead is substantial with the Father, deigned
as to His Human Body to become consubstantial with her."[2]

Blessed indeed among women!

How does the Church of England honour the Blessed Virgin?

On February 2nd she commemorates the Presentation of
Christ in the Temple, a Festival commonly called the
Purification of the Virgin.

March 25th: The Festival of the Annunciation of the
Blessed Virgin Mary.

In the Calendar on July 2nd, she has the Visitation of the
Blessed Virgin Mary; on September 8th, the Nativity of the
Blessed Virgin Mary. In the table of lessons for Holy days,
"The Annunciation of our Lady"; the *Magnificat* is in the
daily Evensong.

In Article II. "The Blessed Virgin."

---

[1] *Eirenicon,* ii. p. 24.   [2] *Id.* p. 24.

In the Homily for Whitsun Day she is spoken of as the "Blessed Virgin."

In the Homily on Obedience, "the Holy and Blessed Virgin Mary" is set forth as an example of obedience.

In the Homily on the right use of the Church, "the Blessed Virgin Mary" is quoted as an example of zeal and fervency in Divine worship.

In the Homily on Repentance, pt. i., "took our nature of the undefiled substance of the Blessed Virgin."

In the Homily against Peril of Idolatry, after saying that the greater the opinion is of the majesty and holiness of the person to whom the image is made—to images of God our Saviour Christ, the "Blessed Virgin Mary" is mentioned.

In the Sermon on the Nativity she is called "the Blessed Virgin."

In the Homily against Wilful Rebellion, pt. ii., "the excellent example of the Blessed Virgin Mary" is set forth, saying also "that in comparison with her, *we are most base and vile.*"

How does the good old Puritan, Bishop Hall, speak of the Virgin?

"Blessed Mary! he does not honour Thee too much, who maketh not a Goddess of Thee."—Quoted from BISHOP FORBES *on Nicene Creed*, p. 194.

How does Bishop Pearson speak of the Virgin?

"What expressions of honour and admiration can we think sufficient now that Christ is in Heaven and that Mother with Him! We cannot bear too reverent a regard unto the Mother of our Lord, so long as we give her not that worship which is due unto the Lord Himself. Let us keep the language of the Primitive Church. Let her be honoured and esteemed; let Him be worshipped and adored."

Give a proof that English Catholics revere the Mother of Our Lord as much as any, yet hold not unscriptural ideas about her?

"She was Mother of our Redeemer, and so from her as the fountain of His human Birth, came all which He did, and was, and is to us.   She, being the Mother of Him who is our Life, became the Mother of Life; she was the gate of Paradise, because she bore Him who restored to us our lost Paradise; she was 'The gate of Heaven,' because He, born of her, 'opened the Kingdom of Heaven to all believers'; she was 'the all undefiled Mother of holiness,' because 'the Holy One, born of her, was called the Son of God'; she was 'the light-clad Mother of Light,' because He who indwelt her and was born of her, 'was the true Light which lighteth every man that cometh into the World.'"[1]

"And where is she?   What has been cannot cease to be. She who was the Mother of God-Man here must be His Mother still.   Little were it to be Queen of Angels.   *The* special bliss must be the special love of the human Mother and the Divine Son."[2]

Should we think of the Blessed Virgin as above all the Angels, above all Saints, above all the Company of Heaven, and closest to the throne of God?

It is not an Article of faith that the Blessed Virgin is in the Highest Heaven now, but whatever Paradise is, wherever She and the Saints of God are now, She surely must be chief and brightest of all.   And after the great Day of Judgment, all who love Jesus must expect now, as a matter of course, to see her then far above all, who will rejoice for ever in God their Saviour.

" Who is she, on whom those Divine eyes, radiant with His Godhead, which survey all things in Heaven and on earth, must rest with an especial love, with the love of a Son to His Mother?   What must be the love and humility of that highest being of the heavenly Hierarchy, whether it be St. Michael or any of the Seraphim, belonging to those ranks which never fell, that he adores the condescension of God, not only in taking into Himself our Nature, but in placing nearest to Himself the God-Man, His purely human Mother above himself, above every possible creature!   For, grand and

____
[1] *Lenten Sermons,* p. 126.   [2] *Id.* p. 127.

magnificent and highly-endowed as may be any the highest creature which God could create, none could have the nearness of her, the Mother of God." [1]

" Plainly we could not love too much her from whom Jesus vouchsafed to receive a mother's care, who loved Him, the All-Holy, and her Redeemer too, as no other mother could love her Son, whom He loved with a Divine, but also with Deified human love ; love with which no other son could love his mother. The love of the Mother and Son, were essentially different from all other love, because He was her Son after the Flesh, but also Almighty God. And that same love must continue on now, only that her God-enabled power of love, in the beatific vision of His Godhead, must be unspeakably intensified." [2]

Do not some persons object to the true Catholic doctrine relating to the Blessed Virgin ?

Alas ! " There is a diseased dread of any reverent mention of her who was taught by the Holy Ghost to say, ' All generations shall call me blessed,' which threatens very serious evil, and even heresy. For the thought of her is inseparable from meditation on the true doctrine of the Incarnation that our Lord was 'God, of the substance of His Father, before the world, and Man of the substance of His Mother, born in the world.' To deny the word Theotokos, is, of course, heresy ; to shrink from it then, is to be ashamed of the truth of God ; to shrink from dwelling on the doctrine conveyed in it, that He 'abhorred not the Virgin's womb,' is secretly to have entertained some heretical counterfeit." [3]

Is it lawful and right in any way for Christians to honour or worship, the Virgin, as they do God, or to pray to her, as they should do to God only ?

It would be a terrible sin to do so.

But do not Roman Catholics worship the Virgin ?

They deny that they do worship her, as they do God ; they

---

[1] *Eleven Addresses*, p. 26.

[2] *Eirenicon*, ii. p. 412.   [3] *Preface to Awill on Advent*, p. lx.

say that it is a lower kind of worship which they give to her, and not the highest, which they say is due to God only.

Why then is the charge of Mariolatry brought against Roman Catholics?

Because, as a matter of *fact*, they *do* use prayers and expressions, in their devotions to the Virgin, which ought only to be addressed to God.

How then do they refute the charge of paying Divine worship to the Virgin?

By saying that whatever may be the words they use, they do not, in using them, *mean* to address the Virgin as they do God.

What danger to the soul results from all this?

There is a continual unconscious injury to faith in our Lord God and Saviour.

How is this?

Plainly, if the Virgin is constantly appealed to in the very same style and language as when addressing Our Lord; plainly if she is constantly asked to do or grant things which God alone can do or grant, injury to faith must result.

"What is any one's God but that from which he seeks his *good?*"[1]

If you were continually to address any person in a subordinate position, in the same terms of honour as you do his Master, then your feeling of honour towards the Master must be lessened. If the Virgin, a glorious created being, be addressed in the *same* way as Our Lord is addressed, then the truth of Our Lord being God and Man must be obscured.

But is it true that the Blessed Virgin is prayed to by Roman Catholics, in a way which seems lawful only when addressing God?

Quite true. The proofs are sadly numerous. The simplest reference is to Liguori's *Glories of Mary*, as quoted in Dr. Pusey's Sermon, "*The Rule of Faith*." Liguori has been raised to the rank of Doctor of the Church, and his teaching formally approved and sanctioned. The quotations given from his

[1] *Occasional Sermons: " Seek God," p. 35.*

work by Dr. Pusey may-be relied upon.　First, because Dr. Pusey was always most laborious and painstaking in the composition of all he published, and when his quotations in the first edition of this sermon were impugned by a Roman Catholic controversialist, he again verified them.　Secondly, this verification of the quotations was lost, and he *verified them again !*—using the Redemptorist edition published with the imprimatur of Cardinals Wiseman and Manning.

Suppose it be objected that we must not judge the Roman Communion in this matter by quoting from foreign writers or from ecstatic writings of Saints ?

The extravagant unscriptural addresses to the Virgin are to be found in Manuals printed and published in England.

Give an instance or two, where the Blessed Virgin is mentioned in the same terms as our Lord.

" O God, who by the Holy Family of the Incarnate Word, has consecrated the whole earth, and hast in Jesu, Mary, and Joseph, given to us the pattern of Holy living, grant that we, who by this *blessed three* implore of Thee the grace of holy living, may together with the Angels come to praise Thee in Heaven . . ."—*Catholic Vade Mecum*, p. 267.

" We cannot in a more proper and agreeable manner show our devotion to the Sacred Heart of the Son, than by dedicating some part of the *said* devotion to the ever pure heart of the Mother."—*Devotion and Office of the Sacred Heart*, p. 167. DUFFY, 1855.

" O Eternal Father, for the most precious blood of Jesus, *and* for the most bitter dolours of Mary, have pity and compassion upon the souls in purgatory."—*The Golden Manual*, p. 547.

Extravagant and unscriptural devotion to the Virgin such as we have been instancing, seems sanctioned by the highest authority acknowledged in the Roman Communion.

Pope Gregory XVI., in an Encyclical Letter, addressed in 1832, " to Patriarchs, Primates, Archbishops, and Bishops of the whole Catholic World," says—

"We address you on this most joyful day (Aug. 15th, the Festival of the Assumption of the Blessed Virgin) . . . that she, who we have well proved our patroness and deliverer in the greatest calamities, may assist us with her favour while We write to you, and by her *heavenly inspiration* may lead our mind into such counsels as may best conduce to the well-being of the flock of Christ."

In the Encyclical of Pope Pius IX. respecting the proposed decree of the Immaculate Conception of the Blessed Virgin, bearing date February 2nd, 1849, we read as follows—

" From our earliest years We have reckoned nothing more dear to us or more excellent than to honour the most Blessed Virgin Mary with singular piety and devotion, and with the inmost affection of Our heart, and to do whatever seemed to Us calculated to contribute to her greater glory and praise, and to the extension of her worship. For you know perfectly, Venerable Brethren, that *all our ground of confidence* rests on the most holy Virgin, forasmuch as God has placed the fulness of all good in Mary, so that if there is in us any hope, any grace, *any salvation, we know that it flows from her*, because such is the will of Him Who has willed that we should have *all things through* Mary."

Pope Pius IX. in his decree, defining the doctrine of the Immaculate Conception of the Blessed Virgin, says—" We rest our most certain hope, and certain confidence, that it will be that the most Blessed Virgih—(who all beautiful and Immaculate)—bruised the poisonous head of the most cruel serpent, and brought Salvation to the world; Who is also the glory of the Apostles and Prophets, and the honour of Martyrs and of all the Saints the joy and crown; who also being the *safest* refuge of all in peril, and most faithful helper, and the most powerful mediatress and reconciless (conciliatrix) of the whole world *with* her only begotten Son, and the most illustrious glory and ornament and most firm protection of the Holy Church, ever slew all heresies, and delivered the faithful people and nations from the greatest calamities of all sorts, and has freed us too from so many gathering perils, will by her most mighty patronage effect that the holy mother, the Catholic Church, all difficulties removed and all errors dispersed, may throughout all nations and all places daily more thrive, flourish, and reign from sea to sea, and from the rivers to the ends of the earth, so that the guilty may obtain pardon, the sick healing, the faint-hearted strength, the afflicted consolation, the imperilled help, and all in error the darkness of mind being dispersed, may return to the way of truth, and there be one fold and one Shepherd. Let all the sons of the Catholic Church most dear to us, hear these our words, and *with a yet more ardent zeal* of piety, religion, and love, continue to worship, invoke, pray, the most blessed Mother of God, the Virgin Mary, conceived without original stain, and to flee unto this sweet Mother of mercy and *grace*, in all perils, distresses, necessities, and doubtful and anxious circumstances. For nothing is to be feared, nothing despaired of, when she is the Captain, she the Author, she propitious, she protecting, who, bearing a motherly mind towards us, *and having in hand the affairs of our salvation*, is anxious about the whole human race, and having been made by the Lord, Queen of Heaven and earth, and exalted above all the orders of Angels and Saints, standing at the Right Hand of her only begotten Son, our Lord Jesus Christ, does by her Mother's prayers, most potently impetrate and find what she seeks, and cannot be frustrated."

The office and work of our Lord, and of the Holy Ghost, seemingly attributed to her thus—

" Negotiate our peace."

" Loosen the sinner's bands."

" Make us mild and chaste."

" Guard us in our way."

" Heart of Mary, *infuse* into my heart charity, mercy, and the love of peace."

" The advocate of mankind in Heaven."

" Mediatrix with the eternal Godhead."

" All our joys do flow from Mary."

" And for us His wrath appeasing."

" Sweet heart of Mary, be my salvation."

It is taught that God the Holy Ghost has communicated to Mary His faithful spouse, His unspeakable gifts, and has chosen her for dispenser of all that He possesses. All His gifts and graces to be distributed amongst souls at her discretion ; such gifts to men to pass through her hands only.

" No one can look uncontroversially at such occasional addresses as there are to martyrs in the fourth century (and those chief prayers at their tombs through their intercession or miraculous aid of God), and such books as *The Glories of Mary, The Month of Mary*, and say that the character of the modern reliance on and invocation of Saints was that of the ancient Church. No one could (it should be thought) observe how through volumes of St. Augustine or St. Chrysostom, there is no mention of any reliance except on Christ alone, and how, in modern books, St. Mary is held out as ' the refuge of sinners ' as having ' the goats committed to her, as Christ, the sheep,' as the throne of grace, to whom a sinner may have easier access than to Christ, and seriously say that the ancient and modern teaching and practice are the same. We could preach whole volumes of the sermons of St. Augustine or St. Chrysostom to our people to their edification and without offence : were a Roman Catholic preacher to confine himself to their preaching he would (it has been said among themselves) be regarded as indevout towards St. Mary, ' as ' one whose religion was more of the head than of the heart."[1]

The fact is plain, that in the Roman Communion, devotion to the Blessed Virgin has become unscriptural and wrong, and therefore injurious to the faith and to the honour of God.

But while we feel this to be the case, we must try in all charity to think that the Roman Catholics when they address the Virgin as they do God, do not mean to ascribe to her the attributes, powers, prerogatives of the Most High, but next to

---

[1] *Paradise of the Christian Soul*, Preface, p. ix.

the doctrine of Papal Infallibility "the vast system as to the Blessed Virgin is the special 'crux' of the Roman system to all of us. It is impossible to condense the statements of a doctrine which presents itself in so many startling forms, coextensive with the present office of our dear Lord to us." [1]

And it must not be forgotten that in the Roman Communion itself there have been very strong complaints of the extravagant addresses to the Virgin. In the sixteenth century a book appeared entitled, *Wholesome Advice of the Blessed Virgin to her Indiscreet Worshippers*. It was published in Paris, and was translated into English and published in London, 1687. Many of the popular modern addresses to the Virgin as quoted in Dr. Pusey's sermon, *The Rule of Faith*, and in his *Eirenicon*, are condemned in it. But this book itself was condemned in Rome.

See SCUDAMORE'S *Letters to a Seceder*, p. 74, *Appendix* K.

What are we to think of the doctrine of the Immaculate Conception of the Blessed Virgin?

This doctrine is to the effect that from the very first moment of the conception of the Virgin in the womb of her mother, she, the Virgin, was, by the grace of God, preserved free from original sin. The Church of England does not teach this doctrine ; she teaches as in her Article XV., that Christ alone is without sin, and not so "all we the rest."

Whether the Virgin was conceived in sin or not, she teaches that Christ was made very man of her substance, and that without spot of sin. And that He took upon Him our frail nature in the Blessed Virgin's womb, and that of her undefiled substance. "That He was born of a pure Virgin."—*Homily on Repentance*, pt. i.

Without less veneration to the Mother of our Lord than any Communion in Christendom, she is content with the declaration of the Angel Gabriel to the Holy Virgin, "Hail! thou that art highly favoured. The Lord is with thee. Blessed art thou among women. The Holy Ghost shall come upon thee, and

[1] *Eirenicon*, pt. i. p. 101.

P

the power of the Highest shall overshadow thee ; therefore also that Holy Thing which shall be born of thee shall be called the Son of God."

EVER VIRGIN.

Is it to be believed that St. Mary, being at once Mother of the Lord Jesus, and yet a Virgin, she continued for ever in the same Virginity according to the tradition of the Fathers, and the constant belief of the Church?

It is difficult to understand how any faithful, reverent mind can possibly think otherwise. All devout persons would ever think of her as a consecrated vessel, holy unto the Lord. The peculiar eminency and unparalleled privilege of that Mother; the special honour and reverence due unto that Son, and ever paid by her; the regard of that Holy Ghost who came upon her, and the power of the Highest which overshadowed her; the singular goodness and piety of Joseph to whom she was espoused, have persuaded the Church of God in all ages to believe that she still continued in the same Virginity, and therefore is to be acknowledged as the Ever Virgin Mary. As if the gate of the sanctuary in the Prophet Ezekiel were to be understood of her, " This gate shall be shut, it shall not be opened, and no man shall enter by it ; because the Lord, the God of Israel, hath entered in by it, therefore shall it be shut." —Bishop Pearson *on the Creed.*

No one can doubt that St. Joseph was told of the appearance of Gabriel to St. Mary, and that he knew all the wondrous message by the Angel. He had four warnings by the Angel of the Lord concerning the conception and the care of the Holy Child. In the first vision being told that the Virgin had conceived by the operation of the Holy Ghost.

We are not to credit St. Joseph with less reverence than Elizabeth, who, when filled with the Holy Ghost, said to the Holy Virgin, " Whence is this, that the Mother of my Lord should come to me ? " Knowing as St. Joseph did, the declaration that the Holy Thing born of the Virgin was the Son of God, it is impossible for any reverent mind to think of him, but as ever the chaste guardian of the Holy Virgin to whom he was espoused.

It has been remarked that after the Birth of our Lord, Holy Scripture always speaks of the " Young Child and His Mother," never to St. Joseph of "thy wife."—STIER *on the Angels,* chapter i.

THE ROMAN CLAIMS.

INFALLIBILITY.

Is the controversy with Roman Catholics a much simpler thing than it used to be ?

Yes; it is now narrowed to a simple issue, namely, the position and office of the Pope.

Was Papal infallibility always an article of faith in the Roman Communion ?

It did not become so till quite recently, that is, in 1870.

Give a few plain proofs that English Roman Catholics did not believe in the doctrine of the Pope's infallibility up to that date.

" It is not an Article of the Catholic Faith, nor are we thereby required to believe that the Pope is infallible." See *Pastoral Address to the Clergy and Roman Catholic Laity, Ireland,* 1826.

Must not Catholics believe the Pope in himself to be infallible ?

" This is a Protestant invention, and it is no Article of the Catholic Faith. No decision of his can oblige under pain of heresy, unless it be received by the teaching body—that is, by the Bishops of the Church."—KEENAN'S *Catechism,* p. 112; " published with the sanction of one Archbishop and four Vicars-Apostolic."

" Never, thank Heaven, have I thought, said, or written anything favourable to the personal and separate infallibility

of the Pope, such as it is sought to impose upon us."—
MONTALEMBERT'S *Dying Protest.*

"The Italian doctrine." "An opinion." "A peculiar
theory."—CARDINAL WISEMAN, *Essays,* vol. ii. p. 122.

"Ever since I was a Catholic, I have held the Pope's
infallibility as a matter of theological opinion."—CARDINAL
NEWMAN, *Letter to Gladstone,* p. 99.

"The chief authors of the passing generation:—Cardinal
Wiseman, Dr. Ullathorne, Dr. Lingard, Mr. Tierny, Dr.
Oliver, Dr. Rock, Dr. Waterworth, Dr. Husenbeth, Mr.
Flanagan—which of these ecclesiastics has said anything
extreme about the prerogatives of the Blessed Virgin, or the
infallibility of the Pope?"—CARDINAL NEWMAN, *Letter to
Dr. Pusey.*

Archbishop Kenrick: "The dogma of Papal infallibility is
not of faith, and cannot become so by any definition even
of a council."—*A Roman Catholic's Reasons against Papal
Infallibility,* p. 76 (Rivingtons).

Roman Catholic principles in reference to God and the King.

"Papal definitions, in whatever form pronounced, taken
exclusively from a general council or universal acceptance of
the Church, oblige none under pain of heresy to an interior
assent."—*The Faith of our Ancestors,* sec. ii. para. 6, date
1680. Copy presented by Roman Catholics to Mr. Pitt, 1788.

"But Mr. Bower never found the infallibility of the Pope
in our creed, and knows very well that no such article is
proposed by the Church, or required of any one."—ALBAN
BUTLER, *Reasons of R. C. Layman,* p. 19.

Bishop Milner: "In the third place, I must remind you and
my friends that I have nothing here to do with the doctrine
of the Pope's individual infallibility. (When pronouncing
ex cathedrâ, as the term is, he addresses the whole Church,
and delivers the faith of it upon some contested article.) Nor
would you, in case you were to become a Catholic, be required
to believe in any doctrines except such as are held by the
whole Catholic Church with the Pope at its head. But with-

out entering into this or any other *scholastic question*," &c.— p. 279.

Irish Catholics declared according to the Act of 33 Geo. III., in 1792-3: "I declare that it is not an article of the Roman Catholic Faith; neither am I required to profess or believe that the Pope is infallible."—*Reasons of R. C. Layman*, p. 49.

In England in 1740, a "declaration and protestation" was signed by 1740 persons, including 241 Priests, in which it is said, "We acknowledge no infallibility in the Pope."

Ambrose Lisle Philipps: "We are far from claiming for the Papacy a separate infallibility, distinct from that which all Catholics are bound to believe in, as the prerogative of the universal Church. Those who make so novel a claim must reconcile it with the grave facts of ecclesiastical history. . . . And we believe, that with these facts undenied and not dis-proved, it would be impossible for the Church to define any such theories to be articles of faith."—*Union Review*, May 1866, p. 95.

Faith of Catholics, edited by Rev. J. Waterworth, and dedicated to Bishop Walsh: "That the former (personal infallibility of the Pope) is not an essential term of Communion, is certain, whatever may be the private opinion of individuals as to whether that infallibility does or does not form a part of the deposit of faith."—See also *Propositions*, xiv. xv.

Is the Pope's authority received by the Irish Roman Catholic Church as supreme in matters of faith or morals?

"We recognize him as the head of our Church, and there-fore give him the executive authority; but that is limited by the Sacred Canons. He cannot create new articles of faith."— BISHOP DOYLE (*Lords*, March 21, 1825; *Report*, p. 387), R. C. L., p. 77.

How is the Vatican Decree of 1870, declaring the Pope infallible, worded?

"The Holy Council approving, we teach and define as a Divinely revealed dogma, that the Roman Pontiff, when he

speaks *ex cathedrâ*, that is, when discharging the offiee of
pastor and teacher of all Christians by his supreme Apostolic
authority, he defines a doctrine about faith or morals, to be
held by the universal Church, is invested, through the Divine
assistance promised to him in blessed Peter, with that infallibility wherewith the Divine Redeemer willed His Church to
be furnished in defining a doctrine on faith or morals; and
therefore such definitions by the Roman Pontiff are of themselves, and not in virtue of the consent of the Church, irre-
formable. And if any one—which God forbid—shall presume
to contradict this our definition, let him be anathema."

What is the result of this Decree?

" *The whole Roman system was changed* by the Vatican
Council. Until its close, the rule of faith at least was the
same. The Roman Church, too, acknowledged with the
Fathers, that the sole source of Faith was God's revelation
of Himself in Holy Scripture; the interpreter of Holy
Scripture was the same; the universal Church from the first,
according to the saying 'quod semper, quod ubique, quod ad
omnibus.' The same body of truth which was attested by
Holy Scripture was taught by the Apostles everywhere, before
a word of Holy Scripture was written. Believed everywhere,
it was transmitted everywhere. The faith of the Church
remained the same. This was brought out by general councils,
in which Bishops, lettered or unlettered, were assembled from
all parts of the world. All attested—'So have we received';
and the concurrent testimony of all, and of every individual,
was accepted as evident proof of a common original. Heresy
enlarged the explanations of the Church; it did not develop
its doctrine, which was the same before as afterwards. The
Bishops of Rome (as they were then called) as the only
Apostolic See of the West had, of course, a great share in
this; but it was only a share. There is evidence of their
gathering the judgments of Western Bishops, in which case
they represented the whole West. At the Council of Nice,
the Bishop of Rome certainly did not preside; at the first

Council of Constantinople one only Western Bishop was present, and he in no relation to Rome." [1]

The system is changed indeed!

Has the Pope ever been declared by the whole Church to be superior to a general council?

Never. The Vatican Decree of 1870 was only a decree of those Bishops who considered themselves in abject obedience to the Bishop of Rome.

Did not the Bishops of East and West in the early general councils of the Church, consider themselves bound to obey the Bishop of Rome, as their sole infallible guide in all matters of faith?

No student of history could honestly assert such a thing.

But if the Bishops of Rome were not considered infallible by the early Church, yet did not councils always consult and decree under the absolute direction and command of the Bishops of Rome?

Most certainly not. "The independent examination of the writings of even eminent Popes by general councils, in order to ascertain their agreement with the Faith laid down by previous councils, which had taken place in the third or fourth general councils, was laid down as a, principle in the fifth." [2]

How does St. Gregory the Great speak of the four great councils?

He says in an encyclical letter to all the Patriarchs: "I receive and venerate the four councils as I do the four Holy Gospels; the fifth council I venerate in like way. All the persons whom the venerable councils aforesaid reject, I reject; those whom they reverence I receive; because, seeing they are established by universal consent, *whoever* presumes either to loose whom they bind, or to bind whom they loose, destroys himself, not them." [3]

"This is not the language of one who might himself have written the decrees of those councils, and whose single voice

<hr>

[1] Preface to *Rule of Faith*, p. iii.   [2] *Id*. p. vi.   [3] *Id*.

would have saved all the toil and sacrifice of life involved in the gathering of aged Bishops from all quarters of the world." [1]

Besides the historical fact that the Bishops of Rome were not regarded in the Primitive Church as they now are in the Roman Communion, what is the simplest plain reason, proving that in the days of the Primitive Church the Bishops of Rome were not looked upon as infallible?

It is simply inconceivable that, as in the Arian times, when the Church was in such terrible trouble, that the Bishop of Rome did not settle the question by his *ex cathedrâ* judgment, if his judgment could have settled the question for the Church.

What happened instead?

In those days travelling was not so easy and rapid as now; yet after a long sad time of bitter and terrible dissension the Council of Nice was called to meet, and at length settled the controversy.

Who is, by consent of all, looked upon as chief amongst the "Fathers"?

St. Augustine.

Is there anything he ever wrote or did showing that he believed in Papal Infallibility?

"The modern Roman doctrine was, of course, unheard of in his time, but he signed a protest against appeals being made to the Bishop of Rome; and as regards the difference between Pope Stephen and St. Cyprian, he says, 'We ourselves should not venture to assert anything of this sort' (viz. what Pope Stephen had asserted), 'unless we were supported by the most concordant authority of the Universal Church; to which he himself (St. Cyprian) would doubtless yield, if at that time the truth of this question had already been solidly established, having been cleared and declared by a plenary Council.' A 'Plenary Council' then, not the Bishop of Rome, was, in St. Augustine's mind, the ultimate authority." [2]

"In like way, St. Augustine blames the Donatists, not for appealing from the synod of eighteen Bishops, assembled at

---

[1] *Rule of Faith*, Preface, p. vi.   [2] *Id.* p. xiii.

Rome under Melchiades, but that they did not acquiesce in the judgment of the 'plenary council to which the cause was then referred.' See, let us suppose that all the Bishops who judged at Rome, were not good judges, there still remained a plenary Council of the Universal Church, in which the cause might be canvassed with the judges themselves; so that if they should be proved to have judged amiss, their sentence might be annulled." [1]

Has any Bishop of Rome ever been held to have the right to set aside any decree of a general council (acknowledged and received by the whole Church), or of his own accord, acting by himself, to amend or correct such a decree?

Never. The Popes used to seek the Confirmation of the Church.

"The judgment of a general council (accepted by the Universal Church) never was reconsidered, but was obeyed. It was a saying of St. Gelasius, an excellent Pontiff, 'A good and Christian Synod once passed, cannot and ought not to be discredited by any reiteration of a new Synod.' The judgment of the Holy Spirit is discredited, whenever it is reconsidered by a new judgment. But a judgment propounded by a Roman Pontiff *is of such sort* that it was *reconsidered* by a new judgment. It was *not* then *that last and ultimate judgment* of the Church." [2]

To come down to later times: what was decreed by the Council of Constance?

"This holy Synod of Constance, being lawfully called together in the Holy Spirit, constituting a general council, and representing the Catholic Church, has its power immediately from Christ; and every one, of whatever state or dignity, even if it be Papal, is bound to obey it in what appertains to the Faith and to the extirpation of the said schism and the reformation of the said Church in its *head* and its members." It also enacted "that if any one of any condition, state, dignity whatever, even if Papal, should contumaciously refuse to

<hr>

[1] *Rule of Faith*, Preface, p. xiii.   [2] *Id.* p. xvii.

obey the precepts of this sacred Synod or any other general council soever lawfully called, he should be subjected to condign penitence unless he repented, and should be duly punished even by recourse to other aids of law if need be."[1]

Did all English Catholics believe in the Infallibility of the Pope, before the Vatican Decree of 1870 declared it to be an article of faith?

No, they did not, and many of them, as we have seen, protested most strongly, that it was no part of their faith.

When did the English Roman Catholics make these protests, and why?

They made many of them some years before the passing of the Roman Catholic Emancipation Act, and to obtain the enjoyment of all civil privileges, on a par with their fellow-countrymen.

When the attempt was made to procure the Vatican definition of Infallibility of the Pope, what was then the feeling of some English Roman Catholics?

It had been suggested to Dr. Pusey by Roman Catholics, " to bring the fact to the remembrance of the English Roman Catholics, that it would involve a great scandal if what was so often repudiated, in order to remove their civil disqualifications, should, after they had gained them, be indirectly made matter of faith."[2]

Is there any evidence that Papal Infallibility is a Divinely revealed truth?

"There is no evidence. Had there been any, the whole history of the Church would have been other. Almighty God did not will that it should be by the voice of one man that heresies should be slain. He had an office for the Universal Church spread throughout the world. He had an office for the Church as a whole, to bear witness of the truth. One voice went up from every clime : ' So have we been taught.' Thus believes the Catholic Church. And thereupon they confessed how the faith lay, in order to show that their own

----

[1] *Rule of Faith*, Preface, p. xviii.   [2] *Eirenicon*, iii. p. 317.

sentiments were not novel, but Apostolical; and what they wrote down was no discovery of theirs, but was the same as was taught by the Apostles." [1]

"The Bishops, however endowed, learned or unlearned, knew the faith of Christ. And the faith which they attested surmounted every shock; the violence of Roman or Persian emperors, of Gothic or Vandal kings, or the wiles of heretics, or gatherings of heretical Bishops, because it was builded on the Rock which was Christ. 'Petrus super petram, non petra super Petrum.' The faith in Christ, Son of God, and, for us, Son of Man, was the Rock against which the gates of hell should not prevail. So it was with the subsequent councils. The councils knew nothing of the infallibility of Popes: the Popes, represented in them, knew nothing of it; the Popes who regarded the acceptance of their letters by councils, as a confirmation of them, knew nothing of it; nor those who retracted what they had said, and owned their fallibility; nor the Church, when in successive councils it reconsidered what Popes had said, and accepted it; not as their saying, but because it agreed with what general councils had before decided; nor Roman Canonists when the digest of canon law was compiled; nor very eminent canonists subsequently. For the first time (1870) in the history of the Church, a council was held, not to over-rule emerging heresies, and declare over-against them, what is the true faith which the Church had ever held. For the first time a council was held, not to subdue heresy, but to subject to anathema those who should deny what, down to the final vote of the council, every one was free to deny and to declare to be destitute of sufficient evidence to make it a matter of faith. A compact majority was determined to carry the decree at any cost, and the minority, at one time very considerable, melted away, and retired mostly from the council, some almost broken-hearted." [2]

Name some of the disastrous consequences of the Vatican Decree declaring the Bishop of Rome to be Infallible.

[1] *Rule of Faith*, Preface, p. xxxiii.   [2] *Id.* p. xxxiv.

"It is a great strain on belief, that, because any one be chosen as Bishop of Rome, whatever his antecedents, sins, crimes, he is, at once, a god upon earth, the Vicar of Jesus Christ; whereas some of the Popes of the Middle Ages were more like the heathen gods, Jupiter or Mars, than images of the Living God. Whether these claims will prepare for the coming of Christ, or, by their oppressiveness on belief of His last antagonist, the Anti-Christ, God, the Omniscient, only knows."[1]

By this Vatican Decree of 1870, has not the work of the re-union of Christendom been terribly injured?

"The Vatican Decree revives much which had passed away, and whose revival the English Roman Catholics, sixty years ago, did not think possible. 'The Pope's claim to temporal power by Divine right,' says C. Butler, 'has not perhaps at this time a single advocate.' It is now with Roman Catholics infallible truth, having been declared in a Papal Bull, and acted upon in the depositions of Henry VIII. and Elizabeth, and in detail, it is infallible truth, that the Pope has a right to depose any prince, to require subjects to renounce their obedience, to rise in arms against him, and drive him from his kingdom."[2]

"The burnings of Smithfield used to be regarded as obsolete. It was counted bigoted to name them. Burning was a civil law, although set in motion by the Church, of which the civil power was the executioner. It is now systematically defended to be put in force, whenever it should seem expedient, or when secular powers shall be inclined to use it."[3]

Are not the heresies and extravagances, so rife in the Devotions to the Virgin, now sanctioned by the (so-called) voice of Infallibility?

"All this has been sanctioned by what is to Roman Catholics, infallible authority. The Bull in which Pius IX. defined by his supreme judgment and authority 'the doctrine of the

---

[1] *Rule of Faith*, Preface, p. xlv. [2] *Id*. p. xxxvii.
[3] *Id*. p. xxxviii.

Immaculate Conception,' was addressed to all in his communion. It was written by him as the teacher of the Church. But in it he declares that ' the most Blessed Virgin ' is constituted between Christ and His Church. All the deliverances of the Christian Church are attributed to her. She, being wholly sweet and full of graces, hath ever delivered the Christian people from calamities of all sorts, and from the snares and assaults of all enemies, and hath rescued them from destruction." [1]

"The doctrine that the most Blessed Virgin is constituted between Christ and His Church, justifies as infallible truth, all which we hoped were the exaggerated expressions of individuals ; it is no longer a question of mere, however powerful, intercession ; it is an office as distinct as our Blessed Lord's own mediatorial office with the Father. As Jesus is ' the way to the Father, and no one cometh to the Father, save by Him,' so now all those sayings, that ' Mary is the way to Jesus,' and that ' none come to Jesus except through her,' seem to be authenticated to Roman Catholics by what is now to them infallible truth ; as infallible as the Gospels." [2]

Roman Catholics are now placed in a very difficult position. They must either accept the new doctrine of Papal Infallibility, and all its consequences, or they must be inconsistent, and say they do accept the doctrine but reject the consequences.

They must either say Pius IX. was infallible in his Syllabus, 1864, and in his decree on the Immaculate Conception of the Virgin, and that Bulls, Decree, Encyclicals, *ex cathedrâ*, utterances of all former Popes were also issued by Infallible Popes, or if they dare not say this, they must say that no Pope was infallible before Pius IX., nor he till 1870. And if he was not infallible till then, they must believe that it was a Divine truth then revealed, the whole history of the Vatican Council not giving likelihood to such an idea.

How do Roman Catholics interpret the text, " Thou art

____

[1] *Rule of Faith*, Preface, p. xli. [2] *Id.* p. xlii.

Peter, and on this Rock will I build My Church, and the gates of hell shall not prevail against it" ?

They say that it proves that the Church is built on Peter, and then they proceed to assert that St. Peter became Bishop of Rome; and that all Bishops of Rome, his successors, have been each and all of them the Supreme Infallible Heads of the Church.

Is it true that St. Peter ever was Bishop of Rome ?

There is no clear proof of it, but there seems very good reason to believe the tradition to be true—that he did go to Rome, and was martyred there.

Was the See of Rome regarded as the chief See in the early days of the Church ?

Yes. "And while Rome deserved the pre-eminence, she had it." [1] But primacy is one thing, supremacy another.

The Bishop of Rome, then, after the days of the Apostles, became the Primate, or the first Bishop in Christendom ?

Yes.

But was he regarded as Supreme over the whole Church, so that not only was he held to be the source of all mission and jurisdiction, but also the Infallible Teacher of the whole Church?

Nothing can be farther from the truth ! All history is against this modern supposition.

How then did the Early Fathers interpret Matt. xvi. 18, *" Thou art Peter," &c. ?*

See BARROW'S *Treatise on the Pope's Supremacy.* See *Note Q.* by Dr. Pusey, in Tertullian, *Library of the Fathers.* For the testimony of mediæval Commentators, see Denton's *Commentary for Holy Days.* Note at the end of St. Peter.

Give one Catholic interpretation of the text.

"To St. Peter, our Lord graciously echoes, as it were, His words, in blessing, 'And I say unto thee'; that is, 'thou hast avouched Me to be thy Lord and thy God, and I, the very Son of God, Whom thou hast confessed, say to thee, Thou art Peter'; or as a father explains it, 'I am the unshaken Rock;

[1] See *Letter to Dr. Jelf,* p. 183.

I, the Corner-stone, Who made both one; I, the Foundation, other than which can no man lay.' Yet thou also art a rock, because thou art established by My strength, so that what are of right My own, shall, by My imparting, be common to thee with Me. On this might, will I build an everlasting temple, and on the firmness of this Faith shall arise the majestic height of My Church, which shall reach to Heaven. This confession the gates of Hell shall not restrain; the bonds of death shall not bind; for this voice is the voice of life." [1]

Even supposing it were granted that St. Peter was the Rock on which Christ founded His Church, where would the Scriptural proof be found that St. Peter's successors (supposing he ever was Bishop of Rome) would be the Supreme Infallible Heads of the Church?

Where indeed?

On the Catholic theory that the Apostles were equal, and St. Peter first among equals, where is there any proof that they and their successors would always have the help and authority of their Master in ruling the Church?

"Lo, I am with you alway, even unto the end of the world." Matt. xxviii. 20.

What great fallacy underlies the Roman theory of St. Peter being, and his successors being, the Rock or the Foundation-stone of the Church?

The Church is built *upon* her foundation, the work of building *up* is ever being continued by the Master Builder. Other foundation can no man lay than is laid, Christ Jesus. Grant that St. Peter is the first great stone laid upon the Rock, then if all the Bishops of Rome succeed him in his position, this first great stone laid upon the Rock is continually being changed, and the whole building is being continually undermined.

What is the Catholic theory?

That the Church is built on Christ; the Apostles being the twelve foundation-stones; the whole structure being ever

<hr>

[1] Vol. ii. p. 283.

added to, built up, resting on the four square foundation-stones of the twelve Apostles.   They are the foundation-stones resting on Christ the Rock.

What, in man's sight, are the saddest consequences of the un-catholic and unhistorical doctrine of the infallibility of the Pope?

The promotion of the increase of unbelief, and the causing of a fresh hindrance to the reunion of Christendom.

Is, then, the reunion of Christendom more hopeless than ever?

By no means.   God often brings good out of evil; when things seem most dark and hopeless, God often is about to interfere and to help.

What is the duty of English Catholics, indeed of all Christians?

To weary not in their intercession for Unity, Peace and Concord.

Give some reasons for thinking that, after all, the Vatican Decree of 1870 may some day be set aside and annulled?

In the first place, it was not the decree of a general council, representing the whole Church.   It was not a free council.

The Bishops were not unanimous.

The minority represented the most ¦important sees; some of them left the council rather than give a final vote.

Some hold that the council was not formally dissolved, but only prorogued, and may re-assemble.

Many Roman Catholics do not *ex animo* believe the Vatican doctrine, and would be only too glad were this great weight upon their consciences removed.

How does the Vatican Decree press upon the mind and consciences of good and earnest Roman Catholics?

Having to believe that to be an article of faith, necessary to salvation, which never was so believed by the Catholic Church, and was only held as a pious opinion by many in the Roman Communion up to 1870.

Not only then is their faith changed, but the position of the Roman Catholics is now seriously altered?

Yes; the claims asserted by the Pope are such as to place civil allegiance at his mercy.—*See* GLADSTONE'S *Vaticanism*, p. 109.

However loyal Roman Catholics may have been, as at the time of the Armada, now that Papal Infallibility is declared, may not their position at any time become most difficult?

Yes; now that Roman Catholics hold that the Pope can excommunicate Christians all over the world, and that in all matters it is best to follow and obey him.

Even Cardinal Newman says—"He can judge and he can acquit; he can pardon and he can condemn; he can command and he can permit; he can forbid and he can punish. He has a supreme jurisdiction over the people of God. He can stop the ordinary course of Sacramental mercies; he can excommunicate from the ordinary grace of redemption; and he can remove again the ban which he has inflicted. It is the rule of Christ's providence that what His Vicar does in severity or in mercy, upon earth, He Himself confirms in Heaven."

"There are kings of the earth who have despotic authority which their subjects obey indeed and disown in their hearts; but we must never murmur at that absolute rule which the Sovereign Pontiff has over us, because it is given to him by Christ, and in *obeying Him* we are obeying his Lord. We must *never suffer ourselves* to doubt that, in his government of the Church, he is guided by an intelligence more than human. His yoke is the Yoke of Christ; he has the responsibility of his own acts, not we; and to his Lord must he render account, not to us. *Even in secular matters, it is ever safe to be on his side,* dangerous to be on the side of his enemies."—NEWMAN'S *Sermon,* "The Pope and the Revolution," pp. 10, 11.

Is it not strange that for over 1800 years the Church never acknowledged the Infallibility of the Bishop of Rome; the modern Roman theory being that the Pope's Infallibility was always believed in?

It is "beyond all expression strange, that for one thousand three hundred years, or were it but for half one thousand three hundred years, the Church performed her high office, and spread over the nations, without any infallible teaching

whatever from the Pope, and then that it should have been
reserved for these later ages first to bring into exercise a gift
so entirely new, without example in its character, and on the
presence or absence of which depends a vital difference in the
conditions of Church life."

"The declarations of the Pope *ex cathedrâ* are to be the
sure guide and mainstay of the Church, and yet she has passed
through two-thirds of her existence without once reverting to
it. Nor is this all. For in those earlier ages, the fourth
century in particular, were raised and settled those tremendous
controversies relating to the God-head, the decision of which
was the most arduous work the Church has ever been called
to perform in the sphere of thought."—GLADSTONE, *Vaticanism,*
pp. 104, 105.

*Many have felt called upon to denounce the controversial
methods of Rome ; what is the opinion of Mr. Gladstone on this
matter ?*

"This sensitiveness is at the best but morbid. The cause
of it may be that for the last thirty years, in this country at
least, Ultramontanism has been very busy in making controversial war upon other people, with singularly little restraint
of language; and has had far too little of the truth told to
itself. Hence, it has lost the habit, almost the idea, of equal
laws in discussion of that system as a system, especially after
the further review of it which it has been my duty to make, I
must say that its influence is adverse to freedom in the State,
the family, and the individual; that when weak it is too often
crafty, and when strong, tyrannical; and that, though in this
country no one could fairly deny to its professors the credit of
doing what they think is for the glory of God, they exhibit in
a notable degree the vast self-deluding forces which make sport
of our common nature."—*Vaticanism*, p. 111.

*Has the Roman Communion always been properly constituted
and organized as a Church in England since the days of the
Reformation ?*

No. As Cardinal Newman wrote in 1866, in his *Sermon*

on "The Pope and the Revolution," p. 14—"Pius IX. has taken the Catholics of England out of their *unformed state and made them a Church.* He it is who has redressed a misfortune of nearly three hundred years' standing. Twenty years ago we were a mere collection of individuals; but Pope Pius has brought us together, has given us Bishops, and created out of us a body politic."

How does Papal Infallibility bear upon the marriage question?

"I have before me the Exposition with the text of the Encyclica and Syllabus published at Cologne in 1874, with the approval of authority (*mit ober Kirchlicher*—approbation). In p. 45 it is distinctly taught that with marriage the State has nothing to do—that it may safely rely upon the Church— that civil marriage, in the eyes of the Church, is only concubinage; and that the State, by the use of worldly compulsion, prevents the two concubinary parties from repenting and abandoning their guilty relation to one another. Exactly the same is the doctrine of the Pope himself, in his *Speeches* published at Rome; where civil marriage is declared to be, for Christians, nothing more than a 'mere concubinage, and a filthy concubinage' (sosso concubinato). These extraordinary declarations are not due to the fondness of the Pontiff for speaking impromptu. In his letter of September 19th, 1852, to King Victor Immanuel, he declares that matrimony carrying the Sacrament is alone lawful for Christians, and that a law of civil marriage, which goes to divide them for practical purposes, constitutes a concubinage in the guise of legitimate marriage. So that, in truth, in all countries within the scope of these denunciations, the parties to a civil marriage are declared to be living in an illicit connection which they are called upon to renounce. This call is addressed to them separately, as well as jointly, the wife being summoned to leave her husband, and the husband to abandon his wife; and after this pretended repentance from a state of sin, unless the law of the land and fear of consequences prevail, a new connection under the name of a marriage, may be formed with the sanction of the Church of Rome."

"It is true indeed, that two hundred thousand non-Roman marriages which are annually celebrated in England, do not at present fall under the foul epithets of Rome. But why? Not because we marry, as I believe nineteen-twentieths of us marry, under the sanctions of religion; for our marriages are, in the eyes of the Pope, purely civil marriages; but only for the technical, accidental, and precarious reason, that the disciplinary decrees of Trent are not canonically in force in this country. There is nothing, unless it be motives of mere policy, to prevent the Pope from giving them force here when he pleases. If, and when that is done, every marriage thereafter concluded in the English Church will, according to his own words, be a filthy concubinage."—GLADSTONE, *Vaticanism*, p. 26.

How does Papal Infallibility bear upon loyalty and civil allegiance in England?

"Had the decrees of 1870 been in force in the sixteenth and seventeenth centuries, Roman Catholic peers could not have done what until the reign of Charles II. they did; could not have made their way to the House of Lords by taking the oath of allegiance, despite the Pope's command. But that is not all. The Pope, *ex cathedrâ*, had bidden the Roman Catholics of England in the eighteenth century, and in the sixteenth, and from the fourteenth, to believe in the deposing power as an article of faith. But they rejected it; and the highest law of their Church left them free to reject it. Has it not bound them now? The Pope in the sixteenth century bade the Roman Catholics of England assist the invasion of the Spanish Armada. They disobeyed him. No unquestioned law of their Church forbade them to disobey. Are they as free now?"—GLADSTONE, *Vaticanism*, p. 68.

Why was it said above that the whole controversy with Roman Catholics is narrowed to a simple issue?

"Because on the modern Roman theory the *ex cathedrâ*

voice of the Pope is as infallible as the very word of God Himself. It is of course the teaching of the Pope that the Roman Communion is *the* One Catholic Church. This being so, it is no use wasting time in showing that the Roman Communion is not *the* Catholic Church, because she teaches this or that uncatholic or unscriptural doctrine. On *her* theory the Pope being infallible, she only teaches the truth, and all that she teaches is the truth, the Catholic faith. It is no use to say, that any one distinctive Roman doctrine is unscriptural or uncatholic; the Roman reply is, 'the Pope sanctions it and teaches it'; therefore it is 'of faith.'"

The Roman controversial method of establishing their claims and position is now as follows—

It is first asserted that the Roman Communion is *the* Catholic Church. Next, that this Catholic Church declares the Pope to be infallible, and the Pope declares the Roman Communion alone to be the Catholic Church; therefore the Roman Communion is the Catholic Church. Q.E.D. Or the Church must have a Supreme Infallible Head. The Pope is this Head, therefore the Roman Communion is *the* Church.

What then is the great mistake continually made by Roman controversialists?

They make a theory, and then say that all things must be adapted to it; that God must therefore have meant this or that.

How so?

"Our convictions must ever follow after, not anticipate, the meaning of Divine Revelation. To argue, for instance, as some do, that Christianity *must* be stronger with a visible Head, and therefore that it *must* be part of the Divine mind that it should have one; that whatever is taught in the actual Church, *i. e.* by all its clergy, *must* needs be matter of faith; that infallible authority *must* needs exist authoritatively to declare on every occasion the truth as to any question which may emerge; these, or any like assertions, that Almighty God *must*, in such or such a way, secure any disclosure which He makes of His mind or

will, are arguments of much the same sort as that which used
to be confined to unbelievers, that, 'if God gave a revelation,
it would be written in the sun.' "[1]

*What remarkable incidental testimony against Papal Infalli-
bility is given in the decree of the Sixth General Council condemning Pope Honorius ?*

" Having read the dogmatic letters written by Sergius,
formerly Patriarch of this God-protected and imperial city,
both to Cyrus, at that time Bishop of Phasis, and to Honorius,
who was Pope of the elder Rome; and in like way, the letter
written in reply by him, *i. e.* by Honorius to the same Sergius,
and having found them to be altogether alien from the Apostolic teaching and the things *defined by the Holy Synods* and all
the eminent Holy Fathers, and that contrariwise they follow
the false teachings of the heretics, we altogether reject them
and abhor them as soul-destroying." [2]

The reader will observe the reference of the council to
Apostolic teaching, "to the things defined by the Holy Synods,"
"and all the eminent holy fathers," and the absence of any
reference to any infallible decisions of any previous Bishop of
Rome.

What is now claimed for the Bishop of Rome ?

" In a word, the whole magisterium or doctrinal authority of
the Pontiff as the supreme Doctor of all Christians, is included
in this definition of his Infallibility.   And also all legislative or
judicial acts, so far as they are inseparably connected with his
doctrinal authority; as, for instance, all judgments, sentences,
and decisions which contain the motives of such acts as derived
from faith and morals.   Under this will come laws of discipline,
canonization of Saints, approbation of religious orders, of
devotions and the like; all of which intrinsically contain the
truths and principles of faith, morals, and piety."

" It takes away the breath even to listen to the enumeration
of these specimens of what is included within the limits of
the definition of the Infallibility of the Pope.   For they are

---

[1] " *This is My Body,*" p. 6.   [2] See *Eirenicon,* iii. p. 193.

only specimens offered, ' for instance,' and as examples of the like."—MASKELL'S *What is the meaning of the Vatican Decree ?* p. 11.

Lastly, what are the two questions which Roman Catholics have hitherto completely failed to solve ?

First, what is the proof, either from Holy Scripture, Antiquity, or History, that Christ endowed St. Peter with supreme infallible authority to govern the Church Universal? Secondly, that He appointed him Bishop of Rome, and ordained that all his successors in that See should inherit all his prerogatives necessary for the autocratic government of the Church?

Having, then, only the assertion of the members of the Roman Communion for the proof of the foregoing claims, can Roman Catholics prove that all Bishops from the days of St. Peter till the present, have been baptized, and been validly ordained Priests, and consecrated Bishops, and that they were, one and all, rightly canonically elected to occupy the See of Rome, and that there has never been any such grave flaw as would void the election of any one Pope?

There are some who think there is grave cause for believing the Papal Succession to have completely failed, and the clear proof to the contrary has yet to be made.

Meanwhile, English Catholics may have the " comfort of knowing that our succession is valid, that our Bishops are the successors of those through whom God planted the Gospel here, and so our Church is *the* appointed channel of God's gifts, and the instrument of salvation for us."[1]

The English Churchman has also the comfort of knowing that the true Catholic theory does not rest the whole safety and life of Christendom on one man, the Bishop of one See.

Any single chain may snap at its weakest link. It is a homely proverb, containing a wholesome caution : " Do not put all your eggs in one basket." The English Catholic knows that, whether there is a failure of any sort in any one See, whether as regards the failure of succession or failure to

---

[1] *Letter of Dr. Pusey,* 1845, p. 1.

defend the Truth (as Honorius), the Church Universal will never fail; that in her the Apostolic Succession is provided for by the care of the Holy Ghost, Who is shed *abroad.* His work is throughout the Church, and not as it were tied down to emanate from one particular spot. On the Roman theory, the failure of the Bishop of Rome is the failure of Christ's Church; the chain is broken. On the Catholic theory, if through the carelessness or sin of the members, the net of the Church is damaged here or there, yet the whole net is not destroyed; it can still work, and the damage be repaired.

Was it only a theory of the late Dr. Littledale that the Papal Succession has been broken long ago by uncanonical elections ?

"What was the appearance of the Holy Roman Church? How exceeding foul, when at Rome courtesans held sway at once most powerful and most foul! At whose will Sees were changed, Bishops given, and (dreadful and horrible to hear) their adulterers thrust into the chair of Peter, pseudo-pontiffs admitted into the Catalogue of Roman Pontiffs, only for the purpose of marking the time! *For who could say that such as these, lawlessly thrust in by harlots, were lawful Roman Pontiffs ?* Nowhere any mention of clergy electing or after-wards assenting. Canons all choked in silence, decrees of Pontiffs smothered, ancient traditions proscribed, and the old customs in the election of the chief Pontiff and the sacred rites and early usage *utterly extinguished !* So had lust, relying on secular power, maddened and stung by phrenzied rage for dominion, made all its own."[1]

In Sanderson Robin's *Whole Evidence against the Roman Claims,* 1851, there is a long section on the failure of the Papal Succession.

Fully allowing that there have been faults on all sides, " that Satan has sown his tares everywhere," what should be the feeling of all who love Jesus as regards the re-union of Christendom ? What should they desire, how behave ?

"Evil days and trial times seem to be coming upon the earth.

<hr>

[1] Vol. i. pp. 165, 166. *Baronius,* A. 900, § 1.

Faith deepens, but unbelief too becomes more thorough. Yet what might not God do to check it, if those who own one Lord and one faith were again at one, and united. Christendom should go forth bound in one by Love—the full flow of God's Holy Spirit, unhemmed by any of those breaks or jars or wranglings—to win all to His Love Whom we all desire to love, to serve, to obey. To have removed one stumbling-block would be worth the labour of a life." [1]

" To all who, in East or West, desire to see inter-communion restored among those who hold the faith of the undivided Church, we say, ' This is not our longing only ; this is impressed on our Liturgy by those who were before us ; for this, whenever we celebrate the Holy Eucharist, we are bound to pray that God would inspire continually the Universal Church with the spirit of truth, unity, and concord.' ' For this I pray daily. For this I would gladly die.' " [2]

What are the first principles of sound unity ?

" Humility and repentance before God."

How should the restless and unsettled be advised ?

" Hold fast what thou hast; act up to what thou believest ; walk on in His strength ; halt not ; and what thou yet lackest, He has said ' He will reveal unto thee.' " [3]

" Thus alone, my brethren, may we hope that in doctrine our sad manifold divisions will cease. Thus they must cease ; for He has said, ' God will reveal it unto thee.' Not by disputing, not by teaching alone, not by learning, not by reading Holy Scripture only, shalt thou know the truth ; but by gaining through God's grace a child-like mind ; by cleansing the eye of the soul ; by obedience. Not by wisdom or prudence canst thou gain the knowledge of the things of God ; from proud wisdom God hides it, and reveals it unto babes." [4]

What caution should be taken well to heart by those tempted to secession ?

" And so we have need, not only to pray that we be guided

---

[1] *Eirenicon,* iii. p. 342.   [2] *Id.* i. p. 335.
[3] *Letter to Dr. Miley,* 1841.   [4] *Leeds Sermons,* p. 358.

into the truth of doctrine, or of life, but also not to rely upon our own prayers too confidently, as though we should of course possess the truth because we pray, while we know not of ourselves whether we are such as are worthy to have 'all truth' disclosed to us; whether we have not all the while some darkness in us, which hinders the shining in of all God's holy truth. Even on this ground may we entrust ourselves the rather to the guidance of God's Church, which we know, and in our Creeds confess to be 'holy,' while we sorrowfully confess our own unholiness, and pray the while that God would 'look well whether there be any way of wickedness in us,' and so 'lead us in the way everlasting of faith and life.' So when we are holy like her, we shall see also for ourselves the truth committed to her to be the truth of God. And on this account alone must it be very dangerous to find fault with any thing we find in her, not only lest we be irreverent and break 'the first commandment with promise,' but lest what we ignorantly blame be just the very truth which is wanting to us, and which some defect in ourselves blinds us from seeing."[1]

[1] Vol. iii. p. 254.

PART II.

MISCELLANEA.

UNITY.

"Have we not all one Father? Hath not one God created us? Are we not all redeemed by the Blood of one Redeemer? Hath not one Lord given one Holy Spirit to bind and knit in one communion and fellowship the whole Body of Christ? Did we not all in Baptism renounce, in the same words, the threefold enemies of our holiness and of our salvation, the flesh, the world, and the devil? Was not the name of the Holy Trinity named on us all, and were we not sealed by the one sign of the Cross, as the sheep of one Shepherd, the disciples of the Crucified? Do we not all belong to one Body? Have we not all had gifts of one Spirit? 'Even as we were called in one hope of our calling, One Lord, One Faith, One Baptism, One God and Father of all, who is above all, and through all, and in you all.' But since we have all besides in common, One God, Who calls us; One Redeemer, Who shed His Blood for us; One source of Grace, the Blood of Christ; One giver of Grace; One and the same channel of Grace to our souls, the same Sacraments which flowed from One Lord's pierced Side; One Beginning, One End; how should we not be capable of one and the same gift of Holiness, which is to be the way to that one End, our rest in the Bliss of God?"[1]

[1] *Parochial and Cathedral Sermons*, p. 167.

SYNODS AND ROYAL SUPREMACY.

"I am satisfied that the Church of England has not conceded to the civil sovereign, any power inconsistent with that which essentially belongs to her as a portion of the Church of Christ." [1]

"Our trust must be, not in man, but in Him Who has promised to be present when two or three are gathered together in His Name. Who has always been believed to be present in synods, and Who will be present if devoutly called upon by the Church, when causes are tried, and by the Bishops assembled to guard the faith and truth of Christ." [2]

SECULAR JUDGMENTS ON CHURCH DOCTRINES.

"A judicial decision, even of the highest court, cannot affect the doctrine of the Church of England. The plain meaning of her formularies must be the same. The judgment, if unfavourable, could affect discipline only. A wrong decision even in a supreme court, cannot alter the faith of the Church." [3]

"No authority less than that of the Church can decide in her name, that she does not receive the Creeds which she uses, in the sense in which the Church has ever received them. If any authority not co-extensive with herself, decides wrongly, he condemns himself, not her. He may embarrass her, may cripple her functions; he cannot alter her Faith." [4]

CHRISTIAN GOVERNMENT.

Must not Churchmen regret that so many of those who make laws for the State are not Christians?

"How can we but weep and have sorrow of heart, when, if it be for our own sins, and the sins of our people, the Ark,

---

[1] *Royal Supremacy*, p. 158. [2] *Id.* p. 171. [3] *Id.* p. 5. [4] *Id.* p. 6.

the Church of God, is sorely shaken, and the hearts of men are perplexed and the work of God is hindered; and, if so be, the State becomes indifferent to truth, and prepares for a final apostacy and admits aliens to rule over her?"[1]

THE REFORMATION.

"The formal act of the schism was not ours; we did not renounce their communion, but they ours. One may be very grateful to God for having brought our Church through the Reformation, and for all the blessings which He has bestowed upon her out of it (as our Liturgy and the use of the Cup in Holy Communion)."[2]

"And yet have a sorrowful feeling that much about the Reformation was not as it should be, and that we are suffering for this still. This is only George Herbert's feeling."[3]

RITUAL.

"We, the clergy, have often need to forego, even in religion itself, in the service of God, in ritual, or ornament, or worship, our own tastes or inclinations, what we think or know to be beautiful or becoming, or even reverent. Truth has suffered more from the immature introduction of ancient forms, which are misunderstood, and so, to our congregations, soulless ritual, than from the gainsaying of the world. For the world, while it gnashed its teeth, bears witness to the might of the truth which angers it; it has triumphed if it can but despise; it has a plea for despising if it represent us as engaged about externals, not contending for God's eternal truth. We may not outrage the world if we would win it. We have to exhibit the truth to it, on the side upon which it will best receive it. We must give up all self, but nothing of God's."[4]

[1] Vol. i. p. 140. [2] *Letter to Churton Church Intelligencer*, May 22, 1843.
[3] *Letter to English Churchman on Subscription to the Articles*, 1844.
[4] *Sermons*, 1872, p. 431.

ALTAR AND TABLE.

"Eucharistic Sacrifice is the same wherever or whereinsoever it is offered. . . . They who offer it now are unconscious mostly of the form and substance of the Altar where they offer it. The Celebration of the Eucharistic Sacrifice makes the Altar." [1]

THE MIXED CHALICE.

"There can be no doubt but that the mixed chalice was used by our Lord in the institution of the Holy Eucharist." [2]

INCARNATE-KNEELING IN THE CREED.

"Of old, the Church, when it uttered the words of the Creed, 'And was Incarnate of the Holy Ghost,' fell down on its knees to worship Him, bowed down to the earth by the sense of His boundless love and gracious lowliness." [3]

THE SIGN OF THE CROSS.

"We too were baptized into our Saviour's Death, our Saviour's Cross; we too bear upon our brows the imprinted Cross unseen of men, but seen of Angels, seen of Satan, the 'seal of God upon our foreheads,' which whoso 'keepeth, that wicked one toucheth him not.'" [4]

"When imagination is busy, you know how the very earliest Christians, those close on the Apostles' times, used the sign of the Cross. I know nothing so powerful in removing evil imaginations, distractions, bad memories and thoughts, as to retrace on the forehead, the seat of thought, the baptismal Cross; used religiously, I never knew it fail. I have known the thoughts by which a person was beset so entirely scattered that he was not even conscious what they had been. The soul

---

[1] *Letter to English Churchman*, Sept. 25, 1841.
[2] *Letter to Daily Express*, June 14, 1877.
[3] "*God is Love*," p. 30. [4] Vol. iii. p. 37.

was like a clean sheet, on which every trace had been utterly effaced; like a serene blue sky, from which every cloud had disappeared."[1]

USE OF A CRUCIFIX.

Is there anything wrong in either wearing a small Crucifix, or in kneeling and praying before a Crucifix ?

No. Of course it would be wrong to offer the worship due to God alone, directly and only to the material Crucifix. To treat it with the deepest reverence as a representation of Christ Crucified cannot be wrong.

"Strange it is that while not the Lutheran only, but the united Lutheran and Reformed bodies in Prussia, have the Crucifix upon their Communion Table, the very name of a Crucifix amongst us awakens only thoughts of idolatrous worship. There can, in principle, be no difference between the Picture of the Crucifixion and the figure of Christ Crucified; both alike set before our eyes Christ Crucified. The Picture ordinarily, by aid of colour sets forth his Sacred Form and Countenance, and the Eyes which seem almost to look on those who look on Him, more vividly to the mind. Yet pictures of the Crucifixion are received and beheld by all with reverence and love; the Crucifix, with dread of some wrong design in it."[2]

"I could not, when asked, but say that the Crucifix in itself was not forbidden by the second commandment, for the second commandment forbids us to make to ourselves any likenesses of the invisible God; the Crucifix represents not the Son, in His Invisible Deity, but in 'the form of a servant,' which He took for us, and in which 'He became obedient unto Death, and that the Death of the Cross.'"[3]

"But further, neither can I think it wrong for any one to

---

[1] *Lenten Sermons*, p. 380.
[2] *Letter to Bishop of London*, 1881, p. 105.   [3] *Id.* p. 106.

pray, either with a picture of our Lord Crucified, or a Crucifix before him, so that it be used only to fix and deepen our thoughts of His Dying Love, and make It present with us. This also I have said, when asked.   But as to this also, I have always spoken of the charity due to the prejudices of others. I need not say to your Lordship that, not images, but the worship of images, was forbidden either by the Council of Frankfort to which we appeal, or by the English Church.   The Article says expressly, 'worshipping and adoration as well of images as of reliques.'   Natural actions, tokens of love, are not 'worship and adoration.'   Who has not seen one kiss the picture of one loved but absent?   Who, well nigh, has not done it?   If then any one, following the outward gesture of St. Mary Magdalene, and in outward act, figuring himself like her, were to kiss this likeness of his Lord's Feet, I own I could not count the action superstitious, nor to imply a temper alien from the English Church." [1]

TEMPTATION TO DOUBT.

" If any allege to thee any imagined laws of matter (whereof we know nothing), whereby it should be supposed that our Lord's precious Body and Blood could not be spiritually, supra-locally present under those outward forms, and would reduce thee to a belief of a presence, varying and uncertain, elicited by and dependent upon the faith, whereby we do receive the grace thereof, say to thyself, ' Of the laws of a spiritual body I know nothing.   One thing I know, that the Truth has said, "This is My Body."

> 'I believe whate'er the Son of God hath told ;
> What the Truth has spoken, that for truth I hold.'

And then remember how holy men were cautioned of old, ' Touch not the Body of Christ with a fevered hand.   Abstain from all uncleanness, and then take the Body and Blood of

---

[1] *Letter to Bishop of London*, 1881, pp. 106, 107.

Christ, and carefully guard thy mouth by which the King has entered.'

"If others (be they who they may) speak against the power of the keys committed by Christ to His Church for the cleansing of the penitent, probe thou the more thine own conscience."[1]

As regards the Rule of Faith, what are the common principles of the ancient Church?

"What is a matter of Faith must be capable of being proved out of Holy Scripture; yet, that not according to the private sense of individuals, but according to the uniform teaching of the Church."[2]

The Faith delivered to the keeping of the Church is one complete, uniform whole, capable neither of being increased nor lessened; perfectly delivered to the Apostles by our Lord; perfectly delivered by the Apostles to their successors; perfectly transmitted in succession by them to faithful men after them.

The Faith was delivered to each Church individually by the Apostle who founded it, and was held and transmitted by it in harmony with the whole. Each needed not to inquire the Faith of the rest, but held it as a hereditary treasure, committed to it, to be transmitted by it.

"The present Church must (if need be), in contradiction to heresy, declare the mind of the ancient Church. Yet what she declares must not be her own mind alone, but according to the teaching of the Fathers."

"The Faith comes to us, not on the authority of the present Church, but of the whole Church from Christ until now."[3]

"The Church of Rome as the Apostolic Church of the West, had great weight, because, in Tertullian's words, 'On it the Apostles poured out all their doctrine with their blood.' In it St. Peter was crucified, St. Paul beheaded, and St. John endured martyrdom in will."

"But it was regarded only as one witness to the truth, and

[1] *Sinful Blindness*, p. 30.
[2] *Rule of Faith*, p. 40.
[3] *Id.* p. 41.

especially to the Churches in the West which were not Apostolic."

ENCOURAGEMENT FOR ENGLISH CHURCHMEN.

"For myself I am even now far more hopeful as to our Church than at any former period! Far more than when outwardly things seemest most prosperous."[1]

"He (God) Who loved us amid negligence so as to give us the earnest desire to please Him, will surely not forsake us, now He has given us that desire."

These words, written at the darkest, saddest period of the Catholic Revival, should encourage all Churchmen in these days when "things are not nearly so bad."

RESTORATION.

"God is not the author of confusion, but of peace, and when every one is eagerly and confidently bringing in his own scheme by which the temple of God shall be re-edified, without regard to the wisdom of past ages, or the experience of our elders, it but little resembles that first peaceful and quiet building when

> 'No workmen's steel, no ponderous axes rung ;
> Like some tall palm the noiseless fabric sprung.'

It savours little of the spirit of those times, in which our more glorious temple was founded, when 'the multitude of them that believed were of one heart and of one soul,' and but little also of that 'wisdom that is from above,' which 'is first pure, then peaceable, gentle, and easy to be entreated.' Let us rather in modesty and humility commit our Church to Him who 'loves it better than we can love it,' and under Him, to those whom His Providence has appointed to govern it, praying Him, Who alone can do so, by His continual pity to cleanse and to defend it, and because it cannot continue in safety without His succour to preserve it evermore by His help and goodness."[2]

[1] *Letter on Dr. Newman's Secession,* October 1845.
[2] *Cathedral Institutions,* p. 161.

LOYALTY TO THE CHURCH.

"Our duties are positive and unconditional; they lie towards our Mother, the English Church, because God has assigned us our lot in her, and are irrespective of anything without her. The duties and blessings of the first commandment with promise 'are in obedience to our Parent as such.' Our duties are to her, because through her we were reborn; within her have we been trained, catechized, instructed, guarded, guided, called, recalled; in her words and in her courts we have worshipped from childhood until now; in her we have had all our 'means of grace'; in her we have whatever be our hopes of glory; at her breasts our Heavenly Father 'nourished and brought us up' as children, and to forsake her would be to 'rebel against' Him; through her He fed us, when young, with milk; in her He feeds us now with Angels' food, the Bread of Heaven; in her He has given us what out of her we could not have had—I need but allude to one precious gift, whose value none can estimate, bestowed on us alone in the whole Western Church, and which I cannot understand how any communicant who loves his Lord could of his own act forego." [1]

"Avoid whatever you think tends to alienate your affections from your Church." [2]

"Do not attend services not of hers."

GROWTH OF CHURCH.

"In grace, they tell us how the body of the Second Adam is formed, His Church, growing out of the formless and deformed mass of our race, in this our prison-house and land of death, consisting of perfected yet also of yet imperfect members, which are being perfected; each with its separate lineaments and forms and office; some more, some less

---

[1] *Letter to Archbishop of Canterbury*, p. 12.   [2] *Letter*, Aug. 1845.

honourable, yet all growing together into one harmonious body, intricate in its harmony, yet harmonizing in its intricacy; all needed for the perfection of the whole, and all needing one another; each member, lay or clergy, teacher or taught, old or young, rich or poor, head or foot, having its separate functions and uses, all growing together unto the one unseen mystical whole, in a secret way, unknown to the world and amid the world's darkness, but under the eye of God: her destinies, hindrances, reverses, growth all written in God's book: until clad with the full number of the elect, having gathered and formed all her appointed members, and grown 'unto the measure of the stature of the fullness of Christ,' she, at her Maker's, Saviour's, Husband's call, be translated wholly out of this 'land of the shadow of death,' to live for ever with and in God, in the land of the living." [1]

CHURCH TROUBLES AND CHEERING SIGNS.

"Few can tell, but those who have felt or seen it, how heavy and oppressive the feeling of insulation is, when a man is spoken of with mistrust and suspicion, and kept aloof."

"If nothing will convince them, death in the Bosom of the Church of England will." [2]

"Our Church is not in a healthy state. It cannot be amid such manifold divisions, denials of the faith, and want of zeal for the conversion of souls in our crowded towns; yet it follows not (God forbid) that life is therefore decaying. We see with our eyes that it is increasing, spreading, deepening. Yet since this is so, there is nothing to fear, nothing about which to despond." [3]

"Tokens of a past winter are not discouraging amid the signs of a returning spring."

"Without having any dread myself that the Church would be weakened by being disestablished, I trust that we shall be

<hr>

[1] *Leeds Sermons,* p. 373.
[2] *Speech, London Church Union.* Oct. 15, 1850.
[3] *Letter to English Churchmen.* October 1855.

even more careful than heretofore to win all people for the sake of the love with which our Master loves them." [1]

" Persecution is a great proselytizer." [2]

" But as a condition of this high and enlarged office, and of all other duties which may seem to be in store for her, as the Reformed Apostolic Church of the West, probation and severity appear to be likely to be allotted to her, as they have been to her branches in Scotland and America." [3]

" I believe there is a great future for the Church of England if she remains what she is." [4]

DANGERS IN RELIGION.

What caution is very needful for those who are devout and have pleasures in the duties of religion, in the worship of God, in Church, or in serving Him in works of mercy?

" The very things of God Himself, if sought for themselves, not for Him, may shut out God. Nay, there is very danger, in the most sacred things, in holy thoughts or fervent words, or transporting feelings, or labours of love, or heart-uplifting sounds, or Divine knowledge, that they may take up the soul the more readily in themselves, and the soul stop short in them, because it fears no danger, being as it were on 'holy ground.' " [5]

" How many praise sermons, how few act on them ! Not to such as we are, but to a Prophet, God saith, ' Thou art unto them as a very lovely song of one that hath a pleasant voice, and can play well upon an instrument ; for they hear Thy words, but they do them not.' How may perceive the beauty of holiness ; how few are holy ! How many can speak well of Jesus ; how few obey Him steadfastly or consistently !" [6]

[1] *Letter to Times*, Nov. 14, 1856.
[2] *Speech, P. W. R. Bill*, Meeting, June 1874.
[3] *Sermon*, November 5, Appendix, p. 77.
[4] *Letter to Times*, August 1872.
[5] Vol. ii. p. 252.   [6] Vol. i. p. 356.

CONTROVERSY.

If we differ with others, and feel it our duty to enter into controversy with them, how should we conduct the discussion?

" We should begin, not with that which is seemingly most at variance with our own thoughts, but with that which we believe in common." [1]

" We should look carefully what those to whom we seem to be opposed are themselves opposing."

" In judging also of the statements of others, we must give careful heed not only to the design of their meaning, but to the sense, whether exact or popular, in which they use whatever doctrinal words they employ."

" Only in whatsoever stage we are, let us beware of judging or disputing about things or practices which we have not tried. It is one sore evil of the age in which we live, that it disputes about everything, whether it understands it or no. Or rather, it disputes against holy duties and practices, because not having tried, it does not understand them, and so disputing, cannot understand them. The truth of God is a solemn thing, and to be treated reverently. For most of us it is dangerous to speak even against error, lest with the tares we root up the wheat also, the truth with error; lest we injure our own minds by speaking in a common way of things which God hath hallowed. How much more, if what men ignorantly speak against be, after all, a part of the truth of God, and they be found ' haply to fight against God.' " [2]

" Leave to the Church the controversies about the Church; the responsibility is hers and her teachers, not yours. Called by God in a Church having the Apostolic descent and the faith as once for all delivered to the Saints, there it is your duty to abide with God. Do you seek to approve yourself to God in her—in your daily duties and in your devotions—and you will find her what she is, the instrument of God for the salvation of

---

[1] *Justification*, vol. 1855, pp. 10, 11, 16.   [2] Vol. iii. p. 208.

your soul. Act as you must if you would be saved anywhere, and you will be saved in her." [1]

" You have long known how persuaded I have been these fifteen years that good men who seem to be opposed to the truth, are not really opposed to it, but to some counterfeit which they mistake for it, and which they suppose to be held as the truth." [2]

" It is of the very nature of error that it should look like truth ; even as a false coin has the royal image set upon it although it be base and adulterate. Mostly, it must be said, such have not gone the way of obedience and self-denial ; have not followed painfully, step by step, the leadings of God and the tracks of His Cross. We see not on such systems ' the prints of the Nails.' " [3]

" I cannot think it right or generous that persons under cover of anonymousness should assail one who writes under his own name." [4]

WARNINGS AGAINST UNSCRIPTURAL TEACHINGS ON CONVERSION AND REPENTANCE.

" Humility, retirement, obedience, fear, are the best accompaniments of penitence ; first to school and discipline self, and then await His further guidance under the shadow of His Church, what further task He has in store for us. Others mistake the stirrings within them for calls to act on other sinners ; their own restlessness, for God's summons to be doing." [5]

" And so souls, being scarce reformed themselves, set themselves, as it may be, to reform the Church. They blame her, because they themselves failed to profit by her ministry, or, instead of edifying the Church by the silent witness of their renewed lives, divide it by taking upon themselves a ministry to which they are not called, in some new or old schism."

[1] *English Churchman*, Dec. 11, 1841.   [2] *Supremacy*, p. 188.
[3] *Leeds Sermons*, p. 360.   [4] *Guardian*, March 25, 1863.
[5] Vol. iii. p. 36.

"If we deem ourselves set upon some great thing, out of the order of God's ordinary providence (as when one unlearned and uncommissioned thinks himself called to take upon himself the office of the ministry), we may well suspect ourselves ; but if, as God certainly often vouchsafes, the call sets him upon breaking off some sin, 'walking more humbly with his God,' doing more zealously the duties of his calling, then he may be assured Who is calling him. He may know that it is the voice of God, which he heareth behind him, saying, ' This is the way, walk ye in it.' "[1]

"If it were right to call any system 'soul-destroying,' it would be that which, making present assurance of salvation its sole end, checks the healthful agony with which God is searching into every defiled recess of the soul, and cleansing it for Himself, and releases it unbidden from its sufferings and its cure."[2]

"All are saved as yet in hope only."[3]

"There is then no safety, brethren, but never to think ourselves safe; Lent after Lent to bind ourselves to Him by penitence ; Easter after Easter to beware, lest in earthly joy or relaxation, we betray Him Whom in Lent we sought ; morning by morning to make Him anew our deeper, only choice, and pray Him to knit it fast unto Himself; evening by evening quickly to amend by prayer for pardon and grace and more earnest purpose, if in aught through human infirmity we have chosen amiss."

"The doctrine often found that ' they who believe they are saved, are saved '; that ' man's salvation depends on his own personal assurance that he is saved '; that ' an act of faith (as it is called) conveys in itself the pardon of past sin,' are, however qualified or inconsistently held by individuals, deadly heresies ; in Wesleyanism, the system thereon founded threatens to be one of the most dreadful scourges with which the Church was ever afflicted, the great antagonist of penitence, as those who have charge of souls most sorrowfully find."

[1] Vol. iii. p. 408.   [2] *Id.* p. 136.   [3] Vol. i. p. 272.

" He would teach us that it is like a hireling to look for a reward, which yet our Blessed Saviour in His human nature, Scripture saith, looked for ; He would take the appearance of an angel of light, and use the holiest doctrines, and teach us that if we profess a belief in Christ we shall be accepted, and shall not be judged according to our works, although Scripture says we shall ; He would make us think it a merit to renounce our works, and that if we renounce them, we shall not be judged by them." [1]

" False then is every system of ' will-worship and would-be humility,' which, under the show of not trusting in works, would make a work of faith, and look to its faith as something of its own, and seek to be saved by what it thinks faith. ' Without faith we cannot please God, or do works pleasing to Him '; yet not by our faith shall we be judged, but by our works. He has assigned to us no other witness of our love for Him than this, ' Keep My commandments.' He has told thee that thou shalt be judged, not according to what thou persuadest thyself that thou feelest, but by what thou dost by thy works." [2]

WARNING AGAINST MERE EMOTIONAL RELIGION.

" The strongest emotions are not necessarily the deepest or the most lasting. The tears of penitence which flow the fastest, often flow the fastest away. The bounding joy in finding anew the forgotten Saviour which is uttered most ardently, may die away the soonest. Hot water freezeth soonest. True conversion to God is not a passing feeling, not exulting gladness in the boundless love of God, not swelling thankfulness for His redeeming mercies ; it lives not in ardent emotions, impulses, nor even in burning desires to live more to God, and to be more faithful to Him. It includes all these, but it goes beyond them. It is to hate what God hates, and love what God loves ; it is to hate one's self

---

[1] *Day of Judgment,* p. 13.　　　　[2] *Id.* p. 22.

for having loved what God hated, and hated what God loved ; and to grieve that too late we loved Him. It is to love Him who died for us, and bore with us, and forgave us ; and loving Him, to cleave to Him. Its seal is perseverance through His grace, unto the end." [1]

Remember—"It is an awful gift to have recovered grace ; to be again entrusted with what we had forfeited."

SAVED BY HIS LIFE.

"Not alone to die for us, did the Son of God leave the glory of His Father ; but to live for us, and in us ; to conquer our great enemy, Satan, in the very nature which he had defeated and corrupted." [2]

FREE-WILL.

"He hath given you free-will that you may freely choose Him, your God, and His Will. He who could dispose of us without our wills, respects our free-will ; He will not force us even to our good. He willed that even the Incarnation should not take place until His creature by His grace, said, 'Behold, the handmaid of the Lord ; be it unto me according to Thy word.' 'He waits for our wills.'" [3]

"Dare to look at Hell, and read there our own deserts, and how God must have loved thy free-love and choice of Himself ; that, at the risk of losing thee, He endowed thee with that nobility of choice to choose Himself." [4]

"Without free-will, man would be inferior to the lower animals, which have a sort of limited freedom of choice." [5]

"Absolute free-will implies the power of choosing amiss, and having chosen amiss, to persevere in choosing amiss. It would be self-contradictory, that Almighty God should create a free agent capable of loving Him, without being capable also of rejecting His love."

<hr>

[1] *Parochial and Cathedral Sermons*, p. 67. [2] Vol. iii. p. 441.
[3] *Sermons*, 1872, p. 459. [4] *Lenten Sermons*, p. 256.
[5] *"What is of Faith ?"* p. 22.

"The higher and more complete and pervading that free-will is, the more completely an evil choice will pervade and disorder the whole being."

"But without free-will we could not freely love God. Freedom is a condition of love."

"In eternity, those who behold Him will know what the bliss is, eternally to love Him. But then that bliss involves the intolerable misery of losing Him through our own evil choice. To lose God and be alienated from Him, is in itself Hell, or the vestibule of Hell."

"But that His creatures may not lose Him, God, when He created all His rational creatures with free-will, created them also in grace, so that they had the full power to choose aright, and could not choose amiss, except by resisting the drawing of God to love Him."

"The only hindrance to man's salvation is, in any case, the obstinate misuse of that free-will with which God endowed him, in order that he might freely love Him."

"God wills that all should be saved if they will it, and to this end gave His Son to die for them, and the Holy Ghost to teach them."

"The merits of Jesus reach to every soul who wills to be saved, whether in this life they knew Him or knew Him not."

"God the Holy Ghost visits every soul which God has created, and each soul will be judged as it responded, or did not respond, to the degree of light which He bestowed on it, not by our maxims, but by the wisdom and love of Almighty God."

"None will be lost, whom God can save, without destroying in them His own gift of free-will."

"Free-will of which men boast, is, in our corrupted nature, a perilous gift. At best it is an awful gift. In our corrupted nature it is a freedom to choose good or evil, with a strong overcoming bias to evil; in our restored nature, it is a power to choose for ourselves that which God appointed for us. To choose by a separate act of our own, unconstrained, uncompelled, that which alone ought to be chosen, the will of God. It is an awful dignity with which we are invested, that, whereas inferior creatures fulfil God's law by the very law of their being, and He Himself is their law, we have it left in our choice whether we will so do. We fulfil His law not by constraint or of necessity, but by a separate act of our own. Amazing and awful gift, this—one which, for its very greatness, we might well shrink from, but that He has been pleased to lay it upon us—for a creature to have to choose by an act of its own, its Creator's will; to have in any degree to concur, so to say, with Him, Who is the only source of power and right; to have to choose for ourselves Him, Who is the only object of right choice; to be in any sort even so far (one dreads to say the very word) independent of Him, as to be able even to choose Him and His laws by any act of our own." [1]

"On one side is the Creator, on the other the creature. We must choose wholly the One, the Creator, or we do choose the other, the creature. We have our choice given between the two. There can be no choice without preference. Whenever there is a choice to be made, if we choose the creature against the will of God, no matter how small it may seem, we are rejecting the Creator. Nay, in one way, its very smallness makes the act more grievous in that, for a small matter, we go against the will of God." [2]

"Jesus came as a Teacher of mankind; but, as has been said, 'rather to be the Object of a revelation than to make one.' He Himself was the centre of His own revelation. He came to reveal Himself as the Saviour of mankind, to suffer for our sins, to die for us, and so to enter into His Glory, and to reign not only as King of kings, and Lord of lords, but to be adored by all, visible and invisible, whom He had created, wherever any created being is in boundless space, who does not abuse that awful prerogative with which God has invested His intelligent creatures, to return love for love, or to refuse it." [3]

[1] Vol. iii. p. 76. [2] *Id.* p. 78. [3] *Prophecy of Jesus,* p. 13.

THE DANGER OF UNBELIEF.

" These things, about which God's creatures dispute so freely, are not matters of keen intellectual subtlety, or trial of skill, or practice of acuteness, or exercise of greater boldness than our fellow-men venture upon ; they are matters of certain truth which God has infallibly revealed, and in rejecting which truth men reject God." [1]

" If men, through their own fault, reject Him (of which not they, but He, the Searcher of hearts, is the judge), they are matters of life and death, of life and death eternal, of that everlasting life in God in Heaven, or that deathless death, apart from Him, in an everlasting loss of God in Hell. It is Jesus, Who died for us, Who so loved us as to die for us, Who, in His love, said it, that we might not die eternally : ' He that believeth not, shall be damned.' "

DEVELOPMENT.

What is meant by the doctrine of development ?
" Taught by the Church to receive that, and that alone, as matter of faith, which was part of the good deposit once for all committed to the saints, and which had been held always everywhere, and by all, we must not venture to receive what is confessedly of a more recent origin, and whose tendency seems at variance with Holy Scripture itself. While acknowledging the authority of the Church in controversies of faith (Art. XX.), he could not understand on what ground that vast system, as to St. Mary, could be rested, except that of a new revelation." [2]

For instance, " It seems inconceivable that St. Peter, St. John, and St. Paul should have believed what is now earnestly taught and believed upon authority within the Roman Church, as to the present office of the Blessed Virgin, or that believing

[1] Vol. 1872, p. 76.   [2] *Eirenicon*, pt. i. pp. 113, 114.

it, they could have written as (*e. g.*) St. Paul through the Holy
Ghost, in the Epistle to the Hebrews; or that if Almighty God
had willed it to be believed in the Church, it should have been
so excluded from Holy Scripture, and the doctrine itself not
have appeared for centuries."

*May the Creeds be explained variously as to their essential
meaning according to the private judgment of individuals ?*

" Surely wherein the Church meant them to have a definite
meaning, that is their meaning to all who belong to the Church.
In those points in which the Church meant to declare her
faith, what she meant to declare is her faith.   The faith cannot
change.   It is like Him from Whom it comes, in Whom it
centres, 'the same yesterday, to-day, and for ever.' It is unchangeable because He is.   It is truth, from the Truth.   It
cannot cease to be the truth, since He from Whom it comes is
Truth.   The Creeds cannot change.   The one truth may be
explained further.   It cannot be altered, cannot cease to be
truth.   What *was* faith, remains faith.   What *was* opinion,
remains opinion.   They cannot interchange.   What was certain
cannot become uncertain.   What was part of ' the Faith once
for all delivered to the Saints,' must remain so.   What was not
cannot become so.   What St. Peter, St. John, St. Paul were
taught by God to believe, and taught the Church, that is the
faith now.   It may vary in expression, not in substance.   It is
not the question, then, how much or how little may seem to
any one to lie in any words of the Creed ; how much any
person without previous knowledge of the subject might imagine
them to contain.   Creeds were formed for the declaration of
certain truths.   They had, in that they were creeds, one definite,
recognized sense.   When persons arose who wished to change
that sense, the Church declared more explicitly in words the
one sense in which she had always understood them." [1]

" How infinitely more sublime a view of the Christian
Revelation is presented by conceiving it originally delivered
to the world in its full, consummate perfection, than by this

----

[1] *Supremacy*, p. 230.

cumbrous and complicated hypothesis of perpetual supple-ments and infallible guarantees! How incomparably more wonderful appears the compass of that wisdom which "once for all delivers" to mankind a brief system of belief and practice, of such depth and power, that comprised within it, and capable of being educed and applied according to the needs of man in the simple exercise of reason, shall be found all that, in all the changes of society, shall ever be required for the perfect education of humanity—than that which is displayed in furnishing supplementary revelations as circum-stances arise, and providing a perpetual inspiration to watch and adjust the variations of the system !

.   .   .   .

"The true glory of the Gospel is that of original maturity, simplicity, and comprehensiveness—not (though under any form we had been bound to unutterable gratitude for the blessing) that of progressive enlargement and gradual com-pletion. Christianity was not designed to become known at last, by striking, from age to age, a precarious and difficult average among hesitating teachers; it was not to be nursed through an infancy and childhood of centuries into a slow and imperfect adolescence. Christianity was born full-grown. Its authentic stamp of Divinity is this—that its Author so marvellously "knew what was in man," that no revolution of man's history could take His Dispensation by surprise; that He should so lay down (if I may venture a figure intelligible to mathematicians) the equation of the human heart, that in that single comprehensive provision all the possible varieties of individual and social man were for ever foreseen and included.

"To the reflective mind this aspect of the characteristic excellency of the Christian Revelation will open views which I cannot but think infinitely superior, both in speculative interest and in practical profit, to any which are ever likely to be suggested by the opposite hypothesis of doctrinal develop-ment."—ARCHER BUTLER *on Development*, pp. 399, 400.

INTELLECT AND ITS DANGERS.

" It is no disparagement to high intellect to say that it has its own special temptations. Powerful intellect has its temptations, as well as great physical powers, or great wealth. The temptations of the most powerful, are the most powerful. I believe that this forcing-house for intellect, in which the plants are to draw one another up, each striving upwards for the light, produces an unhealthy growth. If men are practically taught that cultivation of the intellect is the highest end, they are thereby even encouraged to neglect its correction, repression, subdual, in things which are beyond its range." [1]

" All things must speak of God, refer to God, or they are atheistic. History without God is a chaos without design or end or aim. Political economy without God would be a selfish teaching about the acquisition of wealth, making the larger portion of mankind animate machines for its production. Physics without God would be but a dull inquiry into certain meaningless phenomena. Ethics without God would be a varying rule without principle, or substance, or centre, or regulating hand. Metaphysics without God would make man his own temporary god, to be resolved, after his brief hour here, into the nothingness out of which he proceeded. All sciences may do good service if those who cultivate them know their place, and carry them not beyond their sphere; all may, in different degrees, tend to cultivate the human mind, although no one human mind has time or capacity for all. But all will become antagonistic to truth if they are deified by their votaries; all will tend to exclude the thought of God if they are not cultivated with reference to Him. History will become an account of man's passions and brute strength instead of the ordering of God's providence for His creatures' good. Physics will materialize man, and metaphysics God." [2]

" Intellect, by itself, heightened, sharpened, refined, cool,

---

[1] *Collegiate Teachings*, p. 74.   [2] *Id.* p. 213.

piercing, subtle, would be after the likeness, not of God, but of His enemy, who is acuter and subtler far than the acutest and the subtlest." [1]

REASON.

Is not reason often in direct conflict with Faith ?

" Yes ; but it is also true that reason healed, restored, guided, enlightened by the Spirit of God has a power of vision above nature, and can spiritually discern a fitness and correspondence and harmony in the things of God which through faith it has received and believed." [2]

" Reason, unaided, cannot even penetrate into the sphere of the objects of faith, discern their substance, or measure them by earthly laws." [3]

Those who think reason by itself can settle what is to be believed, what God has revealed, forget the injury of the Fall in Paradise.

" Reason unaided, unsanctified by the Spirit of God, is not ' such as Adam had it before the Fall, unwarped by prejudices, unswayed by pride, undeafened by passions, unallured by self-idolizing, unfettered by love of independence and master of itself because subdued to God.' " [4]

HERESY.

" A false application of truth. This is the parent of almost every heresy, by which people have hidden from their own eyes or from others the truth of God. Dwelling upon one set of truths or of texts which establish them, against another, men deny, in the Name of God, the truth of God." [5]

RATIONALISM.

" I never looked on Rationalism except as a deadly enemy." [6]

[1] *Collegiate Teachings*, p. 215.   [2] *All Faith*, p. 17.
[3] *Id.* p. 16.   [4] *Id.* p. 16.
[5] *Lenten Sermons*, p. 135.   [6] *Letter to Record*, March 11, 1863.

ON THE STUDY OF THE FATHERS.

All cannot, but to those who can, would the study of the Fathers be very useful?

"If any would spend as much time in reading the Fathers as they do on daily or weekly papers, magazines, periodicals, and other ephemeral publications, they could in a few years enrich their life's blood by the marrow and fullness of the teaching of the Fathers. If I might leave one bequest to the rising generation of clergy, who will have (what I have had only incidentally) the office of preachers, it would be, 'In addition to the study of Holy Scripture, which they too studied night and day, study the Fathers, especially St. Augustine.'"[1]

"It is one thing to argue from the Fathers in proof of doctrine, another to listen to them as practical teachers, opening, as they do richly, the meaning of Holy Scripture, or impressing the substance of the great truths of the gospel. To quote or argue from the Fathers requires learning; to learn of them only teachableness."[2]

"It is people's own fault if they make a show of learning, or argue, in a shallow way, from this or that Father who they happen to hear alleged in controversy. The Fathers spoke to the hearts of their own people; the members of the One Body of Christ, in their own day: they will yet speak to the heart, if they read with hearts which God teaches."[3]

COMFORT TO PENITENTS.

"Hast thou lost that first bright crown of virgin souls, who have loved God alone, have ever loved Him, loved Him with

---

[1] *Parochial and Cathedral Sermons*, Preface, p. ii.
[2] *Lenten Readings*, Preface, p. v.   [3] *Id.* p. vi.

their first pure, spotless, ardent, undivided love, yet who can tell the brightness of her crown, who once despised of man : despising herself yet more, with unshamed shame, which maketh not ashamed, burst through to the Feet of Jesus, and washed them with a sinner's burning tears ? " [1]

PURITY.

" Limb by limb they are the same bodies as that which God the Son took, which for us was crucified, which now is in glory at the Right Hand of God. All sin is misery because it is rebellion against so loving a Father ; all aggravated sin has its deeper misery ; that it does, in fact, make a mock, and sets at naught the Cross of Christ. Sins of the flesh have yet this special misery, that they degrade that body which Jesus took, degrade it below the beasts which perish. To sin as to the flesh, is to insult Christ. It is to insult Him, because they are the like bodies to that which He took and glorified, but also because He has made these, our very bodies, His. His they are, because He bought them at so dear a price. His they are, because in Baptism we put on Christ : His they are, because by His gift, the gift of the Holy Ghost, they are the temples of the Holy Ghost, the dwelling-place of the Trinity, as He says, 'We will come unto him, and make our abode in him' : being made members of Christ, the Only Begotten Son of God ; His they are, because He has said, 'He that eateth My Flesh, and drinketh My Blood, dwelleth in Me, and I in him.' " [2]

THE FALLEN.

" And those too, to human sight, lost, degraded, outcasts ; first destroyed, and then destroyers ; first corrupted, and then corrupters ; those hapless wrecks betrayed to their destruction, because they once chose vanity or easiness, or misplaced

[1] *Leeds Sermons*, p. 275.   [2] *Lenten Sermons*, p. 376.

affection, rather than the plain will and command of God—
they too were once the temples of God. Once God dwelt in
them ; once they were His children, heirs—our fellow-heirs of
the bliss of His Presence in Heaven. And now, forsaken they
seem of God and man. Fathers, mothers, brothers, sisters
now own them not ; perhaps they dare not own them, for fear
of injury to those who remain ; or orphans they were with no
mother's care (orphans they not unseldom are, even of those
born as we), who for want, or homelessness, or friendlessness,
broke the law of God ; and man, who makes light of other
breaches of God's law, who forgives himself any breaches of
the law of God, fulfils in them the righteous judgment of
God, and as it were, outlaws them. A short-lived generation,
decaying before they have lived half their years ; sinking into
the grave, weighed down untimely by the sins whose guilt they
share, but whose weight they alone bear, dying like the brute
creation, none knows how, no one well nigh cares to know :
unheeded, unwarned, unprayed for, out of hearing of their
Saviour's Name, and, so far as human sight can see, unrepentant,
unknowing how to repent, and so, if forgiven, forgiven in their
last hour, through His unrevealed Mercy, Who made them for
Himself." [1]

And yet God loves them still ; God must love them still,
for He still gives them life and time for repentance : He who
willeth not that any should perish, willeth that they too should
be "converted and live." He knows that they can repent.
He said of such as they are, that they should by repentance
enter the Kingdom of Heaven before the self-justifying
Pharisees. To one whose sins were such as theirs, who being
forgiven much, loved much ; He himself first appeared after
the Resurrection, before His Disciples, before His Mother,
and made the penitent an apostle to apostles, the bearer of
good tidings to those who should preach the Gospel to the
world.

They may yet turn to God, and if there be a penitent sinner

---

[1] *Parochial and Cathedral Sermons,* p. 467.

over whom angels may rejoice, surely it may well be such as these, who fell through others' sin even more than through their own, and who seem to have been dragged on to their misery rather than themselves to have sought it. A closer knowledge of their unhappy histories fills even man with deep compassion. How much more their God! If there is a sight touching to human sympathy it is to see the returning blush of modesty again tinge the cheeks, whence it seemed to man's eyes to have been bleached and worn away for ever.

"Think of those tens of thousands in our cities, who die an untimely death, *publicæ libidinis victimæ*, and that of Christians." [1]

By thoughtless familiarities such as the young often think to be no harm, reserve was broken, the bloom of modesty was brushed away. Once, one by one they were perhaps like your own sisters; their brothers doubtless thought so. And now, who shall say that every careless word, careless act, did not contribute to their present death? As well say that each blow of the axe did not aid to lay the oak prostrate. Is one less a poisoner because he gives those accumulating doses which in the end destroy life, or because the last comes from another hand? How can they think that Christian purity exists, that there is anything to repent of, when they know only of those who seek them as accomplices of their sin? And yet, unless rescued by some miracle of God's grace, they will each in the Day of Judgment accuse with that agonizing shriek of despair, every one who bribed them to fill up the measure of their perdition: "We were destroyed by you, and you, and you, disciples of the Crucified." "Woe to that man by whom the offence cometh."

"There is a class of short-lived, half-willing, half-unwilling sufferers by man's sins, worn down to an early dishonoured grave by the sins of man and their own. God has his own among them also. For them also, Christ died. One of them was nearest to the Cross and earliest at the grave of Jesus

---

[1] *Parochial and Cathedral Sermons*, p. 366.

when Apostles had fled. There are among them, who wish to be delivered from the bondage in which they are held, who loathe the sin by which they sustain their living death, in whom the chastening hand of God is working by His Grace, weariness of sin, and a longing to be free at least from their misery, which may be transformed into the glorious freedom of children of God." [1]

What must those be very careful about, who by God's grace are not addicted to, or have overcome temptations to sins after the flesh?

"Not only to watch and pray humbly lest they too fall; but also to remember, ' Spiritual sins may be even in more direct antagonism to the Holy Spirit than grosser offences. For the sins of this poor weak flesh of ours may be sins of weakness. Spiritual sins are sins of defiance of the human spirit against the Divine.' " [2]

ST. MARY MAGDALENE.

"On the whole then the identity of the individual who anointed our Lord, seems to follow from the most natural explanation of St. John xi. 2, to have recommended itself to the minds of simple Christians, and unless it be supposed (which is the opinion of Origen only, and very improbable) that there were three acts of anointing, or three women who anointed our Lord; the narratives of St. Matthew and St. Mark are harmonized most naturally with that of St. John (ch. xii.) on the supposition that the anointing related by St. Luke was a distinct act of the same individual. This opinion, which appears (as was said) to have been the most common before Origen, is adopted in several places by St. Gregory the Great from St. Augustine; and partly, perhaps from its naturalness, partly from having been received in the Roman Breviary, has been prevalent in the Western Church. The alleged difficulties as to the Scripture narrative are occasioned solely by the sup-

---

[1] *Lenten Sermons*, p. 419.   [2] Vol. 1872, p. 491.

position, that one act, not two different acts, of the same person are related." [1]

"We then must love all—Jews, Turks, infidels, and heretics; all, however fallen or staining the Christian name; all outcasts from men and mere human sympathy, 'in highways or hedges, streets or lanes of the city.' Yea, we must love them the more, would we have Divine love, because they are shut out from all love but God's." [2]

SINS OF REFINEMENT.

"Refinement of itself may only blind us the more, because its 'sins are the more subtle. Its sins are more malignant, more deliberate, more unawakening, more directed against God, more diabolical. A man sins in them more, face to face against God." [3]

"Antagonism to Christ is not the less dangerous because it is smooth. Its smoothness is the kiss of Orpah, who returned to the world and her gods. It is the kiss of Judas, who betrayed his Lord and God with a 'Hail Master!' Refined sin is mostly more deadly than gross crime.

"The world is more perilous when it blandishes than when it molests; it is more to be mistrusted when it allures to love it, than when it gives warning and constrains our contempt."— St. Augustine.

"A very polished surface will betray even wary feet." [4]

"I much fear that subtle, delicate sins may, in the Day of Judgment, bring a heavier sentence on the sinner than the coarse brutalities of the brutalized. And this, because the will is the spring of all sin; and the clearer the light of God's law without, the brighter and more spotless that mirror of God's law, our human reason, is in any of us, the more inveterate is the maliciousness of the human will, which disobeys God in both." [5]

---

[1] *Leeds Sermons*, p. 394.   [2] *Occasional Sermons,* "*God is Love*," p. 15.
[3] *Lenten Sermons*, p. 282.   [4] Vol. 1872, p. 403.   [5] *Id.* p. 292.

SINFUL LUXURY.

"And sad as is the sight of its heart-aching penury; sad to behold the shifts whereby our fellow-beings strive to keep off starvation; sad as it is to read the hard intellectual faces of those of whom one dare not hope that they believe in God; sad to track it by night in streets chiefly illumined by its gin-palaces; miserable as is the hollow laugh of women who have sold themselves to sin, perhaps out of penury; there is one sadder sight than all—because it is the sin most against the light and love of God—it is the luxury of its many Dives, who know all this, and pass by on the other side, loving their own luxuries, comforts, pleasures, vanities, frivolities, more than the souls for which Jesus died. It is sadder; for He has said, 'The publicans and harlots go into the kingdom of God before you.'" [1]

FASHION AND SIN.

"If mothers in these days seek the fashionable houses of those from whom if they were poor instead of wealthy they would shrink, what do they but connive at and abet the damnation of those once Christians in deed as well as name? What do they but cheer them on in their way to Hell, and repeat to God Cain's impious taunt, 'Am I my brother's keeper?'" [2]

THE PRESENCE OF GOD.

Is God everywhere present?

Yes, in all places; there is no imaginable place where He is not.

"He is not in one way within them, in another way without them, but One and the Same God wholly everywhere. He does not fill one with one part of Himself and another with another part, but is One and the Same in all. He is not stretched out

---

[1] Vol. 1872, p. 132.   [2] *Lenten Sermons*, p. 167.

in order to contain ; not in place, although He is above and below, but the Same, as the Same ruling above and supporting below ; encircling without, with that Same being which filleth within.

" But then since God is everywhere, we move, speak, act, think, in God." [1]

" This might be very blessed, the bliss almost of the blessed in Heaven. But it has its awful side also, since we think, speak, act in God, then every sin which men commit, the foulest, most cruel, most loathsome, most contrary to the nature which God formed, is committed in God." [2]

" If the viewless air which is around thy very frame were all eyes, all bent upon thee in thy sin, what a faint image were it of the One, all-seeing, all-piercing Presence of God, in which ' we live and move,' and in which and against which, if thou sin, thou sinnest." [3]

FEAR OF HELL.

" The dread of Hell brought you probably to repentance. Shrink not from thinking of Hell. No one, probably, who thought much of it, ever fell into it." [4]

" For nothing will keep man from any sin except the love of God or the fear of Hell. And any one who knows anything of the human soul, knows in what countless cases the fear of Hell first drove men to their forgotten God and Saviour, and so they learned to know Him, and to love Him." [5]

What is Conscience ?

" Conscience is not thine own voice. It speaks not at thy will, but against it. It is God's voice within thee, approving, checking, upbraiding, condemning ; unchangeable in itself as the law of God which it enforces, it will speak plainly at times, though thou sin against it, though thou elude it, though thou stifle it, at least until thou have sinned away grace, and God

---

[1] *Vol.* ii. p. 376.   [2] *Id.* p. 377.   [3] *Id.* p. 378.
[4] *Lenten Sermons*, p. 233.   [5] *Letter to Record*, Feb. 19, 1864.

has abandoned thee.   But beware, as you value your salvation,
how you tamper with it ; how, Balaam-like, you persuade yourselves that God may not disapprove what thou knowest, what
He has told thee that He hates." [1]

"There are two sorts of peaceful consciences, and there are
two sorts of troubled consciences.   There is a good conscience
which is peaceful because it mourns its past sin for love of
Him who loved us ; it resists mightily present temptation, in
His might who overcame the Evil one ; it trusts in Him, Who
never fails them who trust Him.   This is a foretaste of Paradise, peace in Him who is our Peace.   'Peace which passeth
all understanding.'   But even the good conscience may be
troubled, either if it roots not out strongly lesser faults, or if it
dwells on the hardness of the struggle rather than on the greatness of the Reward.   If it serves in fear, rather than in love ;
if it dwells on its failings, rather than on the boundless love of
Jesus, or thinks of Him as the Judge more than the Redeemer.

"But peace, as it is the blessing of the good conscience, so
it is the curse of the bad conscience." [2]

"A troubled and remorseful conscience has life, its remorse
is the token of its life.   There is hope of a man amid any sin
I might almost say, amid any mass of sins, if he hates them,
and does not hate them less than he did once.   Nay, there
is a hope of him if he has any real hatred still.   A conscience
wholly at peace and yet sinning, is not alive but dead." [3]

SELF-DECEIT.

"There must be the more scope for it, the greater the light
with which any are surrounded.   Whatever crimes, violations
of man's better nature, brutalities, brutishness, there may be
among heathen nations, there is the less scope for self-deceit.
Among them it can only find room where men stifle the inward
workings of the Holy Spirit, the unknown God." [4]

[1] *Lenten Sermons*, p. 85.   [2] *Parochial and Cathedral Sermons*, p. 3.
[3] *Id.* p. 4.   [4] *Lenten Sermons*, p. 130.

"Self-deceit is almost as varied as the human mind. For it is the working of nature to exempt itself from the uncomfortable operations of God's Holy Spirit upon it, a false conscience dexterously framed to overlay and stifle the voice of the true. It is the outcome and result of repeated lies which the soul tells to itself; first, timidly whispered, then said hesitatingly, then with less and less misgiving, or amid, or after intervals of misgiving, until at last they are told to itself with effrontery resenting all contradiction."

SELF-EXAMINATION.

Is this a most important duty?

"How can it be safe for us, brethren, not to know as fully as we can our past lives? How can we be forgiven our sins unless we repent of them, or repent of them unless we know them?—or know them unless we think of them? Or do ye think that because ye know in a general way where ye passed your lives, what has been your outward calling, your bodily employment with whom ye have lived, conversed; yea, the changes of your circumstances, therefore ye know your inward lives? Your lives are not the mere outward life of the body, they are chiefly the life of the soul; not merely what we did, spake, thought, but *why* we did what we did; whether we lived, acted, thought with a view to God, or to the world ourselves." [1]

"We cannot understand what we are now, unless we look back as far as we may on all we have been." [2]

"Whosoever, I may say, has not all his life through been taking heed to his ways, and has, at whatever time, been brought by the grace of God, to look back on his own past life, has found much evil which he thought not of; much or most of which he thought to be good, to be at least mixed up with and spoiled by real evil." [3]

"There are many ways to Hell; only one to life, the way is narrow; not to take heed is to miss it. 'The snares of death

----

[1] Vol. i. p. 212. [2] *Id.* p. 213. [3] *Id.* p. 214.

encompass us'; not to take heed is to fall into them. Not fully to know thyself, as far as thou canst, is to walk blindly on a precipice, where to fall is to perish for ever." [1]

"One way only there is, as God bids you, 'examine yourselves.' 'Examine your own conscience,' our Church repeats, 'and that not lightly and after the manner of dissemblers with God'; 'examine your lives and conversations by the rule of God's commandments.' If thou hast not yet thoroughly examined thyself, be sure that thou dost not yet know thyself. Thou must examine thyself, that thou mayest know thyself. Thou must examine thyself, that thou mayest keep the knowledge of thyself, and not forget thyself. Thou must examine thyself again and again, as thou wouldst glean after harvest, that nothing be lost. Thou must examine thyself, not by the examples of those around thee, nor by the maxims of the world, nor heeding the praise (if so be) which men give thee, but by the light of God's commandments." [2]

DEBTS.

"Or does vanity and love of personal appearance or the wish to vie with those of larger means tempt thee to contract debts which thou canst not pay, and knowst not how thou ever wilt pay? 'Owe no man anything,' saith God, 'but to love one another.'" [3]

DESPISE NONE.

"There is so much patient, almost sacramental suffering among the poor; among those whom men call outcasts, whom we neglect, who perhaps not through their own fault have not heard the Name of Jesus. That still often uncomplaining suffering must have been God's unknown unperceived grace. Now God is waiting to be gracious to that soul. I doubt not that much mercy is shown in that last hour, although I should

---

[1] Vol. i. p. 215.　　　[2] Vol. ii. p. 109.　　　[3] *Lenten Sermons*, p. 63.

expect it least, for those who delayed repentance to that hour. For theirs was a continued rejection of God." [1]

CURIOSITY.

" Victory were, by God's grace comparatively easy, were it not that the devil's porter, curiosity, opened the gate, and brought in those beasts of hell which lay waste the soul. They who have not in boyhood indulged curiosity, are blessedly exempt from a whole embattled army of trials, which it lets in on the poisoned soul. The baleful poison of the sin of knowledge has not spoiled the imaginations, stirred up passions by nature happily asleep, created longings which belong not to its age, not taken the will captive when innocence would still start back from completed guilt." [2]

> " Curiousness, first cause of all our ill,
> Is yet the plague, which most torments us still."

LEVITY.

" Man's tone of mind upon each several subject is the result of that with which he has approached or engaged in every other. Not only in confirmed cases, as of a buffoon or a jester who cannot, when he would, be serious; but in each shade between the commonplace product of a self-indulgent age, and him who, for and with his Lord, ' died daily '; is that saying verified, ' the natural man receiveth not the things of the Spirit of God, neither can he perceive them because they are spiritually discerned.' " [3]

" Or dost thou in levity and wantonness of spirit, by look or word or touch, risk injuring another's soul, or encourage them in sin, or jest at seriousness? To do aught which may injure another's soul is to be, as far as in thee lies, a murderer of souls."

[1] *Eleven Addresses*, p. 113.
[2] *Lenten Sermons*, p. 121.
[3] *Doctrine of Holy Baptism*, p. 189.
[4] *Lenten Sermons*, p. 64.

SELF.

"For even when men have learnt to renounce, as they hope, their own merits and their own works, and would be nothing of themselves, but for all depend upon Christ; still, self in the one or the other subtle way, creeps in. Yea, often self the more creeps in, because people think they have once for all renounced self, and rely rather on the good profession which they have made and make; than on earnest, continual subdual of self." [1]

KNOWLEDGE.

"I will not willingly exaggerate anything, nor would I attach an undue importance to the knowledge even of Divine things. Every Christian must be assured that without the Spirit of Christ, learning as well as every other good gift of God will become a snare to its possessor; that, unless it be consecrated to God's service, it must of necessity be profaned: that one may understand all mysteries and all knowledge, and yet be but as sounding brass or a tinkling cymbal." [2]

DELAYING TO REPENT.

"Direct disobedience has been converted and saved; we hear of no conversion of one who promised future obedience. The son who said, 'I go not,' afterwards 'repented and went.'" [3]

"What is then the danger of delay, what is its offensiveness, that God warns us, that if we neglect His grace to-day, the to-morrow to which we procrastinate may not be a day of grace to us? It is not that God would not hear us, if we were to choose *then*, what we delay to choose *now*. It is that our delay shows that we have not the love of God *now*, and that we do not wish to have it." [4]

---

[1] Vol. iii. p. 467.
[2] *Cathedral Institutions*, p. 28.
[3] *Lenten Sermons*, p. 205.
[4] *Id.* p. 207.

TEMPTATION.

" Now as to all temptations which are voluntary, there is but one rule of salvation, ' avoid them as you would avoid hell.' To remain wilfully in or near occasion of sin is to trifle with God and your own salvation." [1]

EXCUSES FOR SIN.

The Balaam soul says, " True, God has said, ' Thou shalt not commit adultery.' God forbid that I should so sin ! But God has not forbidden this or that way of dressing, this or that way of speaking, this or that meeting, or intimacy, or connection." [2]

Abhor that which is evil. Yield not to the least beginnings of temptation ; avoid, as far as possible, all occasions of temptation.

THE FRUIT OF UNCONQUERED TEMPTATION TO SIN.

" And yet some one unmastered, over-mastering sin, makes the heart not whole with God, defiles perhaps the temple of the Holy Ghost, the body ; it wounds the conscience, cripples the soul, withdraws it from intercourse with God, its life, chases away the Holy Spirit, scares from Communions the great preservative against deadly sin, or makes the soul go to them faithlessly, hopelessly, unprofitably." [3]

LIES.

" Or despisest thou truth, when it suiteth thee, in exaggeration, to give life to thy conversation, or to avoid some scrape or some passing shame, or to exalt thyself? Dost thou act untruth, palming off as thine what is not thine? Deceit, in act or word, direct or indirect, in ways habitual to those in thy

---

[1] *Lenten Sermons,* p. 260.　　　　[2] *Id.* p. 84.　　　　[3] *Id.* p. 318.

station or thine own, is lying ; and 'liars,' thou knowest, 'shall have their part in the lake of fire.' Thou canst not lie and be a Christian." [1]

RIDICULE.

" Ridicule cannot be employed with impunity as a test of truth ; error and truth often lie so closely together, nay, most religious error has so much of truth mingled up with it, that the very love of truth ought to preclude the love of jesting, not to say that the fearfulness of the subject, and the majesty of Almighty God might well instinctively awe men into sobriety. For, through this close connection of truth and error, mire cannot be cast at error, without defiling the truth also. To take the most palpable errors : Could a man jest at Trans-substantiation, and not thereby unfit his mind for the reception of the Holy Mystery of the Communion ? " [2]

WRONG LOVE.

" Except the loss of God, I cannot conceive a suffering in hell greater than that of the horrible hate of one another, especially of those who, by mutual sin and chiefly by unlawful love, have brought each other thither." [3]

VANITY.

If again thy temptation is to vanity, then all this trickery of dress, wherewith our women caricature the extravagances of a neighbouring nation, and make themselves (if they knew it) the laughing-stock of those whose admiration they would draw —what mockery of God it is, amid everything which can minister to vanity, to pray to God for humility, amid exposure of person of which heathen Rome would have been ashamed, to pray for modesty. [4]

[1] *Lenten Sermons*, p. 63.
[2] *Earnest Remembrance*, p. 4.
[3] *Eleven Addresses*, p. 50.
[4] *Lenten Sermons*, p. 268.

SIMONY.

What is the sin of unworthy traffic in the sale of Livings ?
"Christ is sold continually, in the buying and selling, for unworthy persons, the cure of souls." [1]

BACKSLIDING.

" As it is the greatest triumph of the Grace of God and the joy of the Holy Angels when the lost sinner is found, so it seems the greatest reproach to the power of God's grace and to His Goodness when one who had begun to serve Him grows weary of His service. Remember—' No man having put his hand to the plough, and looking back, is fit for the Kingdom of God.' " [2]

EVIL-SPEAKING.

What is a good rule against this sin ?
Ask ∙thyself not —" *May* I say this evil of my neighbour ? but *must* I say this of him ?   Is it absolutely necessary ? " [3]
" Remember, after a few years, thou canst not again speak an evil word except in Hell." [4]

THE SEVEN DEADLY SINS.

GLUTTONY.

What would you think of *his* sorrow, who with one dead in his house took thought to have a meal of delicacies, and fared sumptuously ?   But a dead soul is a far sadder sight than death of the body. " Let him add to his expenditure," exclaims an ancient father ; " let him get together fatlings of a monstrous

[1] Vol. ii. p. 206.
[2] *Parochial and Cathedral Sermons*, p. 63.
[3] *Id.* p. 224.
[4] *Id.* p. 233.

T

growth; let him refine old wines; and when one shall ask, 'On whom dost thou lavish these things?' let him say, 'I have sinned against God, and am in danger of perishing everlastingly; and therefore I am anxious, and I pine away and torture myself, that I may reconcile unto myself that God whom I have offended by my sin.'"[1]

PRIDE.

"And since pride was the chief source of disease in our corrupted wills, to heal this the Eternal Son of God came as now from His everlasting glory, and as a little child fulfilled His Father's will."[2]

COVETOUSNESS.

"Step by step he was covetous, a hypocrite, a slanderer of those who hindered his covetousness, a betrayer, an infidel, a suicide"[3]—(Judas).

. "'Covetousness,' says Scripture, 'is idolatry.' And yet this is the very end and aim in this our country, the very nerve of what men do, the very ground of their undertakings, to keep or to enlarge their wealth. A spirit of enterprise infects all; it is the very air men live in; prosperity is our idol, the very measure of good or ill, the very end to which they refer all other ends; and what is this but their God?"[4]

LUST.

"If thy temptation, or the temptation of thy time of life, is to fleshly sins, then to pamper the flesh, to feed high, not to use fasting or abstinence, not to keep under the body and bring it into subjection, is to expect God to work a miracle for thee, which may save thee from the effects of thy self-indulgence. Heathen wisdom knew better than this. The heathen proverb,

---

[1] *Tert. de Poenit*, n. xi. p. 368, O.T.   [2] *Vol. i. p. 463.*
[3] Vol. ii. p. 211.   [4] *Occasional Sermons,* " *Danger of Riches,*" p. 20.

my sons ('sine Cerere et Baccho'—you remember it), bears witness to the Apostolic wisdom alike in our weekly day of abstinence, and in the abstinence of Lent." [1]

ANGER.

" He bids you forgive one another, if there be such who do you wrong, to love them for His sake, who bears with them as He has borne with you. He requires you to subdue your passions, to restrain your anger, to watch over all the motives and desires of your hearts, that you allow them in nothing which shall wound the conscience, or hurt your own or your neighbour's soul. He asks of you to be meek and patient, gentle and loving." [2]

ENVY.

"Would, my brethren, we could set before us more our Saviour's life, our Saviour's words of love, our home in Heaven, the sweet peace which shall reign there, the oneness of heart, the loving harmony. There shall be different ranks there; there will have been different attainments; there will be degrees of nearness to the throne of God; there will be different haloes of glory around the heads of the redeemed. It may be that, while all shall behold the face of God and of the Lamb, we may even there depend, in some way, on those higher than ourselves. Yet *there*, there could not be one emotion of rivalry, or jealousy, or pain at preference, or coolness of love. One faintest thought of it would mar Heaven. Ye hope to be admitted there for the sake of Jesus. And with whom? With all, if both are saved; with all, against whom men now speak evil; against whom they sin, whom they slight, whom they despise, whom, by their careless idle words, if not out of malice, they cause to be despised. Why then not live here already with all as we hope that we shall live for ever?" [3]

[1] *Lenten Sermons*, p. 267. [2] *Parochial and Cathedral Sermons*, p. 172.
[3] *Id.* p. 232.

SLOTH.

" Hast thou, in earlier days, allowed thy imagination to be corrupted, so that thoughts which thou knowest to be forbidden thee, come to thee, and thou takest pleasure in them and dwellest on them, or invitest them to thee even although thou wouldest not do the sins to which they relate ? Thou must turn from them wholly, however they beset thee, else thou canst not be altogether a Christian." [1]

" Or dost thou allow sloth to creep over thee, so that it has made thee well-nigh cease to pray, even morning and evening, and thou puttest off the thought of God, wilt not rouse thy soul to things above what thou seest, actest in thy daily life as if God were not, turnest away or holdest sluggishly back if God give thee some gleam of prayer? Jew, Turk, Heathen, will arise in the Day of Judgment to condemn thee. Canst thou think thyself a Christian ? . . ." [2]

" Sloth, then, as a deadly sin, is a far more comprehensive, terrible, almost irreparable evil, than most of us have been apt to think of . . ." [3]

IMPATIENCE UNDER THE PUNISHMENT OF SIN HERE.

" And even if the evil is from thyself, and the plain chastisement of thine own sins, lose not patience even with thyself. Be displeased with thyself that thou hast deserved it ; thankful to God who chastened thee here that He might spare thee hereafter." [4]

SOLEMN WARNING.

Which are among the most solemn words of warning uttered by our Lord?

St. Matt. xx. 16 : " Many be called, but few chosen."

[1] *Lenten Sermons,* p. 62. [2] *Id.* p. 63.
[3] *Id.* p. 187. [4] *Leeds Sermons,* p. 221.

"These words of our blessed Lord do give the intensest awe and pain of any in Holy Scripture; at least they render what Holy Scripture says of eternal punishment most fearful, and bring it most near ourselves." [1]

FORGIVENESS.

"It would seem no such great thing for *us*, who have been so much forgiven, to forgive from the heart any one who wronged us. It is a condition of salvation. If we forgive not, we should perish. Yet to this duty, though essential to salvation, God annexes a reward, 'Forgive, and ye shall be forgiven. Men, upon praying for one who had injured them, have felt themselves bathed with Divine Grace.'" [2]

SOFT EASY TEMPERS.

What is the danger of what is called good-nature?

"Undoubtedly the soft easy temper is very winning. The rough hard temper is unattractive. Yet without God's grace that easy temper will like wax be pliant to any evil; that hard temper (with God's grace) like the rough marble-block, may receive blow upon blow, and in the end retain for ever that Image of its Maker in which He has re-fashioned it." [3]

REVERENCE.

"But apart from that awful issue of our good or ill, reverence, my sons, the presence of God in you, around you now. Remember when tempted, *Who* is by. You could not utter some unseemly jest if your sisters were by. You would reverence their purity. Reverence the holiness of God, whom the pure in heart shall behold. He is nearer, and loves you better than a sister could. You could not make a profane jest from His Word if an elder whom you much reverence

---

[1] Vol. i. p. 155. [2] *Lenten Sermons*, p. 350.
[3] *Parochial and Cathedral Sermons*, p. 77.

were by.   Reverence Him whose Word it is, and make not a profane use of His Word in His very presence.   Remember God is by." [1]

CARE OF THE POOR AND SUFFERING.

"There is a Judgment of which all temporal judgments are but forerunners; a fire which God will not extinguish; suffering, of which there is no mitigation, no end; a doom in which there is no intercessor; and that these are especially reserved for such as in this life showed no mercy to Christ's poor; that while fornicators, unjust, covetous, have no portion (we know) in the Kingdom of Heaven; yet in our Lord's own description of the Great Day, the sin, which He singles out for condemnation, is neglect of Him in His poor and suffering members" (Matt. xxv. 44, 45). [2]

RESPONSIBILITY AS CHRISTIANS.

"'Responsibility.'   The word is almost clean gone out of our common language, except that we speak of the 'responsible Minister of the Crown,' in the sense that the Sovereign has to give no account of her acts to man; and a 'responsible' person or firm, is one which can discharge his or its monied obligations; and we can understand that that responsibility can be complete to the very last farthing.   How is it that we can so discern our relations to this world, and in the midst of the light of the Gospel cannot discern our relations to Almighty God?" [3]

SELF-DENIAL.

(1) "Think then nothing too little; keep hold over thyself; cross thy own desires; deny thyself at one time in sleep that thou mayst pray, or do some duty the better; at another, as to some luxury or food; in what is called (and if not in excess,

---

[1] *Parochial and Cathedral Sermons*, p. 511.   [2] *Source of Love*, p. 45.
[3] *Lenten Sermons*, p. 180.

is) innocent pleasure ; in thy words ; in permitted enjoyments ; relinquish what you wish, and practise what you wish not ; make it your object so to do, in order to school yourself and have the habit of self-denial.

(2) "Then also follow our Lord's rule literally, 'Take up thy Cross *daily.*' Make it a rule *every day* to deny thyself something because the Lord has enjoined it. Watch thyself, and if through human frailty thou forgettest it on any day, humble thyself, be the more diligent, and deny thyself the more resolutely on the next.

(3) "Fail not to observe any, the slightest, intimation given within thee to deny thyself; and if thou be faithful God 'will gird thee, and carry thee whither' of thyself 'thou wouldst not,' but on a way which leads to Him and His eternal glory.

(4) "The fasts which God hath through His Church appointed are an excellent way of learning to bear the Cross. They may have other ends ; they will free thee from many temptations ; they will tend to keep thee humble ; they have the promise that 'thy Father which seeth in secret Himself shall reward thee openly' ; but they are also learning to bear the Cross. Let any observe the weekly fast of the Church on the day whereon his Lord died on the Cross for him ; let him observe it in penitent humble memory of those sufferings and of his own sins, and he will learn more of the doctrine of the Cross ; he will be more drawn to his Lord, and to the Cross of his Lord, than by any profession of the lips." [1]

REMORSE.

"But remorse, although a first step to repentance, is not repentance. For remorse centres in a man's self. It dreads the temporal penalty of its sin ; it dreads more or less distinctly its deserved doom ; it sees in the distance the fires of hell ; it writhes at the thought of itself. While it is mere remorse it does not turn to God. Cain had remorse, and accused God ;

[1] Vol. iii. p. 66.

Esau had remorse for his profane sale of his birthright, and purposed to regain it by fratricide; Ahab had remorse, did some great deeds of humble penitence, but died in his pride and rebellion. Judas had remorse, but hanged himself and went to his own place." [1]

SPIRITUAL DEPRESSION.

What should the soul do in those times when prayer seems not to be heard, and seems wasted; when Communions seem as if nothing had been received; when it seems as if there was a dark heavy cloud between the soul and God?

" What should the soul do in such sickness as this? What should the sick do but go to the Physician? What did the Canaanitish woman? What did blind Bartimæus, when 'many charged him that he should hold his peace? He cried out the more a great deal; Thou Son of David, have mercy on me.'

" Do thou the same. Cry on, looking to Him alone. 'Good Jesus, have mercy on me!' and whatever be thy blindness, Jesus will at the fitting time touch thine eyes, and thou shalt see; whatever thy coldness, He will kindle thy soul. Though it were dead and buried He would raise it up." [2]

PATIENCE.

" Patience seems in many ways the grace which God is especially forming in our Church, which they who keep will abide; they who lose will be driven away." [3]

Give a simple definition of Christian patience?

" Patience is the endurance of any evil, out of the love of God, as the will of God." [4]

PERSEVERANCE.

" But we know that perseverance in any good is the chiefest of God's gifts." [5]

" Pray to persevere, and you will persevere. Those who persevere will be saved." [6]

[1] *Lenten Sermons*, p. 244.
[2] Vol. ii. p. 299.
[3] *Preface to Tertullian*, p. xiv.
[4] Vol. ii. p. 80.
[5] *Eleven Addresses*, p. 3.
[6] *See* vol. ii. p. 179.

HOPE.

"Hope is not a gift only of God, to cheer us on. It is also a virtue, one of the chief virtues, whose end is not man, but God Himself. If we be Christians indeed, we not only may, we ought to have this virtue of hope. Christian character is wanting without it."[1]

"For our hope is not the glory of Heaven, not joy, not peace, not rest from labour, not fullness of our wishes, nor sweet contentment of the whole soul; not understanding of all mysteries and all knowledge; not only a torrent of delight, *it is* 'Christ our God,' the Hope of Glory. 'Nothing which God could create is what we hope for; nothing which God could give us out of Himself, no created glory, or bliss, or beauty, or majesty, or riches. What we hope for is our Redeeming God Himself, His Love, His Bliss, the Joy of our own Lord Himself who hath so loved us, to be our Joy and our Portion for ever."[2]

"My hope is in Thee" (Psalm xxxix. 7).

CHURCH TROUBLES AND PROGRESS TO TRIUMPH.

"He who spared us in the lukewarmness of the last century, will not abandon our Church in the more devoted earnest service which He has given her the wish to render. He has not in vain allowed the Church to undergo every form of trial; He has not upheld her in every hour of trial, and raised up sons for her in every variety of need, to abandon her now. He does not supply fresh grace, suddenly to withdraw it; give the fresh oil of His Holy Spirit to our lamps in order to extinguish them; give fresh growth to the Vine which His Right Hand planted, in order to root it up."[3]

"Whether others exult, or complain, or censure, or talk indifferently, as about news, of what enters into our very souls, let us pray; everything may remind us of our troubles; everything bids us pray."[4]

[1] Vol. ii. p. 24.　　[2] *Id.* p. 39.　　[3] *Supremacy,* p. 213.　　[4] *Id.* p. 214.

What should be the spirit of those who take part under God in the Church revival?

" However we may see that our present decay and negligence should not continue, restoration must not be rashly compassed. It is not a matter of obeying rubrics, but of life or death, of health or decay, of coming together for the better or for the worse, to salvation or to condemnation. Healthful restoration is a work of humility not to be essayed as though we had the disposal of things, and could at our will replace what by our forefathers' negligence was lost; and by our sins bound up with theirs, is yet forfeited. Sound restoration must be the gift of God to be sought of Him, in humiliation, in prayer, in mutual forbearance and charity, with increased strictness of life and more diligent use of what we have." [1]

" We need no organic change in the Church, no Convocation, no laws, no enforcement of outward directions, no public discipline. It were to begin at the wrong end. What we need is, that men's hearts should be restored, the longings after a more inward, or more watchful, more devoted life fostered; the desire of greater strictness with self and conformity to the Will of God strengthened, the indistinct feeling after a higher standard of duty confirmed and more defined. Our duties lie severally to individuals of whom God assigns the charge to any; as a whole, we need to follow, not to guide; for that which we should follow is the only sure guide, the deep working of the Holy Spirit, which is anew more fully penetrating our whole Church and lifting it up, as a whole, as the Ark upon the waters." [2]

" The Church was never stronger than when St. Peter said, ' Silver and gold have I none.' " [3]

---

[1] *Holy Eucharist and Penitent*, p. 30.
[2] Preface, *Entire Absolution*, p. xvi.
[3] *Letter to Burgon.*

WHEN PERSONAL SPIRITUAL PROGRESS SEEMS SLOW.

"Thou mayest not see the change thyself, but He will gradually change thee, and make thee another man. Only yield thyself to His moulding hand." [1]

NOTHING TOO SMALL TO DO FOR GOD.

"The mistake of mistakes is to think that holiness consists in great or extraordinary things, beyond the reach of ordinary men. It has been well said 'Holiness does not consist in doing uncommon things, but in doing common things uncommonly well!' Even in those great Saints of God, the things which dazzle us most are not perhaps those which are the most precious in the sight of God." [2]

SOLITUDE.

"He had the same zeal for a single soul as for His whole people. For as God, He beheld and loved each single soul with an undivided love." [3]

"He wept, though with different tears, over His own friend Lazarus as over Jerusalem.

"He taught the one sinful woman of Samaria with the same gentle patience as Nicodemus; and Nicodemus, who came in fear and cowardice, as the whole people. His tenderest love and pains seems shown to us when He speaks to single souls."

SPIRIT IN WHICH TO HOPE FOR HEAVEN.

"In some one of these mansions, perhaps the very lowest, it may be, that we hope that we ourselves may be. In some order of the blessed spirits, under the feet of all God's elect, last and least, we hope, perhaps, that a place may be found for us." [4]

[1] Vol. iii. p. 182.   [2] *Parochial and Cathedral Sermons*, p. 169.
[3] *Id.* p. 263.   [4] *Id.* p. 148.

TRUST IN GOD.

" Why shall we not trust Him with the things of time, or with ourselves, who must trust Him with our eternity ? Why not trust that, for these few days and years, He will provide for us whom He has made for His Love, if we will have it, in those countless ages which time measures not ? " [1]

WARNING TO WEAK CHRISTIANS.

" It is a hard thing to say (God grant that it may not be so !), but I more and more fear that what is wanted in so many, amid this powerless religiousness, is an entire conversion of heart. ' Thou shalt love the Lord thy God with all thy heart, and with all thy mind, and with all thy soul, and with all thy strength ; and thy neighbour as thyself ! ' Where is this whole-hearted loyal obedience, when self is stealthily enshrined in so many hearts, and God seems to be made for man, not man for God ? A ' weak Christian ' were a contradiction in terms. For to be a Christian at all is to be a member of Christ, who is Almighty God ; it is to have a claim to His might, who has all power in Heaven and earth ; it is to have Him for your in-dweller, Who is all Holiness, all Hallowing. To be a weak Christian is to have but a weak will to be a Christian ; to have been made a Christian, yet half to repent of the love of God towards thee in making thee a Christian." [2]

SENSIBLE DEVOTION.

" He ' realizes ' what prayer is, who knows that by himself he is nothing ; that he can do nothing, but that God can do all things for him ; and prays. He ' realizes ' what Holy Communion is who meditates upon the greatness of God's Gift beforehand, prepares his soul for it, prays his Lord to come under his roof, and lives afterwards, as knowing whereof he has

---

[1] Vol. ii. p. 349.   [2] *Lenten Sermons*, p. 320.

been a partaker. He 'realizes' what repentance is who forsakes his sin, and sorrows that he ever offended his God. He 'realizes' what humility is, who is humble; he, what charity is, who is loving in act and tender in word, and denies himself for Christ's poor." [1]

COMFORT TO THOSE WITH FEW GIFTS.

" Among the Cherubim which upbear His throne, He places the dull heavy ox, as well as the fierce might of the lion, and the eagle of piercing sight and dauntless flight, with the prudence of the man, to show that all powers of nature may do Him service, so they bow themselves to His easy yoke." [2]

EDUCATION.

In these days when there is so much thought and talk of Education, as if it were the one thing needful, what line ought Churchmen to take?

They should remember, " if there be any one act of charity more than another to which our very nature turns; if there be any one that touches the heart, of all in which love however overladen with care or pleasure, or selfishness, still lives, it is the love of those, one of whom our Lord set in the midst and said, ' Whoso receiveth one such little child in My Name, receiveth Me.' Human nature, which knows of their future trials, tribulations, sufferings, and all that development to good or evil to which they are day by day tending, but which they know not of, imagine not, fear not—cannot but yearn over their yet remaining innocence, cannot but long for the well-being of those over whom it yearns. If, then, there be any work of love more than another which love must desire or cherish, it is any plan which shall guard these little ones against those future perils, which shall arm them for a conflict in which their innocence and purity will be maintained or lost; the beauty of their soul shall increase or fade, in which that freshness which

---

[1] Vol. ii. p. 297.　　　[2] *Parochial and Cathedral,* p. 80.

we love in them, as God's work, shall be blighted or matured, and they shall be a blessing or a curse to the parents who bore them, a blessing or a curse to themselves, and their own souls shall be lost or saved ; they shall be among those to whom our Lord shall say, 'Come, ye blessed of My Father, inherit the Kingdom prepared for you ; enter thou into the joy of thy Lord ' ; or, ' Depart, ye cursed, into everlasting fire.' " [1]

" Secular education will not so arm them, knowledge is but a two-edged sword to save or to destroy. Knowledge in itself 'sharpens' ; it does not direct, nor temper, nor guide, nor control the soul, nor teach, much less empower the soul to control itself. Even religious knowledge is not education. It is light, not warmth. By itself it would only make sin more deadly, in that it would be sin against light. Religious education is to train the whole soul, to watch and correct the temper, to strengthen what is weak, soften what is hard, temper what is wrong, check what is heady, and bring the whole soul with all its powers into the obedience of the law of the love of Christ. They only can really educate who are themselves under the power of that love, and the vessels of that love to others."

What is " Knowledge" in Holy Scripture ?

Knowledge in Holy Scripture is not of the understanding, but of the heart and the will.

" The power to read giveth not the love of reading God's Word ; to learn to read is not education ; a various knowledge of things of all sorts is not education ; ' knowledge puffeth up,' and the power of reading, like every other power, is more likely to be abused than to be used aright ; the abuse comes more naturally to man's natural heart than the use. Knowledge of all sorts is but a sharp instrument, which whoso learneth not to use aright will wound himself. Instruction by itself is not education, but the whetting only of an appetite, which, as it is taught to feed on what is healthy or unhealthy, will benefit its possessor or destroy him. 'The fear of the

<hr>

[1] Vol. ii. p. 366—368.

Lord' is the only education, the beginning of wisdom and the Knowledge of the Holy is understanding." [1]

" It is a very remarkable peculiarity'in this country, that the wants elsewhere provided for by the State, are here mostly supplied by private benevolences. Not only have the provisions for the poor, the sick, and indeed for every bodily and mental infirmity been made by individual liberality, but almost the whole business of education, from the dames' or the Sunday school to the universities—our national, our grammar, or collegiate schools—have been provided by individual munificence." [2]

But the most powerful agencies are everywhere indirect.

" The object of education then must be as much to guard these incidental inlets, as the more direct avenues to the mind. The teaching of religion or religious truths is but a small part of religious or Christian education. Christianity is not an insulated system, which can, like any scheme of philosophy, be taught apart or by itself; a true Christian education requires the formation of the whole character on Christian principles; the imparting of all truth in a Christian spirit." [3]

CAUTION TO THE YOUNG.

" Children are taught not to instruct their parents, but to obey them ; and it is mentioned as a token of God's Judgment, when ' babes shall rule,' and 'the child behave himself proudly against the ancient.' " [4]

" And let the young especially remember that it is not by giving vent to their feelings, but by restraining them ; not by blaming others (in doing which they could scarcely avoid sin), but by schooling themselves by meekness, by self-command, by quietness, by peaceableness, by disciplining themselves, and by acting under discipline, by submitting to authority even where they see not precisely the reason, by acting in their

[1] Vol. ii. p. 305.
[2] *Cathedrals*, p. 16, 1833.
[3] *Id.* p. 89.
[4] Vol. i. 105.

petty occasions on faith, that they may best prepare themselves for whatever duties in the great army of their God it may please Him hereafter to call them to." [1]

HUMILITY.

What is the preciousness of Humility?

"Humility is the beginning of all solid good, and of every grace. It opens the heart for them, and guards them, where God has given them. Humility scoops away the barren sand of our self-conceit, that so our foundation may rest solidly upon the Rock which is Christ." [2]

"Then may the building which we raise reach to Heaven by love; for it cannot fail, being founded on the Rock."

DEPENDENCE ON GOD.

"We are, throughout life, by holding what we have as not our own, learning to be fitted to have of our own, in the only way in which created being can have any good, in entire dependence upon Him Who created all, and Whose own all are, since in Him and through Him all have and had their being. As without Him we could not be, so without Him we could not use our function of our being, and neither have what we have, nor use what we seem to have, except to our own ruin. Our strength, and the power to use it, and much more the grace not to abuse it; our thoughts, and the power to control or direct our thoughts, are from Him. Without Him we could not think one good thought, speak one good word, form one good wish, perform one good act. All grace, whereby we do things gracious and grateful to Him, is His; all power to use His grace is a second grace of His; that we fall not more short of His grace than any do, is His." [3]

[1] *Sermon*, November 5th, p. 49. [2] Vol. ii. p. 72.
[3] Vol. iii. p. 248.

CARE OF CHILDREN.

"So has the mercy of God turned our loss into gain. Blessed indeed was Adam before his fall, sinless, passionless, free from our weary strife, clothed with a robe of heavenly righteousness. Yet what his bliss to ours, if we be Christ's? What although ours be as yet in hope only, what to ours, to be one with Christ? What was even that, our lost innocence, to the gift of Christ to be our righteousness? What freedom from strife, to victory through the Spirit, which dwelleth in us? What to be sons of God as creatures, to this our sonship by being very members of the Eternal Son? What were the Father's love for a spotless creature to that love wherewith He loved us, that He gave the Only-begotten Son to die for us, and now, if we be His, loves us in the Son of His Love?"[1]

"Does the Church's belief that her little ones are temples of the Holy Ghost stagger us any longer, through the greatness of the gift, when He who became a Little One, in the manger, for our sakes, was the Very and Eternal God? Can we otherwise than, for love of Jesus, reverence, and love and yearn over and cherish these little ones? Feel we not (at least if we be not deadened by this world's vanities) a drawing forth of our inmost hearts towards them, a tender love, a reverence for them, which, alas! we cannot have for ourselves, and often not for others of riper years? The childhood of Jesus, and their recent birth of God, the impress of His Hands and the sealing of His Spirit, the fresh invocation of the name of the Holy Trinity upon them, and their own freedom, for the most part, from grave actual sin, the presence, maybe, of 'their angels,' who 'do always behold the face of their Father in Heaven,' win from us a reverent love, unlike anything besides in this our corrupted world. The children of the Church are, save her Saints, the purest ornament with which God hath clothed her; they should be her chiefest care."[2]

---

[1] *Occasional Sermons*, "*God is Love,*" p. 33.　　　　[2] *Id.* p. 34.

"To give alms alone, to educate anyhow, is not to receive little ones in Christ's Name; the blessing is too great to be obtained by such costless means."[1]

GUARDIAN ANGELS.

"The care of these little ones, one by one, is given to Angels who behold not the outskirts of God's glory only, nor are at times only illumined by it, but at all times behold the very Face of God, while ministering to them. Each of these unconscious little ones has such a Guardian assigned to it; and, from the great dignity of these their appointed Guardians, we are to learn their great value in our Father's eyes."[2]

· LOVE.

"Love, then, is the sign of life, our safety in Sacraments, the mark of Christ's disciples, the beginning and ending, the Mother and foundation of all virtues, the earnest of the Spirit, inviting and waiting for its fullness. Martyrdom without Love would be death of the soul; faith the confession of devils; Sacraments would be received to our hurt; miracles a testimony against us; the tongues of Angels a tinkling cymbal; the knowledge of mysteries a swelling vanity; but Love, as it cannot be without faith, so ·it gives or replaces knowledge or wisdom, or speech, or (if they be not unlovingly laid aside) even Sacraments themselves, for 'God is Love.'"[3]

"Or, take again St. Paul's description of love. For what sin could it leave place? By what would it be mastered? Not by vexatiousness, for it not only suffereth long but returns evil with good; 'it is kind,' not by envy, for it 'envieth not'; not by pride, for it 'vaunteth not itself'; not by thinking of its good deeds, for it 'is not puffed up'; not by conceit of station or wealth, for it 'doth not behave itself unseemly'; not by selfishness, for it 'seeketh not its own'; not by injuries, for it

[1] *Occasional Sermons*, "*God is Love*," p. 43.
[2] Vol. iii. p. 300.   [3] *Occasional Sermons*, iv. p. 9.

'is not provoked'; not by suspicions, for it 'thinketh no evil'; not by malice, for it 'rejoiceth not in iniquity'; not by error, for it 'rejoiceth in the truth'; not by all ill-treatment, for it 'beareth all things'; not by being deceived, for it 'believeth all things'; not by despondency, for it 'hopeth all things'; not by failure of all good or infliction of all evil, for it 'endureth all things.'" [1]

CHARITY.

"Everything in this day is gigantic, except Charity. Empires, riches, designs, works of art and toil, mercantile enterprise, shipping, everything whereby gains may be acquired, and with them our sins and miseries, are on a gigantic scale. Is Charity, the very daughter and Image of the Infinite God, who is Love, to be alone cramped and stinted in her growth?" [2]

LOVE OF SOULS.

"My brethren, lukewarmness about the salvation of our brethren is no good token for ourselves." [3]

"Our very blessings condemn us if we impart them not. To be careless about others' salvation is to risk our own. *For they only are saved who love.* And can we indeed love God, if we long not that all around us should love Him Who has so loved us, in Whose Love we have found our rest?"

LOVE OF OTHERS.

"I said, 'if it were possible to be saved alone.' I should almost doubt whether it were possible. Quite alone, it would be well-nigh impossible; for it would be to be saved without love." [4]

[1] Vol. ii. p. 361.
[2] *Occasional Sermons*, p. 17. No. III.
[3] *Leeds Sermons*, p. 279.
[4] *Lenten Sermons*, p. 338.

GOD'S LOVE OF EACH SOUL.

"And what God has done for all, He has done for each single soul." [1]

"But then by that continual operation of which our Lord speaketh, 'My Father worketh hitherto, and I work.' And Zechariah, 'Who formeth the Spirit of man within him,' He at thy conception, chose thy individual soul and created it for Himself. Thenceforth, all His doings are individual to thee, the single special acts and tokens and instruments of His love."

"This is what the human heart so craves for—an undivided love, a love which it shall have all its own. This is what God gives us." [2]

"But what He gives to all, He gives indivisibly to each. The indwelling of God the Holy Ghost and the participation of Christ, are the unity of the whole body of Christ the Church; but singly you were made in Baptism a member of Christ; singly, you have that special relation to Christ; singly, in the Holy Eucharist, by that miracle of His Love, you 'eat the Flesh (He says) of the Son of Man, and drink His Blood; you dwell in Christ and Christ in you, are one with Christ and Christ with you'; singly, you belong to Christ, and have that whole indivisible love of Christ, yea, of the All-Holy Trinity. God loves with the whole Power of His Infinite love, all who do not finally shut out His love; yea, He loves thee with His Whole Being, for God is Love."

"Each one is as much the object of that Infinite Mind and Counsel, as if it was the solitary production of His Omniscience." [3]

VALUE OF THE SOUL.

Why are our souls so precious to God?

"To God, the fall of empires, the crash of the world, the dissolving of the whole universe, were as nothing. By His

---

[1] Vol. 1872, p. 48. [2] *Id.* p. 50. [3] *Eleven Addresses*, p. 17.

word were they created ; at His breath they would pass away. More precious to Him than the whole world is the value of one single soul. For the world shall perish, the soul endureth. The world and all its wondrous beauty is but the work of His Hands ; the soul made and remade in the image of God, was redeemed by the Blood of Christ." [1]

SOUL-MURDER.

"The murder of the body may be but the passport to Heaven. The murder of the soul is Satan's own act, the plunging into Hell. Have we love? Have we fear? Have we hearts ?—that they should not break at wounding such love, with the crushing weight of such guiltiness." [2]

DEATH.

" What a task this, when perhaps the hours are numbered, and the soul bewildered with the thoughts of approaching judgment, and Satan, as he often doth, is assailing him with all his force and subtlety, to plunge him into doubt or despair. Is there not enough to do in that last conflict with the Evil One, that last moment of penitence and imploring of pardon, and faith, and hope, and love, not to burden it with aught which can be performed before? It is an axiom of religion, that what is good to be done, before we die, it is good to do now, lest death surprise us." [3]

DEATH-BEDS.

" How many may be recalled, converted, justified, even at the last hour, is one of the hidden mysteries of His Love. A death-bed is one of the great secrets of God, in which He is very busy with the soul, because it is His last hour. What passes even when the soul can no more express itself, is hidden

[1] Vol. ii. p. 88.　　　　[2] *Lenten Sermons,* p. 254.
[3] *Absolution of Penitent,* part ii. p. 7.

from all, save Him who worketh by His Spirit in the soul. Who will still draw it from without, even if it have expelled Him from within—its God. One thing only is certain, that God will not part with one soul whom He has redeemed, if it remains not obdurate to the end."[1]

FEAR OF DEATH.

" One more very solemn thing. Do not put away as gloomy any personal fear, even of being lost, or of death. If it comes often, God has some work for it to do in your soul. He sends it, or (which is one) He lets it come. He sends the fear into your soul, that you may have no cause to fear. He sends you fear, to take away real fear. Let it have its way; only cast yourself with it at the feet of Jesus, and He will hush you more tenderly than your mother could."[2]

NEAR DEATH.

" Even now we do sometimes see the face of God's Saints gleam with unearthly purity and love. Even now, as the parting spirit sometimes sees Heaven open, and hears and almost feels the brushing of Angels' wings who shall carry it, or knows the room to be full of angels, or sees the Redeemer Himself, so does the body catch the light it is approaching."[3]

From those prayerfully preparing to die, " The fear of death in life is commonly taken away in death."[4]

[1] *Sermon, " Prophecy of Jesus,"* p. 46, 1879.
[2] *Lenten Sermons,* p. 232.   [3] *Vol. iii.* p. 423.
[4] *Lenten Sermons,* p. 16.

OUR DEAD IN PARADISE.

LOVE OF SOULS.

How may we think of them ?

" What then must it be now, when for so many centuries God has borne witness to the blessedness of choosing Him as our portion for ever ?—when we are ' compassed with so great a cloud of witnesses ' ; when, not Patriarchs only and Prophets, but Apostles, Evangelists, Martyrs, Teachers, Saints, all, of every age and tongue, and people, and nation, who have been perfected ; young and aged, boys and virgins, the early-perfected and gray-haired holiness, the poor, and they who have made themselves poor for the Kingdom of Heaven, call us by their faithful lives and peaceful deaths ; beckon us, as it were, from Paradise, and tell us, ' We know Whom we have believed ; Whom we sought (yea, who sought us), we have found ; Whom we chose we have ; one thing we asked of the Lord, this we have desired to behold, the fair beauty of the Lord and to visit His Temple. And now we dwell in His courts, and behold His face, and are filled with His Love ; Whom, not seeing, we believed and loved." [1]

" It is a comfort to us, when those whom we love are away, if we can set before us their faces, imagine their looks, picture them in our souls as when they were most loving, gentle, tender, good towards us. Who has not thought of those who have passed away out of our sight to Paradise, as the Martyrs have been allowed to be seen of old, with the same countenance, and look of pure holy love, which they once had here, yet now ' surpassing bright, so that their likeness could scarcely be recognized, because the eyes of the flesh gleamed with angelic radiancy ? ' " [2]

[1] Vol. i. p. 266. [2] Vol. ii. p. 230.

PARADISE.

"For although there are Heavens to which these, our Heavens, are as earth, and Heaven of Heavens, these are in space. They may but help us to ascend in thought with our ascending Lord. We know from Holy Scripture that the third of these, the abode of those who sleep in Jesus, is Paradise. And doubtless the others too have their own inhabitants, some order of Angels." [1]

THE INTERMEDIATE STATE.

. Does the Church of England teach that any souls go straight to Heaven at the moment of death ?

People very often talk as if they thought so. In the Service for the Burial of the Dead, we pray that "we, *with* all those that are departed in the true faith of Thy Holy Name, may have our perfect consummation and bliss, in Thy Eternal and Everlasting Glory "—"and that, at the general Resurrection in the last day, we may be found acceptable in Thy sight ; and receive that blessing, which Thy Well Beloved Son shall *then* pronounce to all that love and fear Thee, saying, Come, ye blessed children of My Father, receive the Kingdom prepared for you from the beginning of the world."

What then does she teach concerning those who depart hence in the Lord ?

That " the souls of the faithful are in joy and felicity," and "rest in Christ."

The Church of England then denies all notion of any purgatory or purifying process ?

No. She only denies the Romish doctrine of Purgatory in Article XXII.

May we not think that any Christian who has lived a good sort of life on the whole, will at once be at perfect peace, in perfect bliss with Jesus ?

[1] Vol. ii. p. 220.

" To thoughtful minds, whom the grace of God has taught something of what sin is, and of the holiness and love of God and of Jesus, it is absolutely inconceivable that—when the soul shall first behold Jesus and, in His sight, with its powers quickened by Him, shall behold its past life as a whole ; when, in His Countenance, it shall behold all which it never before saw of His goodness, and, in contrast with this, all its own ingratitude, baseness, rebellion, negligence, discontent, murmurings, not to speak of deadly, forgiven sin—it should not have intense pain ; pain so intense that one should think that, in this life, soul and body would be severed by its intensity." [1]

It seems then, that there may be great suffering in the way of anguish, shame, sorrow, and regret, at ever having offended, as we all often have, such a Good and Gracious and Holy Lord.

But will there not be physical suffering to undergo, the torment of material fire, as is commonly taught in the Roman Communion ?

Whatever may be taught by numerous devotional writers, remedial punishment by material fire is not an " article of faith " in the Roman Communion, though it is almost everywhere taught and preached as if it was.   It is not an Article of Faith in the Greek Church, and has never been taught as " necessary to be believed " by the Catholic Church.

How God may cleanse, purify, fit souls to dwell with Him, in perfect peace and joy, is not revealed to us ; enough for us to believe that He who has " begun a good work in souls will continue it."

Let it be granted then, that we could not expect at once to feel perfectly at ease, and perfectly happy in the presence of Christ our Judge and Saviour.   Can it yet be right to pray for those who die, that our Lord, as He knows best, will give them rest, and let His perpetual Light of love shine on them ?

It is not only right so to pray, but it would be against the nature and instinct of true love not so to pray.

[1] *Eirenicon,* i. p. 191.

Can it be right to pray for the dead, when to do so seems to imply, that we expect God to reverse His final decision concerning their acceptance or rejection?

Praying for the dead does not mean this. It is simply asking God to have mercy on them, asking for them what we would hope to have for ourselves.

How can any one tell that such prayers can do any good to the departed?

We may ask in reply, How can any one tell that they may not avail?

It cannot be wrong to ask God to have mercy on any one. We are nowhere told *not* to pray for the dead, and we are told that the dead are to be judged, how can it be wrong then for their brethren to pray to the Lord of both for Mercy?

But suppose a man dies a saintly death at the close of a saintly life. What good can prayers do for such an one?

God's love, God's mercy, God's gifts, are not finite and exhaustible, but the contrary. He *can*, for ever and for ever, add every moment some fresh increase of joy or glory to the joy and glory of the most perfect and glorious of all His Saints.

Has the Church of England anywhere said anything which tacitly allows, if not encourages, prayers for the dead?

"They are indistinctly, yet they *are* included in the Eucharistic Prayer. 'By the merits and death of Thy Son Jesus Christ, and through faith in His Blood, we and *all Thy whole* Church may obtain remission of our Sins.'"[1]

Did the early Church pray for the dead?

Yes, from the very first.

St. Ambrose prays, "Give perfect rest to Thy Servant Theodosius, that rest which Thou hast prepared for Thy Saints."—*See* BISHOP FORBES' Article XXII.

"May she rest in peace with the husband, before and after whom she never had any."—ST. AUGUSTINE'S *Prayer for his Mother.*

[1] *Eleven Addresses*, p. 127.

Give one of the chief reasons why many people oppose prayers for the dead?

From a terribly inadequate idea of the Holiness of God, the awfulness of sin, the cost of the Sacrifice on Calvary, and the ingratitude of all, for whom the Precious Blood was shed.

"We cannot wish God to be less Holy than He is. And our own consciences may tell us that, our repentance for our sins having been very imperfect, and our own longings for the sight of God, amid this whirl of duties and religious interests, such as we do not like to think of, we are not fit to behold Him. This, perhaps, more than the direct dread of hell, is the source of the fear of death to many. They trust in God's mercy in Christ that they shall be saved; but they feel themselves unfit to enter into His presence. To be admitted into any vestibule of His presence where they can sin no more, and by longing for that Beatific Vision, may be for ever freed from the slough which has clung to them in this life—this is not too high for their hopes, the thought of this unspeakably allays their fears." [1]

If people really believe that the soul does not die at death, but that then it only leaves the body, still lives and is conscious, there can be absolutely no good reason for not praying for the soul still. It has only gone to another place; prayer can reach *everywhere;* God can help *anywhere;* a soul can be blessed by Him in Paradise as well as on earth.

"The soul lives on, sleeps not, continues its unbroken existence." [2]

So again if people really loved souls as they ought, they could not pray God to bless them when alive, and then cease to do so the moment the last breath is drawn. It will often be found that those who do not pray for the dead, do not pray continually and lovingly for those they profess to love when alive. No Christian man bidding "farewell," when near death, would tell those from whom he was parting, "If I rest in peace in the presence of Jesus, I shall never pray for you whom I

---

[1] *Eirenicon,* iii. p. 109.   [2] *Daniel,* p. 504.

leave and love here." Nor could he say, "Your love in prayers has often helped me *here*, but do not pray for me *there* ; God only answers prayer for souls He loves on earth, and pays no heed to the love that would pray His love to bless in Paradise."

Rather, "The love of the departed avails for us in gaining grace for us in this our perilous voyage. Our prayers avail for them to abridge the time of their waiting, so would God perpetuate Divine love beyond the grave; so would He, in the Communion of Saints, provide that 'they without us should not be made perfect; that they who have attained, should be yet indebted to our love while we are yet more indebted to their love."[1]

"He willed that through eternity we should be bound together, not only as His creatures, or through the oneness of His Spirit in us all, or by our own oneness of relation to Him, our Father and our God; not only by all our natural ties of friendship or of love, but by the endless memories of that sacred love that under Him and through Him we were helped onward by one another to that unspeakable bliss."[2]

PRAYERS FOR THE DEAD.

"Unless these were, in the Word of God, an absolute prohibition of prayer for the departed, how should we go on praying for those whom we love until they were out of sight, and then cease on the instant as if 'out of sight, out of mind,' were a Christian duty? How should we not rather follow the soul to the Eternal Throne, with the Apostle's prayer (as seems probable, for the *departed* Onesiphorus), 'The Lord grant that he may find mercy of the Lord in that day'? But we have no doubt that we *may* pray. For the whole Church so prayed, much nearer to the time when the beloved disciple left this earth, than many of us are to the early memories of our fathers. And, however, in evil days, the public and ritual use

---

[1] *Eleven Addresses*, p. 134. [2] *Parochial and Cathedral Sermons*, p. 329.

of those prayers was laid aside in the Church of England, yet even a Court of Ecclesiastical Law formally decided their lawfulness, according to the doctrine and discipline of the Church of England, and the departed *are*, but indistinctly, yet *are* concluded in our Eucharistic prayer, 'by the merits and Death of Thy Son Jesus Christ, and through faith in His Blood, we and all *Thy whole Church*, may obtain remission of our sins, and all other benefits of His Passion.'"

"I say this, in case any should be afraid so to pray. But since it is lawful, what an unspeakable privilege." [1]

PRAYER OF SAINTS.

Is it right to think that the Saints at rest pray for us?

Certainly. "The intercession of the Saints departed, and at rest, for us who are still militant, is part of the doctrine of the Communion of Saints, and would be a necessary consequence of God-given love, even if it did not appear from Holy Scripture. The contrary is inconceivable." [2]

SPECIAL LOVE OF SOULS.

May we think that in Heaven, while loving God first, and all in Him, that any pure special love we enjoyed on earth may be continued there?

"There in that abode of love, shall no special holy love be lost. God has not formed us, yea, bidden us, in this our nursery for the heavenly life, to love one another, in all our several relations, that all this, after this life, shall cease. We could not think as to the very Human Nature of our Lord, that in the full glory of God, He does not love still with that same special love, with which on earth He loved the disciple whom He loved. He cannot change. For then too He was 'Very God' as well as 'Very Man.' His Human soul loved then with the unchangeable love of the Godhead, with which

---

[1] *Eleven Addresses*, p. 126.   [2] *Eirenicon*, part iii. 33.

it was united. Again, how could He, as Man, not have fulfilled His own command, and not have loved with the love of a son, the Mother who bare Him after the flesh? And how can that have ceased now?"[1]

"Rather it shall be part of our joy, to love all which we loved here; only how *much* more, because every infirmity which in ourselves or in others, ever checked for an instant the flow of love, shall then have been absorbed into the love of God, and God shall fill all with Himself."[2]

LOVE IN HEAVEN.

"And there, in Heaven, we shall all so deeply love, that our deepest love here will be but a shadow of the lowest love there; and we shall love all, and so share the joy of all there, with a more inward joy than here we share the joy of those whose joy is as our own."[3]

SPECIAL GLORY.

"Nothing is *there* but love; and so, such as one's self, of all the meanest, if by His gift he may attain thither, shall in the higher joy and love of all the rest of the saints in bliss, joy as if it were his own. In all we shall behold, in all love God. The praise of all shall gladden us; each voice, which has learned the new song, shall swell with its own special beauty, the everlasting harmony; the glory of each several star in that more blessed firmament shall shed its own special lustre."[4]

"Every one of those millions of millions of beings full of love, and of love of us. And there will be no sameness in their love. Out of each, love will stream forth with its own individual beauty and loveliness of love."[5]

[1] Vol. ii. p. 263.　　　　　[2] *Id.* p. 264.
[3] *Parochial and Cathedral Sermons*, p. 289.
[4] *Leeds Sermons*, p. 317.　　　　[5] *Lenten Sermons*, p. 425.

FREE AND OPEN CHURCHES.

"What St. James condemns in words, that in our modern places of worship which we ourselves build, we seem to act; preferring in God's presence, before whom we come alike as sinners, and before whom we alike confess ourselves unworthy to appear, the rich to the poor, allotting the best places to the rich, and thrusting aside the poor." [1]

ALMSGIVING.

"We do the rich great mischief by flattering them, by accounting much of those little doles, of which they should be ashamed.   I have never preached a sermon to the rich on almsgiving, but I have felt afraid lest I should occasion them to sin against light.   We are so inured to our little gifts out of our large revenues; not 'of our little, gladly to give of that little,' but out of an abundance to give but little!" [2]

WHAT IS THE BEST TIME FOR ALMSGIVING?

"At the Holy Communion, for here we may safely trust our alms, and that liberally, to the distribution of others, because God by His Church invites us; and such was ever His appointment, and the practice of the Ancient Church.   It is sad to see how people show least love, when they come to acknowledge His inestimable Love, to receive 'the pledges of His Love, to their great and endless comfort'; and are then most penurious in their charity, when they come nearest to their Lord, Who bade us love our brethren, *as* He loved us, with a self-denying, self-sacrificing love." [3]

ALMSGIVING IN THE STREETS.

"Even in those sad cases in the streets, in which it may become our duty to withhold our alms, both because giving

<hr>

[1] Vol. iii. p. 73.   [2] *Eleven Addresses*, p. 117.   [3] Vol. iii. p. 142.

would be rather an occasion of sin, and that we may have more for those who really need it, we ought not 'to pass by on the other side' unconcerned or impatient at their importunity. Even when we must say with the Apostles, 'Silver and gold have I none,' we should with the Apostle bestow what we have —our prayers." [1]

THE JEWS.

How shall Christians regard the Jews?

They should, as with all their dealings with all mankind, be full of humility, remembering St. Paul's warning (Rom. xi.) : "Be not high-minded but fear; for if God spared not the natural branches, take heed lest He also spare not thee."

"And who shall say how many thousand, thousand Jews, who confessed the doctrine of Atonement, yet through invincible, hereditary ignorance knew not their Atoner, may not have been pardoned and accepted for His sake, Whose office they implicitly acknowledged, even while they ignorantly rejected Himself?" [2]

"Not in vain hath God preserved His ancient people, a sacrifice 'salted with salt,' the guardian of the ancient Scriptures, the witnesses to the prophecies, which themselves bear witness to the Redeemer of us both. Through what sifting, they shall be restored, we as yet know not; whether the failure of their last false Messiah the Anti-Christ, and God's might put forth therein, shall turn them in repentance to worship Him Whom their Fathers pierced, or through any other way known to His Omniscience, who said, 'so shall all Israel be saved.'" [3]

"Gifts, which are given out of our abundance, may gain us credit among men; they may show a kindly spirit, such as the Jews were bid to cherish, but they are not tokens of Christian love. Alas! would that we were not put to shame by the very Jews! Would that our righteousness came up even to theirs, and that we provided for our poor as they even now

---

[1] Vol. iii. p. 132.　　[2] Vol. 1872, p. 487.　　[3] *Id.* p. 488.

do for theirs ! Would that we, who are God's people, came up to them, who for the time are ' not His people.' " [1]

MOHAMMEDANISM.

"It is in keeping when a religion like Mohammed's, a stereotyping of a cold, unloving Monotheism, abstracting from the Gospel so much of truth as is no tax on human reason, gaining support from the truth of the Unity of God, but freeing itself from the weight of every mystery as to God or man, which it could discard without annihilating to itself the idea of God or man, and asking for no moral victories of faith, demands of man an unspiritual assent." [2]

" Or what of the Mohammedans ? Mohammed, a descendent of Arius and forerunner of Socinus, could only establish his heresy by owning Christ as the ' Word of God.' His was not an independent religion, but a heresy. It too, as far as it was better than the idolatry which it absorbed, was a feint of the ' law ' which went forth from Jerusalem. ' All its positive truths are from revelation, only not made to him who claimed it as his own. Compared to the Gospel it is as darkness to light, yet its twilight rays are from the Gospel.' " [3]

" Mohammedanism, which is rather a heresy from Christianity than a religion, boasts of the rapidity of its armed subdual of mankind. It has no marks by which it can claim that God bore witness to it, ere it was." [4]

" What must have been the inward hollowness, when that impostor, who has stamped his name upon a body (too many torn from the Church itself, and even now ninety-six millions of our race, the lord and oppressor of the Church far and wide, and almost its successor), seemed for a time to threaten the existence of the Christian name, and hem it in on all sides; with no plea except the hatred of idolatry ! Christians to have become the followers of one, blood stained and a sensualist." [5]

---

[1] *Occasional Sermons,* "*Source of Love,*" p. 46.   [2] Vol. 1872, p. 19.
[3] *Id.* p. 127.   [4] *Id.* p. 157.   [5] Vol. i. p. 165.

MUSIC.

"The harmony of music, the most unearthly sound upon this earth, is but an echo of those angel choirs in which the redeemed shall fill up the perfect unison of the new Heaven, and the new earth. No joy of any sense shall be wanting there, but all shall be purified, heightened, glorified. Blessed, eternally blessed, they who bear their part in the songs of heavenly melody in which countless voices of the glorified, with wondrous and inconceivable sweetness, shall, from end to end of the realms of the redeemed, blend in one Alleluia, ' to Him Who sitteth upon the throne, and to the Lamb.'" [1]

"Things of sense or of spirit, the commonest supplies of our needs, or the most refined objects, which employ our under-standing, all were alike made for good ; all are turned, through sin, to evil." [2]

"The very sounds, which seem to float down as from another world, and echo the angels' harps ; the very voice of praise, the language of heaven, we scarcely know whether it is spiritual or material ; how, in our very churches, does it often steal away men's hearts to love itself, not the praise of God, which by its speechless voice it utters ; how, in the world, is it pro-faned to feverish excitement and sensual pleasure, and vanity and sin."

DIVORCE.

"It is a marvel to us, how at least fidelity on the wife's side could become to such an extent a heathen virtue. Contrast with the miseries and iniquities revealed and fostered by the English Divorce Court, Roman faithfulness, through which, in a hot climate, divorce was unknown for two hundred and thirty, some say, for five hundred and twenty, years." [3]

[1] Vol. ii. p. 266.   [2] *Id.* 309.
[3] *Lenten Sermons*, p. 301.

MILLENNIUM AND ELIAS.

"The doctrine of the Millennium depends upon the book of Revelations, and so is independent of the question whether the latter parts of Isaiah and Ezekiel are then to find a more complete fulfilment. It cannot be doubted that they have received a large fulfilment in the Church and its gifts, its privileges, holiness, and peace : a larger fulfilment of the same kind, though fuller in degree, may yet be in store for her. The more modest way seems to be, not peremptorily to decide either way ; either way, we may be prescribing to the Wisdom of the All Wise : it may be that the prophecies, after their first partial temporal fulfilment, are to have no other than their spiritual fulfilment, which is their highest meaning, and we should not require more, as if God must be a debtor to our interpretations. On the other hand, we should not decide peremptorily that it may not please Him to give them a second literal fulfilment : it were but analogous to an expectation, which is found in the Fathers, that Elias may yet come personally before the second Advent of our Lord, although we know in Divine authority, that the prophecy of His coming was fulfilled (*i. e.* had one complete fulfilment, so as to require no other) before His first Advent."[1]

NATURE AND GRACE.

"But the most subtle danger of the spirit of the age is analogous to that, incidental to the natural good in the individual, viz. that it should form a character, in which certain natural virtues should be substituted for Divine Grace."[2]

Why do some souls fall short of God's Grace?

"On *this* ground, that if we are not aiming at something above ourselves, we are living a life of nature, not of grace.

[1] *Tertullian*, p. 130, *note C.*
[2] *Lenten Sermons*, p. 281.

If we live a life of nature we do not use grace, we forfeit grace; and our corrupt nature anew finds its way."[1]

Whatever our life may be, whatever our trial, if we are not aiming to lift up our nature above its level, we sink below it.

CAN THERE BE ANY MERCY IN CAPITAL PUNISHMENT?

"Everything, within or without, bids him 'Prepare to meet thy God'; and the grace of God, which, however forsaken, forsakes us not, has free undisturbed access to the soul. I trust that, as a rule, that dread fulfilment of God's law, 'Whoso sheddeth man's blood, by man shall his blood be shed,' is a most special mercy to the soul of the offender: as contrariwise, that solitary, life-long confinement which man's wisdom, amending God's law, invented to combine compassion to the criminal, with safety to society, was the extremest curse, a murderer of souls."[2]

CAUTION IN ZEAL FOR TEACHING OTHERS NOT TO INJURE FAITH.

See also the Preface to Sermons, by the late ARCHER BUTLER, *by* DEAN WOODWARD.

"It is perilous to touch even a mistaken faith, for since the whole of Divine faith rests to each on one authority, one mistake seems to shake all, which rests on that one authority. Even as to mistaken faith, it is safer to expand and enlarge what is true, so that what is not true should fall off, as it were, of itself, well-nigh unperceived."[3]

WAR.

What should Christians think of war?
"Of all scourges of God wherewith He chastens man for

---

[1] *Parochial and Cathedral Sermons*, p. 64.
[2] Vol. 1872, p. 291.   [3] Vol. 1855. *Real Faith*, p. 47.

sin, the most terrible is the scourge of war. David choose a three days' pestilence, which destroyed 70,000 men, rather than three months' invasion of a conquering foe. Holy Scripture has ratified the ground of his choice, 'Let us fall now into the hand of the Lord, for His mercies are great, and let me not fall into the hand of men.'" [1]

BROTHERHOODS.

"We need not single clergy only, but bodies of clergy, if the light of the Gospel is ever to penetrate the dark corners of our great towns, and in its streets and lanes visit those abodes of festering wretchedness, where tens of thousands drag out a dying life to (but for God's mercy, not man's) an undying death, without hope, and without God in the world." [2]

SISTERHOODS.

"Why should we not also, instead of our desultory visiting societies, have our Sœurs de la Charité, whose spotless and religious purity might be their passport amid the scenes of misery and loathsomeness, carrying that awe about them which even sin feels towards undefiledness, and impressing a healthful sense of shame upon guilt by their very presence? Why should marriage alone have its duties among the daughters of our great, and the single estate be condemned to an unwilling listlessness, or left to seek undirected and unauthorized and unsanctified ways of usefulness of its own?" [3]

These words, though written many years ago, have their weight now.

CAUTION TO DISTRICT VISITORS.

"Only whether we visit the poor or Christ's little ones, it must not be as superiors, but with great inward reverence for

---

[1] *Parochial and Cathedral Sermons*, p. 29.
[2] *Letter to Bishop of London*, 1851, p. 174.   [3] *Id.* p. 174.

Christ; not as though it were some great thing, but in humility; not only to teach them, but (as our Lord gave them us for an example) to learn of them; not as unto man, but as seeing Christ in them, so becoming like them: 'Yours shall be the kingdom of heaven,' which He has promised to such as they, so ministering unto Christ, ye shall yourselves 'receive Christ.'" [1]

ANIMALS.

Is it wrong to think it probable that animals may live again?
"He made them: He extendeth His Providence over them. 'His Mercy' Scripture saith, 'is over all His works'—encompasseth, enfoldeth them all. He feedeth the young ravens which call upon Him; 'not a sparrow falleth to the ground without your Father.' Yet their spirit goeth downwards to the earth, not upwards to God, who gave it. He careth for them as His creatures, and *may have something in store for them.*" [2]—*See* BISHOP BUTLER'S *Analogy*, ii. p. 25.

THE CHURCH'S SEASONS AND FESTIVALS.

"Such was the teaching of the ancient Church; so did everything bind them on to their Lord; the hours of their daily solemn worship spoke to them, and filled them with thoughts of His being contented to receive the bitter sentence of death for them; of His being nailed to the Cross; of His nailing our sins with His own Body there; of His tasting death for our sins, and commending His Blessed Spirit into the hands of His Heavenly Father; their going to rest; of His being laid in the grave for them; their awakening; of His Resurrection; and so each weekly fast bound them more closely to their Saviour's Cross, that they should not start from it; each Lord's Day they rose with Him. And thus 'day unto day uttered speech, and night unto night shewed knowledge.' And as the year flowed on, the Festivals of our

---

[1] "*God is Love,*" p. 44. *Occasional Sermons.*   [2] Vol. i. p. 299.

Lord did not simply commemorate (in modern phrase) ' events which took place 1800 years ago,' but showed Him to their purified hearts, as even then coming into the world, born, suffering, dying, rising, ascending. They longed for His coming; they suffered in His Passion; they rose with Him from the tomb; they 'followed His Ascension'; they awaited His return to judge the quick and dead, and to receive them to His Kingdom. And so in His Sacraments also He was with them; He fed them in the Eucharist; He washed away their sins in Baptism; and Baptism was to them Salvation, and the Cross and the Resurrection, because He opened their eyes to see not only the visible minister, but Himself, working invisibly. Not only the water, but the Blood; and the Holy Spirit, the third witness, applying the Blood, through the water to the cleansing of the soul." [1]

" These festivals are meant to help you on to this better choice. 'As you cannot serve two masters, so neither can you rejoice in God, and in the world.' The joy in the one must continually absorb in itself the joy in the other; 'he who joyeth in the world, joyeth not in God, and he who joyeth in God, joyeth not in the world.' Ye may rejoice being in the world, but the world must not be your joy; ye are not only in the world, ye are in God. . . ." [2]

"All our festivals in some way are in honour of our Lord. Yea, everything which the Church hath, or does, or is, is in some way in honour of Him, her Lord." [3]

First remember that not only are there special times to be observed by Churchmen, but it is also our duty to prepare for them.

The Church's festivals and fasts are special times, seasons of grace, for "although grace is ever around and in those who have not finally rejected it, there are special seasons at which it comes to individuals and to the Church; seasons which, if we miss, we know not what we lose; the wave has passed by,

---

[1] *Doctrine of Holy Baptism*, p. 173.
[2] Vol. iii. p. 460.   [3] *Id.* p. 463.

and we who might have been borne upon its crest, and carried safe, are tossing to and fro on a perilous sea."[1]

"And so whenever God would draw near to man, He would have man prepare for that awful nearness. We cannot on the instant change our whole tone of mind."[2]

"God has taught the Church to place longer seasons of preparation before the greater mysteries of the Faith."[3]

ADVENT.

"Awake! Again the Gospel trump is blown,
From year to year it swells with louder tone."

KEBLE.

"Advent, like penitence itself, has a mingled character of sorrow, and awe, and hope, and joy; sorrow for sin and wasted grace. Awe at judgment to come. Yet hope and joy too, that He who 'shall come to be our Judge,' at this time, 'to deliver man, abhorred not the Virgin's womb.' Our own Liturgy, in every change which was made, brings before us the stricter side, as if to say, 'sow in tears,' that ye may 'reap in joy.'"[4]

"Earnestness in Advent is the harbinger of Christmas joy. The Baptist's preaching of repentance prepares the heart to hear the song of angel-choirs; first we hear 'Glory to God,' then 'on earth peace, goodwill towards men.' Awe of the Day of Judgment must make us fill up the low places of our earthliness, and lower the eminences of our pride, make straight our crooked ways, and soften our asperities and all contrary to love, if we would, in the end, see the Salvation of our God."—*See also* DR. PUSEY's *Preface to Avrillon's Guide to Advent.*

[1] Vol. i. p. 45.   [2] *Id.* p. 49.   [3] *Id.* p. 52.
[4] *Absolution of Penitent*, pt. ii. p. 37.

CHRISTMAS DAY.

"Think on th' eternal home,
The Saviour left for you."

KEBLE.

What should we think of on Christmas Day?

"The intensity, then, of this day's blessed mystery is, 'God with us'; that, to retrace His Image upon us, He, Who is the Co-Eternal Image of the Father, took us into Himself, and stamped again His likeness upon us, by taking the likeness of our sinfulness. That us, who were aforetime alienated from God, He made to be at one with God, by Himself becoming one of us, and giving us of His Oneness with the Father. Us, who were a blot in the Creation of God, outcast from His sight, He has brought back into the harmony and order of His obedient creatures, uniting us to the Father in Himself, replacing our deadness by Himself, Who is Life; our darkness by Himself, Who is Light; our blindness by Himself, Who is Wisdom; our corruption by His Incorruption; our sinfulness by His Holiness; our emptiness by His Fullness, enlarging our infiniteness to receive God, Who is Infinite."[1]

What great lesson is taught us at Christmas?

Humility. "It surpasses all thought, it amazes, it confounds, to think of God becoming man; the Infinite enshrined within the finite; the Lord of all blended with His servant, the Creator with His Creature! It is a depth of mystery unsearchable. We must shrink with awe when we pronounce it. Of old, they fell down and worshipped, when, in our Creed, they uttered it—'God was made Man.'"[2]

"This is the special festival of humility, as of joy, a lowly joy, a joy of the lowly. Our Lord, from the manger, where, for our sakes, He deigned to lie, preacheth to us humility. This was the beginning and end of His teaching. He taught it in action now, by His Birth. He taught it in all His Life and Sufferings."[3]

[1] Vol. i. p. 65.   [2] *Id.* p. 81.   [3] *Id.* p. 87.

CIRCUMCISION.

"'The year begins with thee
And thou begin'st with woe."

KEBLE.

" Reflect to-day, the first shedding of the Precious Blood. The world begins this day with glad greetings and words of hope, and preparations of joy, and undefined looking and longing for future excitement and greater joy in store. Its Saviour begins it with suffering and humiliation, the first shedding of His Redeeming Blood foredating its full outpouring on Calvary, and His humbling Himself to the death of the Cross."[1]

EPIPHANY.

" Let us then, according to our means, seek how we may, amid our joys, of which we are all unworthy, deny ourselves, in order that in this sharp and bitter season, in which our Lord vouchsafed to come into the world for us, we may minister to Him. Seek Him out, where He yet is, unseen by the world, as when laid in the cave at Bethlehem; seek Him where He yet deigns to lie, sick, and ahungered, and athirst, and cold, and naked; and He to Whom, unseen on His manger throne, we offer the gold of our charity, the incense of our prayers, the myrrh of our self-denial, will from His Throne in the highest heaven look graciously upon it; He will soothe our sorrows, and purify our joys; yea, through joy and sorrow He will purify ourselves, until He fits us at last for the joy of His own everlasting Presence, 'in whose Countenance is the fulness of joy, and at whose right hand there are pleasures for evermore.' "[2]

[1] Vol. i. p. 116.   [2] Vol. iii. p. 461.

LENT.

"So angels pause on tasks of love
To look where sorrowing sinners kneel."

KEBLE.

In this "the deepest season of grace in the whole year, in which we would, day by day, fast with our Lord, that, what is to us the medicine of sin or the token of unworthiness, may by this holy and meritorious fasting, be sanctified, the Church tells us anew the blessedness of obeying His call. He calleth us apart from the world to live with Him at least in the stillness of the heart, and subdued affections, and chastened will, and a lowly hatred of ourselves, and humble faith and penitent love, so that we may, at the close, die with Him, be buried with Him, rise with Him, ascend with Him; yea, He again descend to us, that He may dwell in us by His Spirit. He Who accepteth the 'cup of cold water' given to His own in His Name, calleth us to these petty self-denials, to hallow them by His Grace. He calleth us to deny the body, that He may feed the soul; to retire for a time from the pleasures of the world, that He may speak to it 'good words and comfortable words'; to think how we may empty our souls of vanities that He may fill us with His Goodness. He calls us to deny ourselves, that for our decayed selves He may give us Himself."[1]

"And yet it may be, that among the redeemed around the Throne of the Lamb, some who shall wear the brightest crowns will be from among those who passed their years in penitence and joyous sorrow, witnesses to the Heavenly hosts of God's overflowing love, and to what height of life the penitent love, humble love of Christ may raise from what exceeding depth of death."[2]

"And this may, in a degree, be a comfort to us all. For almost all may too well know of themselves how they in

[1] Vol. i. p. 148.   [2] *Id.* p. 235.

former seasons neglected Wisdom's voice, and have since gathered the bitter fruits."

What should Lent be to each?

"Lent should take in and be a discipline of the whole man, in union with the Passion of his Lord and God. Prayer, alms, and fasting, form one holy band, for which Our Blessed Lord gives rules together, and which draw up the soul to Him : for they grow out of and cherish the love to Him, love to His members for His Sake, denial of self." [1]

What should be our great aim in Lent?

Retirement; to be at least a little more alone with God.

"And it is probably one chief reason why Lent, though always healthful, does not bring deeper profit to some whom it does profit; that they do not avail themselves enough of it to gather themselves up in retirement, and there to hold converse with their God. From the first dawning of conversion to the hour of death, *it is in solitude mostly* that God speaks to the soul." [2]

THE PASSION.

"Akin to this tenderness of His sacred Flesh was the tenderness of His Human Soul, which was outraged more than His Human Body was torn, and which endured those outrages for love of us sinners. We are wont to speak of the soul as if, because it is one thing, it were therefore much the same in different human beings. We understand, of course, the difference between a soul in sin and a soul in grace; the soul of one who, like some degraded forms of humanity, is seemingly acted upon by some unknown dealings of grace only; or, if acted upon, is acted upon only thence to derive a fresh occasion of doing despite to the grace of God, and a soul, like those of the Blessed Apostles, 'filled with the Holy Ghost' (Acts [ii. 34 ; iv. 8 ; vi. 3, 5 ; vii. 55 ; ix. 17 ; xi. 24 ; xiii. 9, 52). But these distinctions relate to qualities super-

<hr>

[1] Vol. i. p. 242. [2] *Id.* p. 243.

induced for good or ill, not to the original structure of the soul. Yet human souls, in their original structure and capacity too, vary indefinitely one from another, even as those blessed spirits do, in their several choirs, to whose broken ranks they are, if they persevere, to be advanced, as, to fill them up those souls were created. Our Blessed Lord's Human Soul, having been created to be for ever united with the Person of God the Son, was like to our human souls in all their sinless infirmities ; it was like them as being a soul [in everything belonging to the nature of a soul, without which it could not be such. But the soul of Christ, being created in order to be united with the Word, was created with greater perfections and greater capacities, and was a higher Object of the love of the Holy Trinity Who created it, than all the rest of creation, or all possible creations collectively. Such was the Soul, united with God the Son, seeing all things in the Word, with more than all other created perfections, yet with all the perfection of human tenderness, which had to suffer during those awful hours, in which all malice, human or diabolical, was let loose upon it.

" That tenderness was wounded in all the most opposite ways, yet, by reason of the perfection of His knowledge, in all those ways at once. He never lost sight of one." [1]

EASTER.

> " So buried with our Lord, we'll close our eyes
> To the decaying world, till angels bid us rise."
>
> KEBLE.

What is the joy and gift of Easter ?

"Our very risen Lord Himself. To the Church it is really true, 'The Lord hath risen indeed, and hath appeared to Simon.' Before, all was laid up for us, but we had it not. By the Resurrection is the gift of the Spirit, and engrafting into Him ; by it is forgiveness of sin and removal of punishment, and righteousness, and sanctification, and redemption, and

[1] *Eleven Addresses*, p. 48.

adoption as sons, and brotherhood with Christ; yea, oneness with Him, and eternal inheritance, because all these are in Him, and by it we become partakers of Him and of all which is His; yea, this is the bliss of all our festivals, that they not only shadow out a likeness and conformity between the Head and the members, our Redeemer, and us on whom His Name is called, but there is, through the power of His Cross and Resurrection, a real inworked conformity, a substance and reality.' " [1]

Is there yet more ?

Yes. " In Christ shall all be made alive."

" The bursting of the bars of our prison-house, the restoration of our lost paradise, the opening of the Kingdom of Heaven, the earnest of our endless life, the binding of the strong man, and letting us, his lawful prisoners, free; the bringing in of incorruption; the conquest, in the Head, of the last enemy." [2]

Can there be more than this ?

" There can. The text unfolds to us a yet deeper Mystery, that all this is to us 'in Christ.' 'In Christ shall all be made alive.' The endless life, which they shall live who are counted worthy of it, shall not then be a life such as men seem to live here, where our true life is unseen, as if we were so many creatures of God's Hand, each having his existence wholly separate from his fellows, upheld in being by God, yet, as it seems, apart from God, having his own wills, affections, tastes, pursuits, passions, love, hatred, interests, joys, sufferings."

" Our life in Heaven shall not be, as it seems here, and as it truly is in the ungodly, separate from God, and in the good indistinctly and imperfectly united with Him. It shall be a life 'in God.' 'In Christ shall all be made alive.' We shall live then not only as having our souls restored to our bodies, and souls and bodies living on in the presence of Almighty God. Great and unutterable as were this blessedness, there is a higher yet in store—to live on 'in Christ.' For this implies Christ's living on in us." [3]

This then, as it is the special Mystery of the Gospel, so is it

<hr>

[1] Vol. i. p. 286.   [2] *Id.* p. 296.   [3] *Id.*

of the Resurrection.   To be "in Christ!"   This is the greatness of God's gift in Baptism, that we are thereby "in Christ."

ASCENSION DAY.

"Then shall we see Thee as Thou art,
    For ever fixed in no unfruitful gaze,
    But such as lifts the new created heart
    Age after age in worthier love and praise."

KEBLE.

What is the very mystery of this Day's Festival?

" Heaven is the very mystery of this day's Festival.   We
have not only, with St. John the Baptist, seen the Heavens
open and the Spirit descending from Heaven and lighting
upon our incarnate Lord ; we have not only had His promise
fulfilled : 'Thou shalt see greater things than these.   Verily,
verily, I say unto you, hereafter ye shall see the Heaven open,
and the Angels of God ascending and descending upon the
Son of Man.'   We have seen Heaven part, not only for gifts
to be received by Him for us, and the union between Heaven
and earth which sin had broken, restored, but we have seen
Him, our Head, clothed with our flesh, with ourselves One
God with the Father ; one Man with us, received up as Man
into Heaven and above the Heavens at the Right Hand of
God.   What then have we any more to do with earth, or the
things of earth, its cares or its sorrows, its pleasures or its
vanities, its emptiness or its fullness, Whose Head is in Heaven ?
Where else should the members be ?   The Redeemer is there ;
where else the redeemed ? " [1]

"'Our conversation is in Heaven.'   Many are the meanings
of this word, and every way, the Apostle says, we are in
Heaven.   For the word, in the language in which God wrote
it, means the city or state to which we belong, or citizenship,
or the order and rules of a state by which it is governed, or
the way of life of the citizens ; 'our conversation'—and in all
these ways he places us in Heaven." [2]

[1] Vol. i. p. 419.   [2] *Id.* p. 421.

What is the great comfort and privilege of this, our citizenship ?

"This then is the great blessedness of this our citizenship, as of every other gift of grace or glory, that we have it, not in ourselves, but of and in Christ. We belong to Heaven because we belong to Him; 'members,' the Apostle says, 'of His Body, of His Flesh, of His Bones.' His temple knit into one with Him, Who knitteth in one all things in Heaven and in earth. All in us, which is of Heaven, is of His Spirit in us, His Holy Spirit, the Bond of the Oneness of the Father and the Son, which encircleth all things, taketh us up into Himself."[1]

Why should Ascension be kept as one of the most bright and joyous of all Festivals ?

Because it was a time of transcendent rejoicing in Heaven itself.

"Since 'there is joy in Heaven among 'the Angels of God over one sinner that repenteth,' what must have been the joy over the completed Redemption, to see our Lord, 'the first begotten from the dead' arrayed with the majesty of the Father, 'leading captivity captive,' bringing the fathers who had waited for His coming, to their appointed place, and Himself, above all created being, above the stars, above each rank of Angels at the Right Hand of God!"[2]

Did Jesus at His Ascension into Heaven really take possession of the Highest Place therein ?

"He ascended, not 'above' only, but 'far above'; not into the highest Heavens, but 'far above all Heavens,' than which there is nothing higher. There, where no creature is, or can be: there above all spirits (for the Body of Christ, being united with His Godhead, is above all created spirits); there, in the noblest place which created beings can have (for this is the meaning of 'the Right Hand of God'), encircled, embosomed, impenetrated with the Godhead, united with God, adored together with His Godhead, by all creation, is the Body of Christ our God, our King, our Head, Who calls us 'His Body,' calleth us brethren."[3]

[1] Vol. i. p. 427.   [2] Vol. ii. p. 218.   [3] *Id.* p. 220.

Did Jesus take into Heaven the very same body He had on earth ?

Most certainly. Christ did truly rise again from death, and took again His Body with flesh, bones, and all things appertaining to the perfection of man's nature. " Wherewith He ascended into Heaven, and there sitteth until He return to judge all men at the last day."—Article IV.

"But what can we think of the glory of God, wherein His Human Form lives, wherewith It is radiant; that Light, which lightens all that lives, fills all the Heavenly hosts with light transparent, yet which shrouds by its very brightness the depth of the invisible glory of the Godhead? Yet in that Divine Glory, lives that very Human Form which our loving Lord took for us, unchanged, save that the glory which when He was for us on earth, was veiled, now issues forth, the light and joy of all, throught the spheres of Heaven."[1]

" His Eyes, as the beloved disciple saw them, were 'as a flame of fire' beaming brightly on those who love or desire Him, consuming the impenitent. 'His Countenance shone like the sun in his strength' with spiritual light, and the brightness of grace, and radiant mildness, and enlivening glow. Yet it is the same Countenance which looked upon Peter in his fall; the same look which melted the heart of the dying robber by His side. The same eyes which shone on Mary Magdalene at His feet, live on, shine on, unchanged except in their glory. The love must beam forth even more now; since the Divine Nature, veiled then, shines forth in its strength now; and God is Love. His feet seemed to St. John 'like to fine brass, as if they burned in the furnace,' so transparent and translucent were His very feet with the Divine glory. Yet they are the same feet which St. Mary Magdalene anointed, and 'washed with her tears, and wiped with the hairs of her head.' They are the same feet which for us were pierced; and the prints of the nails, in everlasting glory bespeak and plead silently the depth of His love, the merits of His Passion."[2]

[1] Vol. ii. p. 225.   [2] *Id.* p. 232.

WHITSUN-DAY.

" But when He came the second time
He came in power and love ;
Softer than gale at morning prime,
Hovered this holy Dove."

KEBLE.

What is Whitsun-Day?

" Whitsun-Day is the filling up of the Ascension, when man in God was taken up into Heaven, and sat on His Father's throne; the Day of Pentecost fulfilled the promise of the Father, and as man now dwelt in God, so God, in a new ineffable way, dwelt thenceforth in man." [1]

" But now, such is the wondrous goodness of God, such His overflowing Love towards us, His Divine Joy in imparting Himself to us His most fallen creatures, if we will but receive Him, that this Divine work in us, He worketh in a way wholly Divine. It is not enough for His Love, to give us any, or all the gifts of His Grace; not enough to give us His Love, and 'Righteousness, and Sanctification, and Redemption,' but He is Himself all these and all besides to us. His gifts are the fruits of the Spirit, not without us but within us. His gifts stream forth from His Gift, Himself, His gift is Himself. He giveth us not only, if we will, His various graces; He is to us 'Wisdom and Righteousness, and Sanctification, and Redemption,' and that by indwelling ! " [2]

" All our other great festivals are festivals of our Lord; this is in a manner our own. All other festivals tell us of what God wrought for us. The Day of Pentecost speaks to us of God's great work in us, His humbling Himself to each one of us." [3]

" The gift of this day is Almighty God Himself. Not grace alone, nor gracious influences, nor drawings of His Love, nor loving-kindness, nor His Love shed abroad in our hearts,

---

[1] Vol. i. p. 440.   [2] *Id.* p. 441.
[3] *Parochial and Cathedral Sermons,* p. 459.

contented His Infinite ineffable love to give us, unless He also gave Himself. It overpowers reason, it transcends imagination; the heart itself can scarce contain the thought, but that God has said it. The love of God is shed abroad in our hearts, but 'through the Holy Spirit Who is given to us.' Uncreated love pours created love into our souls, but by being Himself given to us. Thus was the Comforter more than to replace our loving Lord's Bodily Visible Presence. 'I will ask the Father, and He shall give you another Comforter, that He may abide with you for ever, the Spirit of truth, Whom the world cannot receive; because it seeth Him not, neither knoweth Him. But ye know Him, for He shall dwell with you, and shall be in you."[1]

TRINITY SUNDAY.

"By all the grace Thy Heavens still hide,
We pray Thee keep us at Thy side,
Creator, Saviour, strengthening Guide."

. KEBLE.

"Other festivals in our Christian year have set before us the condescension of our God; how God was ·Incarnate; God was born; God, made Man, suffered; God, made Man, died, rose again, ascended in the Manhood which He had taken; and God the Holy Ghost condescended to come down to dwell among us and in us, and, if we would, to take possession of our hearts. To-day is the festival, not of what God has done for us, but of Himself, what He is, what it is His unceasing Bliss to be, Father, Son, and Holy Ghost."[2]

"'We shall see Him as He is.' We shall see Him wholly, Father, Son, and Holy Ghost. We shall see and be blessed in the sight of their mutual Eternal Love. O thought beyond all thought, condescension beyond all conceivable condescension, that we shall see God, not only as He is to us, by bestowing on us His transporting, jubilant, ecstatic love, but we shall see Him in Himself, as He is, Father, Son, and

---

[1] *Parochial and Cathedral Sermons*, p. 473. [2] *Id.* p. 488.

Holy Ghost; how the Father loveth the Son, and the Son is all love to the Father; and the Holy Ghost is ever breathed forth by both, and poureth back His love to both; and the love of all Three Persons is infinite, unceasing, unvarying, the self-same; for God is One, and God is Love." [1]

"The Doctrine of the Holy Trinity shows us His true Majesty; the Doctrine of the Incarnation, His true Humility." [2]

ST. ANDREW.

"To all of us, probably while we were yet children, God hath so spoken through our parents, in our own souls, through His own Word, and has bidden us 'do this,' 'cease to do that'; sometimes more specially, 'leave off this one thing'; sometimes more largely, 'break off all your evil ways, and serve God with a whole heart.' To us also hath He in the one or the other way called, 'Follow thou Me.' And, as we were faithful or not to our first calls, has been the happiness or misery of our life hitherto. Many we had, doubtless, which we mostly no longer remember; some or other more striking ones, when God spoke more loudly, and which, by our listening or no, have left some traces, most of us probably still bear in our memory. But all have had many of them, and all shall give account of all that they have had. Hence the example of these many Apostles may be such a blessing to us, in that in them we see how God rewardeth obedience to the first call." [3]

ST. THOMAS.

"Faint not, nor despond. If thou prayest, 'thy heaviness shall be turned into joy.' Let thy heaviness ever issue in prayer, brief, but longing; and while thou art yet in heaviness on earth, thy prayer, which seems to fall back upon thee, Angels shall waft on their golden censers, and thine Almighty

---

[1] *Parochial and Cathedral Sermons*, p. 487.   [2] *Id.* p. 493.
[3] Vol. iii. p. 409.

Intercessor shall present it before His Father; and unseen, perhaps unfelt, the Holy Spirit shall descend upon thee, and thou shalt, day by day, be renewed, not by any workings of thy own mind, nor by any power over thine own thoughts, nor by any change of thine own feelings wrought by thyself, but by His might, 'Who subdueth all things unto Himself.'

" They are well nigh wasted hours, in which thou broodest sorrowfully over thyself, as though there were no hope, unless they issue in prayer to God. There *is* hope, yea and *assured* salvation, for all who will now hear God's call, and turn to Him. Whatever thy disease, stop not short in thyself; but go forth out of thyself to thy Lord and thy God."

" Brood not in heaviness over thine own state, or what thou imaginest to be thine own state before God. Count everything temptation which holds thee back from God. God willeth that all should be saved. The Price of thy Redemption, Scripture says, is 'the Blood of God,' wherewith 'He purchased the Church.' Thy Saviour on the Cross stretched out His Almighty Arms to embrace the whole world, even thee in thy misery."[1]

ST. PAUL.

" Well might the Apostle in this his outward death and hidden power of life, appointed, as it were, to a perpetual conflict with death (1 Cor. iv. 9), yet upheld in life by the life of his Lord, so that it is not, he says, 'I that live, but Christ liveth in me'; well might he be a spectacle, not to the world only and to men, but to Angels, marvelling to see in our fallen race, a life like their own, the first-fruits of the Mystery of the Passion, the human partaking of the Divine, man living by and sharing the life and love of his Redeemer and his God."

" Yet he, who was a spectacle to Angels, was none to himself. He reflected not on his good deeds wrought in God:

[1] Vol. ii. pp. 193, 195.

he counted not the courses he had run, two years after this, and by revelation of God, he knew that it was finished; now, what did he? He who 'knew' his Lord, and 'the power of His Resurrection' in himself, 'and the fellowship of His Sufferings;' he, to whom those Precious Sufferings had been so imparted, that what were Christ's were, by His communicating, made common with him; he who had been conformed to His death, had received the stamp of its likeness on himself, had been 'moulded into it' (St. Chrys.); what did he? 'Brethren,' he says, 'I count not myself to have apprehended; but this one thing I do; forgetting those things which are behind, and reaching forth unto those things which are before, I press towards the prize of the high calling of God in Christ Jesus.' Of all the past, he recollected this only, that he, when fleeing from Christ, had been pursued, overtaken, apprehended, by Him; 'for which also I was apprehended by Christ Jesus.' And now, he had but one thought, one object before him, one prize hanging before his eyes on high, after which, the more he had attained, the more he must strive in his course. It was on high, and he must see nought on earth; he saw, as though he saw not; heard, as though he heard not; had, as though he held not; suffered, as though he endured not; dead to all outward things; all, sight, hearing, soul, body, wrapt in that One Object toward which he day by day strained and stretched onward, to which he was, day by day nearer; 'If by any means,' he says, 'I might attain to the Resurrection of the dead.' For by that Resurrection should he be brought to Him Who had so loved him; Him Whom he so loved, when he should be raised aloft amid Cherubim and Seraphim (S. Chrys. Hom. 32, on Rom., p. 504, Oxf. Tr.), to hold that prize on high, to Which he had stretched out; hold it for ever, by Whom he was held; might grasp in his hands, enfold with his soul, Him by Whose love he should be enfolded—God Himself."[1]

---

[1] *Leeds Sermons*, pp. 349, 350.

ST. MATTHIAS.

"Now He bids thee, with one earnest strife, cast out of thyself what chokes thy heart, so that thou canst not contain everlastingly His Love. He bids thee, by His grace, enlarge thy heart, that He may fill thee more largely. All of this world will soon have passed away. But God will remain, and thou, whatever thou hast become, good or bad. Thy deeds now are the seed-corn of Eternity. Each single act, in each several day, good or bad, is a portion of that seed. Each day adds some line, making thee more or less like Him, more or less capable of His Love, fitter for greater or less glory, to be nearer to Him, or to be less near, or to be away from Him for ever. Is the strife long and hard? Long and hard it would be, to be ever defeated. But Christ shall lighten it for thee. He will bear it in thee; He will bear thee over it, as He will bear thee over the molten surges of this burning world. Christ will go before thee. He saith unto thee, 'Follow Me, and where I am, there shall thou be with Me.' 'Follow thou Me.' 'Be of good cheer, I have overcome the world.'" [1]

ST. MARK.

"The festivals of the blessed Evangelists and Apostles of our Lord are so ordained in our Church as not only to be days of thanksgiving for the mercies vouchsafed to us through them, but also to convey lessons of duty to us. That of this day is, in what way we, who in God's holy Church have been instructed in 'the heavenly doctrine of His Evangelist St. Mark,' may not be 'carried about with every wind of doctrine,' but 'may be established in the truth of Christ's holy Gospel'; how we may follow, in our measure, the firmness and stead-fastness of this blessed Saint, who, having by his preaching, his life, his labours, the miracles wrought by his hands, planted

[1] Vol. ii. p. 128.

the Gospel widely and deeply, yielding fruits of a strict holiness, at last, in this our Easter season, 'resisted unto blood, striving against sin,' yielded his body to be mangled by the enemies of the Cross, his spirit to join the white-robed army of martyrs, evermore to praise his Lord."

"And yet St. Mark was naturally unsteadfast. (See Newman's *Parochial Sermons*, vol. ii. 'Religious Cowardice.') It is thought that he records against himself, that he was the young man (St. Mark xiv. 51), who, when his Lord was taken, 'fled away naked.' Again, when Paul and Barnabas were 'separated for the work,' he shrank back in time of difficulty, and 'went not with them to the work.' Yet, at last, he was fitted by God for more than ordinary difficulties; he preached the Gospel amid tribes the most savage, founded the Church of Alexandria, of all the strictest, and so the most resolute also in maintaining the faith, and yielded his life in a bold resistance to sin by a lingering martyrdom; an encouragement to us, that however weak or irresolute we may by nature be, our Saviour's strength may be perfected in our weakness, and we too may be fitted to bear our Saviour's Cross, and follow Him."[1]

ST. PHILIP AND ST. JAMES.

"'I am the Way, the Truth, and the Life'; the Way, whereby we are to go; the Truth, whereunto we are to go; the Life, wherein we are to abide: the Way, in which there is no error; the Truth, around which no shadow of falsehood can gather; the Life, which is incompatible with death. Observe the absoluteness and exclusiveness of the words. Not 'a way,' but '*the* way'; not *having* truth or a portion of truth, not as ours, partial or error-mingled truth, but '*the* Truth'; not life-endowed, but '*the* Life.' What others, what any created thing, could have only in part, *that* He held, whole and in its entireness. Others may possess truth and

___
[1] Vol. iii. p. 184.

life, as communicated by Him; He alone was 'the truth and the life,' having them in Himself, so as from Himself to communicate them, but not as communicated to Him, save as He exists Himself, 'Very God of Very God.'"

"The more gifted you could imagine any created being, the more he would start back at the unutterable folly of declaring that he, being created, was 'the Truth.' No man ever said it, save He Who was also God."[1]

ST BARNABAS.

"Of one grace he was the exemplar among his brethren, but throughout in harmony, in nothing jarring, or resisting the pervading influence of that Holy Spirit, which filled him wholly, and attuned every thought in its whole compass to the blissful sympathies of heaven. Firm and self-denying, yet compassionate on the infirm; meek and gentle, yet 'delivering over his life unto death' (as the Apostle bare him witness) (Acts xv. 26), for the name of the Lord Jesus Christ; charitable, .so as to command Apostolic respect, and bring down the praise of God, at once delivering over all he had, not claiming even the distribution of it, seeking neither power nor influence, but taking contentedly the lower place, and through the long succession of years maintaining himself with an unpretending simplicity; with outward advantages of person and of the learning of the priestly tribe, yet in godly sincerity setting others higher than himself; yea he had concentrated in himself all those natural advantages which men boast of, that outward appearance which once deceived even the eye of Samuel, wealth, learning, winning character, high expectations, noble descent (*i. e.* descent from that tribe whose privilege of being near the Lord the great of the world then thought higher than their own); yet all, descent, popularity, wealth, learning, reputation, outward show, he held as nothing. He followed implicitly our Lord's command (St. Matt. xx. 26), 'Whosoever

[1] Vol. 1872, p. 216, 217.

shall be great among you shall be your minister'; he consecrated or gave up all to God, and so received all back from God, the praise of God which he sought, and the praise of men which he sought not; and humbling himself he was exalted, and how much more shall he be exalted at the Great Day."

ST. JOHN BAPTIST.

"St. John Baptist says of our Blessed Lord Himself, 'He whom God hath sent speaketh the words of God; for God giveth not the Spirit by measure unto Him' (St. John iii. 34). 'The sword of the Spirit is the Word of God' (Eph. vi. 17), and even thence hath it its sharpness; and, through the power of the Word, whose Word it is, doth it 'pierce even to the dividing asunder of soul and spirit,' and 'discern the thoughts and intents of the heart' (Heb. iv. 12; Jer. xvii. 10; Rom. viii. 27; Rev. ii. 23), coming from Him, Who is the Searcher of the heart. To the prophet God Himself saith, 'Behold, I will make My Words in thy mouth fire, and this people wood' (Jer. v. 14). It devoured man, as being fire from Him Who 'is a consuming fire'" (Heb. xii. 29).

"Further, since rebuke is of so awful a character, and inflicts suffering, it must be given, not without suffering to ourselves also, who give it. We may not inflict pain without pain; suffering without suffering. Our Ever-blessed and gracious Master, who sends us suffering, Himself first suffered for us. 'The Prophets, who spake in the Name of the Lord,' are set forth 'for an example of suffering affliction, and of patience'" (St. James v. 10).

"The Apostles were, as it were, 'appointed unto death,' and out of the midst of death, bearing about 'the marks of their Lord's suffering' (Gal. vi. 17), they 'reproved the world of sin,' in the words which the Holy Ghost taught. Elijah and St. John delivered their stern messages, clothed in hair cloth."[1]

[1] Vol. i. pp. 105, 106.

" In the desert, He formed Moses for forty years, and St. John Baptist all his life ; He revealed Himself to Moses in the flame of fire in the bush, and to St. John in that which it signified, His Incarnate Son." [1]

ST. PETER.

" The ardent lover of the Lord ; conformed to His death, crucified with Him by the death, long foretold ; yet, in humility, dreading too near an approach to its outward likeness ? Yet little as we can say, one may, out of the manifold graces which his Lord imparted to him, name his deep humility, ardent love, devotion to his Master's honour, prompt, self-denying obedience. And these we see when they were as yet half-unformed, before the Holy Ghost had come down in the fullness of His Presence upon the Church. What reverent awe at the Presence of our Lord, which would even forego that Presence from very humility, 'Depart from me, for I am a sinful man, O Lord.' What instant love, when he who refused to see Him, his Lord and God, prostrate to wash his feet, yet, when threatened with the loss of Him, said, 'Lord, not my feet only, but my hands, and my head !' What ready obedience, ere yet he had been called to give up all, and follow Him (St. Luke v. 5), 'we have toiled all night and taken nothing, nevertheless at Thy word (at one word of Christ) I will let down the net.' Even his very falls were in love for his Lord. Out of human feeling he would not that his Lord should die, and so drew on himself the rebuke, 'get thee behind Me, Satan.' A rebuke still full of mildness, bidding him 'follow after,' not 'go before,' follow his Lord to death, not refuse that He should die for him. In ardent, though as yet uninstructed, zeal of love, he drew the sword on the high priest's servant. Love drew him within the high priest's palace, and that one grievous fall was not only washed away by those bitter tears, but when he had been for-given, restored, loving and beloved, it was avenged by the

[1] Vol. i. p. 243.

austerity of a whole life (St. Greg. Naz. joins him, in this respect, with Elijah and St. John Baptist; and says that he was 'supported with lupines for three farthings' (an 'as') Orat. 14, de amor. paup a. 4), and the aged confessor, the undaunted witness of the truth, arose, it is related, night by night, at cockcrowing, to weep that once he fell.

"Such then being some of those graces in St. Peter, to which the Father revealed the faith, against which the gates of hell should not prevail—ardent love, devotion, humility, ready self-denying obedience—how is it with us?"[1]

ST. JAMES.

"Both were of an earnest, zealous, fiery temper, whence He called them Boanerges, *i. e.* sons of thunder; sincere and zealous for their Master's honour, whence, without knowing the spirit *they* were of, they would imitate, of themselves, what Elias by Divine command had done. Confiding that, for the love they bore to their Master, they could in all things follow Him, and be made like to Him, they pledged themselves to (St. Matt. xx. 22) 'drink of the cup of which He drank, and be baptized with the Baptism wherewith He was baptized'; and He, Who saw their sincerity, accepted their promise, and held them bound to Him and with Him. They, with St. Peter, were the only witnesses of some of the chief things in the life of our Lord: they only were present at the raising of the daughter of Jairus from the dead: they only saw the glories of the Transfiguration, when the Incarnate Divinity shone through the veil of flesh, and gave a glimpse of those glories which they should see hereafter, and which now they more fully behold. To them who had seen His glory, He spake also of His coming humiliation; to them only with St. Andrew, of His coming to destroy Jerusalem, and of His second coming to Judgment. They only, 'Peter,' and these 'two sons of Zebedee,' were admitted to witness His soul

[1] Vol. ii. pp. 294, 295.

'sorrowful and very heavy'; to them only He condescended to look for sympathy, and spake the gracious, confiding words, ' My soul is exceeding sorrowful, even unto death; tarry ye here and watch with Me.' Further of St. James we hear nothing, but that one of the appearances after the Resurrection was to him and six other of the Apostles, as they for the time returned to their fishing on the Lake of Galilee. Then we hear again only of his death, wherein his Lord's promise to him was fulfilled, and he drank of the cup of his Lord, and was baptized with His Baptism of blood : eminent even in his death, in that when ' Herod took in hand to vex certain of the Church,' ' he slew James the brother of John with the sword,' and then ' proceeded to take Peter also '; slaying, it seems, St. James the Greater, as he is called, as being one chief among the Apostles.

" Such and so little does even the Church here below know of the saints of God ! "[1]

ST. BARTHOLOMEW.

" Even so amid trivial things we may be, nay men are, in every station of life, pleasing God ; that is, leading angels' lives, in that they are doing His will on earth, as the angels in heaven ; they are ' servants of His, doing His pleasure.' For to this end, among other ends, did our Redeemer, Who was God and Man, pass through our daily duties, our daily trials, that He might sanctify them, and we no longer think ' common ' what He had, by doing, ' cleansed '; that we might not think slightly of them ; that we might see that in all we might act worthily of Him; that we might not be weary of them. He, in the form of a servant, hungered, that we might learn that even this common craving is hallowed, if we feel that ' man doth not live by bread alone, but by every word that proceedeth out of the mouth of God.' He took food, that we might learn to ' eat and drink to the glory of God.' He

[1] Vol. iii. pp. 198, 199.

rested in sleep as well as watched, that we might learn to lie down in rest, reposing in God.   He wept, that we might learn compassion.   He sorrowed, that we might learn resignation in sorrow.   He, as Man, was subject to the creature whom, as God, He had created, that we might learn the blessedness of simple, child-like obedience.   He worked with His hands, as though He had been what He was called, 'Is not this the carpenter's son?' that we might learn not to be ashamed of whatsoever God has called us to."[1]

ST. MATTHEW.

"Charity, as well as purity, is an absolute command of God, which men neglect at peril of their souls.   It is a command which you must obey, at peril of having the sentence pronounced upon you, 'Depart, ye cursed, into everlasting fire.'   It is a command, which you must obey, as you would not be rebels against the sovereignty of God, and be punished as rebels against Him.   It is a command which you must obey, not as if you were doing some great thing; not as if it were an act of generosity, but in humility, as owning your allegiance to your God.   You do not, I suppose, think it a great virtue to pay your income-tax honestly.   It is simply not to lie and steal.   Charity is a blessed income-tax due to our God, in proportion to our means.   It belongs to our condition of life.   You speak of dress, equipages, appearance, furniture, as suited to your condition of life.   Perhaps some of you have been answering me in your minds, 'We must dress, spend, have this or that elegancy, such or such a table, according to our condition of life.'   And I say to you, that there is a condition of life, antecedent to all these, the due to Almighty God, your Sovereign Lord, 'the King of kings and Lord of lords.'   And as you must, perforce, discharge your dues to the state, antecedently to your expenditure on your condition, so, as creatures of God, as members of

[1] Vol. iii. p. 155.

Christ, you have another due upon you, antecedently and in proportion to your expenditure on self, your due to Almighty God, of which not the tax-gatherer but the poor man is the collector; of your payment of which God, year by year, takes account which, if paid, He will reward a hundredfold; the holding back whereof He will punish, as contempt of Himself and of His love, and of the sufferings of Jesus for you, in Hell." [1]

ST. MICHAEL AND ALL ANGELS.

"The blessed Angels, who ever behold the Face of our Father, ever joy ineffably in the Divine Presence, ever fulfil His Will, and are filled with His glory, and ceaseless praise, Holy, Holy, Holy! they, possessed already of their everlasting bliss, partakers of the Eternity, the Truth, the Will of God, and in Him possessing the fullness of light and of immortal wisdom, who, even while ministering to us, never part from the blissful contemplation of God, the food of whose life is God Himself, can their bliss be increased?—can it be increased by the sight of one, still so loathsome to himself, and so burdensome? 'There is joy in the presence of the Angels of God over one sinner that repenteth.' In him, who seeth not as yet himself, doubtful of himself and his own stedfastness, doubtful almost whether God can love him, the Angels, in Divine light, see their future fellow-citizen in bliss; joy that one more is recovered from our lost world; that the lost is found." [2]

"Yet heavy as the clouds must often be, which man's sins have spread between him and his God, suspending, as it seems, all influx of grace from God, stopping his prayer that it should not pass through, Holy Scripture pierces it for us. While all seems dark below, above that veil of cloud is He, the Unchangeable, in light and serenity and love, forsaking none who forsake not Him finally; meeting us, when fleeing from Him, in displeasure, that we may turn to God in love."

[1] Lenten Sermons, pp. 41, 42.   [2] Leeds Sermons, pp. 267, 268.

ST. LUKE.

"Since, lastly, the Apostle's benediction is not, that we should not be free from suffering, but that (1 St. Peter v. 10) 'the God of all grace, Who hath called us unto His Eternal glory in Christ Jesus, after *ye have suffered for* a while, stablish, strengthen, settle you,' what follows? Surely this, that it behoves us, brethren, to treat suffering, whether in ourselves or others, in a much more solemn way than the generality even of serious Christians are wont to do. In itself, it were a punishment for sin, oppressive, hopeless; through His mercy in Christ, it is His healing medicine, to burn out our wounds and purify us for His Presence. All are tokens of His Presence, the great Physician of our souls, looking graciously upon our spots and sores, checking our diseases ere they take deep root, or cutting deeply and healthfully into our very souls, if He have compassion upon us, when we have deeply offended Him. All, from the most passing pain of the body to the most deep-seated anguish of the soul, are messengers from Him."

"Yet all, if we will regard it, are His Fatherly care, tempering our cup with pain and sorrow, as He sees most needful for us; all, in their degree, loosen our hold of this life (as all pain is an earnest and preparation for our final dissolution); all lead up thitherward, where there shall be no pain; all humble us, as being creatures who require it, and deserve far more; all teach us to look into ourselves, to see for what disease in us this medicine has been sent."[1]

"All, then, pain, sickness, weariness, distress, languor, agony of mind or body, whether in ourselves or others, is to be treated reverently, since in it our Maker's Hand passes over us, fashioning, by suffering, the imperfect or decayed substance of our souls. In itself, it were the earnest of Hell; through His mercy in Christ, it is a purifying for Heaven. Either way, it is a very solemn act."

[1] Vol. iii. pp. 129, 130, 131.

ST. SIMON AND ST. JUDE.

"If we are Christians, we must have zeal; if we are earnest Christians, we must have earnest zeal; if we were Apostolic Christians, we should have Apostolic zeal. For what is zeal? Zeal has two aspects; the one towards God, the other towards man. Zeal towards God is a burning desire for the glory of God, that the whole world should love, honour, serve Him with all their hearts, and minds, and souls, and strength; and since this is not so, it grieves, for love of His Holy Name, that He is so little known, so little loved, so much blasphemed and dishonoured. Zeal towards man is a kindled longing that he should adore and love and honour God, and find in Him all good, and peace, and joy, and bliss, and know the bliss of loving Jesus, and be saved by Him and love Him for ever." [1]

"This zeal we must, in some way, have, if we are not Christians in name, or lukewarm Christians. No one can know how great and good is God, how full of bliss and peace is the thought of Jesus, how great and evil it is to dishonour God, and not feel a pang when he sees or thinks of others who know not God and seeks Him not, nor love Him. It is the most piteous sight in the whole world to see one, for whom Christ died, a stranger to Christ, forgetful of Christ, in word and deed denying Christ. There can be no real love without some measure of zeal."

ALL SAINTS' DAY.

"From many a rural nook, unthought of there,
Rises for that proud world, the Saints' prevailing prayer."

KEBLE.

How should we regard this day?

"This should be a day of subdued, holy joy, peculiar to itself. On other festivals we praise God for some portion of

[1] *Parochial and Cathedral Sermons*, pp. 267, 268.

z

His work of mercy in our Redemption, or for some of that holy band of Apostles and Evangelists, through whom the light of the glorious gospel has reached to us; to-day we praise Him for having perfected what He began, for having completed in man what He wrought for him, To-day is the festival of all the redeemed, whom He perfected." [1]

Of whom should we think to-day?

"Of all whose examples kindled our early faith, Patriarchs, Apostles, Prophets, Martyrs, Confessors, Teachers, Ascetics, Penitents are there; all are at rest from their various labours; all have come out of their varied tribulations, and have washed their robes in the Blood of the Lamb; all are at rest in Abraham's bosom, 'in peaceful abodes' in the keeping of the Lord; they are restored to our lost, yea, a more blissful Paradise; they are 'with Christ,' behold Him, by sight, not by faith; see Him ineffably; joy in his Countenance; see Light in His Light; have begun their endless praise of God. Yea, it is to be hoped that all of us have a still closer interest there; all in some gone before, have their portion in Paradise; all have some who long for and await their coming, in patience, hope, and peace and prayer. All have some link of human affection with the unseen world. All some treasures there, that their hearts may the rather be there also; well might we say, 'It is good for us to be here!'" [2]

Is it not most important that this Festival should be greatly prized and universally observed?

"It may be a sore loss, greater than we can imagine, that although confessing in our Creeds 'the Communion of Saints,' we, for the most part, have so little felt the privilege of being 'fellow-citizens with the Saints, and of the household of God'; of belonging to a body of which such glorious hosts have been already perfected, of being the struggling members of the One Body. Not realizing that they *now live* to God, live a higher life than we, being 'freed from the body of this death,' their histories appear like by-gone tales of what has

<hr>

[1] *Leeds Sermons*, p. 230.   [2] *Id.* p. 231.

been, not the living victories of those still 'living to God, present in His sight, Who wrought these things in and by man.'"[1]

What does Bishop Pearson say on this matter?

" The belief of the Communion of Saints is necessary to inflame our hearts with an ardent affection towards those which live, and a reverent respect towards those which are departed, and are now with God. And if all the Saints of God living in Communion of the Church, deserve the best of our affections here on earth, certainly, certainly when they are dissolved and with Christ, when they have been blessed with a sight of God and rewarded with a crown of glory, they may challenge some respect from us who are here to wait upon the will of God, expecting when such a happy change shall come."—BISHOP PEARSON *on the Creed, Article IX. Fin.*

LIKE GOD.

"Like God! The very gift which Satan taught Adam, by disobedience to seek to gain for himself, not to receive of God: that same surpassing Gift, through the obedience and death of Him, Who is God and Man, will God bestow on man to be like Himself."[2]

"If we would be 'like Him' in glory, we must in our degree be 'like Him' here by grace. If we would have His Image for ever, we must bear even now the Image of the Heavenly, after which, by His mercy, we have been renewed; if we would behold Him in bliss, our heart must be made pure here, that by faith it may here see, Whom by the eye of the body it sees not."[3]

"That likeness here is renewed, in proportion as is our love; since God is love. It is begun, when we are wearied and sickened at ourselves, that we are so unlike Him, so far removed from Him. It is enlarged, when with penitent love we return from the far country whither we have strayed, to

---

[1] *Leeds Sermons,* p. 255.   [2] *Id.* p. 290.   [3] *Id.* p. 298.

confess our unworthiness in our Father's Presence. It is carried on by His grace, through every act of self-denial, or virtue, or love, or penitent suffering, for love of Him; through every groan, that we are unlike Him; every longing to be like Him; every fervent momentary prayer we breathe for His love: for fervent prayer is not our own, but the unutterable groanings of His Spirit Which dwelleth in us. It is renewed by that Heavenly Feast, the Food of Angels, wherein (in the words of our Church) 'our sinful bodies are made clean by His Body, and our souls washed through His most Precious Blood,' yea 'we dwell in Christ and Christ in us; we are made one with Christ, and Christ with us.'"

"It shall be perfected, in those who, by His grace, persevere to the end, in that blessed everlasting Sight, when our vile body shall be made like unto the glorious Body of our Redeemer, our soul shall see the Ever-Blessed Trinity, and in that sight receive of the ineffable Beauty and Glory, and Majesty, and Love which it sees."

"As to Him, so to us, if we are His, the grave is the vestibule to glory. 'The tokens of decay are the cockcrowing to the Resurrection.' 'We shall be like Him, for we shall see Him as He is.' Picture to yourself then, as ye may, the glory of His Glorified Body. Picture It to yourselves, a Body, yet with such glory as created eye could not look upon. View It, transparent with Divine Light, arrayed with Divine Beauty, looking sweetly upon thee with Divine Loveliness, Majestic with Divine Glory, Intelligent with Divine Wisdom, Tender with Divine Compassion, and Love Itself, for God is Love: such, in thy measure, mayest thou be, if thou willest; such may be those whom thou lovest."[1]

OUR BODIES GLORIFIED.

"He speaks again of that lowest part in us, 'Know ye not that your bodies are the temples of the Holy Ghost?' Yes, these poor bodies, which hunger and thirst, are heavy and

[1] *Parochial and Cathedral Sermons*, p. 413.

weary; which shall return to corruption, which shall be subject to the dishonour of the grave, which shall say to corruption, 'Thou art my father,' and to the worm, 'Thou art my mother and my sister'—these, God has chosen to be His dwelling-place; in them He is pleased to dwell; these He hallows; within these *He is forming that glorious body* which shall be after the Resurrection; with these He unites Himself now, that they may be full of His Glory hereafter."[1]

THE BEATIFIC VISION.

When it is said we shall see God, does it mean that we shall see God the Son, Jesus only, the King in His Beauty?

" To see Jesus is to see God, and were a reward, all too great and glorious, but also, ' Eye to eye shall we behold God, even the Everlasting Father, and His Co-equal Son, and the Holy Ghost from Both proceeding, of Both the Bond in love.' Him, our eyes shall behold and not another, yet cleansed by the light of truth and upheld by Him to behold His Majesty."[2]

LOVE GOD WITH ALL THY HEART.

" Oh why is earth so different from Heaven?   Why have we disputing instead of adoring; questioning instead of thanksgiving; coldness instead of the fire of love ?   It is because men live so much in the things of time and sense, and think so little of Him, Who never forgetteth us.   Oh, ' sursum corda, sursum corda!'   One earnest, steadfast, piercing, longing, loving gaze into Heaven will reveal to thee more than all this world's disputings, nay, than any argument, for ' flesh and blood will not reveal it' unto thee, but thy Father which is in Heaven."[3]

" Blessedness will it be, beyond all bliss, blessedness above

---

[1] *Parochial and Cathedral Sermons*, p. 465.
[2] Vol. ii. p. 325.   [3] Vol. 1872, p. 262.

all created joy, for it is the fruit ot the Infinite Love of Jesus, the foretaste of the eternal joy of thy Lord, when, with God-given faith, thou canst say, ' I love Thee, oh, only Salvation of my Soul, for thou hast redeemed me by Thy Blood, my Lord, and my God. Thou, me !' "

ERRATA.

p. 92, line 8 from foot, *for* N. I. *read* N. T.

p. 156, line 12, *for* Communions unknown *read* Communions as a rule unknown: the exception being on Thursday in Holy Week.

p. 272, note 2, for *Remembrance* read *Remonstrance*.

pp. 273, 274 : PRIDE *should come first of the* DEADLY SINS.

INDEX.

LIST OF WORKS BY DR. PUSEY.

PAROCHIAL SERMONS. Three Vols.

CONTENTS OF VOL. I.

(For the season from Advent to Whitsuntide.)

Preface.
1 The End of all Things.
2 The Merciful shall obtain Mercy.
3 Prepare for Seasons of Grace.
4 God with us.
5 The Incarnation, a Lesson of Humility.
6 Character of Christian Rebuke.
7 Joy out of Suffering.
8 God calleth thee.
9 The Fewness of the Saved.
10 Fasting.
11 Review of Life.
12 Irreversible Chastisements.
13 God's Presence in Loneliness.
14 Barabbas or Jesus.
15 Christ Risen our Justification.
16 The Christian's Life in Christ.
17 Our Risen Lord's Love for Penitents.
18 How to detain Jesus in the Soul.
19 The Christian's Life hid in Christ.
20 Increased Communions.
21 Heaven the Christian's Home.
22 The Christian the Temple of God.
23 The Will of God the cure of Self-will.

CONTENTS OF VOL. II.

1 Faith.
2 Hope.
3 Love.
4 Humility.
5 Patience.
6 Self-Knowledge.
7 Life a Warfare.
8 The Besetting Sin.
9 Victory over the Besetting Sin.
10 Prayer heard the more through delay.
11 Re-creation of the Penitent.
12 The Sin of Judas.
13 The Ascension our Glory and Joy.
14 The Teaching of God within and without.
15 The Rest of Love and Praise.
16 Faith in our Lord, God and Man.
17 Groans of Unrenewed and Renewed Nature.
18 Victory amid Strife.
19 Victory through Loving Faith.
20 The Power and Greatness of Love.
21 Our being in God.
22 The Sacredness of Marriage.

CONTENTS OF VOL. III.

(Reprinted from the " Plain Sermons by contributors to the ' Tracts for the Times.' " Revised Edition.)

1 Sudden Death.
2 Conversion.
3 The Cross borne for us and in us.
4 Real Obedience in all things.
5 Christian Life a struggle, but victory.
6 The Value and Sacredness of Suffering.
7 The Christian's a risen life.
8 Victory over the World.
9 Obedience the Condition of knowing the Truth.
10 Pray without ceasing.
11 Conditions of acceptable Prayer.
12 Distractions in Prayer.
13 Baptism the Ground and Encouragement to Christian Education.
14 Holy Communion.—Danger in careless Receiving, death in Neglecting.
15 Holy Communion.—Privileges.
16 S. Barnabas. Christian Kindliness and Charity.
17 S. James. Obeying Calls.
18 The Transfiguration of our Lord the earnest of the Christian's glory.
19 Christian Joy.
20 God's Glories in Infants set forth in the Holy Innocents.

WALTER SMITH & INNES, 31, 32, BEDFORD STREET, STRAND, W.C.

PAROCHIAL AND CATHEDRAL SERMONS.

CONTENTS.

1 False peace.
2 Conversion.
3 Peril of delaying repentance.
4 Peril of relapses.
5 Backsliding
6 Natural good and evil.
7 Lukewarmness.
8 Loss through little sins.
9 Peril of little sins.
10 Evil of little sins.
11 Good of little acts to please God
12 Saintliness of Christians.
13 The witness of the Spirit.
14 Benefit of temptations.
15 Christ's love in acts, the Christian's model.
16 Christ's words of love, the reproof of detraction.
17 Christ's loving thoughts, the reproof of censoriousness.
18 Christian zeal.
19 Prayer.
20 Thanksgiving.
21 God withdraws in loving-kindness also.
22 God advances His kingdom through man.
23 The minuteness and individuality of God's judgment.
24 Every thought, word, deed, shall be judged.
25 Whither art thou going?
26 Murder of souls.
27 Compromises.
28 Lukewarmness.
29 Fasting.
30 Glory of the resurrection.
31 True peace and false peace.
32 Free-will.
33 The love of God for us.
34 The Resurrection of Christ, the Source, Earnest, Pattern of ours.
35 God's condescending love in restoring man by His own Indwelling.
36 Actualness of the Indwelling of God.
37 The Holy Trinity.
38 The Mystery of the Trinity, the revelation of Divine Love.
39 The Being of God in Whom we are.
40 The Adoration of Heaven.

UNIVERSITY SERMONS. Three Vols.

CONTENTS OF VOL. I.

Preface.
1 The Holy Eucharist, a Comfort to the Penitent. 1843.
2 Entire Absolution of the Penitent. 1846.
3 Entire Absolution of the Penitent. Part II. 1846.
4 The Presence of Christ in the Holy Eucharist. 1853.
5 Justification. 1853.
6 The Rule of Faith. Preached 1850. New Edition, with Preface on Papal Infallibility. 1879.
7 All Faith the Gift of God. 1855.
8 Real Faith Entire. 1855.
9 Patience and Confidence the Strength of the Church. 1841.

These Sermons may also be had separately, price 1s. each.

CONTENTS OF VOL. II.

(Preached chiefly between 1859—1872.)

Preface.
1 Grounds of Faith difficult to analyze because Divine.
2 God is our Light in all Knowledge, Natural or Supernatural.
3 Prophecy a series of Miracles which we can examine for ourselves.
4 The Prophecy of Christ our Atoner and Intercessor in Isaiah liii. 12.
5 The Christ the Light of the World to be rejected by His own, to be despised, and so to reign in glory.
6 Power of Truth amid Untruthfulness in Jewish Interpretation of Prophecy.
7 Causes which blinded the Jews to the Prophecies that Jesus should suffer.
8 The Gospel could not be True unless it had certain Truth.
9 Jesus the Way, the Truth, and the Life.
10 The Doctrine of the Atonement.
11 Christ the Lord our Righteousness.
12 Human Judgment the earnest of Divine.
13 The Terror of the Day of Judgment as arising from its Justice.
14 Grieve not the Spirit of God.
15 Value of Almsgiving in the Sight of God.
16 The World an Ever-living Enemy.
17 On Human Respect.
18 Each has his own Vocation.
19 To Believe in Jesus the Teaching of the Holy Ghost.

UNIVERSITY SERMONS—*Continued.*

CONTENTS OF VOL. III.

1 Everlasting Punishment.* 1864. *6d.*
2 Miracles of Prayer. 1866. *6d.*
3 Will ye also go away? 1867. With Preface and Appendix. *6d.*
4 This is My Body. 1871. *1s.*
5 The Responsibility of Intellect in Matters of Faith. 1872. With Appendix on Bishop Moberly's Strictures on the Athanasian Creed. *1s.*
6 Sinful Blindness amidst imagined Light. 1873. *6d.*
7 Christianity without the Cross a Corruption of the Gospel of Christ. 1875. With Note on "Modern Christianity a Civilized Heathenism." *6d.*
8 God and Human Independence. 1876. *6d.*
9 Un-Science, not Science, adverse to Faith. 1878. *1s.*
10 Prophecy of Jesus the certain prediction of the [to man] impossible. 1878. *6d.*
11 "Blessed are the Meek." A Sermon preached at the Opening of the Chapel of Keble College, on S. Mark's Day. 1876. With New Note. *6d.*

[* *Notes to this Sermon will be found in " What is of Faith as to Everlasting Punishment?" See p.* 7.]

LENTEN SERMONS, preached chiefly to young men at the Universities between 1858—1874.

CONTENTS.

*1 Life, the preparation for Death.
2 Why did Dives lose his soul?
3 Almost thou persuadest me to be a Christian.
4 Balaam—Half-conversion, unconversion.
5 The losses of the saved.
6 Eve.—The course of Temptation.
7 Man's self-deceit and God's Omniscience.
*8 Our Pharisaism.
9 Personal responsibility of man, as to his use of time.
10 The prodigal son.
11 The prodigal son.
12 Repentance, from love of God, life-long.
13 David in his sin and his penitence.
14 The grace of Christ our Victory.
15 The conflict, in a superficial age.
16 The Gospel, the Power of God.
17 The Prayers of Jesus.
18 The means of grace the remedy against sin.
*19 The thought of the love of Jesus for us, the remedy for sins of the body.
20 Continual comfort, the gift of God on continual sorrow for sin.
21 Suffering the gift and presence of God.
22 Jesus, the Redeemer, and His redeemed.
23 Jesus at the Right Hand of God, the Object of Divine Worship.
24 Isaiah; his heaviness and his consolation.

* *These may be had separately, price 6d. each.*

SERMONS AT A MISSION AND RETREAT, at the Consecration of S. Saviour's, Leeds. With a Preface. 1845. Together with Eight Sermons by the Rev. JOHN KEBLE, W. U. RICHARDS, ISAAC WILLIAMS, C. MARRIOTT.

CONTENTS.

1 Loving Penitence.
*2 The Nature of Sin.
*3 The Sinner's Death.
*4 God's Merciful Visitations.
*5 The Last Judgment.
*6 Hell.
*7 Love of Christ for Penitents.
*8 The Returning Prodigal.
*9 Virtue of the Cross.
10 Looking unto Jesus the Groundwork of Penitence.
11 Looking unto Jesus the Means of Endurance.
12 Union with Christ, &c.
13 Hopes of the Penitent.
14 Bliss of Heaven, "We shall be like Him"
15 ——— "We shall see Him as He is."
16 ——— Glory of the Body.
17 Progress our Perfection.
18 Daily Growth.

[*The Sermons with an asterisk prefixed are not by Dr. Pusey.*]

OCCASIONAL PAROCHIAL SERMONS. The following Sermons formerly contained in this volume may still be had separately.

The Day of Judgment. 6d.

Christ the Source and Rule of Christian Love. 1s.

The Preaching of the Gospel a Preparation for our Lord's Coming. 6d.

God is Love. Whoso receiveth one such Little Child in My Name receiveth Me. 1s.

Chastisements Neglected, Fore-runners of Greater. 6d.

The Blasphemy against the Holy Ghost. 6d.

Do all to the Lord Jesus. 6d.

The Danger of Riches. Seek God First and ye shall have All. Two Sermons. 1s.

The Church the Converter of the Heathen. Two Sermons. 1s.

THE LOVE OF GOD AND OF JESUS FOR SOULS, AND THE BLESSEDNESS OF INTERCESSION FOR THEM. Addresses during a Retreat of the Companions of the Love of Jesus, engaged in Perpetual Intercession for the Conversion of Sinners. 8vo, cloth, 3s. 6d.

CONTENTS.

1 Object of the Retreat; Renewal of fervour.

2 The love of God for individual souls.

3 God's love for each soul in the Incarnation.

4 The love of God and of Jesus for single souls, as seen in the Passion.

5 Jesus' love for souls, seen in some special Sufferings of the Passion.

6 Love of Jesus in His continual High Priest's Office for us.

7 Love of God the Holy Ghost for individual souls.

8 Horribleness of sin.

9 Necessity of Intercession.

10 Helps for keeping up Intercession.

11 Prayers for departed Companions.

PRIVATE PRAYERS. 2s. LONGMANS AND GREEN.

PRAYERS FOR A YOUNG SCHOOL-BOY. 1s. LONGMANS AND GREEN.

ADVICE ON HEARING CONFESSION. From writings of Saints. Abridged, condensed, and adapted from the ABBÉ GAUME's Manual for Confessors. With Preface embodying English Authorities on Confession, by E. B. Pusey, D.D. 1877. Revised Edition. 8vo, cloth. 6s.

PREFACE separately (in wrapper). 2s. 6d.

CASE AS TO THE LEGAL FORCE OF THE JUDGMENT OF THE PRIVY COUNCIL, in *re* FENDAL *v.* WILSON ; with the Opinion of the Attorney-General and Sir Hugh Cairns, and a Preface to those who love God and His truth. 8vo. 6d.

† CATHEDRAL INSTITUTIONS. 1833.

CHURCH OF ENGLAND (THE) LEAVES HER CHILDREN FREE TO WHOM TO OPEN THEIR GRIEFS. A Letter to the Rev. W. U. RICHARDS. 8vo. With Postscript. 5s.

COLLEGIATE AND PROFESSORIAL TEACHING AND DISCIPLINE in answer to PROFESSOR VAUGHAN. 5s.

CORRECTION OF SOME CRITICISMS ON THE MANUAL FOR CONFESSORS. 1879. 6d.

COUNCILS OF THE CHURCH (THE), from the Council of Jerusalem to the close of the Second of Constantinople, A.D. 381. 6s.

DANIEL THE PROPHET. Nine Lectures delivered in the Divinity School of the University of Oxford. With copious Notes. 1880. 8vo, cloth. 10s. 6d.

DOCTRINE OF HOLY BAPTISM (THE), as taught by Holy Scripture and the Fathers. (Formerly "Tracts for the Times," No. 67.) 8vo, cloth. 5s.

DOCTRINE OF THE REAL PRESENCE (THE), as contained in the Fathers from the death of S. John the Evangelist to the Fourth General Council. 1855. 8vo, cloth. 7s. 6d.

EIRENICON (AN), VOL. I. Letter to the author of "The Christian Year," "The Church of England a Portion of Christ's One Holy Catholic Church, and a Means of Restoring Visible Unity." 1865. 8vo, cloth. 6s.

———————————— VOL. II. First Letter to the Very Rev. J. H. Newman, D.D., "The Reverential Love due to the ever-blessed Theotokos, and the Doctrine of her 'Immaculate Conception.'" 1869. 8vo, cloth. 6s.

———————————— VOL. III. Second Letter to Dr. Newman, "Healthful Re-union as conceived possible before the Vatican Council." (Formerly entitled "Is Healthful Re-union Impossible?" 1870. 8vo, cloth. 6s..

FIFTY-THIRD CHAPTER OF ISAIAH (THE), ACCORDING TO THE JEWISH INTERPRETERS.

    I. TEXTS, edited from Printed Books and MSS. (Ad. Neubaur). Post 8vo. 18s.

GOD'S PROHIBITION OF THE MARRIAGE WITH A DECEASED WIFE'S SISTER (Lev. xviii. 6) not to be set aside by an inference from His limitation of Polygamy among the Jews (Lev. xviii. 18). 8vo. 1s.

HABITUAL CONFESSION NOT DISCOURAGED BY THE RESOLUTION ACCEPTED BY THE LAMBETH CONFERENCE. A Letter to His Grace the Lord Archbishop of Canterbury. 1878. 6d.

INTRODUCTORY ESSAY ON RE-UNION. 6d.

LECTURE AT TEMPORARY CHAPEL, TITCHFIELD STREET. 1850.

LETTER TO LORD BISHOP OF LONDON, in Explanation of some statements contained in a Letter by the Rev. W. Dodsworth. 1851. 16mo. 1s.

RENEWED EXPLANATIONS IN CONSEQUENCE OF MR. DODSWORTH'S COMMENTS ON THE ABOVE. 8vo. 1s.

LIBRARY OF THE FATHERS. (See p. 7.)

† MARRIAGE WITH A DECEASED WIFE'S SISTER, &c., 1849. 3s. 6d.

MINOR PROPHETS (THE). With a Commentary Explanatory and Practical, and Introductions to the several Books. Cloth 4to, £1 11s. 6d.

Or as follows :—

Part I. HOSEA TO JOEL, INTRODUCTION. 5s.

II. JOEL, Introduction—AMOS VI. 6. 5s.

III. AMOS VI. 7 TO MICAH I. 12. 5s.

IV. MICAH I. 13 TO HABAKKUK, Introduction 5s.

V. HABAKKUK, ZEPHANIAH, HAGGAI. 5s.

VI. ZECHARIAH, MALACHI. 6s.

Case for binding Minor Prophets, 2s. 6d.

INDEX by Rev. G. R. ADAMS, 2s.

ON THE CLAUSE "AND THE SON," in regard to the Eastern Church and the Bonn Conference. A letter to the Rev. H. P. Liddon, D.D., Ireland, Professor of Exegesis, Canon of S. Paul's. 1876. 8vo, cloth. 5s.

REAL PRESENCE THE DOCTRINE OF THE ENGLISH CHURCH. (THE). With a vindication of the reception by the wicked, and of the Adoration of our Lord Jesus Christ truly present. 1857. 8vo. 6s.

ROYAL SUPREMACY (THE) NOT AN ARBITRARY AUTHORITY, BUT LIMITED BY THE LAWS OF THE CHURCH, OF WHICH KINGS ARE MEMBERS. Ancient Precedents. 8vo. 6s.

SEARCHINGS OF THE HEART. 1844.

THREE LETTERS TO THE EDITOR OF THE "TIMES" ON "ECCLESIASTICAL LEGISLATION." 1875. Reprinted. With Preface. 6d.

TRACT XC. On certain Passages in the XXXIX Articles, by the Rev. J. H. NEWMAN, M.A., 1841 ; with Historical Preface by E. B. PUSEY, D.D. ; and Catholic Subscription to the XXXIX Articles considered in reference to Tract XC, by the Rev. JOHN KEBLE, M.A. 1851. 8vo, sewed. 1s. 6d.

TRACTATUS DE VERITATE CONCEPTIONIS BEATISSIMÆ VIRGINIS pro Facienda Relatione coram Patribus Concilii Basileæ, Anno Domini MCCCCXXXVII, Mense Julio. De mandato Sedis Apostolicæ Legatorum, eidem Sacro Concilio præsidentium. Compilatus per Reverendum Patrem, FRATREM JOANNEM DE TURRECREMATA, Sacræ Theologiæ Professorem, Ordinis Prædicatorum, Tunc Sacri Apostolici Palatii Magistrum. Postea Illustrissimum et Reverendissimum S. R. Ecclesiæ Cardinalem, Episcopum Portuensem. Primo impressus Romæ, apud Antonium Bladum, Asulanum, MDXLVII. Small 4to (850 pp.), cloth. 7s.

UNLAW. With Preface. 6d.

WHAT IS OF FAITH AS TO EVERLASTING PUNISHMENT; In reply to Dr. Farrar's Challenge in his "Eternal Hope." 8vo, cloth. 3s. 6d.

WORKS BY REV. P. E. PUSEY, M.A.

S. CYRILLI ALEXANDRINI Epistolæ tres œcumenicæ libri quinque contra Nestorium XII., capitum defensio utraque scholia de Incarnatione Unigeniti. Being Vol. VI. Demy 8vo, cloth. 12*s.*

S. CYRILLI ALEXANDRINI de Recta Fide ad Imperatorem de Incarnatione Unigeniti dialogus, de Recta Fide ad Principissas, de Recta Fide ad augustas, Quod unus Christus dialogus apologeticus ad Imperatorem. Being Vol. VII., Part I. Demy 8vo, cloth. 12*s.*

THE THREE EPISTLES OF S. CYRIL OF ALEXANDRIA. With Revised Text and English Translation. Demy 8vo, sewed. 3*s.*

LIBRARY OF THE FATHERS OF THE HOLY CATHOLIC CHURCH,

ANTERIOR TO THE DIVISION OF THE EAST AND WEST.

Translated by Members of the English Church.

S. ATHANASIUS AGAINST THE ARIANS, PART I. 6*s.*

———————— HISTORICAL TRACTS.
———————— THE FESTAL EPISTLES. } 10*s.* 6*d.*

———————— LATER TREATISES, with an Appendix on S. Cyril of Alexandria and Theodoret, by Dr. BRIGHT. 5*s.*

S. AUGUSTINE'S CONFESSIONS, with notes containing his Early Life and Conversion. 6*s.*

———————— SERMONS ON THE NEW TESTAMENT. Two Vols. 15*s.*

———————— HOMILIES ON THE PSALMS. Six Vols. £2 2*s.*

———————— HOMILIES ON THE GOSPEL AND FIRST EPISTLE OF S. JOHN. Two Vols. 15*s.*

———————— PRACTICAL TREATISES. 7*s.* 6*d.*
Chiefly on the doctrines of grace.

A A

S. Ambrose—Letters. 9s.

S. Chrysostom's Homilies on the Gospel of S. Matthew. Three Vols. £1 1s.

———————— Homilies on the Gospel of S. John. Two Vols. 14s.

———————— Homilies on S. Paul's Epistles, including the Homilies on the Epistle to the Hebrews. Seven Vols. £2 12s. 6d.

———————— Homilies on the Acts of the Apostles. Two Vols. 12s.

———————— Homilies to the People of Antioch. 7s. 6d.

S. Cyprian.—The Treatises and Epistles of S. Cyprian, with the Treatises of S. Pacian. 10s.

S. Cyril (Bishop of Jerusalem), Catechetical Lectures on the Creed and Sacraments. 7s.

S. Cyril (Archbishop of Alexandria), Commentary upon the Gospel of S. John. Vol. I. 8s.

———.—— Vol. II. 10s. 6d.

———.—— The five Books against Nestorius, the Scholia on the Incarnation, Christ is One, the Fragments against Theodore, Diodore, and the Synousiasts, with Preface on Nestorius and S. Cyril. 6s.

S. Ephrem's Rhythms on the Nativity, and on Faith. 8s. 6d.

S. Gregory the Great—Morals on the Book of Job. Four Vols. £1 11s. 6d.

S. Irenæus (the Works of). Translated by the late Rev. John Keble. 8s.

S. Justin Martyr (the Works of). 6s.

Tertullian's Apological and Practical Treatises. 9s.

ORIGINAL TEXTS.

S. Augustini Confessiones. 7s.

S. Chrysostomi in Epist. ad Romanos. 9s.

———————AD Corinthios I. 10s. 6d.

———————AD Corinthios II. 8s.

———————AD Galatas et Ephesios. 7s.

———————AD Phil., Coloss., Thessal. £1 10s. 6d.

———————AD Tim., Tit., Philem. 8s.

———————AD Hebræos. 9s.

THEODORETI COMMENTARIUS IN OMNES B. PAULI EPISTOLAS, Edidit C. MARRIOTT, S. T. B. Pars 1. continens Epistolas ad Romanos, Corinthios, et Galatas. 8*s*.

———————————————— PARS II., AD EPHES., PHILIP., Coloss., Thess., Heb., Tim., Tit., et Philem. 6*s*.

ADVENT READINGS FROM THE FATHERS. 12mo, cloth. 2*s*.

DEVOUT COMMUNION. 1*s*. From the "Paradise of the Christian Soul."

FOUNDATIONS OF THE SPIRITUAL LIFE (THE). A Commentary on Thomas à Kempis. By SURIN. 4*s*.

GUIDE TO PASSING ADVENT HOLILY. By AVRILLON. Translated from the French, and adapted to the use of the English Church. 5*s*.

GUIDE FOR PASSING LENT HOLILY. By AVRILLON. With Dr. Pusey's Preface. 5*s*.

LENT READINGS FROM THE FATHERS. 12mo, cloth. 3*s*. 6*d*.

LIFE OF JESUS CHRIST IN GLORY (THE). Daily Meditations from Easter Day to the Wednesday after Trinity Sunday. By NOUET. 5*s*.

MEDITATIONS AND SELECT PRAYERS OF S. ANSELM. 5*s*.

MEDITATIONS ON THE GOSPELS FOR EVERY DAY IN THE YEAR. By the ABBÉ DUQUESNE. 12mo. Vol. I., 3*s*. 6*d*. † Vol. II. Vol. III., 4*s*. 6*d*.

PARADISE FOR THE CHRISTIAN SOUL. By HORST. 6*s*. 6*d*.

SPIRITUAL COMBAT (THE), WITH THE PATH OF PARADISE: and the Supplement; or, the Peace of the Soul. By SCUPOLI. (From the Italian.) Cloth. 1*s*. 6*d*.

SUFFERINGS OF JESUS (THE). Composed by FRA THOME DE JESU, of the Order of Hermits of S. Augustine, a Captive of Barbary, in the Fiftieth Year of his banishment from Heaven. Translated for the first time from the original Portuguese. In Two Parts. 3*s*. 6*d*. each.

YEAR OF AFFECTIONS (THE); or Sentiments on the Love of God, drawn from the Canticles, for every Day in the Year. By AVRILLON. 4*s*.

[*The books with a* † *prefixed are out of print.*]

The following are also out of print:—

EARNEST REMONSTRANCE. A Letter to an Opponent of the "Tracts for the Times." 1836.

APPENDICES TO SERMON ON FIFTH OF NOVEMBER. 1839.

PRAYERS FOR UNITY.

LETTER TO BISHOP OF OXFORD. 1839.

LETTER TO DR. JELF. 1841.

LETTER TO ARCHBISHOP OF CANTERBURY. 1842.

CHURCHES IN LONDON. With an Appendix.

THOUGHTS ON THE BENEFITS OF FASTING. "Tracts for the Times," Nos. 18 and 66.

LETTER ON THE PROPOSED CHANGE OF THE MARRIAGE LAWS. 1842.

[*R. Clay & Sons, Ld., London & Bungay.*